REVIEW OF
RESEARCH IN
EDUCATION

Review of Research in Education is published annually on behalf of the American Educational Research Association, 1430 K St., NW, Suite 1200, Washington, DC 20005, by SAGE Publishing, 2455 Teller Road, Thousand Oaks, CA 91320. Send address changes to AERA Membership Department, 1430 K St., NW, Suite 1200, Washington, DC 20005.

Member Information: American Educational Research Association (AERA) member inquiries, member renewal requests, changes of address, and membership subscription inquiries should be addressed to the AERA Membership Department, 1430 K St., NW, Suite 1200, Washington, DC 20005; fax 202-238-3250; e-mail: members@aera.net. AERA annual membership dues are $180 (Regular Members), $180 (Affiliate Members), $140 (International Affiliates), and $55 (Graduate Students and Student Affiliates). **Claims:** Claims for undelivered copies must be made no later than six months following month of publication. Beyond six months and at the request of the American Educational Research Association, the publisher will supply missing copies when losses have been sustained in transit and when the reserve stock permits.

Subscription Information: All non-member subscription inquiries, orders, back-issue requests, claims, and renewals should be addressed to SAGE Publishing, 2455 Teller Road, Thousand Oaks, CA 91320; telephone (800) 818-SAGE (7243) and (805) 499-0721; fax: (805) 375-1700; e-mail: journals@sagepub.com; website: http://journals.sagepub.com. **Subscription Price:** Institutions: $376; Individuals: $70. For all customers outside the Americas, please visit http://www.sagepub.co.uk/customercare.nav for information. **Claims:** Claims for undelivered copies must be made no later than six months following month of publication. The publisher will supply missing copies when losses have been sustained in transit and when the reserve stock will permit.

Copyright Permission: To request permission for republishing, reproducing, or distributing material from this journal, please visit the desired article on the SAGE Journals website (journals.sagepub.com) and click "Permissions." For additional information, please see www.sagepub.com/journalspermissions.nav.

Advertising and Reprints: Current advertising rates and specifications may be obtained by contacting the advertising coordinator in the Thousand Oaks office at (805) 410-7763 or by sending an e-mail to advertising@sagepub.com. To order reprints, please e-mail reprint@sagepub.com. Acceptance of advertising in this journal in no way implies endorsement of the advertised product or service by SAGE or the journal's affiliated society(ies). No endorsement is intended or implied. SAGE reserves the right to reject any advertising it deems as inappropriate for this journal.

Change of Address: Six weeks' advance notice must be given when notifying of change of address. Please send old address label along with the new address to ensure proper identification. Please specify name of journal.

International Standard Serial Number ISSN 0091-732X
International Standard Book Number ISBN 978-1-5443-4247-4 (Vol. 42, 2018, paper)
Manufactured in the United States of America. First printing, March 2018.

Printed on acid-free paper

REVIEW OF RESEARCH IN EDUCATION

The Challenges and Possibilities of Intersectionality in Education Research

Volume 42, 2018

Jeanne M. Powers, Editor
Gustavo E. Fischman, Editor
Arizona State University

Adai A. Tefera, Editor
Virginia Commonwealth University

Review of Research in Education

The Challenges and Possibilities of Intersectionality in Education Research

Volume 42

AMERICAN EDUCATIONAL RESEARCH ASSOCIATION

Tel: 202-238-3200 Fax: 202-238-3250
http://www.aera.net/pubs

FELICE J. LEVINE
Executive Director

MARTHA YAGER
Managing Editor

JOHN NEIKIRK
Director of Publications

JESSICA SIBOLD
Publications Associate

Contents

Cover images: Dmi T/Shutterstock.com and iStock.com/pawel.gaul

Introduction

Intersectionality in Education: A Conceptual Aspiration and Research Imperative

ADAI A. TEFERA
Virginia Commonwealth University
JEANNE M. POWERS
GUSTAVO E. FISCHMAN
Arizona State University

The purpose of this volume is to contribute to education research by presenting comprehensive and nuanced understandings of intersectional perspectives. Researchers working within an intersectional framework try to account for the dynamic and complex ways that race/ethnicity, class, gender, sexuality, religion, citizenship, ability, and age shape individual identities and social life. We argue it is essential to overcome simplistic, static, one-dimensional, and additive approaches to education research by expanding the use of analytical categories and engaging the multiplicities of people's circumstances within and across teaching and learning settings. This volume is our attempt to open a space for analysis, dialogue, and reflection among scholars about intersectionality, and the possibilities of reimagining the research tools used to address the complex demographic, social, economic, and cultural transformations shaping education. Ideally, this conversation will reach audiences outside of the academy.

Drawing from a long tradition of Black feminist theorizing and activism, Kimberlé Crenshaw (1989, 1991) is credited with proposing the term *intersectionality* as an academic concept. Intersectionality was also nurtured by the theorizing of women of color regarding race, gender, sexuality, and other forms of inequality that occurred as early as the 1960s (Beale, 1970; Chun, Lipsitz, & Shin, 2013; Collins, 2000; Collins & Bilge, 2016; King, 1988; Lorde, 1984; Moraga & Anzaldúa, 2015; Yuval-Davis, 2006).

While it is evident that since its initial formulation there have been robust academic debates about what intersectionality is and what it means in practice

Review of Research in Education
March 2018, Vol. 42, pp. vii–xvii
DOI: 10.3102/0091732X18768504
© 2018 AERA. http://rre.aera.net

(Bilge, 2013; Collins, 2015; Levine-Rasky, 2011; Patil, 2013; Salem, 2016), ideas associated with intersectionality gained particular relevance in the popular media during and after the 2016 presidential election, which was part of the zeitgeist that reenergized global political debates about race, gender, immigration, and religion, although activists were engaging in intersectional organizing in the years preceding the election.[1] As the chapters in this volume demonstrate, the conceptual and methodological tools associated with intersectionality are not just being used among academics but also resonating in union halls, nongovernmental organizations, civic and community organizations, and a growing number of conferences, symposia, and edited journal issues (e.g., Hancock, 2016), including this one.

We consider intersectionality to be both a conceptual aspiration and a research imperative for education researchers. Incorporating the multiplicity of intersecting dimensions into our projects and pedagogical actions is becoming increasingly normative in education research as a field. Engaging with intersectionality in research demands that our scholarship be oriented toward (a) accounting for the ways that race/ethnicity, class, gender, sexuality, religion, citizenship, ability, and age, among other things, shape the structural dynamics of power and inequality in social spaces and individual identities (Carbado, Crenshaw, Mays, & Tomlinson, 2013; Collins, 2015); and (b) strengthening the synergy between critical inquiry and praxis. Education researchers need to move beyond one-dimensional or single-axis analyses that focus on a specific category (e.g., race, class, gender, or ability) or that treat other categories as epiphenomenal more often. Instead, intersectionality opens up conceptual spaces to identify the gaps and silences of single-category analyses and approaches, as well as the mutually constitutive relationships between categories (Clarke & McCall, 2013; see also Carbado et al., 2013; Patton, Crenshaw, Haynes, & Watson, 2016).

While it is important to consider the promises of using intersectional analysis, it is equally important to examine the conceptual and methodological challenges associated with this approach. An important critique of intersectionality is that it is narrowly focused on issues of identity. However, this criticism tends to misinterpret the role of identity in intersectional analyses. An intersectional approach is fundamentally oriented toward analyzing the relationships of power and inequality within a social setting and how these shape individual and group identities. That is, our identities are shaped by our experiences in social groups and how we as members of those groups encounter institutionalized social structures. Within this frame, identity is best understood as a starting point for intersectional analyses and coalition-building, allowing academics and activists within and across identity groups to address the "multiple grounds of identity" (Crenshaw, 1991, p. 1245; see also Guinier & Torres, 2002; Harris & Leonardo, Chapter 1, this volume). In other words, intersectionality directs us to attend to both inter- and intragroup social dynamics (McCall, 2005). This is a necessary step in the process of building social movements that draw on and acknowledge the connections and disconnections created by participants' experiences of "discrimination, marginalization, and privilege" within and across different groups (Carbado et al., 2013, p. 306). As Harris and Leonardo (Chapter 1) also point out, engaging with the concept of intersectionality reminds scholars and activists to "be humble and to look for who is missing in the room" (p. 20).

Because intersectionality is widely understood as a framework to analyze the experiences of women of color, some critics of the theory argue that it has limited relevance for understanding the perspectives of other groups. The fact that intersectional analysis was originally rooted in studies focused on the multiple forms of marginalization that Black women face should not be understood as a limitation. Rather, intersectionality provides a framework to deliberately account for and examine the different ways that intersecting social dynamics affect people within and across groups. Nevertheless, some feminist scholars argue that as intersectionality travels across time and space, the concept can lose its political and radical edge if it is used without taking into account the structural inequalities and differential power relations that contribute to inequality (Carastathis, 2016; Salem, 2016). Furthermore, as Robert and Yu (Chapter 5) point out, an increasing number of scholars in the Global South and East are also engaging in research aligned with an intersectional perspective, demonstrating the potential for new transnational alliances and coalitions that include critical race feminism and decolonial thought (Carastathis, 2016; Lugones, 2010).

Indeed, intersectionality as an aspiration continues to bring both academics and activists together, because it provides much-needed language, ideas, and references that are fundamental for finding respectful spaces that allow scholars and activists to forge alliances aimed at overcoming the long-standing distance and mistrust between them. We hope that this volume contributes to making this conceptual aspiration a reality.

CROSS-CUTTING ISSUES AND THEMES

Reading across the chapters in this volume, there are a number of cross-cutting issues and themes the authors take up that we want to highlight here.[2] First, a number of authors in this issue use metaphors as a way to capture the complex social locations that intersectional analyses aim to engage. The term *intersectionality* invokes a metaphor first described by Crenshaw (1989)—the intersection with two (or more) roads crossing—which aptly connotes how the convergence of multiple categories leaves those at the intersection unprotected and thus harmed by the legal system. Though it was less widely embraced (Carastathis, 2016), Crenshaw (1989) also used the metaphor of the basement for how antidiscrimination law works, describing a basement with a hatch; the hatch represents the remedies provided by antidiscrimination law. In this space, people are standing on top of each other, some on the floor and others standing on shoulders in order of their disadvantages. The people standing on the floor are multiply disadvantaged, while those at the top whose heads "brush up against the ceiling" (p. 151) are singly disadvantaged (e.g., White women). Only the people at the top are able to exit the basement through the hatch or benefit from legal remedies. As Carastathis (2016) notes, the metaphor of the basement vividly illustrates how the people "left in the basement" (p. 97) are those whose experiences and claims are rendered invisible in the legal process. We find the use of metaphors to be a particularly useful way of helping us think through the ways that power, identity, and opportunity collide. Many of the authors in this issue use metaphors to expose the ways people who are often silenced, erased, and overlooked navigate complex social realities.

For example, Butler (Chapter 2) draws on historical and contemporary notions of space—tangible, hidden, and imagined—to bring attention to the spaces in which Black girls and women live and learn. She defines space as both physical *and* epistemological, and asserts the importance of examining Black girls and women by "naming spaces where Black women are excluded or included and by whom" (p. 31). Butler's notion of "Black Girl Cartography"—the study of how and where Black girls are physically and sociopolitically mapped in education—draws on mapping and cartographic methods to elicit stories about place, race, and gender. Similarly, Bullock (Chapter 6) and Ireland, Freeman, Winston-Proctor, DeLaine, McDonald Lowe, and Woodson (Chapter 10) invoke the metaphor of figure hiding and (un)hidden figures to "amend the dominant historical record to include the unlikely and unsung contributors to developments in mathematics and science" (see Bullock, p. 123), including those by Black women. On the other hand, Harris and Leonardo (Chapter 1) interrogate the use of the intersection-as-road metaphor by outlining the limitations of using a two-dimensional space to elicit such a complex concept. In Crenshaw's (1991) original formulation, the metaphor of the intersection helped us better understand the inadequacies of single-axis analyses. These early metaphors can also be restrictive when they come to structure how we understand the phenomena they are used to describe. In addition, Harris and Leonardo's use of their own metaphor, an ellipse, to describe how "race and gender gravitationally tug on each other" (p. 15) reminds us that reenvisioning metaphors can also be generative.

A second important theme is the ethical imperative of social justice. Intersectionality demands both theoretical explorations *and* social interventions. Annamma, Ferri, and Connor (Chapter 3) draw on DisCrit and one of its central tenets of intellectual activism to move beyond singular and deficit views of students of color with disabilities. Thus, the authors call on members of the research community to use DisCrit and engage in intellectual activism by making visible systemic oppressions, particularly those affecting students/people of color with disabilities. By doing this, they argue, one finds important opportunities to "refute traditional ways of being in the academy" (p. 62) and to highlight the "creative and ingenious strategies" (p. 62) that youth who are multiply marginalized employ as they navigate and make visible complex systems of marginalization. Similarly, Bullock (Chapter 6) argues that by embracing intersectionality, critical mathematics educators can bridge what are currently siloed approaches to addressing inequalities in mathematics education, because to "fully interrogate the matrix of domination" scholars will need to collaborate across "*ism* groups" (p. 142). Bullock notes that these collaborations can serve as the foundation for collaborative justice communities aimed at "directly confronting the multiplicative effects of injustice and oppression" (p. 142). At the same time, Robert and Yu (Chapter 5) caution us that intersectionality can also be "theorized and re-theorized into academic talk" and that as the concept becomes more frequently engaged by academics, it can become an empty "buzzword" (p. 97; see also Davis, 2008; Harris & Leonardo, Chapter 1).

The ethical imperative of intersectionality also demands that scholars interrogate our epistemological standpoints and recognize the contributions of seminal scholarship, such as Black feminism, that opened up new ways of seeing and doing education research. This requires critically reflecting on how we engage in one of the most revered practices of the academy—citing other scholars' work. In their review of how the concept of intersectionality has been deployed in education, Harris and Leonardo (Chapter 1, pp. 15) note that in "key instances," authors' engagement with the term is aligned with Crenshaw's (1991) formulation. Yet Agosto and Roland (Chapter 11) found examples of citation practices in the field of educational leadership that did not attribute intersectionality to central scholars such as Crenshaw (1991) and Collins (2015). Robert and Yu (Chapter 5) observed that the intersectionality literature from the southern hemisphere was largely disconnected from the seminal theoretical arguments from the United States, which they suggest may reflect the need for local theories in these settings. This "lack of citation disconnects intersectionality from its genealogical trajectory" (Agosto & Roland, Chapter 11, p. 275) and reaffirms "figure hiding" (Bullock, Chapter 6) or the erasure of bodies that intersectionality so deliberately aims to make visible. Alternatively, Butler (Chapter 2) asserts the importance of recognizing the work of "Black Girl Cartographers," or Black Girl scholars, and the researchers responsible for opening up spaces for intersectional Black feminism. The concern with citation practices also highlights another dilemma that is posed as a concept moves into new epistemological and analytical spaces: How do we extend intersectionality as a knowledge project while also acknowledging the important and foundational work that helped bring us to those spaces? That is, as intersectionality travels, researchers engaging with the concept have to be careful that they do not erase the significant contributions that Black women and other women of color have made, historically and contemporarily, to the concept while simultaneously mapping how it could enrich and extend seminal work in their own fields (McCall, 2005; see also Bilge, 2013).

At the same time, Harris and Leonardo's paired reviews of how intersectionality has been taken up as an analytic framework in the fields of law and education vividly illustrates how intersectionality has been engaged unevenly within and across fields (Chapter 1). They observe that the voluminous legal literature on intersectionality consists largely of secondary analyses by legal scholars; yet the concept and practices implied by intersectionality have had little traction in the field. In other words, practitioners—lawyers, judges, and legislators—continue to view civil rights claims in terms of a single dimension of discrimination. This is the central problem Crenshaw (1989) identified in her seminal analysis of employment discrimination cases published 29 years ago. In education, intersectionality was initially engaged as an analogy in Ladson-Billings and Tate's (1995) generative analysis of Whiteness in education through the lens of critical race theory. Since then, education scholars working within the critical race theory paradigm have used intersectionality as "a key concept that unlocks the education house that race made" (Harris & Leonardo, Chapter 1, p. 13).

Agosto and Roland (Chapter 11) observe that intersectionality has been under-used in the field of educational leadership and has largely focused on analyzing indi-viduals' leadership experiences as they encounter and attempt to alter unequal social structures in schools. The authors also explore the possible connections between intersectionality and transformative leadership, both examples of oppositional knowl-edge projects. They argue that a more extensive engagement with intersectionality can deepen the work of transformative leadership by exposing anti-oppressive ways of relating, knowing, being, and leading, which will help school leaders create more equitable and socially just educational spaces. Similarly, Butler (Chapter 2) reaffirms Crenshaw's (1991) call for more complex analyses that include Black girl matters within intersectionality, given the ways Black girls are often pushed to the margins of educational spaces, rendering their experiences as invisible in education research. By introducing Black Girl Cartography, Butler points to a vital and deliberate space for seeing, hearing, and believing in Black girl matters.

Robert and Yu's (Chapter 5) review of how intersectionality has been used to ana-lyze globally circulating educational policies provides insights into how intersection-ality has traveled to Eastern and Southern contexts and how these travels might enrich the work of Western and Northern scholars. For example, they observe that in China, because the state and civil society are dominated by elites, multiply marginal-ized groups who challenge their relegation to the margins of politics are framed as illegally challenging the state. Robert and Yu conclude that researchers outside China can learn from this case that they may need to interrogate their own assumptions about how social groups are positioned in relation to the state and civil society.

At the same time, Schudde (Chapter 4) observes that the concept of intersection-ality has not traveled across the methodological divide between qualitative and quan-titative research, in part because of logistical barriers such as the difficulties of interpreting complex statistical models and the lack of secondary data with adequate representation of the subgroups needed to conduct intersectional analyses using mul-tiple categories. Taken as a group, these authors suggest that intersectionality is grow-ing in acceptance but that in many subfields rich and deep intersectional research has yet to be done.

A number of contributors also point to the ways that intersectionality can be used to highlight significant problems within a subfield. Thai-Huy Nguyen and Bach Mai Dolly Nguyen (Chapter 7) use intersectionality to complicate a key analytic category in the field of higher education, the first-generation student. Nguyen and Nguyen argue that the lack of clarity and consistency around the term *first-generation student*, which paradoxically calls attention to an important and growing group, obscures our understanding of who these students are and their experiences in higher education institutions. Here, intersectionality is used to help us see aspects of these students' experiences that are "rendered invisible" (p. 150). Because it requires researchers to critically reflect on how individuals are captured in analytical categories, intersectionality can help researchers problematize how the category of first-generation student has been deployed and think through how it can be reimagined to help improve students' lives. Similarly, Hernández-Saca, Gutmann Kahn, and Cannon (Chapter 12) call on education scholars more broadly and special education scholars specifically to build on the work of those in critical special education and disability studies in education to examine inequities related to the intersections of ability, race, and language, among others. Taking up the call for a sociohistorical approach to disability at its intersections (Artiles, Dorn, & Bal, 2016), the authors carefully examine the voices and perspectives of youth and young adults with disabilities who are multiply marginalized, demonstrating the dexterity and resilience with which the youth navigate a complex "matrix of oppression" (p. 302). Hernández-Saca and colleagues thoughtfully push the field of education, particularly special education, to more deliberately examine education inequities from an intersectional perspective.

Schudde (Chapter 4) identifies a methodological problem—how to incorporate the rich insights from the large body of qualitative research that has engaged intersectionality into quantitative analyses—and highlights how intersectionality shares important commonalities with heterogeneous effects approaches in quantitative research. More important, intersectionality and insights from qualitative research can provide important theoretical justification for complex statistical models aimed at furthering our understanding of how intersecting identities shape individuals' educational experiences. Ireland and colleagues (Chapter 10) argue that three bodies of scholarship can be fruitfully synthesized for a better understanding of the experiences of Black women and girls in STEM fields: intersectional analyses of STEM education and workforce development, research on the psychology of gender, and research on the psychology of race. Alemán (Chapter 8) highlights the gaps in educational attainment of Latinx youth compared to their White peers and reviews how scholars have used intersectional frameworks to better understand how these students experience and navigate educational settings. These studies have generated a rich set of concepts, such as *racist nativism, gendered familism,* and *the citizenship continuum,* to denote the complex ways that race, gender, and citizenship (among other things) shape students' educational trajectories.

Finally, Souto-Manning and Rabadi-Raol (Chapter 9) identify a problem of practice, how quality has been defined in early childhood education, and use the insights from critical race theory, critical pedagogy, and translanguaging to critique and reenvision the notion of quality. Their critical review highlights how the National Association for the Education of Young Children's definition of developmentally appropriate practice, the dominant standard for quality in early childhood education, disenfranchises multiply marginalized children. Souto-Manning and Rabadi-Raol conclude by proposing intersectionally just design principles for quality in early childhood education that honor the knowledges, experiences, practices, developmental trajectories, and intersectional identities of children from the global majority. This is a critical intervention because it is focused on the assumptions and practices found in the earliest school settings that students encounter.

Although intersectionality began as a way to examine marginalization, it has also been used to analyze the complex ways that marginalization *and* privilege operate. Robert and Yu (Chapter 5) draw on Choo and Ferree's (2010) observation that when intersectionality is used primarily to give voice to marginalized groups, it can also leave the normative categories that define them as the *other* unmarked, thereby reinforcing deficit assumptions and leaving the structural dynamics that shape group experiences underanalyzed. In Souto-Manning and Rabadi-Raol's critique of the National Association for the Education of Young Children's articulation of developmentally appropriate practice (Chapter 9), an approach to teaching that also serves as the foundation for accreditation standards for early childhood programs, they highlight how White monolingual and monocultural values and experiences are cast as normative, while the family and cultural practices, knowledges, and experiences of multiply marginalized students are framed as deficits. Bullock's analysis of how intersectionality has been used in critical mathematics education research highlights numerous examples of the ways that privilege is relative and contextual. For example, in reviewing an analysis of intracategorical intersectionality (McCall, 2005), Bullock (Chapter 6) observed that English-speaking Latinx students experienced more opportunities to learn in their mathematics classes than did their emergent bilingual Latinx peers because they could more easily understand curricular materials and communicate with their teachers. Ireland and colleagues (Chapter 10) also note that there are some STEM settings where Black women may experience advantage because of gender, race, ability, or social class.

CONCLUDING THOUGHTS

Taken as a whole, the chapters in this volume highlight how intersectional perspectives applied to education research are currently more of a conceptual aspiration than a consolidated comprehensive framework. Thus, it is understandable that, for some researchers, intersectionality may appear to be a fuzzy concept or a vague idea that is difficult to accurately measure. The framing and application of conceptual tools associated with intersectionality may be perceived by some in the field as ideological posturing more than as a well-defined and systematic model of inquiry. In short, advocating for the use of intersectionality in education research may be seen as naive at best and as a dangerously wrong approach at worst. The latter perspective will probably find fertile ground among those who voice the common complaints about our field's lack of a unified and well-codified body of knowledge (Mehta, 2013).

Ultimately, we believe, as is demonstrated by the chapters in this volume, that one of the strengths of intersectionality, as both a concept and an aspiration, is that it requires researchers to account for complexity and diversity within and across learning spaces in ways that incorporate quantitative and qualitative methods and perspectives. Instead of adjusting our scholarship and limiting our research questions to what can be neatly described, counted, measured, and clearly defined, we want to reaffirm our commitment to embracing the challenges of conducting research that accepts the irreducible multiplicity of intersecting dynamics of educational contexts. As Carbado and colleagues (2013) remind us, theory—including intersectionality—"is never done, nor exhausted by its prior articulations or movements; it is always already an analysis-in-progress" (p. 304). As an analysis-in-progress, this volume reflects our moral commitment to contributing to the production of robust and usable knowledge for advancing educational equity and justice.[3]

ACKNOWLEDGMENTS

We would like to thank all of the authors for their time and effort in crafting the chapters of this volume. We are also grateful to the reviewers who shared their expertise and provided important advice to the authors. We are especially thankful to Vivian Gadsden, Felice Levine, John Neikirk, and the American Educational Research Association Journal Publications Committee for their support in making this volume possible, and to Keon McGuire, Margarita Pivovarova, and Amelia Marcetti Topper for their helpful feedback on the introduction.

NOTES

[1]Organizations such as the African American Policy Forum are addressing the erasure of Black women's lives in social movements related to police brutality, powerfully demanding the public to #SayHerName (African American Policy Forum, 2018). Similarly, the Black Lives Matter (n.d.) movement, which was launched by three activists in 2013 in response to the acquittal of George Zimmerman for the murder of Trayvon Martin, reflects the legacy of the efforts by women of color to organize around a platform of intersectional justice (Khan-Cullors & Bandele, 2018).

[2]This volume is not exhaustive of the topics that could have been included on intersectionality. Our hope is that the chapters in this volume provide an impetus for scholarship on additional intersectional topics, including LGBTQI (Lesbian, Gay, Bisexual, Transgender, Queer or Questioning, and Intersex), Indigenous, and religious perspectives, among others.

[3]We use the term *usable knowledge* to refer to the intentional processes that enhance access to and engagement with research-based knowledge, as well as affordances for inquiry and implementation not restricted to the scholarly community (Fischman, Anderson, Tefera, & Zuiker, 2018). In this sense, the usability of intersectional analysis could be advanced by the development of explicit strategies promoting dialogue, reflection, and adaptation—within and beyond disciplinary, professional, or technical communities—to foster and sustain processes of conceptual inquiry and/or educational problem solving.

REFERENCES

African American Policy Forum. (2018). *#SayHerName*. Retrieved from http://www.aapf.org/sayhername/

Artiles, A. J., Dorn, S., & Bal, A. (2016). Objects of protection, enduring nodes of difference: Disability intersections with "other" differences, 1916–2016. *Review of Research in Education, 40,* 777–820.

Beale, F. M. (1970). Double jeopardy: To be Black and female. In R. Morgan (Ed.), *Sisterhood is powerful* (pp. 340–352). New York, NY: Random House.

Bilge, S. (2013). Intersectionality undone: Saving intersectionality from feminist intersectionality studies. *Du Bois Review, 10,* 405–424.

Black Lives Matter. (n.d.). *Herstory.* Retrieved from https://blacklivesmatter.com/about/herstory/

Carastathis, A. (2016). *Intersectionality: Origins, contestations, horizons.* Lincoln: University of Nebraska Press.

Carbado, D. W., Crenshaw, K. W., Mays, V. M., & Tomlinson, B. (2013). Intersectionality: Mapping the movements of a theory. *Du Bois Review, 10,* 303–312.

Choo, H., & Ferree, M. (2010). Practicing intersectionality in sociological research: A critical analysis of inclusions, interactions, and institutions in the study of inequalities. *Sociological Theory, 28,* 129–149.

Chun, J. J., Lipsitz, G., & Shin, Y. (2013). Intersectionality as a social movement strategy: Asian immigrant women advocates. *Signs, 38,* 917–940.

Clarke, A. Y., & McCall, L. (2013). Intersectionality and social explanation in social science research. *Du Bois Review, 10,* 349–363.

Collins, P. H. (2000). *Black feminist thought: Knowledge, consciousness, and the politics of empowerment* (2d ed.). New York, NY: Routledge.

Collins, P. H. (2015). Intersectionality's definitional dilemmas. *Annual Review of Sociology, 41,* 1–20.

Collins, P. H., & Bilge, S. (2016). *Intersectionality.* Malden, MA: Polity Press.

Crenshaw, K. (1989). Demarginalizing the intersection of race and sex: A Black feminist critique of antidiscrimination doctrine, feminist theory and antiracist politics. *University of Chicago Legal Forum, 189,* 139–167.

Crenshaw, K. (1991). Mapping the margins: Intersectionality, identity politics, and violence against women of color. *Stanford Law Review, 46,* 1241–1299.

Davis, K., 2008. Intersectionality as buzzword. *Feminist Theory, 9,* 67–85.

Fischman, G. E., Anderson, K. T., Tefera, A. A., & Zuiker, S. J. (2018). If mobilizing educational research is the answer, who can afford to ask the question? An analysis of faculty perspectives on knowledge mobilization for scholarship in education. *AERA Open, 4*(1), 1–17.

Guinier, L., & Torres, G. (2002). *The miner's canary.* Cambridge, MA: Harvard University Press.

Hancock, A. M. (2016). *Intersectionality: An intellectual history.* New York, NY: Oxford University Press.

Khan-Cullors, P., & Bandele, A. (2018). *When they call you a terrorist: A Black Lives Matter memoir.* New York, NY: St. Martin's Press.

King, D. K. (1988). Multiple jeopardy, multiple consciousness: The context of a Black feminist ideology. *Signs, 14*(1), 42–72.

Ladson-Billings, G., & Tate, W. F. (1995). Toward a critical race theory of education. *Teachers College Record, 97*(1), 47–65.

Levine-Rasky, C. (2011). Intersectionality theory applied to whiteness and middle-classness. *Social Identities, 17,* 239–253.

Lorde, A. (1984). *Sister outsider: Essays and speeches.* Berkeley, CA: Crossing Press.

Lugones, M. (2010). Toward a decolonial feminism. *Hypatia, 25,* 742–759.

McCall, L. (2005). The complexity of intersectionality. *Signs, 30,* 1771–1800.

Mehta, J. (2013). How paradigms create politics: The transformation of American educational policy, 1980–2001. *American Educational Research Journal, 50*, 285–324.

Moraga, C., & Anzaldúa, G. (Eds.). (2015). *This bridge called my back: Writings by radical women of color* (4th ed.). Albany: SUNY Press.

Patil, V. (2013). From patriarchy to intersectionality: A transnational feminist assessment of how far we've really come. *Signs, 38*, 847–867.

Patton, L. D., Crenshaw, K., Haynes, C., & Watson, T. N. (2016). Why we can't wait: (Re)examining the opportunities and challenges for Black women and girls in education. *Journal of Negro Education, 85*, 194–198.

Salem, S. (2016). Intersectionality and its discontents: Intersectionality as traveling theory. *European Journal of Women's Studies*. Advance online publication. doi:10.1177/1350506816643999

Yuval-Davis, N. (2006). Intersectionality and feminist politics. *European Journal of Women's Studies, 13*, 193–209.

Chapter 1

Intersectionality, Race-Gender Subordination, and Education

ANGELA HARRIS
University of California, Davis

ZEUS LEONARDO
University of California, Berkeley

In this chapter, we unpack intersectionality as an analytical framework. First, we cite Black Lives Matter as an impetus for discussing intersectionality's current traction. Second, we review the genealogy of "intersectionality" beginning with Kimberlé Crenshaw's formulation, which brought a Black Studies provocation into legal discourse in order to challenge existing antidiscrimination doctrine and single-axis theorizing. The third, and most central, task of the chapter is our account of intersectionality's utility for social analysis. We examine some of the issues raised by the metaphor of the intersection and some of the debates surrounding the concept, such as the tension between fragmenting and universalizing perspectives mediated by the notion of "strategic essentialism." Fourth, we review how education researchers have explained race and gender subordination in education since Ladson-Billings and Tate's Teachers College Record *article. We conclude with some remarks concerning future research on intersectionality.*

In the summer of 2014, as accounts of brutal and unjustified police killings of Black people circulated across social media and mass media in the United States, a new social movement came to prominence (Freelon, McIlwain, & Clark, 2016). Black Lives Matter (BLM, also called the Movement for Black Lives) emerged from a July 2013 Twitter hashtag and became a mass movement in the wake of the 2014 killing of Michael Brown by Officer Darren Wilson in Ferguson, Missouri. Like other American social movements that have arisen to protest group subordination, BLM

Review of Research in Education
March 2018, Vol. 42, pp. 1–27
DOI: 10.3102/0091732X18759071
© 2018 AERA. http://rre.aera.net

has been tagged as an instance of "identity politics" and criticized for its allegedly single-minded and exclusionary focus—notably, under a competing Twitter hashtag, #AllLivesMatter (Freelon et al., 2016). Yet a closer look at the way the founders of BLM describe their campaign reveals a far more sophisticated analysis. On their website, the BLM founders declare that their movement is explicitly built on principles of *intersectionality*.[1]

As one public health scholar defines it,

Intersectionality is a theoretical framework for understanding how multiple social identities such as race, gender, sexual orientation, SES [socioeconomic status], and disability intersect at the micro level of individual experience to reflect interlocking systems of privilege and oppression (i.e., racism, sexism, heterosexism, classism) at the macro social-structural level. (Bowleg, 2012, p. 1267)

In this chapter, we provide an overview of "intersectionality" as a theoretical framework, assessing its utility and its limitations. We recognize that given the widespread embrace of the term—which provoked some at the 2014 American Studies Association conference to call for its abandonment (Bartlett, 2017)—our investigation is necessarily anything but exhaustive.[2] Reflecting our respective disciplinary homes, our focus in this review is on the literatures of law and education.

METHODOLOGY

A search through "all content" in the Westlaw legal database on June 7, 2017, turned up 2,979 uses of the word "intersectionality" in "all state and federal" sources, with 2,706 uses of the word appearing in the secondary literature. We read and analyzed the 50 most cited articles using the term in the Westlaw database. These "top 50" articles were supplemented, based on our familiarity with the literature, with another 10 to 15 legal articles proposing substitutes for the term. To find works still in press, we searched the combination of the terms *intersectionality* and *discrimination* in the Legal Scholarship Network thread of the Social Science Research Network, obtaining the 50 most recently posted papers using both these terms.[3]

A keyword search on "intersectionality and education" in the ERIC database generated 214 results for books and articles. We whittled down this number by privileging works that use intersectionality as a descriptor of the author's analysis, that is, as an *analytic framework* rather than a proxy for arguments about diversity or multiple identities in education. We do not center a more general uptake of the concept that predates Crenshaw's formulation without any specific connection with her work on race-gender subordination since the end of the 1980s.

As with the search in the legal database, as experts in the field we supplement the ERIC search with knowledge of the research literature in education wherein intersectionality appears in the analysis, such as works inspired by critical race theory (CRT) by authors within that specialization. Since intersectionality in education is still a recent methodological or conceptual innovation, at this point any terminological substitutes for Crenshaw's formulation have been few and negligible, some suggestions notwithstanding (Núñez, 2014), and therefore are not part of the methodology for the search in education.

We are aware that several recent books also examine "intersectionality" and its provenance. These include monographs by Patricia Hill Collins and Sirma Bilge (2016), and by Ange-Marie Hancock (2016), as well as edited collections (see, e.g., Berger & Guidroz, 2010; Grzanka, 2014). We also note that the legal scholar most often credited with the invention of the term—Kimberlé Williams Crenshaw—has her own book in press on the topic.

GENEALOGY

In their monograph exploring "intersectionality" as a modern-day "key concept," Patricia Hill Collins and Sirma Bilge (2016) acknowledge that the word has been taken up in a broad variety of contexts, from the academic to the political to the popular everyday.[4] They also remind the reader that although the term is usually said to have been "coined" by legal scholar Kimberlé Crenshaw in 1991, a more accurate genealogy would follow the concept back to women of color scholar-activists working in liberation-focused social movements at least as far back as the 1960s and 1970s, if not before.[5] A well-known example they discuss is the Combahee River Collective's "A Black Feminist Statement," written in 1977, which analyzes the role of heterosexism and homophobia in Black women's lives along with capitalism, racism, and patriarchy. Collins and Bilge also go back further to highlight the 1970 publication of the anthology *The Black Woman*, edited by Toni Cade Bambara. In their view, this anthology conveyed the message that "black women would never gain their freedom without attending to oppressions of race *and* class *and* gender" (Collins & Bilge, 2016, p. 66). They call special attention to Frances Beal's chapter, which had been originally published as a pamphlet in 1969. In "Double Jeopardy: To Be Black and Female," Beal examines the workings of capitalism, racism, and sexism in Black women's lives. According to Collins and Bilge, "Her approach is systemic: her double critique of patriarchy within the Black Power movement and of racism in the white women's liberation movement also criticizes capitalism" (p. 66).

For Collins and Bilge (2016), uncovering this broader genealogy of "intersectionality" is important because it reveals both the centrality of the concept to social justice movements and the tendency for ideas circulated by professional academics to be privileged over the same ideas circulated by grassroots intellectuals. Indeed, they argue that the widespread (scholarly) attribution of the term to Crenshaw is an effect of academic politics. In their account, university and college programs and departments of Black Studies, women's studies, and ethnic studies were instituted in the 1970s in response to widespread campus insurgency by students of color, who demanded scholarship and teaching relevant to their concerns. Because of their "political" origins, these departments and fields of study were consistently marginalized in colleges and universities, and the faculty associated with them were often suspected of flouting norms of academic rigor. Women of color students and faculty who fought their way into academia to establish and grow these programs brought the ideas associated with what would become "intersectionality" with them, but as Collins and Bilge note, these new "insiders" also fell subject to the pressure to obey institutional norms such as the injunction to conduct "dispassionate" scholarship, to embrace the theory of the "romantic author," and to avoid social "activism." For Collins and Bilge, Crenshaw's supposed 1991 "invention" of intersectionality serves to reconcile these tensions:

> A new umbrella term might enable coalition building among the exponentially growing study areas of race, class, and gender. Naming the field might also help legitimate the kind of scholarship produced within these areas by making it more compatible with academic norms of discovery, authorship and ownership. Attributing the discovery of the term "intersectionality" to Kimberlé Crenshaw fits these academic norms. (Collins & Bilge, 2016, pp. 80–81)

Collins and Bilge (2016) warn, however, that this new academic provenance of "intersectionality" created the risk that the term's debt to radical social justice organizing would be lost. Indeed, Bilge (2013) argues that White feminists have already attempted to claim the term as their own, erasing its origin in the struggles of women of color.

Nevertheless, BLM (and Crenshaw's own organization, the African American Policy Forum) testifies to the continued centrality of intersectionality as a framework for social justice activism. What about academia? In the next section, we reflect on the utility and limitations of intersectionality in social theory generally, before turning to its employment in the disciplines of law and education.

INTERSECTIONALITY AND SOCIAL THEORIZING: SOME GENERAL OBSERVATIONS

Although most recent academic reflections on "intersectionality" acknowledge its ubiquity in contemporary scholarship on identity and difference, the term has had many competitors. Within legal scholarship alone, rival formulations include "interlocking oppressions" (Kalsem & Williams, 2010), "wholism" (Cunningham, 1998), "multidimensionality" (McGinley & Cooper, 2013), "inter-connectivity" (Valdes, 1995), "co-synthesis" (Kwan, 1997), "complex bias" (Kotkin, 2009), and "symbiosis" (Ehrenreich, 2002). Scholars have also offered metaphors other than an intersection for understanding the phenomenon, including the "Koosh ball" and the "Rubik's cube." Collins and Bilge (2016) might argue that these rival formulations were prompted by the continuing institutional lure of intellectual credit. For us, the multiple competing terms also indicate the utility of intersectionality—and its limitations as a tool of critical social theory.

One point seems indisputable: within the world of social theory, we are all intersectionalists (if that is a word) now. Descriptively, "intersectionality" provides a less cynical way to understand the steady emergence of new perspectives and fields of study within academia; scholars informed by the concept are constantly prompted to ask, "What or who is obscured by this analysis or focus of attention?" Prescriptively, "intersectionality" serves as a powerful reminder to pay attention to the margins of all identity-based organizing and analysis. The title of a well-known anthology says it all: *All the Women Are White, All the Blacks Are Men, But Some of Us Are Brave* (Hull, Bell-Scott, & Smith, 1982).

Intersectionality disrupts group-based formulations such as "women," "people of color," and "sexual minorities" in at least three ways. First, intersectionality calls attention to social identities that are consistently treated as marginal or invisible because they are conceptualized as mere subsets of broader, larger, or more "significant" assemblages. Second, intersectionality points to the complex nature of power, undermining all reductive theories of oppression.[6] This move also helps scholars and organizers resist the "oppression Olympics"—the desire to have one identity (usually one's own) or form of subordination acknowledged as more important or fundamental than others (see Smith, 2006). That said, although intersectionality research attests to the interplay between social organization and power, it does not put forth a particular theory of power as such. Third, intersectionality points to the gap between social categorization and the complexity of intersubjective experience: the fact that no single social label—female, Black, bisexual, poor—can ever exhaust what it means for an individual to travel in the world, and therefore that no analysis or label is ever complete.

These disruptions have proved powerful within academia, helping scholars develop new perspectives on old problems and call attention to invisible or ignored justice claims (for a public health example, see Bowleg, 2012). Intersectionality has been generative for scholars in at least three ways. First, the concept has inspired scholar-activists to look for identities and forms of subordination made invisible by hegemonic formulations, and to develop increasingly sophisticated and nuanced understandings of social formations. This increasing sophistication is visible among scholars and activists alike. For example, within legal scholarship, CRT and feminist theory have given rise to "LatCrit" (Latinx critical theory),[7] Asian American jurisprudence, queer theory, and "Dis/Crit" (critical disability theory). Similarly, consciousness of the intersectional nature of sexual minority oppression has produced a series of increasingly complex identity terms used for organizing, from "homosexual" to "gay and lesbian" to "LGBT" to "LGBTQIA+" and beyond. Many of the organizers of these new initiatives, moreover, acknowledge the need to keep their borders fluid in light of the tendency of more privileged identities to obscure the needs and experiences of the less privileged (see, e.g., Matambanadzo, Valdes, & Vélez-Martinez, 2016, p. 443, remarking on LatCrit's emergence from a sense of frustration at the marginalization of Latinx identity within CRT and LatCrit's decision to maintain a "strategic anti-essentialism" going forward).

Second, consciousness of intersectionality has led scholars and scholar-activists to pay attention to the structural interpenetration of various forms of oppression (Matambanadzo et al., 2016, p. 445, avowing a commitment to "critical engagements of sex, gender, and sexuality, together with race, gender, and class, as interlocking categories and systems in programmatic terms"). The days of unthinking intellectual "essentialism" seem to be behind us, at least in the humanities, the social sciences, education, and law. Instead, critical social theorists routinely acknowledge that any specific focus will address some forms of subordination while neglecting others, such as Marxism's class-reductive limitations when attempting to explain race and gender relations, which is not necessary to rehearse here.

Third, given the dynamic nature of social identity formation, intersectionality promises a continuous generativity. Collins and Bilge (2016) observe that this is nicely fitted to an institutional world in which academics always need new topics for conferences, panels, dissertations, and research agendas. More important, however, intersectionality reminds us of the inexhaustibility of the struggle for social justice. For any given analysis, initiative, or campaign of resistance at any given point in time, no matter how narrowly or broadly specified, there will always be a remainder, some identity or experience that is marginalized or made invisible. Intersectionality is in this way well suited to the postmodern view that political and social groups are continually emerging and making claims for recognition and redistribution—that there is no point at which all identities will be recognized and all justice claims satisfied (see Butler, 1990, p. 182; see also Connolly, 1995, p. 186). Justice is an endlessly receding horizon—a recognition that may be disheartening but that accords with experience.

Intersectionality, however, also has its limitations, which have led some scholars to declare a "postintersectionality" moment (see Levit, 2002) and others, as noted above, to call for its linguistic "death." One of these limitations, which has led to various rival formulations, is the "intersection" metaphor itself. In her *University of Chicago Legal Forum* article, Crenshaw (1989) asks us to conceptualize intersectionality based on the metaphor of a roadway:

Consider an analogy to traffic in an intersection, coming and going in all four directions. Discrimination, like traffic through an intersection, may flow in one direction, and it may flow in another. If an accident happens in an intersection, it can be caused by cars traveling from any number of directions and, sometimes, from all of them.[8]

One criticism of the intersection-as-road metaphor is that it calls up a mental representation of two-dimensional space—a limitation shared by the Venn diagram, also used by some scholars to represent intersectionality (see Elengold, 2018, for a discussion). The "Koosh ball" metaphor and "multidimensionality" as an alternative term have emerged in response to this concern.[9] A second critique of the intersection metaphor is that it does not reflect the multiple levels of scale at which each axis of subordination operates—for example, race acts on individual, interpersonal, institutional, and structural levels simultaneously. This has led some critics to worry about uses of intersectionality that, for example, give primacy to "psychology" or subjective "identity" at the expense of structural subordination (see, e.g., Williams, 2002).[10] A third critique of the intersection metaphor is that it implicitly figures all forms of subordination as parallel—lending itself to the reduction of intersectionality to a glib list—"race, class, gender, sexuality, disability"—that fails to explore what is distinctive about each form of oppression, and/or fails to explore any particular axis in any depth.[11] Fourth, the intersection-as-road metaphor might be misunderstood to suggest that the nature of subordination is fixed and unchanging, like a road, rather than endlessly shifting and changing in response to political, social, and economic conditions.

A theory of metaphor is appropriate to invoke insofar as linguistic representation cannot be said to occur after an event or as the attempt to *capture* it post facto. In other words, as a constitutive element of a social activity system, mediation tools like language, and more specifically metaphor, function as dialectical nodes in the relationship between material reality and the meaning, or sign, system (see Leonardo, 2016; Ricoeur, 1975; Vygotsky, 1978). In Vygotsky's (1978) *Mind in Society*, language, speech, and sign are described as part of the "alloy" that makes up meaning and material life. Understood this way, the intersectional metaphor is less a way to represent through a convenient linguistic trope an existing reality but rather structures how we arrive at a particular understanding of a certain reality. Therefore, it is a choice that comes with educational consequences and political commitments. In the literature, the metaphor of an "intersection" has been helpful in grasping the limitations of single-axis explanations in favor of a cross-cutting analysis. As such, this discussion highlights the power of metaphor to define constitutively the terrain under investigation while avoiding the dangers associated with portraying social life as somehow "made of language," otherwise known as linguistic idealism. Volosinov (2006), puts it this way:

> The individual consciousness, for its part, is deprived of any support in reality. It becomes either all or nothing. . . For idealism it has become all . . . For psychological positivism, on the contrary, consciousness amounts to nothing. (p. 12)

In its best moments, intersectionality represents the solder in the alloy between speech and the social conditions that make it possible.

Second, intersectionality's limitation is that it is not itself a "theory" in the scientific sense: It cannot generate any testable predictions about the world and therefore can only supplement rather than replace empirical methods (see Bowleg, p. 1268, calling intersectionality a "theoretical framework" rather than a "theory"). Here, intersectionality's seeming death blow to single-axis theorizing has arguably left a hole in social theorizing. Because "grand theories" such as Marxism and dominance feminism are out of fashion, we are left with the vague sense that all forms of oppression are always everywhere but with no new analytical tools with which to explore and understand these forms and how they operate. Some "postintersectionality" scholars have been moved by this limitation to develop their own theories of how forms of subordination interact (see, e.g., Valdes, 1995, on "interconnectivity"; see also Ehrenreich, 2002). Others have simply enjoined scholars to investigate all forms of subordination at all times (see, e.g., Kwan, 1997), without providing specific tools with which to do so. Still others have argued that the attempt to derive a theory from intersectionality is inappropriate "metatheoretical musing" (see Bilge, 2013, p. 411).

Third, intersectionality contains only a partial account of power. Scholars guided by intersectionality are led to understand that systems of subordination, as they are brought to bear on social identities, never travel alone: For instance, race always operates through gender, and gender through sexuality. However, intersectionality does not tell us which of the multiple layers of oppression and/or experience represented by a given "intersection" is most consequential at any given time, or how and why class, say, works differently from disability.[12] This limitation has impelled scholars both to criticize intersectionality and to offer their own supplemental formulations. For example, Darren Hutchinson worries that "it is impossible to theorize about or study a group when each person in that group is 'composed of a complex and unique matrix of identities that shift in time, is never fixed, is constantly unstable and forever distinguishable from everyone else in the universe'" (as quoted by Elengold, 2018, p. 16). Legal scholar Nancy Ehrenreich argues that intersectionality scholars have ignored the situation in which actors are simultaneously privileged and oppressed, and offers the concept of "hybrid intersectionality" in response (Ehrenreich, 2002, p. 257). Legal scholar Mari Matsuda, like Crenshaw a founder of CRT in law, offers "looking to the bottom" as an ethical and political goal of organizing and social theorizing, thus providing the focus that intersectionality alone lacks—but raising the question—where is the bottom?—(Matsuda, 1987). Other scholars and activists simply use intersectionality as a supplement to their own theories of power, whatever those might be. As Collins and Bilge (2016) point out, however, intersectionality's incomplete theory of power places it one dangerous step away from *diversity*, a term that has been used to efface power analysis altogether (see also Berrey, 2015). Intersectionality differs from the more established tradition of multiculturalism in education. Although the two interventions are certainly compatible, the latter's focus on diversity differs from the former's emphasis on subordination that results from asymmetrical power relations. Addressing diversity without addressing subordination eschews the process whereby race and gender difference is produced ideologically and materially. In other words, uncritically promoting diversity in education and social institutions may not necessarily challenge subordination.

Finally, a fourth difficulty with the academic uptake of "intersectionality" is best laid at the feet of those who have misunderstood its point. As Leslie McCall points out, the concept can be employed toward at least three different theoretical ends: to criticize and dismantle accepted categories (what McCall calls demonstrating "anti-categorical complexity"), to hold up for analysis the experiences of dismissed or ignored groups (what McCall calls employing "intra-categorical complexity"—an example is the work of Black feminists from which the term *intersectionality* emerged), and to permit scholars, holding one category or axis of oppression constant, to investigate its interplay with other axes of oppression (what McCall calls the demonstration of "intercategorical complexity"; McCall, 2005). A rigid fidelity to anticategorical complexity, however, can be used to undermine projects of intra- and intercategorical complexity; the result may be the complaint, sometimes heard, that intersectionality makes categorization itself impossible. As McCall notes, however, this complaint betrays a conflation of the different projects that "intersectionality" makes possible; it is not a limitation of the term itself.

INTERSECTIONALITY IN LAW

Crenshaw is a legal scholar, and her initial use of the term was a critical response to some judicial interpretations of federal employment discrimination law. In this section, we offer some reflections on the uptake of "intersectionality" in jurisprudence—that is, its use by lawyers, legislators, and judges rather than academics.

Although as noted above, a search for "intersectionality" in Westlaw yielded 2,979 uses of the word, the vast majority of the references (2,706) were in the secondary literature. Legislators, attorneys, and judges, by and large, have not embraced the term as have scholars and activists. This would not be troubling if the substance of Crenshaw's original critique were being addressed by other means or under other rubrics. Unfortunately, this is only partially the case.

Some background on Crenshaw's critique of Title VII jurisprudence may be helpful. Title VII of the Civil Rights Act of 1964, a federal statute, prohibits employment discrimination on the basis of "race, color, religion, sex, or national origin." Writing at the end of the 1980s, Crenshaw noted that some judges interpreting this language treated each of the grounds for antidiscrimination protection—race, color, religion, sex, national origin—as separate and mutually exclusive. For these judges, moreover, the benchmark for sex discrimination was the experience of a White woman, and the benchmark for race discrimination, the experience of a Black man. Black women, according to this framework, could only claim to have been discriminated against on the basis of sex if their experiences were identical to those of White women, and conversely could only claim to have been discriminated against on the basis of race if their experiences were identical to those of Black men. "Compound" discrimination—the experience of being discriminated against specifically as a Black woman—was not recognizable under the law.

Crenshaw (1989) argued that this approach to Title VII was wrongheaded. She wrote,

Black women can experience discrimination in ways that are both similar to and different from those experienced by white women and Black men. Black women sometimes experience discrimination in ways similar to white women's experiences; sometimes they share very similar experiences with Black men. Yet often they experience double-discrimination—the combined effects of practices which discriminate on the basis of race, and on the basis of sex. And sometimes, they experience discrimination as Black women—not the sum of race and sex discrimination, but as Black women. (p. 149)

Have courts and legislatures gotten the message? Kate Sablosky Elengold (2018) argues that the answer in the United States is no. She cites a 2011 empirical study of employment discrimination actions, in which the authors, examining a representative sample of judicial opinions over 35 years of federal employment discrimination litigation, concluded that the presence of intersectionality "dramatically reduce[d the] odds of plaintiff victory" (Best, Edelman, Krieger, & Eliason, 2011).[13] Elengold (2018) summarizes their findings:

Plaintiffs exhibiting identification with more than one traditionally subordinated group ("demographic intersectionality," also known as a "complex claimant" or an "intersectional" [claimant]) and/or plaintiffs who allege discrimination on the basis of overlapping ascriptive characteristics ("claim intersectionality" or "intersectional discrimination") are less successful in employment discrimination actions. (p. 6)

This is despite the fact that claims involving intersectionality are increasing. According to Best et al. (2011),

In the 1970s and 1980s, less than 10 percent of EEO [equal employment opportunity] opinions dealt with intersectional claims. . . . [T]he proportion began rising around 1990, and by the second half of the decade, more than a quarter of EEO opinions involved intersectional claims. (p. 1008)

Nevertheless, the study authors found that both claim intersectionality and demographic intersectionality were damaging to plaintiffs in court. Indeed, true to Crenshaw's original critique, "non-white women are less likely to win their cases than is any other demographic group" (Best et al., 2011, p. 992).[14]

Elengold (2018) puts forth several reasons for the continued failure of judges to recognize intersectionality in employment discrimination cases. First is the "protected category" structure of the statute itself, which invites judges to slot worker experiences into distinct boxes and to find "comparators" based on one characteristic at a time. This "check the box" approach makes the interaction between categories of discrimination difficult to recognize, and also may encourage judges to fear the "many-headed hydra" that might result were they to recognize the existence of multiple simultaneous types of discrimination.[15] Second, Elengold notes the reliance of attorneys on "stock stories" of discrimination. Despite Crenshaw's criticisms, these stock stories continue to center on the stories of White female plaintiffs in sex discrimination cases and Black male plaintiffs in race discrimination cases. Third, Elengold takes note of the forms produced by the Equal Employment Opportunity Commission (the federal agency charged with managing Title VII administrative complaints) for would-be litigants to fill out. These forms, like Title VII itself, represent discrimination as a series of separate and distinct boxes to be checked, ignoring the possibility of subcategories or category interaction.

Intersectionality has been somewhat more successfully incorporated into international human rights law and European Union (EU) law. With respect to international law, Campbell (2015) explains that the United Nations (UN) recognizes two "mainstream" human rights treaties, the International Covenant on Civil and Political Rights and the International Covenant on Economic, Social and Cultural Rights. These treaties contain antidiscrimination clauses that are phrased, like Title VII, in terms of a list of protected "grounds" or categories of discrimination. The committees interpreting these treaty provisions have explicitly affirmed the concept of intersectionality.[16] Nevertheless, implementation has been difficult, in part due to the category-bound language of the treaties themselves.

Paradoxically, treaties that on their face recognize only single-axis discrimination have been more user-friendly for intersectional litigants and claims. Several international treaties protect the rights of specific groups, such as the Convention for the Elimination of Discrimination Against Women (CEDAW). As Campbell (2015) observes, CEDAW on its face requires single-axis analysis: There is no reference to categories of discrimination other than "sex" and "women," which has led other scholars to conclude that it does not recognize intersectionality. This apparent weakness, however, Campbell argues, has actually enabled CEDAW's interpreters to employ intersectionality, in the form of "intercategorical complexity." Campbell calls attention to the CEDAW Committee's General Recommendation No. 28, which states that "the discrimination of women based on sex and gender is inextricably linked with other factors that affect women, such as race ethnicity, religion or belief, health, status, age, class, caste, sexual orientation and gender identity" (Campbell, 2015, p. 489). Campbell concludes, "The conception of women in CEDAW is not based on a privileged sub-set of women but encompasses all of their identities" (p. 489).[17]

Intersectionality has also been explicitly embraced by some international law advocates. In November 2000, an expert group organized by the UN Division for the Advancement of Women, the Office of the High Commissioner for Human Rights, and the UN Development Fund for Women convened to and "identified seven areas where gender and racial discrimination overlap—including, *inter alia*, criminal justice, population movements, trafficking and armed conflict—the concept of intersectionality was expressly examined" (Chow, 2016, p. 10).[18] Similarly, interpretation of the Convention on the Elimination of Racial Discrimination has produced a "holistic" structural approach to discrimination that embraces intersectionality.[19] This is perhaps not surprising; as Grzanka (2014) notes, Crenshaw penned a background paper on race and gender discrimination for the 2000 UN World Conference on Racism that explained the concept of intersectionality in some detail.

The antidiscrimination law of the EU has adopted the term *multiple discrimination* rather than *intersectionality*. Bullock and Masselot (2012–2013) explain,

Although multiple discrimination is not defined in any legally binding EU text, in the context of EU law, scholars use multiple discrimination to refer to "all instances of discrimination on several grounds contained in [the Treaty on the Functioning of the European Union, Art. 9] and in other instruments. (p. 62)

Bullock and Masselot (2012–2013) observe that EU advocates have been extremely active in promoting the recognition of intersectionality. Nevertheless, EU antidiscrimination law has been beset by the "list" problem. It is also not clear whether the countries of the EU have properly reckoned with the structural focus of intersectionality. For example, Kantola (2014) observes that EU directives on multiple discrimination have successfully prodded Nordic member states to adopt antidiscrimination provisions covering a variety of different grounds in addition to gender, but she doubts that these developments add up to a "genuine engagement with intersectionality" (p. 12). Instead, she fears, the result is a heightened focus on individual rights, rather than "structures and employers' or public authorities' responsibilities to remove barriers to equality" (p. 13).

It must be concluded, therefore, that in the field of law, scholars have embraced the concept of intersectionality (not without vigorous attempts at substituting other terms and metaphors), but judges and legislators, by and large, have not. More than two decades after the introduction of the idea into the legal literature, full legal recognition of the intersectional nature of discrimination remains elusive.

INTERSECTIONALITY AND EDUCATION

After its recent 25th anniversary, the term, concept, or analytical framework of intersectionality has had a significant impact on the field of education. Many collections under the moniker of CRT in education include a chapter on, section on, or frequent mention of intersectionality (e.g., see Dixson & Rousseau, 2017; Lynn & Dixson, 2013; Taylor, Gillborn, & Ladson-Billings, 2009). We might credit the first CRT-inspired Ladson-Billings and Tate (1995) article in education with jump-starting the use of intersectionality. But when they write, "[W]e discuss the intersection of race and property as a central construct in understanding a critical race theoretical approach to education" (p. 58), their deployment of intersectional thought implicates race with property relations. They gesture to Cheryl Harris's (1995) chapter on "whiteness as property" to argue that CRT in education becomes the fulcrum for a critique of White liberalism as well as a certain lack of militancy they find in multiculturalism. In this early stage of CRT in education, intersectionality represents less the full measure of Crenshaw's innovation but rather a more commonsense term that suggests a *connection* between two levels of analysis bridged by the image of a meeting point between them. Moreover, because Ladson-Billings and Tate center the power of whiteness in education, intersectionality functions through *analogy* rather than as an *analytic concept* in its own right.

When Ladson-Billings and Tate's breakout article engages Crenshaw, it occurs with respect to her 1988 *Harvard Law Review* article's concerns around the ambiguity of civil rights legislation. They do not cite her *University of Chicago Legal Forum* article that appeared a year later in 1989, which contains the inchoate form of intersectional analysis, or the *Stanford Law Review* article from 1991 that would eventually become the main text for understanding the framework of intersectionality. Their argument is more in line with a single-axis explanation centered on race, with class or property relations as a species of the race genus. That is, insofar as property rights are tied to race, race relations are not linked to a Marxist explanation of economic antagonism. This early conceptual framing between education and intersectionality warrants some historical context for two reasons.

One, after several decades of writings that interrogated Eurocentrism, multiculturalism became institutionalized in schools, corporate thinking, and public discourse. Such institutionalization meant that White interests converged with multiculturalism's intent to racially uplift non-White students, the former arguably compromising the latter project in a way that Bell's (2005) work could predict CRT in education becomes an alternative to the dominant framework of multiculturalism. The narrative of race subordination found in CRT competes with multiculturalism's model of multiple acculturation. It is possible to interpret this move as an intellectual break but equally possible to regard it as a continuity, with CRT being the next, and historically specific, stage of race analysis in education, perhaps the heir apparent to multiculturalism. In Ladson-Billings and Tate's first article on CRT in education, the authors challenge the discipline to extend beyond liberal multiculturalism toward a more militant form of race scholarship based on CRT in legal studies as a new or emerging tradition. Two, and with respect to intersectionality, Crenshaw's innovation had not yet taken hold by 1995, with Ladson-Billings and Tate's article having been crafted only a couple years after her original works on intersectionality appeared on the scene; it was not yet the cause célèbre. At this stage, the Ladson-Billings and Tate's (1995) article is not an intersectional argument in Crenshaw's sense despite its use of the term. That established, the 1995 article that "launched a thousand publications" (Leonardo, 2013, p. 4) inaugurates CRT in education out of which intersectionality, whether in Crenshaw's specific sense or a general twoness inherited from Du Bois (1989), becomes a dominant trope, at minimum, or an analytical framework, at maximum.

Ladson-Billings and Tate (1995) opened the door into which an entirely new way of making sense of the immanently racial nature of education enters. Out of this, intersectionality emerges as a key concept that unlocks the education house that race made, not only from the obvious racialized achievement gap but also all the way down the educational enterprise, from disciplinary policies (Parker & Stovall, 2004), to the overdiagnosis and overreferral of Black students to special education (Artiles, Dorn, & Bal, 2016), to teacher education in general (Milner, 2010). From Danielle Davis et al.'s (2015) collection, *Intersectionality in Educational Research*, or S. Hancock and Warren's (2017) *White Women's Work: Examining the Intersectionality of Teaching, Identity, and Race* in the United States, to Bhopal and Preston's (2012) *Intersectionality in Education* in the United Kingdom, intersectionality becomes a favored framework in CRT in education, arguably rivaled only by appropriations of Derrick Bell's (2005) "interest convergence" and counterstorytelling methodology (1992), and Harris's (1995) analogy between whiteness and property.

To editors Bhopal and Preston (2012), the role of intersectional analysis in education has been decisive. Going well beyond the race-gender system, the career of intersectionality in education has been fecund for studying the general process of othering. To Brah and Phoenix (2009), intersectionality has roots in Sojourner Truth's injunction "Ain't I a Woman?" to challenge the essentialist notion of "woman" (and we may add "Black"; see Dumas, 2010; Hall, 1996). Brah and Phoenix "regard the concept of 'intersectionality' as signifying the complex, irreducible, varied, and variable effects which ensue when multiple axis of differentiation. . . intersect in historically specific contexts" (p. 248). Intersectionality's effects on education scholars have been felt to such an extent that it includes any explanation about overlapping systems of oppression, psychological, social, or otherwise.

Once CRT becomes established in education, the term *intersectional(ity)* proliferates in the discipline's lexicon, from K–12 (Thomas & Stevenson, 2009) to higher education studies (Museus & Griffin, 2011), from physics education (Leyva, 2016) to physical education (Flintoff, Fitzgerald, & Scraton, 2008). Its closest ally, LatCrit, highlights immigration status and how the ability to speak languages other than English play a central role in the marginalization of Latinx youth (e.g., Covarrubias, 2011; Perez-Huber, 2010; Yosso, 2005). Even the actual consonant "x" in Latinx or Filipinx, symbolizes an intersection in a way that few letters, other than the "t," can claim. It becomes increasingly difficult to invoke the academic term casually, without any reference to Crenshaw's formulation, even when investigating relations of subordination not limited to a race-gender synthesis. It is similar to going down the rabbit hole of studies of ideology without any trace of Marx. Like Ladson-Billings and Tate (1995), Milner (2013) uses intersectionality generally when he writes,

It is important to note that examining the intersection of race and poverty can provide a lens for researchers and consumers of the findings of research to disentangle the role and salience of race in the educational experiences, opportunities, and outcomes of the libraries for particular students. (p. 28)

Noteworthy is Milner's (2013) use of the word "disentangle," arguably an attempt to isolate the "race effect" in studies of poverty rather than entangle race with class relations as coaxiomatic (cf. Grosfoguel, 2007). One finds a comingling of race and class micro aggressions in Sarcedo, Matias, Montoya, and Nishi's (2015) study where they document what they call "raceclassist microaggressions" that first-generation, low-income college students of color suffer. Appropriating Cheryl Harris's (1995) celebrated chapter on whiteness as property, Leonardo and Broderick (2011) argue that within a racialized study of disability, smartness functions ideologically like a form of property, thus intersecting race/whiteness with ability studies without referring to Crenshaw (cf. K. Young, 2016).

As CRT and intersectionality make their way across the discipline of education, their influence is accommodated into well-established paradigms. For instance, Volume 2 of James Banks's four-volume *Encyclopedia of Diversity in Education* contains extended sections on intersectionality. A long and introductory entry on intersectionality is written by Grant and Zwier (2012), followed by another entry on "Intersectionality of race, class, gender, and ethnicity" by Caruthers and Carter (2012; see also Grant & Zwier, 2011). Although more closely associated with multiculturalism, Grant and Zwier provide a lengthy genealogy of intersectionality in the social sciences, which centers Crenshaw but includes other influences like Patricia

Hill Collins (2000) and Iris Marion Young (1990). As such, Grant and Zwier (2012) broaden the history of intersectionality beyond Crenshaw when they state, "There is not one theory of intersectionality, but different conceptualizations and theoretizations of it, such as 'vectors of oppression and privilege,' 'interlocking systems,' and 'multiple jeopardy'" (p. 1263). Additionally, they add concerns that intersectional analysis' strength is also its weakness, mainly that it demands too much complexity and sophistication from writers and readers. The following entry by Caruthers and Carter, by contrast, places intersectionality squarely within Crenshaw's scholarship even as they expand its analytic borders beyond race and gender. To the latter authors, its applicability in education may be found in the "hypervisibility" of African American males, who are under constant surveillance and punitive relations within schools (cf. Ferguson, 2001).

In key instances, intersectional analysis in education maintains fidelity with Crenshaw's original deployment. To the extent that educational scholars work hard to avoid siphoning off the "race problem" in order to forge a single-axis explanation, intersectionality enjoys engagement as a way to explain how racism and sexism, as co-constitutive systems of subordination, reinforce each other (Powers & Duffy, 2016). Their implication with each other is not meant to be additive but multiplicative, where race and gender subordination mutually impair or disable people of color as always raced, gendered, and inferiorized subjects in the eyes of whiteness and patriarchy. In a sense, intersectional scholars spin an elliptical explanation that revolves around at least two axes. Here, the metaphor of the ellipse is more appropriate than the circle to the extent that the former contains two centers around which social and educational analysis orbits. Intersectionality illuminates the way that race and gender gravitationally tug on each other.

This dynamic is made accessible when we consider that Black girls or boys in school do not experience themselves as ultimately either racialized or gendered subjects, other than the return to a troublesome essentialism that Crenshaw set out to problematize. For instance, Annette Henry (2015) remains close to Crenshaw's imbrication between race and gender relations, beginning with the lived experiences of Black women aligned with Patricia Hill Collins (2000; see Willis, 2015, for an intersectional study of Black women who study abroad). In this sense, blackness is not an empty or mysterious box that scholars fill with nationality, race, class, language, and gender but a site of their simultaneity. Brah and Phoenix (2009) seem to agree when they trace the earlier history of intersectional thought from Sojourner Truth, the Bridge (Called My Back) collective, and onward, placing intersectionality within a larger and longer struggle of women of color against "all final closures" (p. 249), with particular alliances organized around "*cultural specificities*" (p. 251).

This point does not prevent powerful interventions in education, which focus, for example, on Black boys. In other words, there is a specificity to the Black male experience in education and the micro aggressions they suffer, which warrants focused attention (Hotchkins, 2016). At the University of Pennsylvania's Graduate

School of Education, a concerted effort has been under way to change the representation and uplift the prospects of African American and Latino males in education. The *Journal of African American Males in Education* is dedicated solely to issues affecting the population signaled by its title. Obama's initiative, "My Brother's Keeper," is another such effort that focuses on increasing achievement for Black boys, sometimes attracting criticism for suggesting that this population is what needs changing rather than addressing structural mechanisms that limit their chances (Dumas, 2016). Valuable insights on Black males in education notwithstanding, a parallel focus on Black girls or Latinas in schools does not exist in the same magnitude, making the integration between gender and race at the level of analysis a matter of political choice that warrants critical reflection (Morris & Perry, 2017; Murphy, Acosta, & Kennedy-Lewis, 2013).

In this chapter, our interpretation is also that such a premium on the dynamism between interlocking social systems does not preclude *beginning* from racial analysis. A critical analysis of education may begin strategically with race without ending on a single-axis explanation. This is warranted especially if a context wherein race antagonism erupts provisionally requires that race is privileged as the overarching relation under investigation. In other words, as understood here, intersectionality was not meant to displace race as much as it was innovated to recognize its full measure of power that *accounts* for gender, class, and language rather than their absence. Said another way, an intersectional race analysis is arguably stronger in its ability to trace the objective and far-ranging effects of race than its weaker form found in single-axis analysis (cf. Harding, 1991, on strong vs. weak objectivity in the sciences). But this does not suggest that race is always an inappropriate beginning for any study, just as BLM spreads (and not always by Black activists) precisely when Black lives are under extreme threat through police shootings and other state-sponsored violence. The same may be said about privileging gender analysis when discrimination against queer and trans students attracts public scrutiny, including challenging bathrooms based on gender "assignment" in public institutions like schools.

Beginning analysis is a matter of context and strategic choice, of how to proceed based on what is immediately at stake, and likelihoods for success based on history and experience in social movements. To begin, as Said (1985) reminds us, is provisional and not originary, is secular not religious (i.e., grounded on sacred texts and issues), and occurs in fits and starts rather than an unfolding teleology toward a predetermined end. In this political condition, intersectionality is educative to the extent that it provides guidance, principles, and the possibilities of praxis across difference rather than laying claims to an essentialist subject of both oppression and liberation from it. It does not designate ahead of time and at which juncture of analysis intersectionality makes its appearance.

At its best, intersectionality is the ability to name racism even while acknowledging that racism is not the only culprit in a particular crime. Intersectionality graces Gillborn's (2015) article title even as he puts sharp focus on racism in education, admitting preemptively that his readers may be confused by the contradiction of "link[ing] the idea of 'intersectionality' and the 'primacy' of racism in the same sentence" (p. 277). He argues, "'Intersectionality' is a widely used (and sometimes misused) concept in contemporary social science" (p. 278); to this, we might include education. Reminding us that the African American Policy Forum, run and directed by Crenshaw, defines intersectionality as a tool of analysis and resistance, Gillborn warns against liberalizing the concept. Delgado (2011) regrets that "intersectionality can easily paralyze progressive work and thought because of the realization that whatever unit you choose to work with, someone may come along and point out that you forgot something (p. 1264)" (as cited by Gillborn, 2015, p. 279). This point is key as intersectionality ascends into popularity and descends into commonsense usage. Based on his study of Black middle-class parents in the United Kingdomn (see Ball, Rollock, Vincent, & Gillborn, 2013; Gillborn, Rollock, Vincent, & Ball, 2012), Gillborn argues that the entanglement among race, gender, and ability relations affects middle-class Black parents in a way that complicates their class privilege (i.e., fails to protect them). In this way, the multiple social forces in education bring up the "primacy of race and racism" at the empirical, personal-biographical, and political levels.

To be extra clear, Gillborn (2015) disabuses himself of being mistaken as a race determinist. He adds,

I do not assume that racism is the only issue that matters . . . neither do I believe that racism is always the most important issue in understanding every instance of social exclusion and oppression that touches the lives of minoritized people. Similarly, I am not suggesting that there is some kind of hierarchy of oppression, whereby members of any single group (however defined) are assumed to always be the most excluded or to always have a perfect under-standing of the processes at work. (p. 284)

With the success that intersectionality has enjoyed in education comes certain dangers. As Gillborn, Delgado, and Crenshaw herself have diagnosed, much like the maligned or malunderstood term *critical*, intersectionality's edge is experiencing a certain rounding. Although it clearly has stood the test of time and shown its power to explain race and gender subordination, intersectionality also faces domestication. Although it challenges the problems of essentialism and provides education scholars the ability to explain subordination more, it is in danger of explaining it less by flattening out the concept. The discipline would do well to guard against this trend.

That said, the intersectional framework has experienced particularly fruitful connections with dis/ability studies. Annamma, Connor, and Ferri (2013) inaugurated "DisCrit," or the intersectional uptake of critical disability studies with CRT in education. DisCrit consists of at least three intellectual commitments: (a) to legitimate studies of subjects with disabilities outside of the medicalized/interventionist discourse, including mainstream special education; (b) to advance *ability* as a theoretical construct in its own right to explain intertwining social relations such as race and gender; and (c) to challenge normativity as a regulating principle (Annamma, Connor, & Ferri, 2016b). As a move to racialize ability and disable-ize race (see

Erevelles, 2002), DisCrit aligns itself with Crenshaw, whose "work on intersectionality [they find] useful for theorizing the ways in which race and ability are likewise intertwined in terms of identity" (Annamma, Connor, & Ferri, 2016a, p. 16), despite the authors' admission that ability concerns rarely appear in Crenshaw's work. The challenge for DisCrit and synergies aside is that at the same time it aligns itself with CRT, it fights against being confounded with it, right down to the tenets it closely appropriates from CRT (Mutua & Robinson, 2017). Some disarticulation may be necessary.

CONCLUSION AND FUTURE DIRECTIONS IN INTERSECTIONAL RESEARCH ON EDUCATION

One overarching implication of intersectional analysis is that dismantling one form of hierarchy necessitates an equally robust assault on other forms of subordination. Because racism and sexism recruit capitalism, sexuality, methodology, and epistemology to their work, problem-posing proceeds organically. In education research, it means seeking a composite methodology and analytic that speak to this complexity. It is unarguable that intersectionality occupies a special place in critical understandings of race and gender stratification in education, distinguishing mainstream uses of intersectionality from its *critical* version. Equally, it is important to push intersectionality into novel and significant ways so as to build frameworks that express their debt to Crenshaw's formulation as well as take intersectionality into new directions.

For this, we return to Crenshaw's original intervention that intersectionality may be a metaphor but should not be reduced to a convenient motif that peppers scholarly arguments. Beyond explaining the lives of Black women, for example, *critical intersectionality* aims to improve their social condition as part of an overall intellectual project. The move to speak to the multiplicity of subordination cannot be accomplished absent a clear attempt to explain and alleviate the challenges experienced by Black women and other marginalized groups. Taking heed of this warning, intersectional analysis maintains its integration of how the compounding effects of social forces, such as patriarchy and racism, limit the lives of despised or denigrated races and genders in education, the law, and social life in general. It should explain more, rather than less, this very process.

Our interpretation of the literature leads us to conclude that intersectionality displaces neither race nor gender as readymade social systems in order that these previously concrete forces melt into abstractions. It does not straitjacket analyses that begin with race or gender as hopelessly essentialist but builds from them as starting points for an appropriate intersectional synthesis. At this point, intersectional analysis becomes a relative practice insofar as there exists no standard to designate ahead of time how many axes to intersect and in what manner within one's analysis. As such, intersectionality is less identity-centered and more the apprehension of conditions that shape and make meaningful these same identities as they crisscross and make cuts in each other.

To this end, research on intersectionality marks a new space for theorizing race and gender subordination in education as well as possible responses to it. It requires that concepts like micro aggression graduate to a complexity that documents the intersectional effects of conditions whereby race, class, sexuality, and gender are no longer separable at the politico-existential level even if they may be disaggregated at the conceptual level for explanatory purposes. Intersectional microaggressions (Nadal et al., 2015) occur precisely as the meanings of gender, race, and other social systems exert multiplicative, rather than additive, pressure on vulnerable communities. It means that resistance takes on an intersectional dimension when protest against the minimization of Black lives is articulated, for example, with a deep appreciation for Islamo- and Chicanophobia. Intersectional resistance becomes valued for its ability to work at nonessentialized understandings of social suffering despite the ostensible inadequacies of the language we use to name it, such as Black Lives Matter or the struggle in the discrimination against queer or trans lives. This is the self-reflective moment of the intersectional framework, which interrogates the conditions of intelligibility that make intersectional thought possible in the first place.

The apparatus of schooling is an intersectional meeting point, rather than the melting pot, of forces in the interpellation of the student as a subject on one hand and the nation creation project that is education on the other. This means that theory, method, and practice are distinguishable as conceptual tools but inseparable as politics. As such, intersectionality becomes a guiding framework at *all levels* of analysis, from inception (of an idea), to conception (of the study), and intervention (into the problem; see Maramba & Museus, 2011). At its broadest, intersectionality becomes a standpoint from which to view educational problems and possibilities, human limitations and liberations.

It is intersectionality as a form of intervention in the lives of people of color and women, or specifically women of color, with which we want to end here. Said another way, intersectional analysis' power is accorded by its intellectual project that is at the same time an educative-political project, or education in the broadest sense possible as the creation of a critical citizenry. Several decades later and with recent events that make this work more pressing, such as the public emboldening of White supremacist groups, attacks on universities, and procurement of "hate" speech even if it has legal standing, developing intersectional work in education makes the intellectual simultaneously political. As the former, one of the deep tasks of academic work is involved in the development of ideas and production of knowledge. As the latter, it reminds us that knowledge is best understood as politics in its conceptual form. Together, the intersection between the intellectual and political becomes a proxy for praxis.

A posting on its website announces that BLM "stands with Standing Rock" in opposition to the Dakota Access Pipeline, a project resisted by the Standing Rock Sioux and their allies through direct action in the winter of 2015:

As there are many diverse manifestations of Blackness, and Black people are also displaced Indigenous peoples, we are clear that there is no Black liberation without Indigenous sovereignty. Environmental racism is not limited to pipelines on Indigenous land, because we know that the chemicals used for fracking and the materials used to build pipelines are also used in water containment and sanitation plants in Black communities like Flint, Michigan. The same companies that build pipelines are the same companies that build factories that emit carcinogenic chemicals into Black communities, leading to some of the highest rates of cancer, hysterectomies, miscarriages, and asthma in the country. Our liberation is only realized when all people are free, free to access clean water, free from institutional racism, free to live whole and healthy lives not subjected to state-sanctioned violence. America has committed and is committing genocide against Native American peoples and Black people.[20]

This eloquent statement indicates that intersectionality has become a central commitment of one of the most vibrant new social movements in the United States. As we have seen, however, this deep understanding of and commitment to intersectionality is not shared in the academy. Despite the fact that we are all nominally "intersectionalists" now, social theorists in law and education continue to struggle to incorporate fully the lessons of this subtle but endlessly generative concept, although in the field of praxis intersectionality continues to bear fruit.[21] Intersectionality reminds us of the importance of coalitions and allyship; it reminds us to be humble and to look for who is missing in the room. Above all, however, intersectionality reminds us—BLM reminds us—that our liberation is only realized when *all* beings are free.

NOTES

[1]Black Lives Matter, "A HerStory of the Black Lives Matter Movement," http://black-livesmatter.com/herstory/.

[2]A Google search on October 28, 2017, for instance, yielded 3,630,000 results for the word "intersectionality."

[3]Because our analysis is not comparativist in nature, the following review does not concentrate on authors' particular contexts and their nation-specific arguments. Our methodology focuses instead on the uptake of intersectionality as a framework for race research, especially our sense of its growing influence in U.S. scholarship.

[4]They write,

College students and faculty in interdisciplinary fields such as women's studies, ethnic studies, cultural studies, American studies, and media studies, as well as those within sociology, political science, and history and other traditional disciplines, encounter intersectionality in courses, books, and scholarly articles. Human rights activists and government officials have also made intersectionality part of ongoing global public policy discussions. Grassroots organizers look to varying dimensions of intersectionality to inform their work on reproductive rights, anti-violence initiatives, workers' rights, and similar social issues. Bloggers use digital and social media to debate hot topics. Teachers, social workers, high-school students, parents, university support staff, and school personnel have taken up the ideas of intersectionality with an eye toward transforming schools of all sorts. Across these different venues, people increasingly claim and use the term "intersectionality" for their diverse intellectual and political projects. (Collins & Bilge, 2016, p. 1)

[5]Crenshaw herself points out that Sojourner Truth's famous intervention at the 1851 Women's Convention in Akron, Ohio—her "Ain't I a Woman?" speech—could be understood as an example of "intersectionality" (Crenshaw, 1989, p. 153). Indeed, contrary to the

standard origin story, Crenshaw's 1991 *Stanford Law Review* article was not even her own first use of the term. "Mapping the Margins" relied on, and referred to, a 1989 article published in the *University of Chicago Legal Forum* called (somewhat awkwardly) "Demarginalizing the Intersection of Race and Sex: A Black Feminist Critique of Antidiscrimination Doctrine, Feminist Theory and Antiracist Politics" (Crenshaw, 1989). It was in this earlier article that Crenshaw first used the word "intersectionality."

[6]Patricia Hill Collins puts this well:

Intersectionality's ability to draw attention to and account for *inter*-social relations—including those on the margins—challenges binary thinking, shifting the analytic focus on the fluidity among, interrelationships between, and co-production of various categories and systems of power. As a result, epistemologically, intersectionality highlights the various standpoints that "inter" social locations occupy; these alternative standpoints challenge truth claims advanced by historically powerful social actors. (Collins, 2012, p. 454)

[7]Indeed, the recent emergence of the term *Latinx* can be seen as a case study in intersectional consciousness. The term is currently used as a nongendered substitution for the gendered term *Latino/a*, which in turn emerged in response to the masculine-gendered term *Latino*.

[8]Crenshaw (1989, p. 149).

[9]Legal scholars Ann McGinley and Frank Rudy Cooper (2013), for example, acknowledge the value of "intersectionality" but adopt "multidimensionality" instead, explaining,

The metaphor of intersectionality suggests two cars traveling down roads that collide at an intersection. The metaphor of multidimensionality more readily suggests a world that exists at many levels, with trains underground, planes above, and other automobiles on the roads. At the level of metaphor, although intersectionality theory might be understood as two-dimensional, multidimensionality theory clearly encompasses three dimensions. It is not that one cannot read the original intersectionality articles to imply multiple dimensions, but we think one is more likely to consider multiple identities and contexts when thinking about the multidimensionality of identities. (p. 335; see also Hutchinson, 1997, p. 641)

[10]Somewhat similarly, Patricia Hill Collins (2012) argues that intersectionality should be identified in a number of different domains. McGinley and Cooper (2013) argue that the cultural realm of intersectionality is too often ignored, and argue that "multidimensionality" does this job better.

[11]As Judith Butler (1990) notes, reeled-off lists like "race, gender, class, sexuality" "invariably close with an embarrassed 'etc.' at the end of the list . . . these positions strive to encompass a situated subject, but invariably fail to be complete" (p. 182). The implicit equation of the "class" dimension of subordination as homologous to other dimensions has come under particular fire from academics. For one well-known example, see Fraser and Honneth (2003).

[12]For a similar criticism of a cognate term now prevalent in sociology—"super-diversity," see Foner, Duyvendak, and Kasinitz (2017).

[13]The authors of this study explored two different senses of "intersectionality:"

[W]e formulate and investigate two different constructs: demographic intersectionality, in which the courts are the site of intersectional disadvantages or discrimination, and claim intersectionality, in which the law does not adequately redress intersectional discrimination that occurs in the labor market. Demographic intersectionality can be thought of as a type of inequality in litigation, while claim intersectionality can be thought of as a mismatch between discrimination as conceptualized by law and discrimination as experienced in the labor market. (Best et al., 2011, p. 993)

[14]According to the study's authors:

Bivariate relationships between both claim and demographic intersectionality and case outcomes yield strong support for intersectionality theory. First, plaintiffs making intersectional claims are less than half as likely to win their cases as are other plaintiffs (15 percent compared to 31 percent; see Table 4). Second, race and sex disadvantages do not operate independently. White male plaintiffs were more likely to lose their cases than white women were (61 percent as compared to 55 percent; see Table 4). This female advantage, however, does not apply to black women, who are slightly more likely than black men to lose their cases (71 percent as compared to 69 percent; see Table 4). (Best et al., 2011, p. 1009)

[15]A similar structure of multiple "grounds" articulated within antidiscrimination legislation has apparently retarded attempts to legally recognize intersectionality in Canada, South Africa, and the United Kingdom (Campbell, 2015).
[16]Campbell (2015) explains,

There is no reference to intersectional discrimination in the text of either the International Covenant on Civil and Political Rights or International Covenant on Economic, Social and Cultural Rights, but both CESCR and the HRC have addressed intersectional discrimination in the General Comments. CESCR observes that "some individual or groups of individual face discrimination on more than one of the prohibited grounds . . . such cumulative discrimination has a unique and specific impact . . . and merits particular consideration and remedying" (idem). In the context of gender discrimination the HRC notes that "discrimination against women is often intertwined with discrimination on other grounds . . . states parties should address the ways in which instances of discrimination on other grounds affect women in a particular way . . ." (HRC, General Comment No. 28, § 30). This remains an essentially grounds-based approach that examines the interaction between enumerated or analogous status-based grounds. (p. 484)

[17]Chow (2016), however, is concerned that the emphasis on structural intersectionality in CEDAW (a) has obscured the fact that multiple identities are not invariably negative, (b) has encouraged a purely "additive" approach to intersectionality, and (c) has obscured women's resilience and creativity in resisting their own oppression. Chow views the approaches to intersectionality embraced by interpreters of CEDAW as overly focused on "intercategorical complexity" and recommends more "intracategorical" analysis to understand how categories themselves are produced and reproduced.
[18]The group wrote,

The idea of "intersectionality" seeks to capture both the structural and dynamic consequences of the interaction between two or more forms of discrimination or systems of subordination. It specifically addresses the manner in which racism, patriarchy, economic disadvantages and other discriminatory systems contribute to create layers of inequality that structure the relative positions of women and men, races and other groups. Moreover, it addresses the way that specific acts and policies create burdens that flow along these intersecting axes contributing actively to create a dynamic of disempowerment. (As cited in Chow, 2016, p. 10)

[19]General Recommendation No. 25 of the Convention on the Elimination of Racial Discrimination Committee on Gender-Related Dimensions of Racial Discrimination, for example, requires the states party to the convention to give consideration to four different aspects of racial discrimination experienced by women: (a) its "form and manifestation," (b) the circumstances under which it occurs, (c) its consequences, and (d) the "availability and accessibility of remedies and complaint mechanisms" (see Chow, 2016, p. 16). Chow argues that in this context, UN human rights treaty bodies have been able to "make visible the sophisticated ways in which 'social differences and inequalities are embedded in existing hegemonic power relations'" (p. 16).

[20]http://blacklivesmatter.com/solidarity-with-standing-rock/.

[21]Patricia Hill Collins (2012) argues that from this perspective, intersectionality and pragmatism are aligned and have much to offer each other.

REFERENCES

Annamma, S. A., Connor, D., & Ferri, B. (2013). Dis/ability critical race studies (DisCrit): Theorizing at the intersections of race and dis/ability. *Race Ethnicity and Education, 16,* 1–31.

Annamma, S. A., Connor, D., & Ferri, B. (2016a). Dis/ability critical race studies (DisCrit): Theorizing at the intersections of race and dis/ability. In D. Connor, B. Ferri, & S. A. Annamma (Eds.), *DisCrit: Disability studies and critical race theory in education* (pp. 9–32). New York, NY: Teachers College Press.

Annamma, S. A., Connor, D., & Ferri, B. (2016b). A truncated genealogy of DisCrit. In D. Connor, B. Ferri, & S. A. Annamma (Eds.), *DisCrit: Disability studies and critical race theory in education* (pp. 1–8). New York, NY: Teachers College Press.

Artiles, A., Dorn, S., & Bal, A. (2016). Objects of protection, enduring nodes of difference: Disability intersections with "other" differences, 1916-2016. *Review of Research in Education, 40*(1), 277–820.

Ball, S., Rollock, N., Vincent, C., & Gillborn, D. (2013). Social mix, schooling and intersectionality: Identity and risk for black middle class families. *Research Papers in Education, 28,* 265–288.

Banks, J. (Ed.). (2012). *Encyclopedia of diversity in education* (Vol. 2). Thousand Oaks, CA: Sage.

Bartlett, T. (2017, May 21). When a theory goes viral: Intersectionality is now everywhere. Is that a good thing? *Chronicle of Higher Education.* Retrieved from https://www.chronicle.com/article/The-Intersectionality-Wars/240095

Bell, D. (1992). *Faces at the bottom of the well: The permanence of racism.* New York, NY: Basic Books.

Bell, D. (2005). The role of fortuity in racial policy-making: Blacks as fortuitous beneficiaries of racial policies. In R. Delgado, & J. Stefancic (Eds.), *The Derrick Bell Reader* (pp. 40–45). New York: New York University Press.

Berger, M. T., & Guidroz, K. (2010). *The intersectional approach: Transforming the academy through race, class, and gender.* Chapel Hill: University of North Carolina Press.

Berrey, E. (2015). *The enigma of diversity: The language of race and the limits of racial justice.* Chicago, IL: University of Chicago Press.

Best, R. K., Edelman, L. B., Krieger, L. H., & Eliason, S. R. (2011). Multiple disadvantages: An empirical test of intersectionality theory in EEO litigation. *Law & Society Review, 45,* 991–1025.

Bhopal, K., & Preston, J. (Eds.). (2012). *Intersectionality and race in education.* New York, NY: Routledge.

Bilge, S. (2013). Intersectionality undone: Saving intersectionality from feminist intersectionality studies. *Du Bois Review, 10,* 405–424.

Bowleg, L. (2012). The problem with the phrase women and minorities: Intersectionality—an important theoretical framework for public health. *American Journal of Public Health, 102,* 1267–1273.

Brah, A., & Phoenix, A. (2009). Ain't I a woman: Revisiting intersectionality. In E. Taylor, D. Gillborn, & G. Ladson-Billings (Eds.), *Foundations of critical race theory in education* (pp. 247–258). New York, NY: Routledge.

Bullock, J., & Masselot, A. (2012–2013). Multiple discrimination and intersectional disadvantages: Challenges and opportunities in the European Union legal framework. *Columbia Journal of European Law, 19*(1), 57–82.

Butler, J. (1990). *Gender trouble.* New York, NY: Routledge.

Campbell, M. (2015). CEDAW and women's intersecting identities: A pioneering new approach to intersectional discrimination. *Revista Direito GV, 11*(2), 479–504.

Caruthers, J., & Carter, P. (2012). Intersectionality of race, class, gender, and ethnicity. In J. Banks (Ed.), *Encyclopedia of diversity in education* (Vol. 2, pp. 1270–1272). Thousand Oaks, CA: Sage.

Chow, P. Y. S. (2016). Has intersectionality reached its limits? Intersectionality in the UN human rights treaty-body practices and the issue of ambivalence. *Human Rights Law Review, 16,* 453–481. Retrieved from https://papers.ssrn.com/sol3/papers.cfm?abstract_id=2753549&download=yes

Collins, P. H. (2000). *Black feminist thought: Knowledge, consciousness, and the politics of empowerment* (2nd ed.). New York, NY: Routledge.

Collins, P. H. (2012). Social inequality, power, and politics: Intersectionality and American pragmatism in dialogue. *Journal of Speculative Philosophy, 26,* 442–457.

Collins, P. H., & Bilge, S. (2016). *Intersectionality.* Cambridge, England: Polity Press.

Connolly, W. E. (1995). *The ethos of pluralization.* Minneapolis: University of Minnesota Press.

Covarrubias, A. (2011). Quantitative intersectionality: A critical race analysis of the Chicana/o educational pipeline. *Journal of Latinos and Education, 10*(2), 86–105.

Crenshaw, K. (1989). Demarginalizing the intersection of race and sex: A black feminist critique of antidiscrimination doctrine, feminist theory and antiracist politics. *University of Chicago Legal Forum, 1989*(1), 139–167.

Crenshaw, K. (1991). Mapping the margins: Intersectionality, identity politics, and violence against women of color. *Stanford Law Review, 43,* 1241–1299.

Cunningham, E. C. (1998). The rise of identity politics I: The myth of the protected class in Title VII disparate treatment cases. *Connecticut Law Review, 30,* 441–502.

Davis, D., Brunn-Bevel, R., & Olive, J. (Eds.). (2015). *Intersectionality in educational research.* Sterling, VA: Stylus Publishing.

Dixson, A. D., & Rousseau, C. K. (2017). *Critical race theory in education: All God's children got a song* (2nd ed.). New York, NY: Routledge.

Du Bois, W. E. B. (1989). *The souls of black folk.* New York, NY: Penguin Books.

Dumas, M. (2010). What is this "black" in black education: Imagining a cultural politics without guarantees. In Z. Leonardo (Ed.), *Handbook of cultural politics and education* (pp. 403–422). Rotterdam, Netherlands: Sense.

Dumas, M. (2016). My brother as "problem": Neoliberal governmentality and interventions for black young men and boys. *Educational Policy, 30*(1), 94–113.

Ehrenreich, N. (2002). Subordination and symbiosis: Mechanisms of mutual support between subordinating systems. *University of Missouri-Kansas City Law Review, 71,* 251–324.

Elengold, K. (2018). Clustered bias. *North Carolina Law Review, 96.* Retrieved from http://scholarship.law.unc.edu/cgi/viewcontent.cgi?article=5722&context=nclr

Erevelles, N. (2002). (Im)material citizens: Cognitive disability, race, and the politics of citizenship. *Disability, Culture and Education, 1*(1), 5–25.

Ferguson, A. (2001). *Bad boys.* Ann Arbor: University of Michigan Press.

Flintoff, A., Fitzgerald, H., & Scraton, S. (2008). The challenges of intersectionality: Researching difference in physical education. *International Studies in Sociology of Education, 18*(2), 73–85.

Foner, N., Duyvendak, J. W., & Kasinitz, P. (2017). Introduction: Super-diversity in every-day life. *Ethnic and Racial Studies*. doi:10.1080/01419870.2017.1406969

Fraser, N., & Honneth, A. (2003). *Redistribution or recognition? A political-philosophical exchange*. New York, NY: Verso.

Freelon, D., McIlwain, C. D., & Clark, M. D. (2016). *Beyond the hashtags: #Ferguson, #Blacklivesmatter, and the online struggle for offline justice*. Washington, DC: American University Center for Media & Social Impact. Retrieved from http://cmsimpact.org/wp-content/uploads/2016/03/beyond_the_hashtags_2016.pdf

Gillborn, D. (2015). Intersectionality, critical race theory, and the primacy of racism: Race, class, gender, and disability in education. *Qualitative Inquiry, 21*, 277–287.

Gillborn, D., Rollock, N., Vincent, C., & Ball, S. J. (2012). "You got a pass, so what more do you want?" Race, class and gender intersections in the educational experiences of the Black middle class. *Race Ethnicity and Education, 15*, 121–139.

Grant, C., & Zwier, E. (2011). Intersectionality and student outcomes: Sharpening the struggle against racism, sexism, classism, ableism, heterosexism, nationalism, and linguistic, religious, and geographical discrimination in teaching and learning. *Multicultural Perspectives, 13*, 181–188.

Grant, C., & Zwier, E. (2012). Intersectionality and education. In J. Banks (Ed.), *Encyclopedia of diversity in education* (Vol. 2, pp. 1262–1270). Thousand Oaks, CA: Sage.

Grosfoguel, R. (2007). The epistemic decolonial turn: Beyond political-economy paradigms. *Cultural Studies, 21*, 211–223.

Grzanka, P. R. (2014). *Intersectionality: A foundations and frontiers reader*. Boulder, CO: Westview Press.

Hall, S. (1996). What is this "black" in black popular culture? In D. Morley, & K. Chen (Eds.), *Stuart Hall* (pp. 465–475). London, England: Routledge.

Hancock, A. (2016). *Intersectionality: An intellectual history*. New York, NY: Oxford University Press.

Hancock, S., & Warren, C. (Eds.). (2017). *White women's work: Examining the intersectionality of teaching, identity, and race*. Charlotte, NC: Information Age.

Harding, S. (1991). *Whose science? Whose knowledge?* Ithaca, NY: Cornell University Press.

Harris, C. (1995). Whiteness as property. In K. Crenshaw, N. Gotanda, G. Peller, & K. Thomas (Eds.), *Critical race theory* (pp. 276–291). New York, NY: The New Press.

Henry, A. (2015). "We especially welcome applications from members of visible minority groups": Reflections on race, gender and life at three universities. *Race Ethnicity and Education, 18*, 589–610.

Hotchkins, B. (2016). African American males navigate microaggressions. *Teachers College Record, 118*(6), 1–36.

Hull, G. A., Bell-Scott, P., & Smith, B. (Eds.). (1982). *All the women are white, all the blacks are men, but some of us are brave*. New York, NY: The Feminist Press.

Hutchinson, D. L. (1997). Out yet unseen: A racial critique of gay and lesbian legal theory and political discourse. *Connecticut Law Review, 29*, 561–646.

Hutchinson, D. L. (2002). New complexity theories: From theoretical innovation to doctrinal reform. *University of Missouri-Kansas City Law Review, 71*, 431–446.

Kalsem, K., & Williams, V. (2010). Social justice feminism. *UCLA Women's Law Journal, 18*, 131–194.

Kantola, J. (2014). The paradoxical gendered consequences of the EU policy on multiple discrimination: The Nordic case. *European Integration Online Papers, 18*(7). Retrieved from http://eiop.or.at/eiop/pdf/2014-003.pdf

Kotkin, M. J. (2009). Diversity and discrimination: A look at complex bias. *William & Mary Law Review, 50*, 1439–1500.

Kwan, P. (1997). Jeffrey Dahmer and the cosynthesis of categories. *Hastings Law Journal, 48*, 1257–1292.

Ladson-Billings, G., & Tate, W. F. IV. (1995). Toward a critical race theory of education. *Teachers College Record, 97*(1), 47–68.

Leonardo, Z. (2013). *Race frameworks: A multidimensional theory of racism and education.* New York, NY: Teachers College Press.

Leonardo, Z. (2016). Tropics of whiteness: Metaphor and the literary turn in White Studies. *Whiteness and Education, 1*(1), 3–14.

Leonardo, Z., & Broderick, A. (2011). Smartness as property: A critical exploration of intersections between whiteness and disability studies. *Teachers College Record, 113,* 2206–2232.

Levit, N. (2002). Introduction: Theorizing the connections among systems of subordination. *University of Missouri-Kansas City Law Review, 71,* 227–250.

Leyva, L. (2016). An intersectional analysis of Latin@ college women's counter-stories in mathematics. *Journal of Urban Mathematics Education, 9*(2), 81–121.

Lynn, M., & Dixson, A. (Eds.). (2013). *Handbook of critical race theory in education.* New York, NY: Routledge.

Maramba, D., & Museus, S. (2011). The utility of using mixed-methods and intersectionality approaches in conducting research on Filipino American students' experiences with the campus climate and on sense of belonging. *New Directions for Institutional Research, 15*(1), 93–101.

Matambanadzo, S. M., Valdes, F., & Vélez-Martinez, S. I. (2016). Afterword: LatCrit theory @ XX: Kindling the programmatic production of critical and outsider legal scholarship, 1996-2016. *Whittier Law Review, 37,* 439–512.

Matsuda, M. (1987). Looking to the bottom: Critical legal studies and reparations. *Harvard Civil Rights-Civil Liberties Law Review, 22,* 323–400.

McCall, L. (2005). The complexity of intersectionality. *Signs, 30,* 1771–1800.

McGinley, A., & Cooper, F. R. (2013). Identities cubed: Perspectives on multidimensional masculinities theory. *Nevada Law Journal, 13,* 326–340.

Milner, R. H., IV. (2010). *Start where you are, but don't stay there.* Cambridge, MA: Harvard University Press.

Milner, R. H., IV. (2013). Analyzing poverty, learning, and teaching through a critical race theory lens. *Review of Research in Education, 37*(1), 1–53.

Morris, E., & Perry, B. (2017). Girls behaving badly: Race, gender and subjective evaluation in the discipline of African American girls. *Sociology of Education, 90,* 127–148.

Murphy, A., Acosta, M., & Kennedy-Lewis, B. (2013). "I'm not running around with my pants sagging, so how am I not acting like a lady?" Intersections of race and gender in the experiences of female middle school troublemakers. *Urban Review, 45,* 586–610.

Museus, S., & Griffin, K. (2011). Mapping the margins in higher education: On the promise of intersectionality frameworks in research and discourse. *New Directions for Institutional Research, 15*(1), 5–13.

Mutua, K., & Robinson, O. (2017). Book review: DisCrit: Disability studies and critical race theory in education. *Teachers College Record.* Advance online publication.

Nadal, K., Davidoff, K., Davis, L., Wong, Y., Marshall, D., & McKenzie, V. (2015). A qualitative approach to intersectional microaggressions: Understanding influences of race, ethnicity, gender, sexuality and religion. *Qualitative Psychology, 2,* 147–163.

Núñez, A. (2014). Employing multilevel intersectionality in educational research: Latino identities, contexts, and college access. *Educational Researcher, 43,* 85–92.

Parker, L., & Stovall, D. (2004). Actions following words: Critical race theory connects to critical pedagogy. *Educational Philosophy and Theory, 36,* 167–182.

Perez-Huber, L. (2010). Using Latina/o critical race theory (LatCrit) and racist nativism to explore intersectionality in the educational experiences of undocumented Chicana college students. *Educational Foundations, 24*(1), 77–96.

Powers, B., & Duffy, P. (2016). Making invisible intersectionality visible through theater of the oppressed in teacher education. *Journal of Teacher Education, 67*(1), 61–67.

Ricoeur, P. (1975). *The rule of metaphor*. Toronto, Ontario, Canada: University of Toronto Press.

Said, E. (1985). *Beginnings: Intention and method*. London, England: Granta.

Sarcedo, G., Matias, C., Montoya, R., & Nishi, N. (2015). Dirty dancing with race and class: Microaggressions toward first-generation and low-income college students of color. *Journal of Critical Scholarship on Higher Education and Student Affairs, 2*(1), 1–17.

Smith, A. L. (2006). Heteropatriarchy and the three pillars of white supremacy: Rethinking women of color organizing. In A. Smith, B. E. Richie, J. Sudbury, & J. White (Eds.), *INCITE! Women of color against violence: The color of violence* (pp. 66–73). Boston, MA: South End Press.

Taylor, E., Gillborn, D., & Ladson-Billings, G. (Eds.). (2009). *Foundations of critical race theory in education*. New York, NY: Routledge.

Thomas, D., & Stevenson, (2009). Gender risks and education: The particular classroom challenges for urban low-income African American boys. *Review of Research in Education, 33*(1), 160–180.

Valdes, F. (1995). Sex and race in queer legal culture: Ruminations on identities and inter-connectivities. *Southern California Review of Law and Women's Studies, 5*(1), 25–74.

Volosinov, V. (2006). *Marxism and the philosophy of language*. Cambridge, MA: Harvard University Press.

Vygotsky, L. (1978). *Mind in society* (4th ed.). Cambridge, MA: Harvard University Press.

Williams, J. C. (2002). Fretting in the force fields: Why the distribution of social power has proved so hard to change. *University of Missouri-Kansas City Law Review, 71*, 493–506.

Willis, T. (2015). "And still we rise": Microaggressions and intersectionality in the study abroad experiences of black women. *Frontiers, XXVI*, 209–230.

Yosso, T. (2005). Whose culture has capital? A critical race theory discussion of community cultural wealth. *Race Ethnicity and Education, 8*, 69–91.

Young, I. M. (1990). *Justice and the politics of difference*. Princeton, NJ: Princeton University Press.

Young, K. (2016). How student teachers (don't) talk about race: An intersectional analysis. *Race Ethnicity and Education, 19*, 67–95.

Chapter 2

Black Girl Cartography: Black Girlhood and Place-Making in Education Research

Tamara T. Butler

Michigan State University

Drawing on research in education, Black Girlhood studies, and conversations connected to girlhood and cartography, this chapter calls for transdisciplinary analyses of Black girls' sociocultural and geopolitical locations in education research. In reviewing education research documenting the practices and interrogating the experiences of Black girls, I propose the framework of Black Girl Cartography. In addition to an analysis of education research, I offer a series of theoretical and methodological openings for transformative and liberatory work grounded in Black Girl knowledge and practices.

BLACK GIRL CARTOGRAPHIES

"Intersectional Black feminism," or intersectionality rooted in Black feminist practices and theories (Blige, 2010, 2013; Carastathis, 2014; Collins, 2000), names the multiple axes of difference and makes clear how equitable and ethical interventions should be conceived. In other words, since Black women experience oppressions along the lines of space, place, race, gender, sexuality, and class, liberation should be imagined along those same lines. For example, in 1990, eight teenagers raped and murdered Harbour, a 26-year-old Black woman who was also a mother in Dorchester, Massachusetts (Crenshaw, 1991). Kimberlé Crenshaw (1991) discusses the ways that Harbour's story did not draw as much media attention as White women who were assaulted or reported missing that year. Yet there was little discussion about the interplay of patriarchy, misogyny, and the structural inequities that shaped Dorchester into a dangerous location for young women of color. How might the impending gentrification of the historically poor neighborhood transform it into a place of violence against Black female bodies, and the erasure of said violence? Similar questions can be asked of Baltimore, Maryland (Alphonza Watson), New Orleans,

Review of Research in Education
March 2018, Vol. 42, pp. 28–45
DOI: 10.3102/0091732X18762114

Louisiana (Chyna Gibson and Ciara McElveen), Cleveland, Ohio (Tonia Carmichael, Crystal Dozier, Tishanna Culver, Le'Shanda Long, Michelle Mason, Kim Yvette Smith, Nancy Cobbs, Amelda Hunter, Telacia Forston, Janice Webb, and Diane Turner), St. Petersburg, Florida (Dominique Battle, Ashaunti Butler, and Laniya Miller), Seattle, Washington (Charleena Lyles and her unborn child), and Detroit, Michigan (Aiyana Jones and Shelly Hilliard). The same holds true for Black girls, whose oppressions, in addition to those listed, are also linked to the liminality of age (Winn, 2010).

In Kinloch's work with youth in Harlem, three Black female participants bring attention to what it means to be a Black female attending school in and living in an urban community. Kinloch's (2010) former research assistant, Rebekkah Hogan (research participant) asserts, "I occupy an interesting location in the matrix of gentrification" (p. 116). Although she is older than the high school student participants, she still lives in Harlem, and her assertion speaks to the ways Black girlhood is tied to geospatial location. She continues by reflecting on how Harlem is a place of belonging for her, as she is able to move through spaces (e.g., a Dominican bakery, a Senegalese grocery store) without question due to the color of her skin. However, her class status simultaneously dislocates her from working-class community members, as she is "educated" with a "middle-class job" that allows her to afford the increasing rent in the disappearing neighborhoods (Kinloch, 2010, p. 116). Another poignant moment for Black girls in the text emerges during an interview at Harlem High School (pseudonym). During the interview, Samantha (17-year-old Black female student) asserts that "they'd rather for us to struggle" (Kinloch, 2010, p. 52) in reference to developers and government officials who are not making life easier for current Harlem residents, especially those who are working-class or living fixed-income households. Through the space of the interview, the girls "were sharing stories about gentrification, place, and race that they did not share during the course of their schooling, but that had an impact on their out-of-school lived experiences" (p. 52). Through Samantha's assertion and Kinloch's observation, we come to see that Black girls—and the researchers who work with them—are attentive to the ways race, class, gender, and additional interlocking identities tied to place funnel into urban classrooms.

As a result, I am working toward a praxis-oriented framework that I am calling "Black Girl Cartography," or the study of how and where Black girls are physically and sociopolitically mapped in education. For this chapter, I focus on the types of knowledge Black women education researchers connect to Black girls' geopolitical and social locations (e.g., race, gender, age, sexuality, ability, and class). Specifically, I consider how Black Girl cartographers—scholars and researchers responsible for most of the education research featured here—push intersectionality in education to be more critical of the connections between oppressions and geopolitical and sociocultural locations, by opening with a discussion of location as addressed in intersectional Black feminism. The second section, "Black Girl Cartography: Mapping our Stories," offers an overview of what is required of scholars who use (and seek to use) the framework to consider how Black Girlhood is informed, reformed, or stifled by the geopolitical space of school. The piece continues with a discussion of how I came to this framework and set of publications about Black girls. Through a selective review of education research during a decade of Black Girlhood Celebration (Kwakye, Hill, & Callier, 2017), I focus on two emergent themes: "Black Girl navigational practices" and "Black Girl charting." The chapter closes with a series of theoretical and methodological possibilities, returning to the notion of Black girls' (and women's) knowledge as pathways to social transformation and liberation.

INTERSECTIONAL BLACK FEMINISMS[1]: CHARTING RESISTANCE

From Anna Julia Cooper's "train station" (1891–1892) to the Combahee River Collective's idea of "interlocking" (1977/1995) to Deborah King's revision of "jeopardy" (Beale 1969) with her conception of "multiple jeopardy" (1988) to Hortense Spillers' "interstices" (1984) to Kimberlé Crenshaw's "intersection" (1989) and beyond, there have been attempts to create metaphors capable of capturing experiences of oppression that seem to twist and turn so as to resist being tracked. (Dotson, 2013, p. 3)

Black girls and women's liberatory practices have been, and will continue to be, rooted in the spaces that we demand, seek, create, and cultivate. In 1977, a collective of Black feminists, lesbians, and Black feminist lesbians issued "A Black Feminist Statement" calling attention to the interlocking oppressions stemming from racism, sexism, heteropatriarchy, and classism that Black women experience. The Combahee River Collective's Statement highlighted the sociopolitical intersections of these oppressions and articulated the ways Black feminism should be considered "the logical political movement" to liberate "all women of color." For the Collective, the Black feminist practices toward liberation are rooted in the epistemologies of Sojourner Truth, Frances E. W. Harper, Ida B. Wells Barnett, Mary Church Terrell, and Harriet Tubman. The group's name, Combahee River Collective, intentionally alludes to a site of Tubman's liberatory practices. Tubman's guidance of 150 Black Union soldiers along South Carolina's Combahee River resulted in the freedom of approximately 750 enslaved peoples (Guy-Sheftall, 1995). The campaign's success relied heavily on Tubman's sociopolitical locations as a Black enslaved woman, which deeply informed her knowledge of the land and the people. To me, a major component of "intersectional Black feminism" (B. Cooper, 2015, p. 15) that emerges from the rhetorical work of the Statement is sociopolitical locations—race, class, gender, and geopolitical location—of resistance.

The Combahee River Collective's work to connect to a genealogy of Black women's resistance is echoed in the work of contemporary scholars thinking about Black women's knowledge and location. In *Demonic Grounds*, McKittrick (2006) focuses on how Black women navigated the Americas, a place she describes as "a geographic landscape that is upheld by a legacy of exploitation, exploration, and conquest" (p. xiv). I argue that the Americas are a geopolitical landscape, created by legal documents rooted in patriarchy, capitalism, and Eurocentric concepts of empire.[2] Therefore, we come to see how Black women engage in fugitivity—acts of resistance, escape, and survival—throughout the transatlantic slave trade in other geopolitical spaces: the hulls of slave ships, the tops of auction blocks, and hidden spaces of homes. Black women recognized that their bodies were vulnerable to violence and exploitation, and in that held deep visions of liberation and survival. As McKittrick (2006) asserts, "Black matters are spatial matters" (p. xiv). In other words, conceptions of Blackness are tied to reclaiming a sense of belonging, weaving one's self into genealogies of resilience, and conjuring new imaginings of existing. The Combahee River Collective's name and Statement signal to the ways in which Black women have been fighting for, making and demanding epistemological and physical spaces.

For this chapter, I am defining space as formally uncharted locations that are still inhabited, used, and created. Physical space can occur within a recognized place (e.g., building, ship, home, city, state, body of water), while epistemological space refers to locations in a field of study or discipline. In analyzing these spaces, we begin to develop a more nuanced understanding of how "Black women and girls, trans* people and queer people become victims of anti-Black state violence" (Lindsey, 2015, p. 233) and epistemic violence (Dotson, 2011; Spivak, 1988). Black feminist philosopher Kristie Dotson (2013) demands that analyses of Black women's oppressions require naming spaces where Black women are excluded or included and by whom. For her, an analysis of Black women's oppressions requires "politics of social spatiality" (Dotson, 2013, p. 17). In her reading of Anna Julia Cooper, "Black women simply did not have a 'field' of space," Dotson (2013) asserts "that lent to interpreting Black women's place in American social landscapes" (p. 19). A. J. Cooper's (1891) encounter with two rooms—one for "ladies" and one for "colored people"—reinforces Fannie Barrier Williams's (1905) description of Black women existing "beneath, beyond, and outside of US social imaginaries." Therefore, the rhetorical work of Black feminists who penned the Combahee River Collective Statement were grounded in a politics of spatiality, one that reasserted Black women's presence in American physical and social landscapes.

Black feminist legal theorist Kimberlé Crenshaw (1989) builds on Black feminism's interest in mapping and analyzing Black women sociopolitical locations. Denouncing "single-axis framework" for the analysis of Black women's experiences, she calls attention to "intersections." In 1991, she critiqued how media, women's shelters, and the judicial system (e.g., police officers, jurors, judges) neglected, underserved, and dismissed sexual violence perpetrated against women of color victims/survivors. Her three-part discussion illuminates how the intersecting axes of race, gender, and class often displace women of color victims, as they are unable to find solace, shelter, and assistance. I am particularly drawn to what intersectionality reveals about location. Through Dotson (2011, 2013) and Crenshaw's lenses, we see that intersectionality is not just about interlocking identities, but it is also about how those identities interlock with geopolitical locations. Geopolitical locations undergird the notion that places are created through laws, ordinances, and zoning codes. Rezoning laws, unemployment, as well as racial and class discrimination in the housing industry gentrified places like Dorchester, Massachusetts, in the 1990s. Once we factor in misogyny, patriarchy, and dehumanizing ideas around Black women's bodies into this economically disenfranchised neighborhood, young Black poor or working-class women living in such a neighborhood, like Kimberly Rae Harbour, become vulnerable to violence. Therefore, intersectional Black feminists are concerned with understanding how geopolitical locations compound the social inequities that Black women experience.

BLACK GIRL CARTOGRAPHY: MAPPING OUR STORIES

To engage in the work of Black Girl Cartography, we are required to be in explicit conversations about place, race, and gender. Such conversations can begin with research methods that explore mapping as a method to reveal inequities and interlocking oppressions (Annamma, 2017). Mapping as a method generates questions such as: What is the narrative behind why the researcher selected this town, city, or neighborhood? What are the girls saying about the town or city? Where is the research "site" in relation to the spaces/places where the girls avoid or spend time? How are girls making use of a place? In answering these questions, we can begin to see how Black girl research relies on the social geography—frequency of movement, entering and exiting, spaces of inclusion and exclusion—of Black girls. This also begins to reveal how a place may or may not welcome Black girls, and how that informs the girls' practices. For example, if girls do not frequent the local library, but are more likely to be found at a community center, how will the researcher account for the girls' place-making practices in the research? By exploring such narratives, we are moving away from sterile and exploitative research practices and instead begin to call into question our research motives and how they may or may not align with the girls' practices, ways of knowing, and being.

Mapping is also applicable to theoretical mapping of Black girls. Gholson's (2016) study of how Black girls are relegated to the research gaps in mathematics education echoes a larger issue of regarding where and how Black girls are situated in social imaginations.[3] In her critical analysis of policy reports published by the College Board Advocacy and Policy Center, she notes how the data reporting process erases Black girls. While one report disaggregates by race and ethnicity, the other only disaggregates by gender. As a result, Black girls are hidden in statistics for "Black" students or "female" students, but neither report makes room for both a holistic analysis of how Black girls are performing in mathematics. Therefore, she is putting forth a call for radical creative research that cultivates knowledge about Black girls. Without such research, Black girls are pushed to the "proverbial shadows of inquiry in mathematics education" (Gholson, 2016, p. 298) and studied in passing. For example, Black girls may become visible when research focuses on "endangered" Black male students or to discuss the Black-White achievement gap. Black girls are rendered "ungeographic" in the field and, as she notes, are left to "engage in the domestic housekeeping of theoretical spaces so that others' identities can be salient and knowable within mathematics education" (Gholson, 2016, p. 298). Therefore, her work brings attention to the ways that race, class, gender, location, and knowledge production are intricately linked. When mathematics education research cannot recognize "Black girl" as an identity, interventions for and pedagogy stemming from such an identity are unimaginable. As a result, Black girls are scripted as incapable of learning mathematics and incapable of providing substantial contributions to the field.

In addition to exploring one's stories of entry and "rationale," Black Girl Cartography requires self-reflection. When Black Girl cartographers dig into the stories behind our research questions, sites, and implications, we find that we are face-to-face with our younger selves. I am defining Black Girl cartographers as researchers, scholars, advocates, and individuals who self-identify as a "Black Girl" and who have a deep concern for Black girls' health, lives, well-being and ways of being. Our commitments to Black girls extend beyond the page and the walls of the academy; instead, we express an interest in sustaining, imagining, and mapping (or protecting) sites of "learning, self-love, and critical discourse where women and girls can come together to share" (Phelps-Ward & Laura, 2016, p. 818). Black Girl cartographers' writings emerge as testaments, letters, and entries to younger selves and future selves, to women and girls that we have grown with and some whom we may never meet. To one another, we offer new ways of using Black feminism and womanism to explore our own stories (Baker-Bell, 2017; Cutts, 2012; Lindsay-Dennis, 2015; K. T. Edwards, Baszile, & Guillory, 2016). Through this work, we begin to see how our own educational experiences have guided us back into classroom spaces so that we may be more intentional about our practices. As a result, we find ourselves centering the stories of Black women (Butler, 2017), being attentive to the lived experiences of Black girls (Love, 2017), and thinking about what it means to become a Black woman learner and teacher (Bailey & Miller, 2015; E. Edwards, McArthur & Russell-Owens, 2016; Ford, 2016). We also teach others to do the same. Therefore, Black Girl Cartography requires a commitment of engaging in an ongoing dialogue with past, present, and future Black girls and women, especially one's self.

METHODS FOR LOCATING BLACK GIRL CARTOGRAPHERS IN EDUCATION RESEARCH

The Combahee River Collective reminds us that to be an intersectional Black feminist is to be engaged in an ongoing practice of reflexivity—where we call into question our everyday politics, beliefs, and behaviors. As a Black Girl cartographer, my work of charting the creative practices of Black girls is grounded in the notion that I am not first and I am not alone. I am consistently thinking about my connection to other scholars who are doing the work with and on behalf of Black girls in the present and in the future. Becoming a Black Girl cartographer requires drawing on lessons that we learned from our experiences as Black girls and/or working with Black girls (Dillard, 2000; Lindsay-Dennis, 2015). Unfortunately, for some education researchers, "there is so much about Black identity"—and Blackgirl identity[4]—"that doesn't get called into practice" (Smith & Smith, 1981, p. 119). Therefore, I intentionally called my

Blackgirlness into practice to craft this chapter. When I present, I often begin with the assertion that I am a Geechee Girl whose research is focused on documenting the stories of Black women who are willing to share them with me so that I may share with others. I use the term *Geechee Girl* to evoke identities and knowledges informed by race, gender, and place; therefore, I am a Black girl from the Southeastern United States, specifically from South Carolina Sea Island community of Johns Island. The lenses through which I see the world rely heavily upon relationships grounded in trust, reciprocity, responsibility, and respect (Torrez, 2018) for self and others. This is key because these lenses inform the research methods, citational practice, and structure associated with this and other projects.

Through the radical citation practice (Tuck, 2017) of citing Black women scholars who work with/for Black girls, this chapter attempts to make visible how educators and education researchers are engaging in this intergenerational moment around Black Girlhood. Although advocates, scholars, relatives, and more have been doing the work of honoring, documenting, and nurturing Black Girlhood, 2006 ushered in an era: Black Girlhood Celebration (Kwakye et al., 2017) on a larger platform. To highlight the contributions and achievements of Black women and girls, Beverly Bond launched "Black Girls Rock!" as an organization and Black Entertainment Television awards show. In 2009, Toni Carey and Ashley-Hicks-Rocha began the campaign #BlackGirlsRun to challenge health disparities among Black women and girls. In 2013, CaShawn Thompson started a movement with "Black Girls Are Magic" (#BlackGirlMagic) and Renina Jarmon revealed that it is because "Black Girls are From the Future." In their 2014 report on policing and schooling, the African American Policy Forum declared that Black Girls Matter. These dates, declarations, and movements are important because they are milestones along Black Girlhood's journey into the mainstream. They are also encapsulated in the year parameters I used for my search: research published between 2007 and 2017. To construct this chapter, I relied on #BlackGirl networks on social media (Facebook and Twitter) to crowd-source citations and publications from scholars who focus on Black girls in education. In addition to receiving five publications through the social media announcement, I connected with scholars whose research focuses on Black girls in other areas of study (e.g., public health, disability studies, sociology, law, and art education).[5] I also searched electronic databases such as ProQuest, JSTOR, and Google Scholar for empirical studies and theoretical discussions about Black girls. ProQuest and EBSCO Host searches of "Black girls," "Black female adolescents," and "education" generated education research that focuses on Black girls in urban schools, communities, and afterschool programs. The search yielded 24 publications, including 3 books and 21 peer-reviewed articles, which I analyzed using the following questions:

1. Are the authors using Black feminist or womanist frameworks? (If yes, proceed to Question 2. If no, do not use here. Save for later.)
2. How are the authors conceptualizing the practices and knowledges of Black girls?

TABLE 1
Themes and Focal Studies on Black Girls in Education

Overarching Theme	Emergent Themes	Studies
Black Girl cartographer research methodologies: Black feminist and womanist methods	Reflexive storytelling	Baker-Bell (2017) Bailey and Miller (2015) Butler (2017) Cutts (2012) E. Edwards, McArthur, et al. (2016) Ford (2016) Lindsay-Dennis (2015) Love (2017)
Black Girl Cartography: Schools are hostile geopolitical spaces for Black girls	Black Girl navigational practices	Hines-Datiri and CarterAndrews (2017) Brown (2013) Hill (2011, 2016) Johnson (2017) Kinloch (2010, 2012) Lane (2017) Watson (2016)
	Black Girl charting: Curricula and digital spaces	Greene (2016) Muhammad and Haddix (2016) Nyachae (2016) Ohito (2016) Phelps-Ward and Laura (2016) Price-Dennis (2016)

3. Did the authors create the site (i.e., program or class) or was the site in place (i.e., a school)?
4. Do the authors discuss the research site? If so, how?

Two major themes that emerged from the research are "Black Girl navigational practices" and "Black Girl charting" (see Table 1). In these studies, the scholars—Black Girl cartographers—often documented how schools functioned as geopolitical sites or spaces where adults and peers attempted to (and sometimes successfully) stop Black girl collective practices, punish Black girl movements, and fragment Black girl identities. Therefore, Black Girl navigational practices are connected to the ways that girls work together in the face of individual meritocracy, choose movement over stagnation, and choose to bring their whole selves when schools demand fragmentation. "Black Girl charting" focuses on the tools—curricula and digital space—students and facilitators use to carve out spaces for Black girls to thrive.

BLACK GIRLS NAVIGATING PRACTICES
Figured Worlds: Schools as Geopolitical Spaces

Black Girl cartographers interrogate how Black girls unpack their relationships between race, gender, class, and geospatial location. Such work speaks to Dotson's (2013) notion of Black feminists' move toward a "politics of spatiality" (p. 17), or calling attention to the theoretical and physical spaces that Black women create, require, and sustain. Emerging from the theoretical work and lived experiences of self-identified Black girls and women, inquiries in the field of Black Girlhood studies (Brown, 2013; Hill, 2011, 2016; Lindsey, 2013) are attentive to the intersections of race, gender, class, and sexuality, especially in schools.

While Black Girlhood studies point specifically to Black girl spaces, girlhood cartography studies interrogate the intersections of race, gender, dis/ability, sexuality, *and* location. Scholars mapping and charting Black girl practices reveal how said girls are epistemically and physically excluded from notions of girlhood. In their work on dis/abled girls and Girl Power, Erevelles and Mutua (2005) assert that elements of Girl Power that are grounded in ableism and heteronormativity, "independence, assertiveness, and strength laced with patriarchal notions of beauty and attractiveness" (p. 127) move dis/abled girls to the periphery of girlhood (Schalk, 2013). Research emerging from dis/ability critical race theory, or DisCrit (Annamma, 2017; Annamma, Connor, & Ferri, 2013) and Black disability studies (Schalk, 2017) explores the intersections of race and dis/ability, but not the intersections race, dis/ability, gender, and sexuality. For education, the conversations about race and dis/ability move toward interventions for students of color and special education (Blanchett, 2014; Tefera, Thorius, & Artiles, 2014) and move the field closer to seeing Black dis/abled girls. By placing cartographies of girlhood in conversation with Black Girlhood studies, we can craft a framework to understand how schools function as geopolitical spaces and how Black girls navigate said spaces. In doing so, we develop a heightened sense of urgency about what Black girls' presence (or absence) in research means for the state of the field, and more important, for the lives of Black girls.

For Black Girl cartographers, disciplinary actions construct schools as hostile geopolitical spaces that often threaten Black girls' learning and their livelihood. Hines-Datiri and Carter Andrews (2017) examine how Black girls are policed in learning spaces. They position schools where zero tolerance policies are implemented as figured worlds built on notions of whiteness and femininity.[6] Such positioning echoes the work of Black Girl cartographers (Bailey & Miller, 2015; Evans-Winters & Esposito, 2010; Halliday, 2017; Hill, 2016; Johnson, 2017; Lane, 2017) who examine schools as heteronormative, patriarchal, racist, sexist, and ableist geopolitical practices that limit Blackgirl ways of being. As a result, these spaces force Black girls "to accept, reject, or negotiate identities of criminalization and misplaced femininity" (Hines-Datiri & Carter Andrews, 2017, p. 14) to not be pushed out of classrooms.

However, Black girls creatively navigate these misplaced identities and work together to reclaim classrooms as sites of belonging.

Navigational Practices

Black Girl cartographers also highlight how Black girls carve out spaces in urban schools to engage in sustainable practices of teaching and caring for one another. In *Crossing Boundaries* (Kinloch, 2012), Damya and Christina reimagined the classroom as a site for edification and guidance. Throughout the course of the year, graduating seniors Damya (17-year-old African American female student) and Christina (19-year-old Afro-Jamaican female student) had an "antagonistic relationship" where the two often engaged in heated verbal exchanges (p.99). However, during a peer writing exchange, Christina asked Damya to partner with her, read her paper, and provide feedback. Kinloch notes that because "Christina respected Damya," she chose Damya in hopes that she would engage in "a very special kind of listening" with her that requires "open hearts and minds" (Delpit, 1995, p. 46, quoted by Kinloch, 2012, p. 99). Through their peer review, Damya expressed a deep concern for Christina, who although she was a high school senior, had "not mastered academic codes and conventions in ways that would allow her to assert a stronger academic voice" (p. 98). Kinloch highlights how Christina and Damya reclaimed the contentious classroom space as one to build constructive relationships. By working through each other's stories and leaning on each other's strengths, we come to see how Black girls "author themselves in new agentive ways" (Hines-Datiri & Carter Andrews, 2017, p. 14). As a result, Black girls' efforts to work together pushes back against educational spaces that are rooted in individualism and meritocracy.

Black Girl cartographers map classrooms as sites where girls still grapple with connections between identities and place. Watson (2016) speaks with six girls attending City High School (pseudonym), located in a "large urban city in the northeastern United States" (p. 242). While the girls expressed that they felt safe at City High School, the girls also expressed concerns about the school's inability to counter pervasive narratives of Black girls. For example, Christine shares insight about stigmas that limit Black girls' movement through the school, stigmas "that Black girls are supposed to be loud and ratchet and ghetto" (p. 245). While some girls negotiate or reject "loud and ratchet and ghetto," Christine's observation raises questions about how community members and educators have mapped certain ways of being onto place. How are notions of urban, ghetto and defiant unpacked productively among scholars, girls, teachers, and researchers? In the case of Kim and Samantha, Kinloch (2010) pushes back on concepts that link urban spaces to negative behaviors. For her, Black girls emerge as "street survivors," whom she describes as individuals with "a sophisticated awareness about the community, its history, and street codes (e.g., language; dispositions; appearance; popular venues/spots like the Apollo)" (Kinloch, 2010, p. 49). Therefore, urban spaces for Black girls are sites of complex relationships and sophisticated practices rather than sites of one-dimensional ways of being and knowing.

Through their work, Black girl practices emerge as temporal and spatial acts of intentional resistances, innovative productions, and creative engagements. The same can be said for Black trans*girls, Black queer girls, Black gender nonconfirming girls, and more iterations of being Black girl that theoretically and physically disrupt space, or "bring wreck" (Pough, 2004). Their presence and practices force the field to interrogate how spaces, such as schools and communities, are constructed and maintained by heteronormative, racist, sexist, and ableist ideologies. Two examples of bringing "wreck" that transforms school spaces can be found in the embodied practices of writing (Johnson, 2017) and moving (Hill, 2011, 2016). In her work with queer youth of color, Johnson (2017) highlights the writing of Anika, a 17-year-old Black queer female who uses the pen for truth telling and to raise questions about visibility and "heteronormative hegemony" (p. 27). "Why can't you see me?" she writes, "Is it because I love your sister?/Because I dress like your brother?" (p. 27). To disrupt notions of how gender is curated, constructed, and (mis)read, Anika challenges those reading both her writing and her body. As a result, she urges readers to consider how she wants to be read as she navigates spaces. Hill (2016) explores a research participant's (Unique, "16-year-old raised in a Cameroonian American household") assertion that, *Not all of us are idiots and start twerkin' in the middle of the hallway for no good reason! I actually read books"* (p. 6, emphasis in original). "The act of twerkin' in the middle of the [school] hallway," Hill offers (2017), could be read as "an act of resistance where foregrounding the Blackgirl body transforms the school hallway into a place of comfort and/or where Blackgirls claim authority" (p. 6). Though she does not use the word "map" or "cartography" in her work, Hill's (2017) discussion of Blackgirl body movements map schools, more specifically the liminal spaces of hallways, as spaces where Black girls begin to challenge oppressive structures that seek to police their bodies. Such work not only points to the resistant and generative cartographies of Black girls, it also points to what we should be considering in research that centers the lived experiences of Black girls—their whole selves moving through and transforming spaces.

Black Girl Charting: Curricula and Digital Spaces

Black Girl cartographers explore the interstitial space of curricula in search of how Black girls are represented in, working with, or critiquing texts. In their review of Black Girl literacies, Muhammad and Haddix (2016) include a section on research connected to Black girls, children's and young adult literature and urban fiction. They conclude that children's and young literature focused on Black girl bodies, specifically "body image, skin color" and "representations of Black girls' hair" (p. 318), while urban fiction usually focused on young Black female (16–23 years of age) protagonists who face and overcome difficulties. In their study of Rita Williams-Garcia's *One Crazy Summer*, Howard and Ryan (2017) focus on how Black Girl Power manifests in the 12-year-old character Delphine Gaither. "Black girls on the cusp of adolescence can draw on their lived experiences" of Black tween characters like Delphine "and become agents of change" (Howard & Ryan, 2017, p. 178). While it is important to think about the themes that are explored in literature, especially when they positively impact girls' perceptions of self, it is equally important to consider how children's, young adult, and urban literature map Black girl geographies as well. For example, of the five young adult books that are mentioned in the review, two books are set in inner-city/urban communities (*Bronx Masquerade* by Nikki Grimes and *The Skin I'm In* by Sharon Flake), one book is set in an all-white school in Connecticut (Jacqueline Woodson's *Maizon at Blue Hill*), one book is set in Georgia/change of setting to Georgia (Rita Williams-Garcia's *Like Sisters on the Homefront*), and one book is set in a high school, though the geopolitical location is unclear (Sharon Draper's *November Blues*). Collectively, these texts signal as to where Black girls are most prevalent or at least can thrive in the literary imaginations of writers and readers. Similarly, urban fiction, "street literature, hip-hop literature, Black pulp fiction, ghetto lit, and gangsta lit" (Muhammad & Haddix, 2016, p. 319), signals to readers that certain types of Black girls have deep ties to urban geographies. As a result, notions of resilience in the face of more contemporary issues are reserved for Black girls "with some sort of social injury" (p. 319). Some spaces are unknown (and shall remain unknown), but should be used in classrooms. Through a Black feminist reading of Jamaica Kincaid's "Girl," Ohito (2016) brings attention to Black girl texts that can be incorporated into ELA classrooms. She asserts that Kincaid's short story decenters the Western world and "confirms that other worlds beyond that which is governed by Man are not only present but also possible" (p. 450). As a result, texts like "Girl" open up conversations about Black Girl spaces of belonging and knowing. The ongoing challenge to Black Girl cartographers is making known (or marking) the additional geopolitical spaces where Black Girls thrive, make meaning, care for one another, and negotiate. Such texts can be incorporated not only into K–12 classrooms but also into teacher education programs in an effort to help preservice teachers envision, consider, and imagine multiple locations for Black Girlhood.

Similarly, Black Girl curricula can also prove to be rich ground to help Black girls develop strong sense of self, community, and vision for future possibilities. As cocreator of the *Sisters of Promise* curriculum, Nyachae (2016) and her partners place the stories and lived experiences of Black girls at the center of their teaching practices. The program curriculum, which was created by "Black women teachers for Black girls within the margins of school" (p. 787), intentionally takes account the girls' sociocultural and geopolitical location—Black girls from the northeast region of the United States who qualified for free or reduced lunch. Through their work, Nyachae and her cofacilitators implemented a program that "empowers Black girls, exposes the oppression of Black women in contemporary American society, and critically examines the world as it relates to each Black girl's intersectionality" (p. 794). The program engages in a "politics of spatiality" (Dotson, 2013) by considering each girl's experience through the lenses of place, race, gender, and age. By "intentionally creating the afterschool space with and for Black girls to discuss theory, reflect upon experiences, and address societal issues" (Butler, 2016, p. 316), Nyachae and her cofacilitators reconstructed urban girls as cocreators of knowledge with ways of knowing, being, and critiquing arising from their experiences as Black girls from the northern United States.

Black Girl cartographers also highlight how Black girls engage in the interstitial spaces of multimodal curricula. By producing and disseminating more complex conceptions of Black Girlhood, girls often used digital tools to expand their sociogeopolitical boundaries and "functioned as conduits for circulating counternarratives to a global audience" (Price-Dennis, 2016, p. 358). For six girls participating in the summer "Facebook online street literature book club" (Greene, 2016, p. 279), the digital platform and its disconnection from school spaces offered them a "platform to focus on agency, identity construction, or meaning-making" (p. 285). Greene encourages educators to rethink how they ask Black girls to engage digital spaces. Instead of constructing assignments that are narrow in scope, function, and audience, educators are urged to "mirror the level of freedom of expression and linguistic autonomy often present in Black girls' digital practices" (p. 285). Through such efforts, digital spaces emerge as good ground for the cultivation of Black Girls' "radical creativity and incisive knowledge" (Dotson, 2014, p. 13; see also Phelps-Ward & Laura, 2016; Price-Dennis, 2016). By sifting through curricula created and facilitated by Black Girl cartographers, we learn about the interstitial spaces where we can seek, find, listen to, work alongside, and learn from Black girls across the field of education.

FUTURES OF BLACK GIRL CARTOGRAPHY IN EDUCATION

Black Girl cartographers are committed to learning by walking alongside Black girls. In Belo Horizonte, Brazil, Henery (2011) learns how Black women's physical labor and geopolitical knowledge shaped the community. As wives, mothers, and domestic laborers, the women's footsteps carved out new pathways in the favelas in the form of "a geographic pattern, rhythm, and ethic of black women's work that . . . gave shape to the neighborhood" (p. 92). By walking with the women, Henery recounts how "Black women's social dynamics" (p. 92) shaped the Brazilian terrain. Similarly, Black Girl cartographers are "walking" with Black girls who are charting and shaping various terrains of learning. When education research works through the framework of Black Girl Cartography, we see where Black girls cultivate care that is rooted in justice, respect, reciprocity, and futurity. Seeing Black girls is the first required action in activism for and with Black girls, as it then pushes toward hearing girls, believing girls, understanding Black Girl matters, and articulating why Black girls matter. I return to McKittrick to think about implications for Black Girl matters, cartography, and the field of education.

If black women's geographies illustrate that our ideological models and the three-dimensional physical world can, indeed, be alterable and reimagined, *where* do their sense of place, and their conceptual interventions take us? Can black women's geographies also open up the possibility to rethink, and therefore respatialize, our present sociogeographic organization? (McKittrick, 2006, p. 122)

To answer McKittrick's questions is to consider how education researchers can become ethical and responsible Black Girl cartographers. Part of ethical engagement is recognizing limits and learning to seek answers in new ways. With all the possibilities of Black Girl Cartography, I do recognize that cartography can be a limiting framework in that it may make static people who are in motion and occupying multiple spaces simultaneously, as well as try to make legible practices that are embodied, ever changing, and indescribable (as we do not yet have the language to effectively translate practices). Writing about the terrains through which Black girls travel and/or make is limited in that it is incapable of fully depicting the multidimensional practices, knowledges, and spaces of Black girlhood (Price-Dennis, Muhammad, Womack, McArthur, & Haddix, 2017). I acknowledge that there are several Black girls who are not "mapped" in this chapter, girls who are important to the framing of Black Girl Cartography. Therefore, the framework is in-flux and in-progress as it is being shaped by the cartographic knowledges of trans* Black girls, Black dis/abled girls, Black girls living outside of the United States, Black girls of various spiritual and religious beliefs, multilingual Black girls, and more. Charting their critical cartographic knowledges requires more conversations with scholars, researchers, and advocates who are walking alongside those who have not been mapped here.

Muhammad and Haddix (2016) assert, in their call for the centering of Black Girl literacies, that "if we reimagine English education where Black girls matter, all children would benefit from a curricular and pedagogical infrastructure that values humanity" (p. 329). Echoing the Combahee River Collective's assertion that everyone else's freedom would be a result of Black women's freedom, Muhammad and Haddix remind us that each child's education and liberation are connected to the education and liberation of Black girls. For example, Black Girl cartographers (Hines-Datiri & Carter Andrews, 2017; Morris, 2015; Wun, 2016) who examine the ways zero tolerance policies result in the overpolicing of Black girls in schools highlight how disciplinary responses push Black girlhood out of schooling landscapes. Their work calls into question why Black girls do not seem to matter in schools. Cartographers who focus on Black girls' digital practices bring attention to how Black girls reclaim space and forge communities, especially if they have been physically or socially ostracized (Phelps-Ward & Laura, 2016; Greene, 2016). Collectively, Black Girl cartographers remind us that education research rooted in responsibility and critical reflexivity can contribute to the long-standing activism of Black women. Such work names the structures and institutions that are responsible for inequities, articulates how Black girls' experiences are shaped by said structures, and considers how Black girls are working within/against the structures. Therefore, Black Girl cartographers are documenting the ways that Black girls are leading to more sustaining, holistic, and liberatory practices. In carrying the legacy of Harriet and unnamed liberators, Black Girl cartographers remember (and remind us) that everyone's liberation is, and possibilities for liberatory education are, intricately linked to Black Girl knowledge.

NOTES

[1]Britney Cooper discusses how and why scholars should take up Black feminist scholarship as relevant theoretical frameworks of analysis that can and should be interrogated, expanded, and critiqued. In her critique of the ways non-Black feminists dismiss the critical epistemological work of Black feminists, B. Cooper (2015) writes, "It is almost as if intersectional Black feminism is treated like those annoying emergency broadcast announcements on radio and television" (p. 15).

[2]Critical geographer Mona Domosh (2017) documents how federal agricultural programs were responsible for maintaining a poor Black working class in Alabama. Through, what she is calling "critical historical geography of race," we can begin to consider how race/racism, gender/gender discrimination, *and* location informed the "making and unmaking of U.S. culture, politics, and power" (Domosh, 2017, p. 766). In order words, such work considers how people's geopolitical location informs where they work, where they live, how much they are paid, and how they are viewed in legislation.

[3]In her review of S. B. Edwards and Harris' (2017) *Hidden Human Computers*, Alexis Pauline Gumbs (2016) discusses the connections between Black women's knowledge of space and time and the need for the book, which is by and about Black women in STEM (science, technology, engineering, and mathematics) fields.

[4]To underscore the holistic realities Black girls (and women) experience as racialized, gendered, age, and sexualized individuals, scholars use identifiers such as "Blackgirl" (Hill, 2016) and "Blackgirlwoman" (Hill, 2016; Womack, 2013) to describe themselves and research participants. The rhetorical intentionality of removing the space(s) between the identities also emphasizes the inability to analyze the positions, conditions, and contributions of Black girls from one axis (e.g., race, gender, class, age, sexuality, dis/ability, etc.), as well as the incompleteness of such analyses. "Blackgirl" and "Blackgirlwoman" recognizes that Black girls enter informal and formal classroom spaces with their interlocking identities, which schools attempt to fragment through punishment and policing (Hines-Datiri & Carter Andrews, 2017).

[5]Grateful to the individuals who responded to the social media announcement (names in parenthesis are people whom the individual "tagged" or referenced): Sherell McArthur, Delicia Greene, Victor Jones (Raygine DiAquoi, Elana Burton-Douglas, Myosha McAfee, and Jaynemarie E. Angbah), Lauren Powell (Courtney Woods), Keisha McIntosh Allen, Tiffany Rose (Joan Nicole), Salandra Bowman, Cameo King, Christina Bush (Kenly Brown), Frances Olajide (Eve Ewing, Daphne M. Penn, Ebony Bridwell Mitchell), Alyssa Elmore, Karisa Peer-Yap (Monique Lane), Esther Ohito (Aja Reynolds), and Melissa Crum.

[6]For readings on the policing of Black girls and the school-to-prison pipeline and Black girls, see Crenshaw, Ocen, and Nanda (2015) and Morris (2015).

REFERENCES

Annamma, S. A. (2017). Disrupting cartographies of inequity: Education journey mapping as a qualitative methodology. In D. Morrison, S. A. Annamma, & D. D. Jackson (Eds.), *Critical race spatial analysis: Mapping to understand and address educational inequity* (pp. 33–50). Sterling, VA: Stylus.

Annamma, S. A., Connor, D., & Ferri, B. (2013). Dis/ability critical race studies (DisCrit): Theorizing at the intersections of race and dis/ability. *Race Ethnicity and Education, 16*(1), 1–31.

Bailey, M., & Miller, S. J. (2015). When margins become centered: Black queer women in front of and outside of the classroom. *Feminist Formations, 27*, 168–188.

Baker-Bell, A. (2017). For Loretta: A Black woman literacy scholar's journey to prioritizing self-preservation and Black feminist-womanist storytelling. *Journal for Literacy Research, 49*, 526–543.

Blanchett, W. J. (2014). African American students and other students of color in special education. In H. R. Milner, & K. Lomotey (Eds.), *Handbook of urban education* (pp. 271–284). New York, NY: Routledge.

Blige, S. (2010). Recent feminist outlooks on intersectionality. *Diogenes, 225*, 58–72.

Blige, S. (2013). Intersectionality undone: Saving intersectionality from feminist intersectionality studies. *Du Bois Review, 10*, 405–424.

Brown, R. N. (2013). *Hear our truths: The creative potential of Black girlhood.* Champaign, IL: University of Illinois Press.

Butler, T. T. (2016). "Stories behind their hands": The creative and collective "actionist" work of girls of color. *English Teaching, 15*, 313–332.

Butler, T. T. (2017). #Say[ing]HerName as critical demand: English education in the age of erasure. *English Education, 49*, 153–178.

Carastathis, A. (2014). The concept of intersectionality in feminist theory. *Philosophy Compass, 9*, 304–314.

Collins, P. H. (2000). *Black feminist thought: Knowledge, consciousness, and the politics of empowerment* (Rev. 10th anniv. ed.). New York, NY: Routledge.

Cooper, A. J. (1891). Woman versus the Indian. In C. Lemert, & E. Bhan (Eds.), *The voice of Anna Julia Cooper: Including a voice from the South and other important essays, papers, and letters* (pp. 88–108). New York, NY: Rowman & Littlefield.

Cooper, B. (2015). Love no limit: Towards a Black feminist future (in theory). *The Black Scholar, 45*, 7–21.

Crenshaw, K. (1989). Demarginalizing the intersection of race and sex: A Black feminist critique of antidiscrimination doctrine, feminist theory and antiracist politics. *University of Chicago Legal Forum, 1989*(1), Article 8. Retrieved from http://chicagounbound.uchicago.edu/uclf/vol1989/iss1/8

Crenshaw, K. (1991). Mapping the margins: Intersectionality, identity politics, and violence against women of color. *Stanford Law Review, 43*, 1241–1299.

Crenshaw, K., Ocen, P., & Nanda, J. (2015). *Black girls matter: Pushed out, overpoliced, and underprotected.* Retrieved from https://static1.squarespace.com/static/53f20 d90e4b0b80451158d8c/t/54d21c9ee4b0535ab80a10ed/1423056030631/BlackGirls Matter_ExecutiveSummary.pdf

Cutts, Q. (2012). A critical pedagogy of place. *Journal of Curriculum Theorizing, 28*, 142–150.

Dillard, C. B. (2000). The substance of things hoped for, the evidence of things not seen: Examining an endarkened feminist epistemology in educational research and leadership. *International Journal of Qualitative Studies in Education, 13*, 661–681.

Domosh, M. (2017). Genealogies of race, gender, and place. *Annals of the American Association of Geographers, 107*, 765–778.

Dotson, K. (2011). Tracking epistemic violence, tracking practices of silencing. *Hypatia, 26*, 236–257.

Dotson, K. (2013). *Knowing in space: Three lessons from Black women's social theory.* (Unpublished manuscript). Retrieved from: http://ssrn.com/abstract=2270343

Dotson, K. (2014). "Thinking familiar with the interstitial": An introduction. *Hypatia, 29*, 1–17.

Edwards, E., McArthur, S. A., & Russell-Owens, L. (2016). Relationships, being-ness, and voice: Exploring multiple dimensions of humanizing work with Black girls. *Equity & Excellence in Education, 53*, 63–77.

Edwards, K. T., Baszile, D. T., & Guillory, N. A. (2016). When, where, and why we enter: Black women's curriculum theorising. *Gender and Education, 28*, 707–709.

Edwards, S. B., & Harris, D. (2017). *Hidden human computers: The Black women of NASA.* Minneapolis, MN: Adbo.

Erevelles, N., & Mutua, K. (2005). "I am a woman now!" Rewriting cartographies of girlhood form the critical standpoint of disability. In P. Bettis, & N. G. Adams (Eds.), *Geographies of girlhood: Identities in-between* (pp. 127–134). New York, NY: Routledge.

Evans-Winters, V. E., & Esposito, J. (2010). Other people's daughters: Critical race feminism and Black girls' education. *Educational Foundations, 24*, 11–24.

Ford, J. C. (2016). "Very simple: I just don't lie": The role of honesty in Black lesbian K–12 teachers' experiences in the U.S. Southeast. *Journal of Lesbian Studies, 21*, 391–406.

Gholson, M. L. (2016). Clean corners and algebra: A critical examination of the constructed invisibility of black girls and women in mathematics. *Journal of Negro Education, 85*, 290–301.

Greene, D. T. (2016). "We need more 'US' in schools!" Centering Black adolescent girls' literacy and language practices in online school spaces. *Journal of Negro Education, 85*, 274–289.

Gumbs, A. P. (2016, August 19). Black bodies and dark matter: Calculating possibility. *The Feminist Wire*. Retrieved from http://www.thefeministwire.com/2016/08/black-lives-dark-matter-calculating-possibility/

Guy-Sheftall, B. (Ed.). (1995). *Words of fire: An anthology of African-American feminist thought.* New York, NY: New Press.

Halliday, A. (2017). Envisioning black girl futures: Nicki Minaj's anaconda feminism and new understandings of black girl sexuality in popular culture. *Departures in Critical Qualitative Research, 6*(3), 65–77.

Henery, C. (2011). Where they walk: What aging Black women's geographies tell of race, gender, space, and social transformation in Brazil. *Cultural Dynamics, 23*, 85–106.

Hill, D. C. (2011). Why you tryna silence her body? The role of education in shaping the black female body. *Qualitative Research Journal, 11*, 102–109.

Hill, D. C. (2016). Blackgirl, one word: Necessary transgressions in the name of imagining Black girlhood. *Cultural Studies <-> Critical Methodologies, 47*, 1–9.

Hines-Datiri, D., & Carter Andrews, D. (2017). The effects of zero tolerance policies on Black girls: Using critical race feminism and figured worlds to examine school discipline. *Urban Education*. Advance online publication. doi:10.1177/0042085917690204

Howard, C. M., & Ryan, C. L. (2017). Black tween girls with Black girl power. *Language Arts, 94*, 170–179.

Johnson, L. P. (2017). Writing the self: Black queer youth challenge heteronormative ways of being in an after-school writing club. *Research in the Teaching of English, 52*, 13–33.

Kinloch, V. (2010). *Harlem on our minds: Place, race and literacies of urban youth.* New York, NY: Teachers College Press.

Kinloch, V. (2012). *Crossing boundaries: Teaching and learning with urban youth.* New York, NY: Teachers College Press.

Kwakye, C. J., Hill, D. C., & Callier, D. M. (2017). 10 Years of black girlhood celebration: A pedagogy of doing. *Departures in Critical Qualitative Research, 6*(3), 1–10.

Lane, M. (2017). Reclaiming our queendom: Black feminist pedagogy and the identity formation of African American girls. *Equity & Excellence in Education, 50*(1), 13–24.

Lindsay-Dennis, L. (2015). Black feminist-womanist research paradigm: Toward a culturally relevant research model focuses on African American girls. *Journal of Black Studies, 46*, 506–520.

Lindsey, T. B. (2013). "One time for my girls": African-American girlhood, empowerment, and popular visual culture. *Journal of African American Studies, 17*(1), 22–34.

Lindsey, T. B. (2015). Post-Ferguson: A "herstorical" approach to black violability. *Feminist Studies, 41*, 232–237.

Love, B. (2017). Difficult knowledge: When a Black feminist educator was too afraid to #SayHerName. *English Education, 49*, 197–208.

McKittrick, K. (2006). *Demonic grounds: Black women and the cartographies of struggle.* Minneapolis: University of Minnesota Press.

Morris, M. W. (2015). *Pushout: The criminalization of Black girls in schools*. New York, NY: New Press.

Muhammad, G. E., & Haddix, M. (2016). Centering Black girls' literacies: A review of literature on the multiple ways of knowing of Black girls. *English Education*, *48*, 299–336.

Nyachae, T. M. (2016). Complicated contradictions amid Black feminism and millennial Black women teachers creating curriculum for Black girls. *Gender and Education*, *28*, 786–806.

Ohito, E. O. (2016). Refusing curriculum as a space of death for black female subjects: A Black feminist reparative reading of Jamaica Kincaid's "girl." *Curriculum Inquiry*, *46*, 436–454.

Phelps-Ward, R. J., & Laura, C. (2016). Talking back in cyberspace: Self-love, hair care and counter narratives in Black adolescent girls' YouTube vlogs. *Gender and Education*, *28*, 807–820.

Pough, G. D. (2004). *Check it while I wreck it: Black womanhood, hip-hop culture, and the public sphere*. Boston, MA: Northeastern University Press.

Price-Dennis, D. (2016). Developing curriculum to support Black girls' literacies in digital spaces. *English Education*, *48*, 337–361.

Price-Dennis, D., Muhammad, G. E., Womack, E., McArthur, S. A., & Haddix, M. (2017). The multiple identities and literacies of black girlhood: A conversation about creating spaces for black girl voices. *Journal of Language and Literacy Education*, *13*(3), 1–18.

Schalk, S. (2013). Ablenationalism in American girlhood. *Girlhood Studies*, *9*(1), 36–52.

Schalk, S. (2017). Interpreting disability metaphor and race in Octavia Butler's "The evening and the morning and the night." *African American Review*, *50*, 139–157.

Smith, B., & Smith, B. (1981). Across the kitchen table: A sister-to-sister dialogue. In C. Moraga, & G. Anzaldúa (Eds.) *This bridge called my back: Writings by radical women of color* (pp. 113–127). New York, NY: Kitchen Table: Women of Color Press.

Spivak, G. (1988). Can the subaltern speak? In C. Nelson, & L. Grossberg (Eds.), *Marxism and the interpretation of culture* (pp. 271–312). Champaign, IL: University of Illinois Press.

Tefera, A., Thorius, K. K., & Artiles, A. (2014). Teacher influences in racialization of disabilities. In H. R. Milner, & K. Lomotey (Eds.), *Handbook of urban education* (pp. 256–270). New York, NY: Routledge.

Torrez, J. E. (2018). Responsibility, reciprocity, and respect: Storytelling as a means of university-community engagement. In M. Castañeda and J. Krupczynski (Eds.), *Civic engagement in diverse Latinx communities* (pp.143–158). New York, NY: Peter Lang.

Tuck, E. (2017). *Citation is political! Presentation at the Curriculum Inquiry Writing Fellows Retreat*. Toronto, Ontario, Canada: Ontario Institute for the Study of Education.

Watson, T. (2016). "Talking back": The perceptions of Black girls who attend city school. *The Journal of Negro Education*, *85*, 239–249.

Williams, F. B. (1905). The colored girl. *Voice of the Negro*, *2*, 400–403.

Winn, M. T. (2010). Betwixt and between: Literacy, liminality, and the ceiling of Black girls. *Race Ethnicity and Education*, *13*, 425–447.

Womack, E. (2013). *Uncovering the literate lives of Black female adolescents* (Unpublished dissertation). The Ohio State University, Columbus.

Wun, C. (2016). Unaccounted foundations: Black girls, anti-Black racism, and punishment in schools. *Critical Sociology*, *42*, 737–750.

Chapter 3

Disability Critical Race Theory: Exploring the Intersectional Lineage, Emergence, and Potential Futures of DisCrit in Education

Subini Ancy Annamma
University of Kansas

Beth A. Ferri
Syracuse University

David J. Connor
Hunter College, City University of New York

In this review, we explore how intersectionality has been engaged with through the lens of disability critical race theory (DisCrit) to produce new knowledge. In this chapter, we (1) trace the intellectual lineage for developing DisCrit, (2) review the body of interdisciplinary scholarship incorporating DisCrit to date, and (3) propose the future trajectories of DisCrit, noting challenges and tensions that have arisen. Providing new opportunities to investigate how patterns of oppression uniquely intersect to target students at the margins of Whiteness and ability, DisCrit has been taken up by scholars to expose and dismantle entrenched inequities in education.

In 2016, Bresha Meadows, a 14-year-old Black girl, killed her father following years of abuse inflicted on her family.[1] Reporter Melissa Jeltsen (2017) wrote of Meadows's case:

According to Bresha's family, the young girl had started to fall apart in the months leading up to the shooting. Her grades plummeted. She began cutting herself. And she ran away, telling her aunts in Cleveland that she was afraid her father might kill them all. He beat her mother in front of her, she said, and threatened them with a gun. She said she was scared for their lives. (Para 9)

Although the average pretrial length of detention is 22 days (Office of Juvenile Justice and Delinquency Program, 2013), by May of 2017, Bresha had been incarcerated for over 250 days and labeled[2] with posttraumatic stress disorder, depression, and anxiety. Bresha's story is not only about racial or gender-related violence but also about

Review of Research in Education
March 2018, Vol. 42, pp. 46–71
DOI: 10.3102/0091732X18759041
© 2018 AERA. http://rre.aera.net

disability. Instead of compassion for the abuse she experienced, Bresha was treated as a dangerous entity, criminalized and punished for being a multiply marginalized[3] disabled Black girl in distress. Her story illustrates how race and disability are not only deeply linked with other social locations but also how racism and ableism, intersecting with additional oppressions, often have serious and sometimes deadly implications.

Intersectionality has opened promising lines of inquiry for dismantling interlocking systems of oppression (Crenshaw, 1989) in education. In initially framing disability critical race theory (DisCrit) as an intersectional framework, we aimed to more fully account for the ways that racism and ableism are interconnected and collusive normalizing processes (Annamma, Connor, & Ferri, 2013). Providing new opportunities to investigate how intersecting patterns of oppression target students at the margins of Whiteness and ability, DisCrit has since been taken up by scholars to expose and dismantle entrenched inequities in education. In this chapter, we (a) trace the intellectual lineage of DisCrit; (b) review the body of interdisciplinary scholarship incorporating DisCrit to date, and (c) propose the future trajectories of DisCrit, noting challenges and tensions evidenced in the work thus far.

TRACING A LINEAGE OF ACADEMICS, ACTIVISTS, AND ARTISTS

In tracing the lineage for DisCrit, we believe it is important to acknowledge the rich scholarly work that contributed to its genesis. Indeed, given the complex tangle of race and disability that has reverberated throughout U.S. history, we cannot do justice in this short chapter to all those who should be recognized. What we can do, however, is share from our collective perspective a cross-selection of individuals who have strongly influenced our own thinking about intersectionality—in particular, the interstices of being raced and dis/abled[4]—that ultimately led us to develop DisCrit in the service of producing new knowledge.

We begin by locating the foundations of DisCrit in Black and critical race feminist scholarship and activism. Take, for example, Anna Julia Cooper, author of *A Voice from the South: By a Black Woman of the South* (1892/1988), and educator, principal, activist, and scholar. Cooper's book and other publications have been recognized as one of first articulations of Black feminism as it substantively explored what it meant to be a Black woman in America. A century later, Kimberlé Crenshaw (1989) further revealed how the law subjugated Black women as they could neither claim discrimination based on race (because Black men were being promoted) nor gender (because White women were also being promoted). Crenshaw (1991) noted how *interlocking forms of oppressions* created unique barriers for Black women and frustrated their ability to claim legal remedy either as women or as persons of color. In her foundational articulation of Black feminism, Patricia Hill Collins (1990) drew from intellectual ancestors such as Angela Davis, Nikki Giovanni, Lorraine Hansberry, bell hooks, Zora Neale Hurston, June Jordan, Audre Lorde, Sojourner Truth, and Alice Walker to illustrate how knowledge claims emerging from Black women's intersectional positioning provided a unique reading on the workings of power, which she identified as a matrix of domination. Although disability did not figure prominently in much of this work, because of its intersectional nature, the pioneering work of Black feminists has nonetheless been foundational to the development of DisCrit.

The transdisciplinary field of critical race theory (CRT) in which race, centered in law, is seen as an organizing principle of power that affects all aspects of society was also integral to DisCrit's foundations (Crenshaw, Gotanda, Peller, & Thomas, 1995; Delgado & Stefancic, 2001). CRT recognizes racism as central to creating group (dis) advantage, highlights knowledge claims forged in the experiences of communities of color, rejects ahistoric accounts of entrenched inequities, and promotes interdisciplinary research that aims to eliminate racial (and intersecting) forms of oppression (Matsuda, 1993). Applying CRT to education reveals pervasive inequities despite decisions, such as *Brown v. Board of Education*, intended to counter them (D. Bell, 2004; Ladson-Billings & Tate, 1995). CRT is also a means of reconceptualizing intractable problems (Tate, 1997). Ladson-Billings's (2006) critique of "the achievement gap," for instance, more accurately conceived the problem as reflective of an educational debt owed to students of color rather than some deficit in the children themselves. By centering race within interlocking and oppressive structures of society, CRT provides a means to understand how racism and White supremacy function in education, while seeking to disrupt them (Leonardo, 2004; Solórzano & Yosso, 2002; Yosso, 2002).

As scholars who began our professional lives working in special education, we recognized how youth of color fared far less well than their White counterparts in schools. We were also aware of the ways that disability functioned to "other" students whose differences were envisaged from a deficit lens. Moreover, we recognized that disability was a political identity, socially constructed in tandem with race and class, rather than an objective medical condition. Struck by how the field of special education ignored or denied racial issues, collectively and individually, we focused much of our academic work on issues such as the overrepresentation of children of color in special education, achievement/opportunity gaps, the school-to-prison pipeline, and discrepancies in outcomes of disabled students of color (e.g., graduation, employment, college). Working in a small community of scholars within special education, we called attention to how dis/ability *and* race merited further attention, noting that labeling and practices associated with special education appeared to be maintaining and expanding racial segregation among students (Artiles, 2013; Artiles, Dorn, & Bal, 2017; Bal & Trainor, 2016; Erevelles, 2002; Erevelles & Minear, 2010; Harry & Klingner, 2006; Leonardo & Broderick, 2011; Losen & Orfield, 2002; Waitoller & Thorius, 2016).[5] Unfortunately, outside of this small circle of scholars, the field of special education has remained quite resistant to engage in the racialized nature of education and dis/ability in meaningful or sustained ways.[6]

Concerned about the persistent problems of deficit-based understandings of difference, overrepresentation in negative outcomes, and the limited range of research methodologies accepted by the field, we aligned our scholarly work with the emerging field of disability studies (DS; Connor, Gabel, Gallagher, & Morton, 2008). In doing so, we perceived DS's focus on ableism as an organizing principle in personal, societal, educational, and historical structures. In addition, we embraced a core value of DS, which privileges knowledge based on lived experiences of disabled people. Subsequently, we began to see the value of drawing on both CRT and DS (as well as feminist studies) in our research. Ferri and Connor (2005), for example, examined public discourse surrounding debates over the two largest historically excluded groups of students in American public schools—African American and disabled children. Drawing on archival research, their findings illustrated how special education became a tool to maintain racial hierarchies after the *Brown* decision. Driven by the desire to have student's lives and voices represented in professional literature that traditionally portrayed them in unidimensional ways, we also documented experiences in and out of school at the interstices of race, dis/ability, and class (Connor, 2008) and gender (Annamma, 2014; Ferri & Connor, 2010).

Linking CRT and DS to frame and analyze the lives of disabled youth of color provided far more nuance than had we simply attended to one element of identity or form of oppression. At the same time, we realized there was a disjuncture in that each field could be engaging more fully with the other. In his critique of DS, Chris Bell (2006) attributed the paucity of DS scholarship addressing issues of race to its White, middle-class location within the academy. Likewise, issues of dis/ability remain largely under-explored in CRT, which has led to "bifurcated social and legal process[es]" that conflate undesirable identities with deficit, while simultaneously ignoring ableism (Goodwin, 2003, p. 229). In other words, both DS and CRT have failed to adequately address intersectionality, focusing primarily on single-axis explanations of structural inequity.

Although there is room to more fully develop the potential power of explicitly integrating both frameworks, some DS scholars have engaged in work about race and disability. Reid and Knight (2006), for instance, used a DS perspective to look at racial disparities in the increased number of college students with learning disabilities, illustrating how some disability labels leveraged access for wealthy White students, while serving as a barrier for Black students. Erevelles (2002) also revealed how citizenship is a form of struggle in which dis/ability and race are implicated. In addition, Mitchell (2006, 2007) has explored ways in which gender, race, and dis/ability involve a life-long negotiation. Similarly, some race and CRT scholars have sought to demonstrate how ability is conferred or withheld along lines of race, gender, and social class. Vincent, Rollock, Ball, and Gillborn (2012), for instance, explored ways Black middle-class parents were aware of how perceptions of their children's ability were constructed by teachers and what parents tried to do to "to present (their child) as a 'good' (i.e. enthusiastic, able, relatively compliant) learner with high aspirations and ambition" (p. 270). Critical race feminist scholar Michele Goodwin (2003) explored ableism in the case of Wanda Jean Allen, illustrating how Allen's multiple social locations of being Black, poor, lesbian, and intellectually disabled worked in tandem to position her as bad, dangerous, and shameful. Audre Lorde (1997) took a personal exploration of her own cancer and how illness affected racialized and gendered experiences. We are heartened, too, by the number of dissertations examining varied topics such as autism and race (Hetherington, 2012), vitiligo as involuntary Whiteness (Sierra-Zarella, 2010), high-stakes testing and ability construction (Tefera, 2011), and the intergenerational social reproduction of disability (Welch, 2002). We imagine this collective work as evidence of the beginnings of a sustained interest in studying the interworkings of race and dis/ability within CRT.

There have also been scholars who have simultaneously integrated CRT *and* DS in innovative and powerful ways. For example, Asch (2001) urged DS scholars to incorporate both CRT and feminism, and Campbell (2008) culled from CRT and the concept of internalized racism to explore internalized ableism within disabled people. Several highly original and provocative studies have included analyses of race, dis/ability, social class, and gender in terms of school discipline (Watts & Erevelles, 2004), inclusive/exclusive education (Erevelles, Kanga, & Middleton, 2006; Petersen, 2009), and state-sanctioned violence (Erevelles & Minear, 2010), among others. In addition, Smith (2004) incorporated DS and critical Whiteness studies, foreshadowing Leonardo and Broderick's (2011) focus on Whiteness and DS, specifically to explicate how smartness and Whiteness operate in schools. Beratan (2008) called attention to institutional ableism within laws and policies that maintain oppressive educational structures. Liasidou (2008, 2011, 2013, 2014) has incorporated critical discourse analysis in examining the intersections of race, class, and disability in terms of inclusive policy. Finally, Ferri's (2008) analysis of Lynn Manning's autobiographical performance of *Weights* highlights how the play illuminates the interstices of race, disability, gender, and class in provocative ways.

Artists and activists, beyond the ones listed above, were also deeply influential in our shifting commitment to an intersectional framing of race and dis/ability. Patti Berne, Anita Cameron, Mia Mingus, Leroy Moore, and Alice Wong, to name a few, have led the conversation, naming how interlocking systems of oppression have affected the lives of disabled people of color. They have created essential organizations led by disabled people of color, such as Sins Invalid and Krip Hop Nation, and developed significant concepts such as Disability Justice and Access Intimacy. Currently, a new generation has joined the work of these trailblazers and continued the lineage of resistance including Lydia Brown, Dustin Gibson, Mia Ives-Rublee, T. L. Lewis, Vilissa Thompson, among others. These emerging voices have pushed intersectional coalitions to let disabled people of color lead as authors of their own lives and solution producers to the inequities they face. Our aim in naming this varied genealogy is to rupture the distance between artists, activists, and academics by recognizing that we owe our evolution in thinking to the knowledge generated from these multiple communities.

Thus, the lineage of DisCrit is both diffuse and rich, exposing commonalities and tensions garnered from its intersectional foundations. The genesis of intersectionality within Black feminism and its further engagement with CRT and DS illuminates the interstices of dis/ability and race within education. Taken together, this multidimensional work demonstrated the viability of developing a specific framework to facilitate engagement with interlocking systems of oppression, to resist them, and to imagine new ways of thinking and advocating for equity. In what follows, we move from tracing the robust lineage of DisCrit to documenting and analyzing how scholars have taken up DisCrit's intersectional commitments to produce new strands of knowledge.

REVIEW METHOD

To trace the many paths that DisCrit has traveled since its initial publication in 2013, we began by searching more commonly used databases such as JSTOR and ERIC using the term "DisCrit." However, here were only nine results for DisCrit and associated terms in JSTOR, some dating back to 1943 and only tangentially related, if at all. We then searched for "disability critical race theory," which resulted in 185,630 hits, as there was no Boolean search option out of "critical race theory." Searching "disability studies *and* critical race theory" resulted in 10,150 works, but again with limited relevance to DisCrit, although many were part of the intellectual genealogy of DisCrit. Understanding that it takes 2 to 5 years to be included in many databases, we turned to alternatives such as Google Scholar, Academia.edu, and ResearchGate. In Google Scholar, our 2013 paper came up as the first result in a search using "DisCrit." It was cited 93 times, including 85 unique citations (13 were our own subsequent publications). In addition to our own paper, the search term DisCrit resulted in 721 results. Adding quotations ("DisCrit") resulting in 423 hits. By excluding work that was unrelated (e.g., related to mining or an algorithm) and eliminating duplicates and non-English-language publications, we were left with an additional 17 results. "Disability critical race theory" with quotations resulted in 32 results, 12 of which were duplicates and 21 that mentioned disability studies and/or critical race theory, but not DisCrit, and therefore were not included in our analysis. Similarly, searching for "disability studies" AND "critical race theory" landed 1,800 hits with both (DS and CRT) and single (DS *or* CRT), but no additional results after 2013. The same searches were done both in Academia.edu and ResearchGate resulting in 18 studies in total, and 2 additional results after exclusions for duplicates, dates, and unrelated subjects. To ensure we included emerging work from the field, we also searched ProQuest and found 26 recent dissertations that referenced DisCrit. We originally included conference papers from Disability Studies in Education Association and Critical Race Studies in Education Association but decided to focus solely on published work. Finally, we culled from our own knowledge of recently published works. In total, we ended up with a total of 122 articles, 12 book chapters (8 of which were from our DisCrit edited volume), and 26 dissertations that fit our selection criteria. We then reviewed each paper (each author read a third of the total) and found that 31 of the total number of papers we identified substantively engaged with DisCrit. We defined substantively engagement as (a) *theoretical pieces* that critiqued, disrupted, and/or extended DisCrit and (b) *empirical papers* that used DisCrit as part of the conceptual framing or analytical tools or that illustrate the affordances of DisCrit in exploration of data. We then read each of the 31 papers again (each author was given a new third that they did not review in the first round) to examine (a) themes explored; (b) DisCrit tenets engaged either theoretically (extends, disrupts, or critiques of the framework) or empirically (in the conceptual framing or as an analytical tool); (c) unique contributions; and (d) implications. In our review, we found that many of the papers explicitly and implicitly engaged in one or more specific tenet of DisCrit. We decided, therefore, that it would be instructive to sort the papers according to the tenets that were either explicitly named or most substantively engaged. When it was difficult to pinpoint the tenet(s) that authors were substantively engaging, a second reader was employed to provide help in determining which of the tenets were addressed—in each of these instances, authors were able to reach consensus. Following this process, we then identified exemplars for each tenet. These were selected to highlight contributions that engaged DisCrit in innovative or substantive ways. We also noted those authors that extended DisCrit or brought additional complexity into their analyses. Because we were interested in determining whether authors were broadening the scope of research on race and disability (beyond, e.g., documenting the overrepresentation of students of color in special education), we also created a chart to summarize the range of topics that the authors were addressing. This summary chart was instructive to illustrate the scope of issues that have been analyzed using a DisCrit framework to date. Overall, our multilayered analysis proved to be useful in accounting for the myriad ways that authors representing this growing body of literature are incorporating DisCrit.

STRETCHING THE BOUNDARIES OF DISCRIT

Positioning DisCrit as an exemplary intersectional analysis (Cook & Williams, 2015; Garcia & Scott, 2016; Ulysse, Berry, & Jupp, 2016), scholars have begun to explore racism and ableism as interlocking oppressions (Kohli, 2016; Lalvani, Broderick, Fine, Jacobowitz, & Michelli, 2015) in fields such as counseling (Peters, 2017), higher education (Ledesma & Calderón, 2015), psychology (Wagner, 2016), and education policy (Ard & Knaus, 2013).

Highlighting the need for intersectional approaches to the study of race and disability, DisCrit encouraged scholars to employ a variety of perspectives and theories in theoretical and empirical work. In addition to crossing disciplinary borders, DisCrit has traversed international boundaries. In the United Kingdom, it has been used to explore the ways Black middle-class parents struggle to prevent or access special education for their children (Rollock, Gillborn, Vincent, & Ball, 2014). DisCrit has informed analyses of racism and ableism that are complicated by legacies of colonialism and globalization in the global south (Stienstra & Nyerere, 2016), by poverty in indigenous communities in Guatemala (Grech, 2016), and special education placement in Canada (Adjei, 2016). Finally, DisCrit has helped lay bare some of the contradictions between language and epistemological commitments, such as Leonardo's (2015) reconsideration of discussing Whiteness as racial dyslexia.

Taken together, this diverse set of scholarship points to the need for intersectional analyses of racism and ableism and offers the potential to deconstruct underlying oppressive ideologies. In the remaining sections of this chapter, we explore the body of this intersectional scholarship to date that has substantively engaged with DisCrit, thereby stretching its boundaries in terms of theory, methodology, and empirical research. We first examine the topics engaged by various authors employing DisCrit. Next, we provide one or more exemplars of scholarly works for each of the seven tenets. Finally, we conclude with a discussion of what we imagine as the future of DisCrit.

Thematic Engagement

Much of the scholarship exploring the intersections of race and dis/ability in education to date has focused on highlighting the persistent problem of students of color being disproportionately placed in special education, particularly in the most subjective categories of learning disabilities, mild intellectual disabilities, and emotional disabilities. Indeed, a concern about the overrepresentation of Black, Latinx, and Native American students receiving special education labels, being placed in the most restrictive and segregated placements, receiving harsh disciplinary sanctions, and being funneled into jails motivated our own scholarly work and provided the impetus to develop DisCrit as an explicitly intersectional theoretical framework to explore the collusive nature of race and disability. This work is absolutely valuable and necessary. Yet, like Crenshaw's (1989) initial artic-ulation of intersectionality, we, too, envisioned that DisCrit could also help frame a wider set of issues.

Our analysis of DisCrit research has demonstrated that DisCrit is indeed a flex-ible and nuanced theoretical and methodological tool for exploring the intersections of race and disability, along with other social markers, across a wide range of issues (see Table 1). Scholars have used DisCrit to critically explore a host of issues related to educational equity as well as to demonstrate the need to infuse teacher education with critical theory. Beyond educational contexts, DisCrit has informed research on health care disparities, postschool transition outcomes, as well as implications of DisCrit in the context of policy and law. Methodologically, researchers have employed a plurality of research traditions (from quantitative, to qualitative, to mixed methodologies). They have also pointed to limitations in data sets that frus-trate intersectional analyses and have found it necessary to develop alternative (and creative) methods in order to fully attend to some of the most marginalized and voices (e.g., incarcerated girls of color with disabilities and young women with intel-lectual disabilities). Table 1 highlights some of the diverse topics addressed in the literature that we reviewed.

DisCrit Tenet Exemplars

To highlight how various scholars incorporated DisCrit, we selected exemplars (from the 31 sources analyzed) in which author(s) deeply engaged with a specific tenet of DisCrit. Although many authors that we reviewed explicitly drew on one or more tenet, because of space, we highlight just a brief example for each tenet. In shar-ing these models, we hope to provide a robust discussion of how particular tenets could inform varied analyses. In providing these exemplars, we illustrate both the diversity and the affordances of DisCrit in advancing knowledge about the

TABLE 1
An Overview of Thematic Engagement With DisCrit

Themes Addressed	Examples
Health care/rehabilitation disparities; Politics of care	Ben-Moshe and Magaña (2014)
School-to-prison pipeline; Incarcerated girls of color with disabilities; Alternative schools	Annamma (2013, 2014, 2015a); Annamma, Morrison, and Jackson (2014); Dávila (2015); Mahon-Reynolds and Parker (2016); Stanard (2016)
Need for critical theory in teacher education to address gender, race, linguistic diversity, class, and disability; Teacher dispositions (beliefs, attitudes)	Banks (2015); Fergus (2016); Mendoza, Paguyo, and Gutiérrez (2016); Gillborn, Rollock, Vincent, and Ball (2016); Whitney (2016); Young (2016)
Whiteness/ability/goodness as property	Adams (2015); Annamma (2015b)
Discourse; Counternarrative; Resistance; Resilience	Annamma (2016); Migliarini (2017); Whitney (2016); Young (2016)
Postschool transition of adolescent girls with intellectual/cognitive disabilities (impact of gender, race, class)	Cowley (2013)
Inclusion 2.0 (broadening the scope of inclusion); Space as variable	Baglieri (2016); Waitoller and Annamma (2017)
Education debt/Opportunity gap	Thorius and Tan (2016)
Overrepresentation/Disproportionality	Fenton (2016); Gillborn et al. (2016); Kozleski (2016); Mahon-Reynolds and Parker (2016)
Law/policy/critical legal studies	Fenton (2016)
Identity	Banks (2017); Hikida (2015); Whitney (2016)
Genetics; Eugenics; Science	Gillborn (2016); Freedman and Ferri (2017)
Microaggressions	Dávila (2015)
Positioning of parents (focus on Black middle class)	Gillborn (2015); Gillborn et al. (2016)
Multiculturalism	Baglieri (2016)
Intersectional research with large data sets	Kozleski (2016)
Policy/reform	Tomlinson (2016); Waitoller & Super (2017)
Intersectional commitments in discourse, laws, and/or policies	Adams and Erevelles (2016); Annamma, Jackson, and Morrison (2017); Broderick and Leonardo (2016); K. Collins (2016)
Shifts in pedagogy	Waitoller & Thorius (2016)
Accounting for class/materiality, as well as race and disability	Ben-Moshe and Magaña (2014); Ferri and Connor (2014)

intersections of dis/ability and race. Each exemplar was selected based on the criteria of whether it explicitly and substantially engaged with the tenet in the framing of the study and/or its analysis.

Tenet 1: DisCrit focuses on ways that the forces of racism and ableism circulate inter-dependently, often in neutralized and invisible ways, to uphold notions of normalcy.

A leading scholar within CRT, Gillborn (2008) has been long troubled by historical hierarchies of racial dis/abilities. Gillborn (2016) expresses concerns about how "crude and dangerous ideas about the genetic heritability of intelligence, and the supposed biological basis for the Black/White achievement gap are alive and well within the education policy process but [are] taking new and more subtle forms" (p. 365). Specifically, Gillborn takes to task major scholars of genetics and education, both fields of study that are historically rooted in racialized ableism. That is, those who have imagined people of color to be less intelligent have relied on the belief that disability and race are deeply connected (Valencia, 1997). As Baynton (2001) states,

(T)he *concept* of disability has been used to justify discrimination against other groups by attributing disability to them. . . . When categories of citizenship were questioned, challenged, and disrupted, disability was called on to clarify and define who deserved, and who was deservedly excluded from, citizenship. (p. 33, italics in original)

Gillborn (2016) illustrates this phenomenon of allocating disability to limit access to the property rights typically attributed to Whiteness in his examination of genetic determinism. The phrase "softly, softly" in the article's title refers to indirect, and even subliminal invocations of race within genetic discourse. He warns that such ". . . *inexplicitness* should not be mistaken for an absence of racialized thinking . . ." (p. 366), and, in fact, "*racial genism*—the belief that genes shape the nature of ethnic group achievement and inequities—has returned with a vengeance but in a new and more dangerous form" (p. 336).

In the first part of his article, Gillborn (2016) details the return of genetic determinism within debates about educational policy in the United Kingdom. Using critical discourse analysis, he makes visible examples of implicit scientific racism and genetic determinism espoused by contemporary researchers and politicians that subsequently become circulated within the media. Analyzing range of books, articles, lectures, and public interviews, Gillborn persuasively illustrates the inexplicitness of race in discussions of fixed intelligence, intellectual aptitude, and academic achievement as reified by test scores. By doing so, he reveals how notions of normalized racial hierarchies are predicated on dis/ability and upheld by a racialized and ableist discourse. In the second part of the article, Gillborn critiques a variety of claims about heredity and intelligence, critiquing the trustworthiness of researchers' claims, adequacy of research methods and tools, and the deliberate indirectness when engaging race. Gillborn (2016) concludes, "The hereditarians have not changed their mind about race and intelligence—they just don't broadcast it anymore" (p. 382). With that subtle connection between race and intelligence being ever present yet unnamed, the author uncovers how it is easier for the media and others to take up this discourse without being labeled racist. In brief, Gillborn illustrates (a) how race and dis/ability are inextricably enmeshed in subtle and indirect ways that seep "softly, softly" into the public imagination and (b) how the virtual invisibility yet centralized existence of race verifies the need for intersectional theoretical frameworks such as DisCrit. Gillborn's work traces this intellectual history to show how racism and ableism have always been deeply connected. DuBois (1920), too, addressed this same issue:

For a century or more it had been the dream of those who do not believe Negroes are human that their wish should find some scientific basis. For years they depended on the weight of the human brain, trusting that the alleged underweight of less than a thousand Negro brains, measured without reference to age, stature, nutrition or cause of death, would convince the world that black men simply could not be educated. Today scientists acknowledge that there is no warrant for such a conclusion. (p. 326)

Throughout history, attempts to link disability, in the form of lower intelligence, to Black and Brown bodies has resurfaced in countless ways. Most recently, this thinking would have us believe that achievement gaps in test scores signify that intelligence is fixed and intrinsic. Gillborn's theorizing does the work that White DS often misses; it renounces beliefs that race, genetics, and intelligence are inextricably linked, explicitly naming and rejecting this newest iteration of racialized ableism by linking it to its eugenic legacy.

Tenet 2: DisCrit values multidimensional identities and troubles singular notions of identity such as race or dis/ability or class or gender or sexuality, and so on.

Banks's (2017) explicitly employs DisCrit to "better understand the educational experiences of African American male students labeled with learning disabilities, as described in their own words" (p. 97). Banks does not simply provide a unidimensional analysis but makes visible the ways racism and ableism inform each other, specifically for Black male students with a disability who are attending college. As one participant noted, "These people are never going to stop labeling me" (p. 96), indicating the effects of feeling perpetually marked as deviant within the education system through his race, gender, and disability label. In determining the consequences of being multiply situated in terms of race, disability, and gender, one participant shared,

In my education career [because I was] an African American male and had ADHD, teachers put me in two boxes—disabled and African American. Then with me above six-feet tall, they expected me to be aggressive. [Teachers] have had to check themselves, but after I talk to them about my learning style, they would see me in a whole different light. (Banks, 2017, p. 105)

Working against master narratives that position Black male students as uninterested in education and simultaneously aggressive in their behavior, this student navigated these intersecting oppressions by explicitly discussing his learning needs as a way to ensure success and teacher cooperation. Another participant highlighted the need to counter official discourses, codified in disability-related paperwork, which positioned him in a negative light:

They looked at me and read what was on the paper and then they judged me off that and put me in special education for the first time. So yeah, I think you always have to prove yourself to people. (Banks, 2017, p. 103)

Banks's (2017) work illustrates how Black students with dis/abilities are positioned differently than White students with a disability and Black students without a disability. Yet the author also uses these counternarratives to highlight the ways multiply marginalized disabled Black male students (re)position themselves, engaging in thoughtful resistance to marginalizing systems. In doing so, the author demonstrates the additional labor that falls on disabled Black males so that they have access to resources and opportunities that should be available to all students. Banks invokes DisCrit to discuss the interdependent circulation of racism and ableism that manifests in multiple, complex ways that run deep within state policies, school practices, and professional and personal discourses and beliefs.

Tenet 3: DisCrit emphasizes the social constructions of race and ability and yet recognizes the material and psychological impacts of being labeled as raced or dis/abled, which sets one outside of the western cultural norms.

Demonstrating its influence beyond U.S. contexts, Migliarini (2017) employs DisCrit as a theoretical tool (along with Butler's concept of subjectivation) to examine the ways that 10 "dis/abled asylum-seeking and refugee students" in Italy experienced educational and social exclusions and inequities as a result of the "normalizing processes of racism and ableism" (p. 183). To fully consider the interworkings of disability, race, and other forms of oppression, Migliarini (2017) drew on Tenet 3 to account for ways that the students in the study were positioned at the margins. By attending to both macro- and micro-exclusions, she was able to document the various ways that students were positioned as embodying deficit. Importantly, in examining how "migratory status" interacts with race and disability, Migliarini illustrates how predetermined neoliberal notions of social integration that place a value on autonomy over interdependence, as well as a politics of respectability, combine to funnel refugee and asylum-seeking teens into low-paid and low-skilled jobs, despite the teens' own desires to attend college and pursue a broader range of professional careers.

Adding Butler's attention to discourse, Migliarini's (2017) study suggests that in addition to focusing on forms of constraint and marginalization, attending to forms of agency illustrates the myriad ways that marginalized subjects find ways to enact subjectivity and resistance, despite their social positioning. For instance, although professionals pushed the youth in her study to learn Italian language as a way to ensure that they would be able to enter the work force and obtain a job, participants focused on gaining proficiency in Italian in order to make friends or to "pass the exam" so they could access higher education. Thus, language learning took on very different meanings—representing different ends despite similar means. By looking both at constraint and performative politics in "discursive relations of power" (p. 11), Migliarini uses DisCrit to illustrate both the intersecting and "enduring patterns" of educational inequality and exclusion and the theoretical tools that can help highlight and support the discursive agency necessary to counter diffuse forms of marginalization.

Tenet 4: DisCrit privileges voices of marginalized populations, traditionally not acknowledged within research.

In addition to traditional forms of qualitative interviewing techniques, many researchers engaging this tenet of DisCrit have found it necessary to devise alternative and innovative strategies to center the "voices" of traditionally marginalized research participants. These have included attending to counternarratives (Banks, 2015), uncovering subtle or unexpected forms of agency (Cowley, 2013), enacting participatory or side-by-side research designs and incorporating mapping or collage as data collection (Annamma, 2016). Enacting Tenet 4, scholars highlight how various mechanisms of surveillance and control often undermine access to participants' perspectives. Whether it is a parent, a teacher, or other gatekeeper, or even a university institutional review board—which often equate disability with vulnerability—gaining access to marginalized voices takes both persistence and commitment. Moreover, because so many people with disabilities are warehoused in the "institutional archipelago"—the "diverse services and spaces that all trace back to undifferentiated confinement" (Ben-Moshe, Chapman, & Carey, 2014, p. 14)—taking participant voices seriously can require negotiation of multiple forms of gatekeeping. DisCrit scholars have nonetheless gained access to voices that are often suppressed or ignored—positioning their participants as knowledge generators, capable of authoring their own stories and creating solutions to the inequities they face (Annamma, 2014; Connor, 2008; Ferri & Connor, 2010).

Some researchers have incorporated traditional research designs but highlight the material impacts of being multiply marginalized in understudied populations. In her study about how Latinx students experienced special education, for instance, Dávila (2015) explored and extended the concept of micro-aggressions as experienced by students multiply situated in terms of race/ethnicity and disability. Davila's data included ethnographic classroom observations and interviews with 20 student participants. Using a framework informed by CRT and DisCrit, Dávila (2015) notes, "Disability does not simply replace race in these instances, but represents a complex interplay between race and disability in the lives of Latino/a students in special education" (p. 454). Findings of micro-aggressions included low teacher expectations (often internalized by students), general disregard, and bullying.

In chronicling instances of educators' micro-aggressions in the form of sarcasm and persistently demeaning remarks toward students, Dávila (2015) highlights their cumulative effects over time. Instances described by students are often shocking. For example, one student recalls a teacher's aide sitting next to him during an exam, narrating:

She looked at my test and it was blank and she said, "You make me sick." I laughed at her and was like "what?" I laughed about it. I didn't get mad . . . she was like, "OK," she caught herself, like "OK, I made a mistake in saying that," so she tried to be friendly and help me out. "No, I don't need your help," she tried to grab my test. . . . (Dávila, 2015, p. 456)

In her discussion, Dávila (2015) writes of the "collective impact" (p. 461) of witnessing humiliating micro-aggressions; although targeting one student, it is nonetheless absorbed by all those present. As one girl explains, "Teachers will say, 'What kind of question is that?' Are you retarded or something?'" (p. 462). By foregrounding students' voices, Dávila conveys how Latino/as labeled with a disability experience self-contained classes, placing these classrooms in stark contrast to typical depictions of special education within "big glossy" text books frequently used in teacher education (Brantlinger, 2006).

Whether drawing on traditional qualitative traditions or bending these traditions in ways that provide alternative spaces to privilege marginalized voices, DisCrit researchers illustrate the importance of attending to direct testimony of the lived realities of individuals who are multiply oppressed in terms of race and dis/ability, along with other markers. In contrast to research designs that collapse (and therefore dehumanize) lived experience, these studies also position participants of research as co-constructors of knowledge about their lives—honoring their subjectivity and ability to speak back to power through counter narratives and expressions of agency and resistance.

Tenet 5: DisCrit considers legal and historical aspects of dis/ability and race and how both have been used separately and together to deny the rights of some citizens.

Waitoller and Super (2017) use DisCrit as an analytical lens to examine how entrenched inequities have temporal roots and are often perpetuated by the legal system and enacted within public policy. The authors explore how "school choice" is part of a larger neoliberal project of "restructuring urban space . . . grounded in Chicago's racialized history" (p. 34). Waitoller and Super explore narratives of school selection by Black and Latinx parents of children with disabilities. They found that though their decisions were framed in the language of choice, parents discursively signaled a politics of desperation (Stovall, 2013), wherein they were forced to make school decisions that left their children of color with disabilities unprotected.

Beginning with a discussion of neoliberalism—how it has influenced policy and drastically changed the education landscape in Chicago—the authors then explore how charter schools affect students of color (without disabilities) and those students with disabilities (not disaggregated by race) separately. The authors then use DisCrit to push this unidimensional analysis to understand how students of color with disabilities experience historically and legally compounding forms of exclusion within charter schools. Understanding space as an active ecology that mediates human activity, the authors illustrate the history of uneven spatial development in a racialized city. As public schools closed in Chicago, charter schools appeared on the landscape as an alternative. Neoliberal supporters argued this increase of charters represented an increase of choice for urban parents. However, Black and Latinx parents on the ground reported fewer options of schools that served disabled children. Waitoller and Super (2017) documented how

closing neighborhood schools and opening charter schools directly decreases school options for Black and Latinx students who require more extensive supports to be included in schools. . . . So, while White students with dis/abilities enjoy the benefits of Whiteness as they lived in areas of the city benefited by the neoliberal restructuring of urban space, and while some Black and Latinx students may enjoy the benefits of claiming smartness and goodness as property (i.e., being considered integrateable to charter schools or selective enrollments), Black and Latinx students with dis/abilities cannot claim neither Whiteness, smartness, nor goodness, and are oppressed by the intersections of these three ideologies. (pp. 10–11)

Ultimately, the authors report that parents of disabled children of color express a politics of desperation that informed the entirety of the educational decision making. Moreover, their children's educational trajectory was made worse by the destruction and disinvestment of neighborhood public schools. Thus, the creation of seemingly well-resourced charters enacted a source of harm to these families of color and, specifically, their children with disabilities. By engaging a spatial analysis, Waitoller and Super (2017) were able to pinpoint how the politics of desperation was enacted differently based on what area of Chicago parents of students of color with dis/abilities resided. The authors' work extended the politics of desperation framework to specifically examine education "choices" made by parents of children of color with dis/abilities. Furthermore, drawing on DisCrit, Waitoller and Super uncover how Black and Latinx parents of children with dis/abilities, who could claim neither Whiteness nor ability as property, were deeply affected by neoliberal policies that spatially restructured access to education choices for their children.

Tenet 6: DisCrit recognizes Whiteness and ability as property and that gains for people labeled with dis/abilities have largely been made as the result of interest convergence of White, middle-class citizens.

Broderick and Leonardo (2016) build on their prior work focusing on smartness as property by exploring how goodness is likewise a form of property conferred on Whiteness. Goodness is thus granted to students who most align with normative identities. That is, goodness is often conferred on a student based on racial positioning—not earned through behavior or disposition—thereby reinforcing White supremacy. Moreover, they show how goodness is also a precondition for smartness,

such that a "smart" kid conceived as bad does not benefit maximally from this construction, whereas a "good" kid who does not perform smartly on assessments may be perceived as "smarter" than his or her academic performance warrants. . . . In other words, the label of smartness is not a taken for granted good-in-itself, but is judged by the contextual regulation of student subjects, such as "too smart for their own good" (that is, precocious) or girls who are too smart (emasculating of boys). (Broderick & Leonardo, 2016, p. 57)

The authors note how without goodness, smartness provides a "wild card," an uncontrollable force that many fear if it coincides with undesirable characteristics associated with race and gender. Thus, White boys' misbehavior is met with a "boys will be boys" attitude, while Black boys are seen as menacing. The authors also call attention to ways goodness is withheld as well as distributed as processes of disablement and enablement. Illustrating how Broderick's White son Nicky, who had been constructed as a "good kid," and comparing him to his Black friend, Jamal's, experiences, they state,

Having been constituted as a "good boy," Nicky reaped the material advantages of race, class, and ableist privilege, manifest in goodness as ideological property, even if he did not understand them as advantages at the time. Through the asymmetric and inequitable distribution of rewards and punishments for behaviors in the classroom both Nicky and Jamal were actively interpolated into racialized identities as "good" and "bad" boys. Nicky was actively groomed to accept his expected role of White complicity with the racist practices of schooling, just as Jamal was materially constituted, over and over, to accept his designated and denigrated subjectivity as a "bad boy." (Broderick & Leonardo, 2016, p. 60)

Broderick and Leonardo (2016) underscore how DisCrit can help recognize Whiteness and ability as property and help deconstruct labeling and discursive practices that undergird classroom routines.

Tenet 7: DisCrit requires activism and supports all forms of resistance.

Activism is often envisioned as marches and sit-ins and placed in opposition to "ivory tower" research in which academics are far removed from the communities they claim to study and from those whom their ideas will most impact. Yet we believe this dichotomy obscures forms of what we might call intellectual activism. We noted, for instance, several studies that employed DisCrit as forms of intellectual activism. In particular, these scholars (a) situated multiply marginalized students of color, their families, and their communities as knowledge generators, capable of naming the processes that animate statistics centering on disproportionality (Whitney, 2016); (b) reexamined normative discourse, policies, and practices through a multidimensional analysis, making visible the intertwined oppressive forces that multiply marginalized students face (Adams, 2017); and (c) highlighted the ways that disabled students of color (re)position themselves when encountering individuals and systems committed to imagining them as problems (Annamma, 2017).

In a recent article, Mayes (2017) situates a Black male disabled student and his mother as knowledge generators. Previously labeled as gifted, Mayes documents how the student experienced marked shifts in his educational experiences once he sustained a traumatic brain injury (TBI). Though Douglas's story is unique, it highlighted important discursive moves and pedagogical practices that animate racial disproportionality in special education and discipline statistics. Mayes (2017) shows how once he sustained a TBI, teachers no longer saw Douglas as academically gifted. Stripped of this identity, teachers drew on racist and ableist stereotypes to position him.

Essentially, his giftedness and academic prowess became obsolete once he sustained a TBI as of his teachers focused on his race and dis/ability the same, seeing those are markers of his laziness and inability to do the work. (p. 13)

An important enactment of Tenet 7, Mayes (2017) and many of the authors cited in this chapter situated disabled students of color as experts of their lives (Banks, 2017; Cowley, 2013; Whitney, 2016). We describe this work as a form of intellectual activism as it refuses to imagine disabled people of color, many of whom have been warehoused in spaces less visible, as embodying deficit or as damaged, incapable of authoring their own stories, which is the traditional way that disabled children of color have been positioned in research, if they have been included at all. To ascertain the subjugated voices of disabled people of color, researchers entered into many formal, yet forgotten education spaces,[7] such as segregated special education classrooms, special schools, alternative school placements, and juvenile jails.

What Adams (2017) and Gillborn (2016) accomplish within their own multidimensional analysis of common discourse and practices is uncover the ways these processes both dis/able and enable specific individuals and groups of people (Leonardo & Broderick, 2011). Each reexamined specific taken-for-granted discourses, policies, and practices through a multidimensional analysis. In doing so, they discover how typically accepted discourses, policies, and practices enact hidden ideologies about who deserves resources in education. This is intellectual activism because it rejects a singular view of identity and resists commonly accepted deficit views about why multiply marginalized children of color struggle in specific learning environments.

Finally, intellectual activism requires that DisCrit scholars refuse to accept deficit notions about disabled people of color that pathologize their learning and/or behavior. Instead, several authors in this chapter sought to understand the learning and behavior of multiply marginalized disabled people of color within contexts (Banks, 2015; Dávila, 2015; Migliarini, 2017). By making visible systemic oppressions and how those oppressions were enacted, these scholars illustrate how learning ecologies can be filled with violence for some learners. Yet once the context becomes clear, this work also highlights how disabled students of color reposition themselves by employing creative and ingenious strategies (Annamma, 2017). Engaging in intellectual activism, the scholars both refute traditional ways of being in the academy and also document ways students resist the processes and practices that position them as less than.

Ultimately, multidimensional framing and analysis is a challenge, however, because it requires that researchers to look beyond the most privileged within any oppressed groups (Crenshaw, 1989). In other words, this work often seeks out the voices and perspectives of those who are multiply marginalized. Moreover, to resist deficit ways that students of color labeled with dis/abilities are traditionally positioned, researchers must also account for the ways racism and ableism are mutually constitutive. Scholars engaging DisCrit must capture how oppressions intersect to describe how "some human beings are not simply 'human' enough"

(Adjei, 2016, p. 2). In each study we reviewed, we were repeatedly struck by the innovative ways researchers sought to understand specific contexts and larger processes that positioned multiply marginalized children of color, their parents, and communities as less than, *and* the ways those multiply marginalized people resisted educational inequities.

CONCLUSION: DISCRIT'S FUTURE

In conducting this review, we are deeply impressed, encouraged, and humbled by the ways in which scholars have taken up DisCrit to uncover how multiply marginalized people experience oppression. As a framework, DisCrit aims to create new knowledge rooted in intersectional commitments, seeks to understand how interlocking oppressions of racism and ableism work in tandem, and pushes the boundaries of intersectionality. It is not and was not meant to be an all-encompassing theory, but one that would thrive by being interwoven with other critical theories and perspectives. Using DisCrit as an intersectional framework, scholars have exposed the social processes that contribute to entrenched inequities and traced how racism and ableism are interdependent in the search for equity. They have introduced new concepts, including the ability line (Broderick & Leonardo, 2016), dis-locating practices (Adams & Erevelles, 2016), and color-evasiveness (Annamma, Jackson, & Morrison, 2017), all of which we hope will be further explored, deconstructed, and expanded in the future. Their collective work helps us consider how to stretch the boundaries of DisCrit by pointing to additional theoretical frameworks that resonate or extend DisCrit, such as Migliarini's (2017) use of Butler's subjectification, Young's (2016) use of LatCrit, Waitoller and Super's (2017) spatial analysis, or Fenton's (2016) use of critical legal theory.

In thinking about the future of DisCrit, we remain cautiously optimistic that the framework will continue to expand and deepen with more engagement across disciplines. We hope to see more studies that take up all seven tenets in a sustained way. We would also like to see more engagement with certain tenets—in particular, we have seen fewer studies that *explicitly* consider how to incorporate the call of Tenet 7 for troubling traditional notions of activism. That is, we found several studies that engaged in an expansive notions of activism, but by articulating their purposeful engagement with activism, scholars could more strategically employ Tenet 7. Studies such as Broderick and Leonardo's (2016) that trace both the *affordances of privilege as well as oppression* and scholarship that accounts for within-group privilege and oppression are also an important line of research to extend. Decentering Western and U.S.-centric perspectives point to ways to further develop DisCrit. Finally, we hope to see DisCrit expanded outside of special education issues. We believe that DisCrit is less about disability and race being included in a list of oppressed identities and more about understanding how the interdependence of racism and ableism affect all people.

In closing, we wish to circle back to Bresha Meadows's story. After 10 months of incarceration and a concerted effort by several organizations led by the social media #FreeBresha campaign, Bresha was offered a plea deal. She will spend a year and a day in prison and another 6 months in a mental health treatment center (or longer if deemed "necessary"). Her case illustrates how racism and ableism actively work together to situate particular children as in need of incarceration. We stand with the Bresha's family, and the #FreeBresha campaign, which states,

(W)e believe that true care cannot and should not be delivered in the context of punishment. The #FreeBresha campaign is in solidarity with Bresha Meadows and her family who have been forced to make hard choices to try to reduce further harm in a coercive context of violent prosecution and incarceration. . . . It is truly unconscionable that Bresha has been targeted by prosecutors for taking desperate action to survive domestic violence. . . . If a Black girl who is abused in her home does all the things adults tell children to do when faced with violence—tell an adult, report it to the police, trust family services—and, one by one, each system fails her, what exactly do prosecutors imagine she should do next? Bresha tried to run away from the violence, but police forced her to return home. There was nothing else left to do but be beaten and possibly killed or defend her life.

In sum, Bresha Meadows is a disabled Black girl who faced dangers in her life and in the educational system that failed her *at every turn*. This failure positioned Bresha as a dangerous Black girl, erasing her other identities while highlighting her criminality (Annamma, 2018). We believe that DisCrit was created to better understand what disabled girls of color like Bresha, who are multiply marginalized, face. We believe DisCrit can help us #SayHerName as a Black girl who has been #SurvivedandPunished, and recognize ways Bresha's disability calls for intersectional analysis of #DisabilityJustice. In first envisioning what would eventually become DisCrit, we aimed to expand our own understanding about how entrenched inequities in education are not unidimensional and to uncover the complex social processes that propel them forward. It is clear from this review that DisCrit will continue to develop as it is put in conversation with other theories, methodologies, and framings. We believe it has the potential to be expanded beyond what we originally intended. We also know it must be improved and further developed. Overall, our hopes for DisCrit are that it continues to be critiqued, extended, and disrupted in productive ways as it stretches to dismantle education inequities.

NOTES

[1]In a protective order her mother filed against her father, her mother stated, "In the 17 years of our marriage, he has cut me, broke my ribs, fingers, the blood vessels in my hand, my mouth, blackened my eyes. I believe my nose was broken." She wrote, "If he finds us, I am 100 percent sure he will kill me and the children. . . . My life is like living in a box he created for me, and if I stepped out of that box, he's there to put me back in that box."

[2]We name this act of labeling to highlight ways that race and dis/ability are co-constructed, yet rarely acknowledged as such.

[3]We use the term *multiply marginalized* to address the way disabled students of color and others at the intersections of multiple oppressions experience the world differently as a result of a complex interaction of social injustices.

[4]We recognize the contestation over other forms of the word *disability*, such as *dis/ability* and *(dis)ability*, which some have critiqued as euphemisms that obscure disability. In this chapter, we attempt to use (a) *ability* when we are talking about a socially constructed and privileged

norm (similar to Whiteness); (b) *disability* when we are talking about either disability-related oppression or disability identity/culture; and (c) *dis/ability* to highlight the constructed and interdependent nature of both ability and disability. These discursive moves are aimed not to circumvent disability but to refute taken for granted deficit meanings of disability, to distinguish the ways society disables (and enables) people, and to recognize dis/ability's contested boundaries.

[5]See also earlier work examining race and disability (Artiles & Trent, 1994; Blanchett, 2006; Dunn, 1968; Erevelles et al., 2006; Ferri & Connor, 2010; Ford, 1998; Kiiewer, Biklen, & Kasa-Hendrickson, 2006; Reid & Valle, 2004; Watts & Erevelles, 2004; and more).

[6]For example, the work of Morgan, Farkas, Hillemeier, and Maczuga (2012) symbolizes special education's negation or evasion of issues of race and disability.

[7]For the purposes of this review, Annamma defines "formal, yet forgotten, educational spaces" as ones that are traditionally ignored in the education literature due to the binary discourse between formal and informal education spaces. This binary between formal and informal learning ecologies has been useful to contrast the constraints and affordances of these different types of spaces. However, this binary can ignore the variance of formal education spaces, situating them as all similar. By essentially smoothing over the extreme differences in education access and opportunities that occur throughout formal spaces, we are missing possibilities for research, policy, and practices to be remediated.

REFERENCES

Adams, D. L. (2017). *Implementation of schoolwide positive behavior supports in the neo-liberal context of an urban elementary school* (Doctoral dissertation). Available from ProQuest dissertation and thesis database. (Order No. 3723218)

Adams, D. L., & Erevelles, N. (2016). Shadow play: DisCrit, dis/respectability, and carceral logics. In D. Connor, B. Ferri, & S. A. Annamma (Eds.), *DisCrit: Critical conversations across race, class, & dis/ability* (pp. 131–143). New York, NY: Teachers College Press.

Adjei, P. B. (2016). The (em)bodiment of blackness in a visceral anti-black racism and ableism context. *Race Ethnicity and Education*. Advance online publication. doi:10.1080/136133 24.2016.1248821

Annamma, S. A. (2013). *Resistance and resilience: The education trajectories of young women of color with disabilities through the school to prison pipeline* (Dissertation). Available from ProQuest dissertation and thesis database. (Order No. 3561913)

Annamma, S. A. (2014). Disabling juvenile justice: Engaging the stories of incarcerated young women of color with disabilities. *Remedial and Special Education, 35*, 313–324.

Annamma, S. A. (2015a). Disrupting the school-to-prison pipeline through disability critical race theory. In L. D. Drakeford (Ed.), *The race controversy in American education* (pp. 191–211). Santa Barbara, CA: Praeger.

Annamma, S. A. (2015b). Innocence, ability and whiteness as property: Teacher education and the school-to-prison pipeline. *Urban Review, 47*, 293–316. doi:10.1007/s11256-014-0293-6

Annamma, S. (2016). Disrupting the carceral state through education journey mapping. *International Journal of Qualitative Studies in Education, 29*, 1210–1230.

Annamma, S. A. (2017). Mapping consequential geographies in the carceral state: Education journey mapping as a qualitative method with girls of color with dis/abilities. *Qualitative Inquiry, 24*, 20–34.

Annamma, S. A. (2018). *The pedagogy of pathologization: Dis/abled girls of color in the school-prison nexus*. New York, NY: Routledge.

Annamma, S. A., Connor, D., & Ferri, B. (2013). Dis/ability critical race studies (DisCrit): Theorizing at the intersections of race and dis/ability. *Race Ethnicity and Education, 16*(1), 1–31.

Annamma, S. A., Jackson, D., & Morrison, D. (2016). Conceptualizing color-evasiveness: Using dis/ability critical race theory to expand a color-blind racial ideology in education and beyond. *Race, Ethnicity and Education*. Advance online publication. doi:10.1080/13 613324.2016.1248837

Annamma, S., Morrison, D., & Jackson, D. (2014). Disproportionality fills in the gaps: Connections between achievement, discipline and special education in the school-to-prison pipeline. *Berkeley Review of Education*, 5(1). Retrieved from https://escholarship.org/uc/item/0b13x3cp

Ard, R. L., & Knaus, C. B. (2013). From colonization to RESPECT: How federal education policy fails children and educators of color. *ECI Interdisciplinary Journal for Legal & Social Policy*, 3(1), 2–32.

Artiles, A. J. (2013). Untangling the racialization of disabilities: An intersectionality critique across disability models. *Du Bois Review: Social Science Research on Race*, 10, 329–347.

Artiles, A. J., Dorn, S., & Bal, A. (2016). Objects of protection, enduring nodes of difference: Disability intersections with "other" differences, 1916 to 2016. *Review of Research in Education*, 40, 777–820.

Artiles, A. J., & Trent, S. C. (1994). Overrepresentation of minority students in special education: A continuing debate. *Journal of Special Education*, 27, 410–437.

Asch, A. (2001). Critical race theory, feminism, and disability: Reflections on social justice and personal identity. *Ohio State Law Journal*, 62, 391.

Baglieri, S. (2016). Toward unity in school reform: What DisCrit contributes to multicultural and inclusive education. In D. Connor, B. Ferri, & S. A. Annamma (Eds.) *DisCrit: Critical conversations across race, class, & dis/ability* (pp. 167–181). New York, NY: Teachers College Press.

Bal, A., & Trainor, A. A. (2016). Culturally responsive experimental intervention studies: The development of a rubric for paradigm expansion. *Review of Educational Research*, 86, 319–359.

Banks, J. (2015). Gangsters and wheelchairs: Urban teachers' perceptions of disability, race and gender. *Disability & Society*, 30, 569–582.

Banks, J. (2017). "These people are never going to stop labeling me": Educational experiences of African American male students labeled with learning disabilities. *Equity & Excellence in Education*, 50, 96–107.

Baynton, D. C. (2001). Disability and the Justification for Inequality in American History. In P. Longmore & L. Umansky (Eds.), *The new disability history: American perspectives* (pp. 33–57). New York: New York University Press.

Bell, C. (2006). Introducing white disability studies: A modest proposal. In L. J. Davis (Ed.), *The disability studies reader* (2nd ed., pp. 275–282). New York, NY: Routledge.

Bell, D. (2004). *Silent covenants: Brown v. Board of Education and the unfulfilled hopes for racial reform*. New York, NY: Oxford University Press.

Ben-Moshe, L., Chapman, C., & Carey, A. (2014). *Disability incarcerated: Imprisonment and disability in the United States and Canada*. New York, NY: Palgrave Macmillan.

Ben-Moshe, L., & Magaña, S. (2014). An introduction to race, gender, and disability: Intersectionality, disability studies, and families of color. *Women, Gender, and Families of Color*, 2, 105–114.

Beratan, G. D. (2008). The song remains the same: Transposition and the disproportionate representation of minority students in special education. *Race Ethnicity and Education*, 11, 337–354.

Blanchett, W. J. (2006). Disproportionate representation of African Americans in special education: Acknowledging the role of white privilege and racism. *Remedial and Special Education*, 35(6), 24–28.

Brantlinger, E. (2006). The big glossies: How textbooks structure (special) education. In E. Brantlinger (Ed.), *Who benefits from special education?* (pp. 45–75). Mahwah, NJ: Lawrence Erlbaum.

Broderick, A., & Leonardo, Z. (2016). What is a good boy: The deployment and distribution of "goodness" as ideological property in schools. In D. Connor, B. Ferri, & S. A. Annamma (Eds.), *DisCrit: Critical conversations across race, class, & dis/ability* (pp. 55–69). New York, NY: Teachers College Press.

Campbell, F. A. K. (2008). Exploring internalized ableism using critical race theory. *Disability & Society, 23*, 151–162.

Collins, K. (2016). A DisCrit perspective of the State of Florida v. George Zimmerman: Racism, ableism, and youth out of place in community and school. In D. Connor, B. Ferri, & S. A. Annamma (Eds.), *DisCrit: Critical conversations across race, class, & dis/ability* (pp. 183–201). New York, NY: Teachers College Press.

Collins, P. H. (1990). *Black feminist thought: Knowledge, consciousness, and the politics of empowerment* (1st ed.). New York, NY: Routledge.

Connor, D. J. (2008). *Urban narratives: Portraits in progress, life at the intersections of learning disability, race, & social class.* New York, NY: Peter Lang.

Connor, D. J., Gabel, S., Gallagher, D., & Morton, M. (2008). Disability studies and inclusive education: Implications for theory, research, and practice. *International Journal of Inclusive Education, 12*, 441–457.

Cook, D. A., & Williams, T. (2015). Expanding intersectionality: Fictive kinship networks as supports for the educational aspirations of Black women. *Western Journal of Black Studies, 39*, 157–166.

Cooper, A. J. (1988). *A voice from the South.* New York, NY: Oxford University Press. (Original work published 1892)

Cowley, D. M. (2013). *"Being grown": How adolescent girls with disabilities narrate self-determination and transitions* (Doctoral dissertation). Available from ProQuest dissertation and thesis database. (Order No. ED553501)

Crenshaw, K. (1989). Demarginalizing the intersection of race and sex: A black feminist critique of antidiscrimination doctrine, feminist theory and antiracist politics. *University of Chicago Legal Forum, 8*. Retrieved from https://chicagounbound.uchicago.edu/uclf/vol1989/iss1/8

Crenshaw, K. (1991). Mapping the margins: Intersectionality, identity politics, and violence against women of color. *Stanford Law Review, 43*, 1241–1299.

Crenshaw, K., Gotanda, N., Peller, G., & Thomas, K. (1995). *Critical race theory: The key writings that formed the movement.* New York, NY: New Press.

Dávila, B. (2015). Critical race theory, disability microaggressions and Latina/o student experiences in special education. *Race Ethnicity and Education, 18*, 443–468.

Delgado, R., & Stefancic, S. (2001). *Critical race theory: An introduction.* New York: New York University Press.

DuBois, W. E. B. (1920). Race intelligence. *The Crisis, 20*(3). Reprinted: 60th Anniversary Issue of *The Crisis, 77*(9), 326. Retrieved from https://books.google.com/books?id=NV2MtmlurRYC&lpg=PA326&ots=ZxE5h3yzM-&pg=PA326#v=onepage&q&f=false

Dunn, L. M. (1968). Special education for the mildly retarded: Is much of it justifiable? *Exceptional Children, 35*, 5–22.

Erevelles, N. (2002). Cognitive disability, race, and the politics of citizenship. *Disability, Culture, and Education, 1*(1), 5–25.

Erevelles, N., Kanga, A., & Middleton, R. (2006). How does it feel to be a problem? Race, disability, and exclusion in educational policy. In E. Brantlinger (Ed.), *Who benefits from special education?* (pp. 77–99). Mahwah, NJ: Lawrence Erlbaum.

Erevelles, N., & Minear, A. (2010). Unspeakable offenses: Untangling race and disability in discourses of intersectionality. *Journal of Literary & Cultural Disability Studies, 4*, 127–145.

Fenton, Z. (2016). Disability does not discriminate: Toward a theory of multiple identity through coalition. In D. Connor, B. Ferri, & S. A. Annamma (Eds.), *DisCrit: Critical conversations across race, class, & dis/ability* (pp. 203–212). New York, NY: Teachers College Press.

Fergus, E. (2016). Social reproduction ideologies: Teacher beliefs about race and culture. In D. Connor, B. Ferri, & S. A. Annamma (Eds.), *DisCrit: Critical conversations across race, class, & dis/ability* (pp. 117–127). New York, NY: Teachers College Press.

Ferri, B. A. (2008). Changing the script: Race and disability in Lynn Manning's weights. *International Journal of Inclusive Education, 12*, 497–509.

Ferri, B. A., & Connor, D. J. (2005). Tools of exclusion: Race, disability, and (re)segregated education. *Teachers College Record, 107*, 453–474.

Ferri, B. A., & Connor, D. J. (2010). "I was the special ed. girl": Urban working-class young women of colour. *Gender and Education, 22*, 105–121.

Ferri, B. A., & Connor, D. J. (2014). Talking (& not talking) about race, social class, & dis/ability: Toward a margin-to-margin approach. *Race Ethnicity and Education, 17*, 471–493.

Ford, D. Y. (1998). The underrepresentation of minority students in gifted education problems and promises in recruitment and retention. *Journal of Special Education, 32*(1), 4–14.

Freedman, J., & Ferri, B. A. (2017). Locating the problem within: Race, learning disabilities, and science. *Teachers College Record, 19*(5), 1–28.

Garcia, P., & Scott, K. (2016). Traversing a political pipeline: An intersectional and social constructionist approach toward technology education for girls of color. *InterActions: UCLA Journal of Education and Information Studies, 12*(2), 1–25.

Gillborn, D. (2008). *Racism and education: Coincidence or conspiracy?* London, England: Routledge.

Gillborn, D. (2015). Intersectionality, critical race theory, and the primacy of racism: Race, class, gender, and disability in education. *Qualitative Inquiry, 21*, 277–287.

Gillborn, D. (2016). Softly, softly: Genetics, intelligence and the hidden racism of the new geneism. *Journal of Education Policy, 31*, 365–388.

Gillborn, D., Rollock, N., Vincent, C., & Ball, S. (2016). The black middle classes, education, racism, and dis/ability: An intersectional analysis. In D. Connor, B. Ferri, & S. A. Annamma (Eds.) *DisCrit: Critical conversations across race, class, & dis/ability* (pp. 35–54). New York, NY: Teachers College Press.

Goodwin, M. (2003). Gender, race, and mental illness: The case of Wanda Jean Allen. In A. K. Wing (Ed.), *Critical race feminism: A reader* (pp. 228–237). New York: New York University Press.

Grech, S. (2016). *Disability and poverty in rural Guatemala: Conceptual, cultural and social intersections.* London, England: London School of Hygiene and Tropical Medicine.

Harry, B., & Klingner, J. (2006). *Why are so many minority students in special education?* New York, NY: Teachers College Press.

Hetherington, S. A. (2012). *"They think we don't have the knowledge": The intersection of autism and race* (Doctoral dissertation). Available from ProQuest dissertation and thesis database. (Order No. 3508412)

Hikida, M. T. (2015). *The interactional co-construction of reader identities: A nested case study of "struggling" readers* (Doctoral dissertation). Retrieved https://repositories.lib.utexas.edu/handle/2152/32581

Jeltsen, M. (2017, May 5). Bresha Meadows, teen who killed allegedly abusive dad, given second chance. *Huffington Post.* Retrieved from http://www.huffingtonpost.com/entry/bresha-meadows-sentencing-killed-father_us_5922e800e4b094cdba55b95d

Kiiewer, C., Biklen, D., & Kasa-Hendrickson, C. (2006). Who may be literate? Disability and resistance to the cultural denial of competence. *American Educational Research Journal, 43*, 163–192.

Kohli, R. (2016). Behind school doors: The impact of hostile racial climates on urban teachers of color. *Urban Education*. Advance online publication. doi:10.1177/0042085916636653

Kozleski, E. (2016). Reifying categories: Measurement in search of understanding. In D. Connor, B. Ferri, & S. A. Annamma (Eds.), *DisCrit: Critical conversations across race, class, & dis/ability* (pp. 101–115). New York, NY: Teachers College Press.

Ladson-Billings, G. (2006). From the achievement gap to the education debt: Understanding achievement in US schools. *Educational Researcher, 35*(7), 3–12.

Ladson-Billings, G., & Tate, W. F. IV. (1995). Toward a critical race theory of education. *Teachers College Record, 97*(1), 47–68.

Lalvani, P., Broderick, A. A., Fine, M., Jacobowitz, T., & Michelli, N. (2015). Teacher education, InExclusion, and the implicit ideology of separate but equal: An invitation to a dialogue. *Education, Citizenship and Social Justice, 10*, 168–183.

Ledesma, M. C., & Calderón, D. (2015). Critical race theory in education: A review of past literature and a look to the future. *Qualitative Inquiry, 21*, 206–222.

Leonardo, Z. (2004). The color of supremacy: Beyond the discourse of "white privilege." *Educational Philosophy and Theory, 36*, 137–152.

Leonardo, Z. (2015). Poverty and education in the social sciences: Three definitions. In W. G. Tierney (Ed.), *Rethinking education and poverty* (pp. 77–93). Baltimore, MD: John Hopkins University Press.

Leonardo, Z., & Broderick, A. (2011). Smartness as property: A critical exploration of intersections between whiteness and disability studies. *Teachers College Record, 113*, 2206–2232.

Liasidou, A. (2008). Critical discourse analysis and inclusive educational policies: The power to exclude. *Journal of Education Policy, 23*, 483–500.

Liasidou, A. (2011). Unequal power relations and inclusive education policy making: A discursive analytic approach. *Educational Policy, 25*, 887–907.

Liasidou, A. (2013). Intersectional understandings of disability and implications for a social justice reform agenda in education policy and practice. *Disability & Society, 28*, 299–312.

Liasidou, A. (2014). The cross-fertilization of critical race theory and disability studies: Points of convergence/divergence and some education policy implications. *Disability & Society, 29*, 724–737.

Lorde, A. (1997). *The cancer journals: Special edition*. San Francisco, CA: Aunt Lute.

Losen, D. J., & Orfield, G. (Eds.). (2002). *Racial inequity in special education*. Cambridge, MA: Harvard Education Press.

Mahon-Reynolds, C., & Parker, L. (2016). The overrepresentation of students of color with learning disabilities: How "writing identity" plays a role in the school-to-prison pipeline. In D. Connor, B. Ferri, & S. A. Annamma (Eds.), *DisCrit: Critical conversations across race, class, & dis/ability* (pp. 145–155). New York, NY: Teachers College Press.

Matsuda, M. J. (1993). *Words that wound: Critical race theory, assaultive speech, and the first amendment*. Boulder, CO: Westview Press.

Mayes, R. D. (2017). "They will leave you lost": Experiences of a gifted Black male with a traumatic brain injury. *Urban Review*. Advance online publication. doi:10.1007/s11256-017-0433-x

Mendoza, E., Paguyo, C., & Gutiérrez, K. (2016). Understanding the intersection of race and disability: Common sense notions of learning and culture. In D. Connor, B. Ferri, & S. A. Annamma (Eds.), *DisCrit: Critical conversations across race, class, & dis/ability* (pp. 71–86). New York, NY: Teachers College Press.

Migliarini, V. (2017). Subjectivation, agency and the schooling of raced and dis/abled asylum-seeking children in the Italian context. *Intercultural Education, 28*, 182–195.

Mitchell, D. D. (2006). Flashcard: Alternating between visible and invisible identities. *Equity & Excellence in Education, 39*, 137–145.

Mitchell, D. D. (2007). *Crises of identifying: Negotiating and mediating race, gender, and disability* (Doctoral dissertation). Available from ProQuest dissertation and thesis database. (Order No. 3286164)

Morgan, P. L., Farkas, G., Hillemeier, M. M., & Maczuga, S. (2012). Are minority children disproportionately represented in early intervention and early childhood special education? *Educational Researcher, 41,* 339–351.

Office of Juvenile Justice and Delinquency Program. (2013). *Statistical briefing book.* Retrieved from https://www.ojjdp.gov/ojstatbb/

Peters, H. C. (2017). Multicultural complexity: An intersectional lens for clinical supervision. *International Journal for the Advancement of Counselling, 39,* 176–187.

Petersen, A. J. (2009). "Ain't nobody gonna get me down": An examination of the educational experiences of four African American women labeled with disabilities. *Equity & Excellence in Education, 42,* 428–442.

Reid, D. K., & Knight, M. G. (2006). Disability justifies exclusion of minority students: A critical history grounded in disability studies. *Educational Researcher, 35*(6), 18–23.

Reid, D. K., & Valle, J. W. (2004). The discursive practice of learning disability: Implications for instruction and parent–school relations. *Journal of Learning Disabilities, 37,* 466–481.

Rollock, N., Gillborn, D., Vincent, C., & Ball, S. J. (2014). *The colour of class: The educational strategies of the Black middle classes.* New York, NY: Routledge.

Sierra-Zarella, E. (2010). *Involuntary whiteness: Autoethnographic explorations of vitiligo* (Doctoral dissertation). Available from ProQuest dissertation and thesis database. (Order No. 3434605)

Smith, P. (2004). Whiteness, normal theory, and disability studies. *Disability Studies Quarterly, 24*(2). Retrieved from http://dsq-sds.org/article/view/491/668

Solórzano, D. G., & Yosso, T. J. (2002). Critical race methodology: Counter-storytelling as an analytical framework for education research. *Qualitative Inquiry, 8*(1), 23–44.

Stanard, C. (2016). *A DisCrit narrative case study: How are the cards stacked in school for African American students with disabilities?* Retrieved from https://digitalcommons.kennesaw.edu/cgi/viewcontent.cgi?referer=https://www.google.com/&httpsredir=1&article=1002&context=speceddoc_etd

Stienstra, D., & Nyerere, L. (2016). Race, ethnicity and disability: Charting complex and intersectional terrains. In S. Grech & K. Soldatic (Eds.), *Disability in the global South* (pp. 255–268). Cham, Switzerland: Springer.

Stovall, D. (2013). Against the politics of desperation: Educational justice, critical race theory, and Chicago school reform. *Critical Studies in Education, 54*(1), 33–43.

Tate, W. IV. (1997). Critical race theory and education: History, theory, and implications. *Review of Research in Education, 22,* 195–247.

Tefera, A. A. (2011). *High-stakes testing: An ethnographic phenomenology of African American and Latino students with "dis" abilities* (Doctoral dissertation). Available from ProQuest dissertation and thesis database. (Order No. 3483190)

Thorius, K. A. K., & Tan, P. (2015). Expanding analysis of educational debt: Considering intersections of race and ability. In D. Connor, B. Ferri, & S. A. Annamma (Eds.), *DisCrit: Critical conversations across race, class, & dis/ability* (pp. 87–97). New York, NY: Teachers College Press.

Tomlinson, S. (2016). Race, class, ability, and school reform. In D. Connor, B. Ferri, & S. A. Annamma (Eds.), *DisCrit: Critical conversations across race, class, & dis/ability* (pp. 157–166). New York, NY: Teachers College Press.

Ulysse, B., Berry, T. R., & Jupp, J. C. (2016). On the elephant in the room: Toward a generative politics of place on race in academic discourse. *International Journal of Qualitative Studies in Education, 29,* 989–1001.

Valencia, R. R. (1997). *The evolution of deficit thinking: Educational thought and practice* (1st ed.). London, England: Routledge.

Vincent, C., Rollock, N., Ball, S., & Gillborn, D. (2012). Intersectional work and precarious positionings: Black middle-class parents and their encounters with schools in England. *International Studies in Sociology of Education, 22*, 259–276.

Wagner, K. I. (2016). *Disabling psychology: A crip analysis of deaf and blind psychotherapists in practice* (Doctoral dissertation). Available from ProQuest dissertation and thesis database. (Order No. 10151027)

Waitoller, F. R., & Annamma, S. A. (2017). Taking a spatial turn in inclusive education. In M. T. Hughes & E. Talbott (Eds.), *The Wiley handbook of diversity in special education.* Advance online publication. doi:10.1002/9781118768778.ch2

Waitoller, F. R., & Super, G. (2017). School choice or the politics of desperation? Black and Latinx parents of students with dis/abilities selecting a charter school in Chicago. *Education Policy Analysis Archives, 25*(55). Advance online publication. doi:10.14507/epaa.25.2636

Waitoller, F. R., & Thorius, K. A. K. (2016). Cross-pollinating culturally sustaining pedagogy and universal design for learning: Toward an inclusive pedagogy that accounts for dis/ability. *Harvard Educational Review, 86*, 366–389.

Watts, I. E., & Erevelles, N. (2004). These deadly times: Reconceptualizing school violence by using critical race theory and disability studies. *American Educational Research Journal, 41*, 271–299.

Welch, A. B. (2002). *African American families in special education: From one generation to the next* (Doctoral dissertation). Available from ProQuest dissertation and thesis database. (Order No. 3044909)

Whitney, E. H. (2016). *Multimodal composition as inclusive pedagogy: An inquiry into the interplay of race, gender, disability and multimodality at an urban middle school* (Doctoral dissertation). Available from ProQuest dissertation and thesis database (Order No. 1839283908)

Yosso, T. (2002). Toward a critical race curriculum. *Equity & Excellence in Education, 35*, 93–107.

Young, K. S. (2016). How student teachers (don't) talk about race: An intersectional analysis. *Race Ethnicity and Education, 19*(1), 67–95.

Chapter 4

Heterogeneous Effects in Education: The Promise and Challenge of Incorporating Intersectionality Into Quantitative Methodological Approaches

Lauren Schudde iD

The University of Texas at Austin

To date, the theory of intersectionality has largely guided qualitative efforts in social science and education research. Translating the construct to new methodological approaches is inherently complex and challenging, but offers the possibility of breaking down silos that keep education researchers with similar interests—but different methodological approaches—from sharing knowledge. Quantitative approaches that emphasize the varied impacts of individual identities on educational outcomes move beyond singular dimensions capturing individual characteristics, drawing a parallel to intersectionality. Scholars interested in heterogeneous effects *recognize the shortcomings of focusing on the effect of a single social identity. This integrative review explores techniques used in quantitative research to examine* heterogeneous effects *across individual background, drawing on methodological literature from the social sciences and education. I examine the goals and challenges of the quantitative techniques and explore how they relate to intersectionality. I conclude by discussing what education researchers can learn from other applied fields that are working to develop a crosswalk across the two disparate, but interconnected, literatures.*

Various dimensions of individuals' identities—including race, class, gender, and sexuality—overlap and intersect. Intersectionality posits that rather than operating as "mutually exclusive entities" (Collins, 2015, p. 2), the dimensions combine to produce an individual's experience and shape broader social inequalities. Most extant literature on intersectionality relies on a limited range of methodological approaches, partially due to the complexity of the concept (McCall, 2005). To date, the theory of intersectionality has largely guided qualitative efforts in social science and education

Review of Research in Education
March 2018, Vol. 42, pp. 72–92
DOI: 10.3102/0091732X18759040
© 2018 AERA. http://rre.aera.net

research. Limiting inquiry on intersectionality to a narrow set of methodological tools restricts the scope of knowledge on the subject (McCall, 2005). Translating the construct to new methodological approaches is inherently complex and challenging but offers the possibility of breaking down silos that keep education researchers with similar interests—but different methodological approaches—from sharing knowledge.

Quantitative approaches that emphasize the varied impacts of individual identities on educational outcomes move beyond singular dimensions capturing individual characteristics, drawing a parallel to intersectionality. Scholars interested in *heterogeneous effects* (HE; also referred to as differential, conditional, marginal, and heterogeneous treatment effects [HTE]) recognize the shortcomings of focusing on the effect of a single social identity. HE allows scholars to examine how various identities, skills, and positions affect the experience and outcomes of individuals (Elwert & Winship, 2010; Museus & Griffin, 2011; Rhodes, 2010; Turney, 2015). This integrative review explores techniques used in quantitative research to examine differential effects across individual background, drawing on methodological literature from the social sciences and education. I examine the goals and challenges of approaches to capture HE and explore how they relate to intersectionality by leveraging McCall's (2005) examination of intersectionality. I conclude by discussing what education researchers can learn from other applied fields that are working to develop a crosswalk across the two disparate, but interconnected, literatures.

BRINGING HE AND INTERSECTIONALITY INTO CONVERSATION

Individuals' experiences and responses to those experiences vary across individuals based on who they are (Berger & Luckmann, 1966; Elwert & Winship, 2010). HE, like intersectionality, anticipates that background characteristics, skills, and group memberships influence individuals' experiences and the effects of those experiences. Despite commonalities in the assumptions and goals of intersectional and HE research, this alignment has received little attention. At best, mixed-methods researchers acknowledge that quantitative methods can benefit from intersectional theory but emphasize the role interview data could play in illuminating patterns of individual and group experiences that are difficult to capture through large-scale survey data alone (Griffin, Bennett, & Harris, 2011). Nevertheless, many quantitative researchers in the field of education rely on secondary survey data, which leaves them with little to no influence on sampling strategy and survey items. To understand the impact of student identity, including membership in multiple groups, on outcomes of interest, researchers must have a way to account for intersectional identities without collecting additional data.

The literature on intersectionality in education and the social sciences does not fully explore the "wide range of methodological approaches" that can be used to study "multiple, intersecting, and complex social relations" (McCall, 2005, p. 1773). McCall (2005) describes common approaches to capturing complex social relationships, including the approach most widely used in quantitative scholarship. Leveraging existing analytical categories to examine relationships and shifting dynamics of inequality, quantitative approaches capture intersectional identities and related "intercategorical complexity" by using predefined social groups (McCall, 2005, p. 1773). Although less holistic than qualitative approaches that deconstruct analytical categories and less critical than approaches focused on identities that "[cross] the boundaries of traditionally constructed groups" (McCall, 2005, pp. 1773–1774), the intercategorical approach allows researchers to draw on large data sets to examine the interplay of predefined identity characteristics (e.g., Black, female, homosexual) in producing unequal outcomes. The intercategorical approach also has the capacity to use large-scale data and evaluate the generalizability of results, which can counterbalance its limitations.

While much of the quantitative literature fails to recognize variation in individual responses as intersectionality, many applications exploring HE are squarely focused on interpreting the way that individuals react differently to a similar environment or experience. The work examining effect heterogeneity[1] acknowledges the way that various identities, programs, and environments interact to "shape complex social inequalities" (Collins, 2015, p. 2). In other words, extant quantitative research does intersectional work (though it is limited in the specific intersections observed through existing categories), but the language differs.

Applied researchers who wish to examine effect heterogeneity should do so with great intentionality, developing theory to inform their hypotheses about varied returns to specific experiences (e.g., Bedeian & Mossholder, 1994; Elwert & Winship, 2010). Incorporating concepts from intersectionality can inform the quantitative literature. Leveraging theory from intersectionality could also improve researchers' ability to interpret HE results, often presented in the form of statistically significant interactions between two or more variables. However, I found several logistical barriers to integrating an intersectional framework into quantitative approaches, including limitations of existing data that lead to difficult tradeoffs in research design and challenges in interpreting complex results.

Drawing on McCall's (2005) work as a theoretical framework for examining the quantitative approaches to capture effect heterogeneity, I examined the methodological literature with an eye toward how extant quantitative approaches can be used to capture intersectionality, how intersectionality can inform future quantitative work, and how extant data (including nationally representative survey data and administrative data) align with the goals of intersectionality. This chapter proceeds as follows: First, I describe the methods I employed for the literature review, including inclusion criteria for studies selected for the review. Next, I synthesize the methodological literature on approaches to capture HE, challenges for implementation, and considerations to overcome those challenges. I conclude by discussing the segmentation of the education literature by methodological approach and the role that intersectionality can play in bridging the divide between quantitative and qualitative scholarship and in advocating for more theoretically grounded statistical models.

STRATEGY FOR LITERATURE REVIEW

To find relevant literature on HE and understand the current state of methodological practice and challenges, my primary goal was to identify methodological literature on HE from social science and education. The methodological literature on

HE offers a means to examine the underlying assumptions and goals of the approaches as they relate to intersectionality. I used EBSCOhost to search for *heterogeneous effects*, as well as alternative forms of the term (*heterogeneous treatment effects, differential effects, conditional effects, marginal effects*) and methodological terms associated with the approach: *modified regression* and *interaction term*. I narrowed the search to work published from 1989 (the year of Crenshaw's first publication on intersectionality) to 2017 and allowed for journals, working papers, and reports. The initial EBSCOhost search offered 2,952 search results from EconLit, 2,227 from ERIC, and 3,588 from SocINDEX.

I worked to narrow the results based on the following inclusion criteria. Given my focus on methods to examine HE, the first inclusion criterion required that research focus on methodological approach—for example, how to obtain HE, difficulties in interpretation and challenges in application, and how to improve the statistical approach—rather than application alone. The second inclusion criterion required that papers describe HE in the context of using observational data, as the intercategorical approach to intersectionality largely relies on predetermined categories available in existing data (McCall, 2005).

The majority of the search results were applications of regression using interaction terms rather than discussions of the approach, its challenges, and interpretations. It was not feasible to identify (and eliminate) applications through search terms. I was able to winnow the results to further align with my focus on observational data by adding a "NOT" Boolean operator for the terms "randomized controlled trial" and "meta-analysis." The new search offered 2,948 from EconLit, 2,164 from ERIC, and 3,538 from SocINDEX on which I performed a title review. To sort through the search results, I first examined titles, keeping only papers that did not explicitly note a particular population/data set/application. When I reached 500 consecutive entries that did not meet the inclusion criteria, I stopped the search. The search based on title resulted in 51 unique papers after sorting through the first 2,100 results (I found 55 papers in total, but 4 were working paper drafts of published versions already included).

For the remaining 51 papers, I examined the abstract and article to determine if they met the inclusion criteria. On closer review, several did not discuss estimating HE, but how to produce estimates when individuals received varied treatments (i.e., where individuals are exposed to different levels of an intervention)—thus they were not focused on effect moderation but, rather, different treatments ($n = 11$). Several other papers were too narrowly focused on the application to fulfil the first criterion ($n = 7$). After the full review, I identified 32 for inclusion in the synthesis.

I gathered additional literature on methodological approaches through ancestor searches, adding papers based on the reference lists of those in my initial search ($n = 14$). Finally, I incorporated papers based on my background knowledge, primarily to describe additional implications of the statistical approaches or support the discussion of intersectionality ($n = 24$). To offer additional insights on the methodological approaches, I incorporated examples from the National Center of Education Statistics (NCES) data documentation, literature on sampling weights, and information on power analysis. Sources that were not obtained through the literature search or ancestor search are denoted with an asterisk in the reference list.

I organized the synthesis of the literature into three themes: common statistical approaches, major challenges in application, and overcoming those challenges when using observational data to examine HE. Within the results, the most common approach for estimating HE uses interaction terms in regression analysis. A second approach extends the first by using propensity score strata, rather than individual covariates, to assess variation in effects. In leveraging these techniques, several challenges emerged in discussions regarding HE, including concerns over adequately supporting statistical models with theory, difficulty in interpreting the results, and the potential pitfalls of insufficient sample size to examine effects among subgroups. I follow-up with additional considerations for using existing large-scale data and the role of administrative data as a potential means to overcome the challenges of small sample size.

APPROACHES TO CAPTURE EFFECT HETEROGENEITY

Intersectionality, starting with Crenshaw's (1991) work on Black women, focuses on the multidimensionality of an individual's experience and stands in contrast to a "single-axis analysis" (p. 139) that would otherwise distort those experiences (i.e., examining the experience of being Black or female disparately). Most social scientists, particularly those interested in inequality, agree that responses to experiences vary across individuals and between groups (Elwert & Winship, 2010; Kam & Trussler, 2007; Manski, 2007; Wodtke & Almirall, 2015; Xie, 2011, 2013). For education researchers, we might anticipate variation in students' responses to a given educational experience based on their background (i.e., certain background characteristics modify the impact of the experience on the measured outcome). Modified regression and HTE across propensity scores are two statistical approaches that allow researchers to explore variation in individual responses. I describe the two approaches below.

Modified Regression

Regression analysis estimates the relationship between covariates (also referred to as independent variables or predictors) and the outcome (the dependent variable). A hypothesis of differential effects anticipates that a *moderator*, or more than one moderator, influences the strength of the relationship between two other variables. When the effect of a given variable depends, in some way, on the value of another variable, there is an *interaction* between the two variables (VanderWeele & Knol, 2014a). In a regression, the role of moderator—a covariate that may dampen or amplify the effect of another variable—is typically captured through a multiplicative interaction term. The magnitude of the relationship between the independent variable of interest and the outcome varies as a function of another predictor (Flanders, DerSimonian, & Freedman, 1992; Preacher, Curran, & Bauer, 2006; Wodtke & Almirall, 2015). In an educational setting, the independent variable of interest, for example, might include exposure to an educational program, but it also could be a particular background characteristic or group membership. The presence of the interaction effect is typically evaluated by the statistical significance of the interaction term in the regression results. The interpretation of the interaction is critical and requires further investigation, which researchers often conduct by plotting and evaluating the slopes of different values of the modifying variable (for illustration, see Preacher et al., 2006). The inclusion of interaction terms also renders the coefficient for the dependent variable more difficult to interpret (Flanders et al., 1992).

Although interaction terms are simple to include in regression models, main-effects-only regression models are still the norm throughout social science and education research (Choo & Marx Ferree, 2010; Elwert & Winship, 2010; Rhodes, 2010; Turney, 2015). Most published research using regression accounts for individual background measures in predicting the outcome but fails to account for interactions between those measures. Yet understanding complex social processes requires "seeing and seeking complexity" (Choo & Marx Ferree, 2010, p. 146) when building statistical models rather than starting with the simplest model.

Why do researchers who theoretically believe in effect heterogeneity rely on main-effects-only regression models? Elwert and Winship (2010) proposed that scholars assume that main-effects coefficients represent a "straightforward average" (p. 327) of heterogeneous individual-level effects. Researchers also rely on average effects because sample sizes may be too small to include interaction terms between the independent variable of interest and more than a few common modifiers (gender, race, income, etc.) and the variables necessary to explicitly model heterogeneity remain unmeasured and/or unknown. To illustrate that ignoring effect heterogeneity, as in most main-effects-only regressions, is prone to failure, Elwert and Winship (2010) used simulation, comparing results from models with unmodeled effect heterogeneity and results that capture effect heterogeneity. They found that unmodeled effect heterogeneity led to biased estimates (Elwert & Winship, 2010). Thus, capturing effect heterogeneity through interaction terms is important, but developing statistical models that "seek complexity" requires theoretical grounding, as I describe in the section on challenges in application.

Effect Heterogeneity Across Propensity Score Strata

A more recent approach for capturing variation in effects follows much of the same motivation as modified regression. Rather than including interactions between two or three measures to test for variation in the outcome, it leverages a composite of background characteristics and examines variation across the resulting score, referred to as a *propensity score*. A *propensity score model* estimates the predicted probability of participation using observed characteristics, summarizing that probability into one number (Hu & Mustillo, 2016; Morgan & Winship, 2007). While standard propensity score methods focus on average treatment effects, much like regressions without interaction terms, recent research explores HE by leveraging a "stratification multilevel model" (Hu & Mustillo, 2016, p. 71). To test for variation in results across the probability of experiencing a given treatment, scholars use propensity scores from the initial model to disaggregate effects of the treatment (Xie, Brand, & Jann, 2012).

The approach outlined by Xie et al. (2012), which they call "HTE," examines effects across intervals of propensity scores. In addition to describing the technique, they offer a program, HTE, to execute the approach in Stata. HTE compares effect sizes for those with the lowest probability of receiving treatment with those with increasingly higher probabilities of selection by dividing the propensity score distribution into strata (i.e., treatment * propensity to participate in treatment, where the propensity scores are divided into intervals). Analyzing the pattern of treatment effects as a function of the propensity score (i.e., Do students with a higher propensity for selection benefit more than those with a lower propensity?) has to potential to uncover the "implications of the distribution of social resources, policy interventions, and events across the population" (Xie et al., 2012, p. 320).

Rather than examining how one background factor or identity moderates the outcome, researchers can use this method to understand how individuals' backgrounds—including the composite intersecting identities—influence selection into treatment and variation in effects. For example, Brand and Xie (2010) used data from the National Longitudinal Survey of Youth 1979 (NLSY79) and the Wisconsin Longitudinal Study to model college students' propensity to earn a bachelor's degree. The propensity score model included several background measures such as race, parents' income and educational attainment, gender, high school class rank, and cognitive ability. The scholars then examined how economic returns to a bachelor's degree varied across students' propensity to earn a degree. By relying on a summary measure of pretreatment characteristics, the HTE approach avoids exhausting precious degrees of freedom compared with testing an array of interaction effects across individual covariates (as in modified regression; Turney, 2015). Using a hierarchical linear model with students nested in propensity score strata, Brand and Xie (2010) examined the pattern of effects on earnings. They found a statistically significant negative pattern of effects across propensity score (students with the lowest probability of completing college demonstrated the biggest returns for earning a degree), which Brand and Xie interpreted as evidence that those who are least likely to earn a degree benefit the most from doing so.

Despite the novelty and advantages of HTE, scholars using the approach face some challenges in interpreting results. Individuals within each propensity score stratum do not share the same exact intersecting identities. Descriptive statistics of each propensity score stratum can demonstrate the most common identities in the group. In Brand and Xie's (2010, Table 3) study, male college students in the stratum with the lowest propensity to complete college were disproportionately non-White and grew up in households with relatively low parental income and educational attainment compared with the sample average. However, because the stratum includes various intersections of identities, it is difficult to summarily conclude which students (based on particular identifies) are most likely to benefit from a degree.

For the purpose of modeling intersectionality, the propensity score method is more flexible than the modified regression approach because it captures various intersecting identities in one interaction term. For the same reason, however, it is less intuitive for interpreting the implications of the results for specific subgroups. While the approach has parallels with the goals of intersectionality, Brand and Xie (2010) did not invoke intersectionality or explicitly consider it when discussing the implications of their results. Doing so may have offered them additional language with which to describe the composition of students in specific strata and the complex pattern of effects.

Further Approaches to Examine Effect Heterogeneity

Because effect heterogeneity is "endemic to nearly all social contexts" (Wodtke & Almirall, 2015, p. 3; see also Xie et al., 2012), capturing that variation can offer valuable insights for social theory and inform program and policy implementation. As such, there are additional statistical approaches to assess HE, depending on the research question and data available. Through path analyses, researchers can examine moderation by incorporating interaction terms, in addition to exploring mediation (Fairchild & MacKinnon, 2009; Henseler & Chin, 2010). Other approaches, like an instrumental variable approach, align with causal inference but allow interaction terms to test for effect heterogeneity (Heckman, Urzua, & Vytlacil, 2006; Moffitt, 2008). Generally, these approaches grapple with many of the same challenges as those in modified regression when incorporating interactions into the models. For additional information, the aforementioned citations offer some insights on challenges specific to each approach.

CHALLENGES IN APPLICATION

From a methodological standpoint, it would not be terribly difficult for more scholars to include interaction terms in their regression models (Elwert & Winship, 2010; Franzese & Kam, 2009; Rhodes, 2010). Yet there are several notable challenges to doing so. In this section, I highlight four main challenges: supporting models with theory, examining tradeoffs in research goals when determining whether to examine HE, complex interpretation, and identifying data with adequate sample size to explore hypothesized interactions.

Supporting Statistical Models With Theory

Theory is a vital component of the process of building statistical models with interaction terms, whether scholars leverage modified regression or HTE. Rather than encouraging the inclusion of interaction terms in search of significance (sometimes referred to as "data snooping"), the methodological literature encourages strong theoretical justification for the statistical models (Aiken & West, 1991; Bedeian & Mossholder, 1994; Bobko & Russell, 1994; Elwert & Winship, 2010). Using theory to inform model building is necessary to understand the need for and the interpretation of interactions. Work from qualitative research and extant intersectional theory can guide quantitative researchers as they build models and accumulate evidence regarding the role intersecting identities play in how individuals respond to experiences (Green, Evans, & Subramanian, 2017; Ragin & Fiss, 2016; Turney, 2015). This approach is especially valuable in applied fields like education, where the impact of programs and environments for different types of students has implications for practice and policy.

To align with intersectional theory, quantitative researchers using modified regression may wish to include multiple interactions terms and leverage three-way interactions when supported by theory (e.g., race * gender * class rather than just race * class). With more interactions (and, thereby, intersections), the model is better able to account for variation across identities. To date, it appears that most papers with interaction terms in education still focus primarily on two-way interactions, which offer insight into HE but often across singular dimensions of student background. The difficulty in incorporating three-way interactions may partially be driven by the difficulty justifying the inclusion of three-way interactions with minimal prior research to cite as an example. McCall (2005) argued that the evaluation of multiple interaction effects using intersectional theory may be discouraged by academic journals because reviewers often stress the need to cite already developed bodies of research and because editors pressure authors to cover more material in less space, which makes it difficult to theoretically justify a large number of interaction terms (McCall, 2005). Qualitative scholarship may be able to provide theoretical justification for exploring various interactions, as qualitative work often offers detailed information on participants' background. Even if faced with conflicting findings across extant qualitative research, quantitative researchers could leverage that as evidence that additional assessment is necessary (Turney, 2015).

Like modified regression, the HTE approach is best suited to research questions that anticipate variation in outcomes based on individual background, where participants in a given program/experience may receive different benefits based on how likely they were to participate. Efforts to examine HTE have sparked debate among researchers interested in causal inference and effect heterogeneity. Breen, Choi, and Holm (2015) argued that evidence of HE may actually be attributed to selection bias, cautioning researchers using the method on observational data collected in social settings. Leveraging the same nationally representative data as Brand and Xie (2010), they demonstrated how, in the presence of additional selection bias (e.g., a variable left out of the model) or a competing differential effect (where some students in the higher strata benefit more from college than their peers with lower propensities), it is possible to artificially identify a differential effect. Their critique illustrates the need for a rich set of covariates, detailed consideration of potential confounders, and careful exploration of alternative explanations for differential effects. To effectively leverage HTE, education researchers should closely consider why variation across propensity to participate might be present in response to the independent variable of interest and test alternative explanations using the data. By leveraging additional theory and examining competing hypotheses, the HTE approach offers insights that may help researchers understand whether and how groups of students respond differently to a given educational treatment.

Tradeoffs: Competing Goals in Applied Research

In applied, policy-relevant research, there is an inherent interest in variation in effects across different groups of individuals. But applied work often navigates a tension between the need to examine differential effects and the desire to offer simple population-level statistics (see Morabia, 2014; VanderWeele & Knol, 2014a, 2014b). Education scholars may learn lessons from a recent debate in epidemiology. Epidemiologists are increasingly interested in using interaction terms to discern whether some individuals stand to benefit more from an intervention than others—a pressing need in the face of limited resources (a challenge similarly faced in education; VanderWeele & Knol, 2014a). These questions are important for programmatic decisions and implementation, but scholars face a parallel incentive to simplify results, presenting broad patterns of population-level trends rather than complex narratives (Morabia, 2014). Focusing on average effects moves scholars away from a complex vision of individuals and masks the way in which background characteristics and prior experiences predispose them to do better or worse than peers.

Yet even when epidemiologists include interaction terms in regressions, they often fail to include more than one modifier variable, despite theory that would support additional model complexity (Morabia, 2014). Minimizing complex statistical models save researchers from a "plethora of interactions" that could "render population thinking and group comparisons essentially useless" (VanderWeele & Knol, 2014b, p. 79). To consider the tradeoffs between exploring HE and relying on average effects, VanderWeele and Knol (2014b) recommended that scholars, from the outset of their research, evaluate their goals and purpose in building a model that includes interactions. Do they seek to understand variation in effects more broadly? Do they seek to target certain subpopulations to determine how to maximize the effectiveness of an intervention or how to uncover mechanisms for improving its effectiveness? Whereas the first goal would leverage interaction terms for descriptive purposes, the second fuels evaluation of which subgroup to treat or how to be most effective in the face of limited resources. Researchers must consider the theory and goals driving their research as they build their statistical models and identify the best approach. The inclusion of interaction terms must align with the overarching goals of the project.

Interpreting Complex Interaction Effects

The inclusion of interaction terms inherently makes models more difficult to interpret. While the incorporation of moderators in a statistical model should be supported by theory, theory does not necessarily make the output—which now includes a series of main-effects and interactions—easier to interpret. If researchers rely solely on regression coefficients, they may find it difficult to produce concrete and straightforward interpretations of the results. Results can be made more concrete—and easier to interpret—by computing predicted values for specific subgroups of individuals (Long & Freese, 2006).

Recent updates in statistical software have improved the tools available to help scholars interpret complex interaction effects (Jann, 2013; Williams, 2012). In 2011,

Stata incorporated a new set of commands to help researchers produce predicted probabilities of specific subgroups that can be applied to interpret interactions. The margins and contrast commands increase the ease with which users can compute the predicted probability for a given hypothetical individual. Williams (2012) produced illustrative examples of the interaction of female * age to calculate the predicted probability that men and women will end up with diabetes. Marginsplot, which helps build visuals from the interactions, increases the ease with which researchers can illustrate interactions (Williams, 2012). Jann (2013) leverages margins and marginsplot to show how users can illustrate varied patterns of effects across subgroups based on the interactions included in their models. The Stata command produced by Xie et al. (2012) relies on similar calculations across propensity score strata as the margins command and produces parallel graphics to marginsplot, facilitating the interpretation of HE across propensity score stratum.

While recent advances in statistical software increase the ease with which researchers can test and display specific interactions, the advice to rely on theory to guide statistical models still holds. Though HTE and marginsplot produce figures to illustrate variation in effects, the interpretation of those results relies on the researchers' knowledge of the literature. Extant research on intersectionality may be useful to inform the interpretation of complex interactions across multiple categories.

Sample Size and Statistical Power

When incorporating interaction terms into a model, researchers may find that very few individuals fall into certain categories (e.g., very few Black students are present in a given school). Small subgroup sample sizes can make it difficult to run the analysis or detect an effect. This challenge may contribute to the lack of three-way interactions in the literature. Since a three-way interaction (e.g., race * parent education * gender) requires even smaller subgroups of individuals in overlapping categories, identifying the impact, even if the intersection is potent for the outcome, may be more difficult. Failing to find a statistically significant impact that is otherwise present is referred to as a *Type II error*. While the hypothetical model may better account for variation across identity (if supported by theory, compared with a model that incorporates a two-way interaction), the number of students in each "combined" group of identities may be small, putting strain on the model, and resulting in the omission of some combined groups in the results.

Similar to standard modified regression, the HTE approach also requires attention to subgroup sample size—in this case, the propensity score strata. This problem is slightly less concerning in HTE than in modified regression because the approach relies on summary scores, minimizing the reliance on subgroups based on one specific covariate (Turney, 2015). However, researchers may still find small numbers of individuals with estimated propensity scores in some strata. Hu and Mustillo (2016) provide a review of recent developments in propensity score methods and provide practical tips to evaluate sensitivity to sample size within strata and methods to adjust the number of strata.

Given the emphasis on statistical significance in publishing, small cell size has important implications. For researchers interested in publication, the risk of failure to detect an effect is a powerful disincentive to pursue research questions that would rely on small subgroups (which have a greater risk for Type II error). There is a tradeoff between the potential contribution of including interaction terms and the limitations of secondary data to capture moderating relationships, largely due to sample size. Bobko and Russell (1994) noted the importance of considering statistical power for examining group-level difference early in research development. Ideally, this notion would arise in study design (i.e., data collection), but researchers using secondary data may also want to maintain this consideration during early analytic planning. If the power is insufficient to study an important subgroup or phenomenon across a given set of identities, researchers might revise their plans (Bobko & Russell, 1994). In some cases, researchers can raise their threshold for considering an effect statistically significant, above the typical p value of .05 (Marshall, 2007). Publically available computer programs[2] can help scholars estimate the power of their planned modified regression to detect a hypothesized effect. Such programs use empirically based algorithms to allow researchers to estimate statistical power by providing values for factors known to affect power, such as anticipated magnitude of the moderating effect and sample size of moderator-based groups (Aguinis, Beaty, Boik, & Pierce, 2005). These resources are quite valuable for researchers interested in examining intersectionality using subgroups in observational data, but otherwise uncertain "How small is too small?" in regard to sample size.

Of course, assessing the appropriate size of a sample to merit exploring interactions is more complex than simply adhering to power analysis results. Even with the risk of nonsignificant results, exploring HE can still be valuable (Bobko & Russell, 1994; Vandenbrouke, 2013; VanderWeele & Knol, 2014a). Effect heterogeneity often provides new insights compared with the alternative option of assuming average effects. The information gleaned can offer insights into the responses of narrow subpopulations—we can learn a lot from the pattern of results, even if it is unlikely that we will find statistically significant results. Performing a power analysis is one way for researchers to be informed about the sample size that would be required to identify a given effect. What is most important is that scholars feel confident that they have enough students in the subsample of interest to believe that the patterns reflect general trends, rather than idiosyncrasies in a tiny subgroup of sampled students.

This set of considerations aligns well with the themes in the intersectionality literature. There is value in examining theory-driven variation in student responses to programs and experiences, even if doing so does not return statistically significant results. Testing for interactions is about scientific reasoning and theory. There is no ideal outcome of the analysis, at least in terms of intellectual curiosity (though publishing bias leans toward statistical associations)—we should ask the question if answering it could bolster or refute theory (Morabia, 2014; Vandenbrouke, 2013).

OVERCOMING CHALLENGES: IS LARGE-SCALE DATA READY FOR INTERSECTIONAL ANALYSIS?

Related to the challenges noted above, I describe the current rationale and approach for drawing samples in NCES data sets. I consider whether the sampling strategy aligns with the examination of group-level differences and interactions, which is necessary to leverage intersectionality. I also describe sampling weights and their limitations in overcoming the problem of small sample size for subgroups and examine the possibility of "big data," including state administrative data, in providing adequate sample sizes to conduct intersectional analyses.

NCES Data: Implications of Sampling Design for Intersectional Inquiry

Collecting large-scale survey data with the goal of achieving a nationally representative sample of students is challenging. In education, there is no comprehensive list from which to draw a random sample from the target population, whether it be kindergartners, high school sophomores, or first-time college students (Thomas & Heck, 2001). Even with a hypothetical list in hand, a random sample could not ensure that students with certain characteristics would be adequately represented, yet this representation is particularly important for researchers interested in specific subgroups of students and intersections with other identities (Thomas & Heck, 2001). NCES addresses these issues with a multistage cluster sampling strategy, which involves oversampling students based on characteristics predetermined to need additional representation in the sample, such as racial minorities (i.e., some individuals have a higher probability of selection; Tourangeau et al., 2009).

Each NCES study has its own design in drawing a complex multistage sample. For instance, the Early Childhood Longitudinal Study–kindergarten cohort (ECLS-K) follows a sample of kindergarteners. To select a nationally representative sample of kindergarteners in 1998–1999, NCES started with a list of counties or groups of counties (Tourangeau et al., 2009). After selecting geographic areas, NCES selected schools within the region, and then children from within the schools. Not all children had an equal probability of being selected. To obtain ensure precise estimates, NCES oversampled Asian and Pacific Islanders (Tourangeau et al., 2009, pp. 4-2). As additional waves of data were added to the ECLS-K 1998–1999, new priorities for subsample preservation arose and NCES adjusted the probability of selection (Tourangeau et al., 2009, pp. 4-1). NCES indicates that oversampling was crucial to achieve adequate numbers of underrepresented subgroups of students—in this case, Asian and Pacific Islanders in Wave 1 and transfer students and language minorities in Wave 3 (Tourangeau et al., 2009).

Overall, it is important to note that NCES data, like most nationally representative data, are not designed specifically for intersectional data analysis. Restricting the sample to focus on certain students, for instance, in investigating the Black–White test score gap using the ECLS-K, has its limitations. Breaking down those subgroups even further may result in challenges such as low cell size. Although NCES oversamples racial minority students to improve researchers' ability to study certain subgroups of students, NCES would likely need to oversample additional underrepresented groups (e.g., stratifying the sample based on sexuality, disability status, or other background characteristics) to ensure adequate representation for intersectional analyses.

NCES has not published any reports of power analyses conducted to evaluate adequate sample size for student subgroups prior to data collection, though the language in their ECLS-K technical report suggests that some sort of analysis was conducted to determine the appropriate sample size for Asian and Pacific Islanders (Tourangeau et al., 2009). Ideally, as research demands change, the sampling design and data structure will shift to allow for adequate representation of various other groups of students. As of now, researchers interested in leveraging existing data must contend with the limitations of the data. In the next section, I examine the role of sampling weights and whether they alleviate concerns about small sample size when using nationally representative data.

Accounting for Sampling Design

Multistage sampling strategies yield samples that include disproportionate numbers of some individuals and do not align with subgroup representation in the population. Results that fail to adjust for sampling strategy are biased, where the extent of bias varies based on how the researchers restricted their analytic sample and selected variables (Thomas & Heck, 2001). Researchers must address issues related to oversampling, where students have unequal probabilities of selection, and clustering, where students within some groups are more similar than those across groups. Thomas and Heck (2001) recommended that researchers using complex sample data incorporate either design-based strategies (e.g., sampling weights to account for selection probabilities) or model-based strategies (e.g., models, such as multilevel models, that account for clustering) into their research design.

Leveraging sampling weights. Sampling weights are used to align the sample's distribution for a set of variables with the population from which the sample was drawn (Winship & Radbill, 1994). Oversampling based on racial identification—as in the ECLS-K—may result in a sample with a higher percentage of some students than is proportionally present in the population. In this case, sampling weights can be constructed to adjust the distribution toward what it would have been had Asian students not been oversampled. The trouble arises when research moves beyond descriptive statistics—which many social scientists and education researchers aim to do—because sampling weights bias the estimation of standard errors (Solon, Haider, & Wooldridge, 2015).

Winship and Radbill (1994) and, more recently, Solon et al. (2015) acknowledged the bias produced by using sampling weights in multivariate statistical procedures such as regression. Many pressing and important inquiries in applied research focus on estimating statistical associations and cause-and-effect rather than population descriptive statistics. Both sets of approaches described to estimate HE aim to allow researchers to understand the impact of independent variables on an outcome and examine modifiers of that effect. When the goal is to understand the impact of one variable (or many variables) on another, then the use of sampling weights may not be appropriate.

While many researchers rely on weighted regressions to draw population-level inferences (indeed, some of the literature supports this method, e.g., Aiken & West, 1991; Overton, 2001), weighted regression estimates are often less precise—they have larger standard errors—than unadjusted regressions (Dickens, 1990; Solon et al., 2015; Winship & Radbill, 1994). The problem appears to be due to the assumption that individuals' error terms are independent of one another, when they likely have group-level factors in common that are not accounted for by the weights (Dickens, 1990; Solon et al., 2015).[3] Decisions are also made in the research process that render the use of sampling weights less applicable. For instance, the researcher may narrow the sample in a way that makes it difficult to know how representative it is of the population.

Overall, researchers must use caution when relying on sampling weights to overcome sampling design decisions. The purpose of sampling weights is not to address small sample sizes but to adjust the descriptive statistics of the sample to resemble the population. As such, using sampling weights does not resolve the problem of low statistical power. For the purposes explored in this chapter, scholars interested in understanding educational impacts among certain subgroups or in examining group-level differences may consider using unweighted analyses (if they restrict their sample in a way that makes population inferences unnecessary) or using a strategy such as multilevel modeling to control for clustering related to the sampling design. I elaborate more on this issue next. If nothing else, researchers using the national data should consider the implications of sampling design when formulating their analytic plan.

Accounting for clustering. As noted in the previous section, sampling weights can account for oversampling. However, they do not account for clustering where perhaps some students in the sample share similar characteristics because they are from the same geographic region or attend the same school. Furthermore, sampling weights must be used at a one level of analysis; the researcher must focus on either students or schools rather than studying both levels of analysis simultaneously (Thomas & Heck, 2001; Winship & Radbill, 1994). Multilevel approaches take clustering into account by decomposing estimates for each variable into the part contributed from within a group/cluster—the individual student—and the part due to variation between clusters—often the schools from which the students were sampled.[4] Another strategy includes using robust standard errors adjusted to account for clustering. Adjustments can be performed easily in most statistical software. For instance, in Stata, researchers can use the vce(cluster) option while performing regressions (Stata, 2017).[5] This approach can be combined with sampling weights, if the researcher has not narrowed the sample in a way that makes sampling weights inappropriate.

"Big Data": State Administrative Data and Other Large Data Sources

Large-scale survey data may be underpowered for some intersectional analyses, making it difficult to identify HE across subgroups with small sample sizes. Is the solution to find "bigger" data? While increasing the sample size for NCES data is unlikely, due to resource constraints, more researchers are turning to administrative data to capture entire populations of individuals (Card, Chetty, Feldstein, & Saez, 2010). Relying on administrative data has its pros and cons. While the data are more likely to be sufficiently powered to test interactions across multiple covariates, potentially detecting HE for various subgroups, the available measures tend to be limited (Card et al., 2010; Scott-Clayton & Qiao, 2017).

Large-scale nationally representative surveys collect detailed self-reported data, which is sometimes combined with administrative data (e.g., transcripts), producing a rich set of covariates on which researchers can draw. In administrative data, the set of information for any individual in the population is finite. This is a problem for researchers interested in testing for variation in effects across various identities. Furthermore, statistical models missing covariates that influence on the outcomes may be biased (Cunha & Miller, 2014; Scott-Clayton & Qiao, 2017).

Yet researchers have increasingly turned to administrative data to answer pressing policy problems, including in the field of education. While much of this research relies on state administrative data, recent research also leverages even larger data sets, including tax records (e.g., Chetty, Hendren, Kline, & Saez, 2014). Large sample sizes make the data sufficiently powered to test a variety of interactions, despite limitations in terms of the depth and breadth of available identity measures. This tradeoff means that some intersections can be explored, depending on the data source, but that researchers interested in examining intersectionality must consider which predetermined categories are of interest and to pursue the data only if those categories are available. Access to administrative data sources can be more difficult to navigate and require a larger investment of money or time to obtain a data license than NCES studies (Card et al., 2010; Cunha & Miller, 2016).

EFFECT HETEROGENEITY AND INTERSECTIONALITY: A PATH FORWARD

Intersectional theorists aim to overcome the tendency to "conflate or ignore intra-group differences" (Crenshaw, 1991, p. 1241) and variation in individual experiences across multiple identities. Although intercategorical approaches for capturing intersectionality are limited in their ability to capture the complexity of individual experiences, examining HE offers the potential for researchers to illuminate intersectional effects across predefined groups (McCall, 2005). Increasing the role of intersectional analyses in quantitative research offers new means by which to examine variation in responses to lived experiences. Encouraging greater dialogue between the (mostly qualitative) scholarship on intersectional research and quantitative education research has the potential to improve theory formation for hypothesized interactions and to offer generalizable results using large-scale data.

Scholars increasingly acknowledge the need for overlap between quantitative approaches and intersectional theory. A recent issue of *Race, Ethnicity, and Education* explored whether quantitative methods can "support a critical race agenda in educational research" (Garcia, López, & Vélez, 2018, p. 150). In the issue, Gilborn, Warmington, and Demack (2018) take a skeptical stance, arguing that quantitative methods "cannot match qualitative approaches in terms of their suitability for understanding the numerous social processes that shape and legitimate . . . inequity" (p. 3). The authors acknowledge the role that quantitative methods play in highlighting structural barriers and inequalities faced by different groups of individuals but warn that statistics often disguise inequities and protect the status quo. This skepticism highlights why researchers should be mindful of the purpose, design, and limitations of the data sets they use. They should also use caution in interpreting the lack of HE across subgroups as evidence of equal returns to the same experience or intervention; they must be mindful of the potential for Type II errors.

In other applied fields, a growing subset of quantitative researchers explore how intersectionality and quantitative approaches can inform one another. Population health researchers (e.g., Bauer, 2014; Green et al., 2017) and poverty scholars (e.g., Ragin & Fiss, 2016) acknowledge the need to incorporate intersectionality into theory and interpretation of quantitative analyses. Green et al. (2017) argue that by combining intersectionality with other social theories related to the production of inequality in health outcomes, researchers are better poised to interpret interactions among measures of social identity as part of "interlocking systems of oppression" (pp. 215–216). Ragin and Fiss (2016, p. 13) emphasize that only through considering a "combination of characteristics"—as opposed to the independent contribution of various independent variables—can researchers understand poverty and inform the complex policy changes to overcome it. Population health and poverty research have several similarities to education, given both fields' interests in the effects of programs and policies on individual outcomes and the driving concern of how to improve outcomes among subgroups of individuals. Thus, these resources may be useful to education researchers to inform the field's conversation about intersectionality, pushing past traditional methodological divisions.

CONCLUSION: ARE INTERSECTIONAL AND QUANTITATIVE APPROACHES COMPATIBLE?

Although large-scale data are not intentionally designed for conducting intersectional analyses, researchers use quantitative data to explore how individuals' characteristics, skills, and group memberships moderate responses to a variable of interest. In this chapter, I synthesized the literature from quantitative methods to consider the merits and challenges of approaches available to explore HE considering the extent to which they align with intersectionality. I also explored the potential of new developments, whether it be statistical software or administrative data, to improve researchers' ability to incorporate intersectionality into quantitative approaches.

There is tension between qualitative and quantitative research that becomes even more apparent in this line of inquiry. Quantitative work is criticized for taking on a deficit-based approach (Reid, Epstein, Pastor, & Ryser, 2000; Schreiner & Anderson, 2005). Meanwhile, qualitative scholars often must respond to critiques about sample size, generalizability, and the need for rigor. The disconnect between studies using quantitative techniques to examine effect heterogeneity and the primarily qualitative and theoretical literature on intersectionality comes as no surprise.

However, each side stands to be enriched by the other. Incorporating intersectionality would strengthen the toolkit available to researchers as they examine HE, supporting theory for statistical models and offering concrete examples from which to interpret results. Likewise, qualitative researchers could benefit from the capability of large-scale data to test the generalizability of their findings. Exploring patterns illustrated in the extant intersectional literature through quantitative data may bolster support for findings and pinpoint areas for inquiry in new contexts.

Innovations in statistical software and the availability of large-scale data make examining effect heterogeneity feasible for a broader array of researchers. The literature on methodological approaches emphasizes the need to leverage theory to support models that test for HE and to interpret the results. This chapter represents an attempt to illustrate the overlap in interests among scholars studying effect heterogeneity and intersectionality. In the field of education, both lenses stand to provide "new angles of vision" to understand how practices, policies, and structures influence social inequality (Collins, 2015).

NOTES

[1]Throughout the chapter, I alternate between referring to the exploration of variation in effects as effect heterogeneity and heterogeneous effects, or HE.

[2]Programs to detect statistical power for various forms of modified regression are available at http://www.hermanaguinis.com/mmr/index.html. Instructions for use are available in Aguinis (2004).

[3]For more in-depth information on the origin of bias due to sampling weights, see Dickens (1990), Solon et al. (2015), and Winship and Radbill (1994).

[4]For more information on multilevel modeling, see Muthen and Satorra (1995) and Raudenbush and Bryk (2002).

[5]Cameron and Miller (2015) offer a useful overview on approaches to deal with clustering.

ORCID ID

Lauren Schudde   https://orcid.org/0000-0003-3851-1343

REFERENCES

An asterisk has been used to denote references collected based on background knowledge rather than the literature search strategy and ancestor search.

Aguinis, H. (2004). *Regression analysis for categorical moderators*. New York, NY: Guilford Press.

Aguinis, H., Beaty, J. C., Boik, R. J., & Pierce, C. A. (2005). Effect size and power in assessing moderating effects of categorical variables using multiple regression: A 30-year review. *Journal of Applied Psychology, 90*, 94–107. doi:10.1037/0021-9010.90.1.94

Aiken, L. S., & West, S. G. (1991). *Multiple regression: Testing and interpreting interactions*. Newbury Park, CA: Sage.

Bauer, G. R. (2014). Incorporating intersectionality theory into population health research methodology: Challenges and the potential to advance health equity. *Social Science & Medicine, 110*, 10–17. doi:10.1016/j.socscimed.2014.03.022

Bedeian, A. G., & Mossholder, K. W. (1994). Simple question, not so simple answer: Interpreting interaction terms in moderated multiple regression. *Journal of Management, 20*, 159–165. doi:10.1177/014920639402000108

*Berger, P. L., & Luckmann, T. (1966). *The social construction of reality: A treatise in the sociology of knowledge*. New York, NY: Doubleday.

Bobko, P., & Russell, C. J. (1994). On theory, statistics, and the search for interactions in the organizational sciences. *Journal of Management, 20*, 193–200. doi:10.1177/014920639402000111

Brand, J. E., & Xie, Y. (2010). Who benefits most from college? Evidence for negative selection in heterogeneous economic returns to higher education. *American Sociological Review, 75*, 273–302. doi:10.1177/0003122410363567

Breen, R., Choi, S., & Holm, A. (2015). Heterogeneous causal effects and sample selection bias. *Sociological Science, 2*, 351–369. doi:10.15195/v2.a17

*Cameron, A. C., & Miller, D. L. (2015). A practitioner's guide to cluster-robust inference. *Journal of Human Resources, 50*, 317–372. doi:10.3368/jhr.50.2.317

*Card, D., Chetty, R., Feldstein, M., & Saez, E. (2010, September). *Expanding access to administrative data for research in the United States* (NSF SBE 2020 White Paper 2010). Washington, DC: National Science Foundation.

*Chetty, R., Hendren, N., Kline, P., & Saez, E. (2014). Where is the land of opportunity? The geography of intergenerational mobility in the United States. *Quarterly Journal of Economics, 129*, 1553–1623. doi:10.1093/qje/qju022

Choo, H. Y., & Marx Ferree, M. (2010). Practicing intersectionality in sociological research: A critical analysis of inclusions, interactions, and institutions in the study of inequalities. *Sociological Theory, 28*, 129–149. doi:10.1111/j.1467-9558.2010.01370.x

*Collins, P. H. (2015). Intersectionality's definitional dilemmas. *Annual Review of Sociology, 41*, 1–20. doi:10.1146/annurev-soc-073014-112142

*Crenshaw, K. (1991). Mapping the margins: Intersectionality, identity politics, and violence against women of color. *Stanford Law Review, 43*, 1241–1299. doi:10.2307/1229039

*Cunha, J. M., & Miller, T. (2014). Measuring value-added in higher education: Possibilities and limitations in the use of administrative data. *Economics of Education Review, 42*, 64–77. doi:10.1016/j.econedurev.2014.06.001

Dickens, W. T. (1990). Error components in grouped data: Is it ever worth weighting? *Review of Economics and Statistics, 72*, 328–333. doi:10.2307/2109723

Elwert, F., & Winship, C. (2010). Effect heterogeneity and bias in main-effects-only regression models. In R. Dechter, H. Geffner, & J. Y. Halpern (Eds.), *Heuristics, probability and causality: A tribute to Judea Pearl* (pp. 327–336). London, England: College Publications.

Fairchild, A. J., & MacKinnon, D. P. (2009). A general model for testing mediation and moderation effects. *Prevention Science, 10*, 87–99.

Flanders, W. D., DerSimonian, R., & Freedman, D. S. (1992). Interpretation of linear regression models that include transformations or interaction terms. *Annals of Epidemiology, 2*, 735–744.

Franzese, R., & Kam, C. (2009). *Modeling and interpreting interactive hypotheses in regression analysis.* Ann Arbor: University of Michigan Press.

*Garcia, N. M., López, N., & Vélez, V. N. (2018). QuantCrit: Rectifying quantitative methods through critical race theory. *Race Ethnicity and Education, 21*(2), 149–157. doi:10.1 080/13613324.2017.1377675

*Gillborn, D., Warmington, P., & Demack, S. (2018). QuantCrit: Education, policy, "big data" and principles for a critical race theory of statistics. *Race Ethnicity and Education, 21*(2), 158–179. doi:10.1080/13613324.2017.1377417

Green, M. A., Evans, C. R., & Subramanian, S. V. (2017). Can intersectionality theory enrich population health research? *Social Science & Medicine, 178*, 214–216. doi:10.1016/j.socscimed.2017.02.029

Griffin, K. A., Bennett, J. C., & Harris, J. (2011). Analyzing gender differences in black faculty marginalization through a sequential mixed-methods design. *New Directions for Institutional Research, 2011*(151), 45–61. doi:10.1002/ir.398

Heckman, J. J., Urzua, S., & Vytlacil, E. (2006). Understanding instrumental variables in models with essential heterogeneity. *Review of Economics and Statistics, 88*, 389–432.

Henseler, J., & Chin, W. W. (2010). A comparison of approaches for the analysis of interaction effects between latent variables using partial least squares path modeling. *Structural Equation Modeling, 17*, 82–109.

Hu, A., & Mustillo, S. A. (2016). Recent development of propensity score methods in observational studies: Multi-categorical treatment, causal mediation, and heterogeneity. *Current Sociology, 64*, 60–82. doi:10.1177/0011392115589599

Jann, B. (2013, June 7). *Predictive margins and marginal effects in Stata* (11th German Stata Users Group Meeting, Potsdam). Retrieved from https://www.stata.com/meeting/germany13/abstracts/materials/de13_jann.pdf

Kam, C. D., & Trussler, M. J. (2007). At the nexus of observational and experimental research: Theory, specification, and analysis of experiments with heterogeneous treatment effects. *Political Behavior, 39*, 789–815. doi:10.1007/s11109-016-9379-z

Long, J. S., & Freese, J. (2006). *Regression models for categorical dependent variables using Stata* (2nd ed.). College Station, TX: Stata Press.

Manski, C. (2007). *Identification for prediction and decision.* Cambridge, MA: Harvard University Press.

Marshall, S. W. (2007). Power for tests of interaction: Effect of raising the Type I error rate. *Epidemiologic Perspectives & Innovations, 4*(1), 4. doi:10.1186/1742-5573-4-4

*McCall, L. (2005). The complexity of intersectionality. *Signs, 30*, 1771–1800. Retrieved from http://www.gla.ac.uk/media/media_200317_en.pdf

Moffitt, R. (2008). Estimating marginal treatment effects in heterogeneous populations. *Annales d'Economie et de Statistique, 91*, 239–261. doi:10.2307/27917247

Morabia, A. (2014). Interaction–epidemiology's brinkmanship. *Epidemiologic Methods, 3*, 73–77. doi:10.1515/em-2014-0017

Morgan, S., & Winship, C. (2007). *Counterfactuals and causal inference: Methods and principles for social research.* New York, NY: Cambridge University Press.

Museus, S. D., & Griffin, K. A. (2011). Mapping the margins in higher education: On the promise of intersectionality frameworks in research and discourse. *New Directions for Institutional Research, 2011*(151), 5–13. doi:10.1002/ir.395

Muthen, B. O., & Satorra, A. (1995). Complex sample data in structural equation modeling. *Sociological Methodology, 25*, 267–316. doi:10.2307/271070

Overton, R. C. (2001). Moderated multiple regression for interactions involving categorical variables: A statistical control for heterogeneous variance across two groups. *Psychological Methods, 6*, 218–233. doi:10.1037/1082-989X.6.3.218

Preacher, K. J., Curran, P. J., & Bauer, D. J. (2006). Computational tools for probing interactions in multiple linear regression, multilevel modeling, and latent curve analysis. *Journal of Educational and Behavioral Statistics, 31*, 437–448. doi:10.3102/10769986031004437

*Ragin, C. C., & Fiss, P. C. (2016). *Intersectional inequality: Race, class, test scores, and poverty.* Chicago, IL: University of Chicago Press.

Raudenbush, S. W., & Bryk, A. S. (2002). *Hierarchical linear models: Applications and data analysis methods* (Vol. 1). Thousand Oaks, CA: Sage.

*Reid, R., Epstein, M. H., Pastor, D. A., & Ryser, G. R. (2000). Strengths-based assessment differences across students with LD and EBD. *Remedial and Special Education, 21*, 346–355. doi:10.1177/074193250002100604

Rhodes, W. (2010). Heterogeneous treatment effects: What does a regression estimate? *Evaluation Review, 34*, 334–361. doi:10.1177/0193841X10372890

*Schreiner, L. A., & Anderson, E. (2005). Strengths-based advising: A new lens for higher education. *NACADA Journal, 25*(2), 20–29. doi:10.12930/0271-9517-25.2.20

*Scott-Clayton, J., & Qiao, W. (2017, January). *Estimating returns to college attainment: Comparing survey and state administrative data based estimates* (CAPSEE Working Paper). Retrieved from https://capseecenter.org/estimating-returns-to-college-attainment/

Solon, G., Haider, S. J., & Wooldridge, J. M. (2015). What are we weighting for? *Journal of Human Resources, 50*, 301–316. doi:10.3386/w18859

Stata. (2017). *Vce_options—Variance estimators* (Online manual). Retrieved from https://www.stata.com/manuals13/xtvce_options.pdf

*Thomas, S. L., & Heck, R. H. (2001). Analysis of large-scale secondary data in higher education research: Potential perils associated with complex sampling designs. *Research in Higher Education, 42*, 517–540. doi:10.1023/A:1011098109834

*Tourangeau, K., Nord, C., Le, T., Sorongon, A. G., Najarian, M., & Hausken, E. G. (2009). *Early childhood longitudinal study, kindergarten class of 1998–99 (ECLS-K): Combined user's manual for the ECLS-K eighth-grade and K–8 full sample data files and electronic codebooks.* Washington, DC: National Center for Education Statistics.

Turney, K. (2015). Beyond average effects: Incorporating heterogeneous treatment effects into family research. *Journal of Family Theory & Review, 7*, 468–481. doi:10.1111/jftr.12114

Vandenbrouke, J. P. (2013). The history of confounding. In A. Morabia (Ed.), *A history of epidemiologic methods and concepts* (pp. 313–326). Basel, Switzerland: Birkhäuser.

VanderWeele, T. J., & Knol, M. J. (2014a). A tutorial on interaction. *Epidemiologic Methods, 3*, 33–72. doi:10.1515/em-2013-0005

VanderWeele, T. J., & Knol, M. J. (2014b). Interactions and complexity: Goals and limitations. *Epidemiologic Methods, 3*, 79–81. doi:10.1515/em-2014-0016

Williams, R. (2012). Using the margins command to estimate and interpret adjusted predictions and marginal effects. *Stata Journal, 12*, 308–331.

Winship, C., & Radbill, L. (1994). Sampling weights and regression analysis. *Sociological Methods & Research, 23*, 230–257. doi:10.1177/0049124194023002004

Wodtke, G. T., & Almirall, D. (2015). *Estimating heterogeneous causal effects with time-varying treatments and time-varying effect moderators: Structural nested mean models and regression-with-residuals.* Ann Arbor: Michigan Population Studies Center.

Xie, Y. (2011). Causal inference and heterogeneity bias in social science. *Information Knowledge Systems Management, 10*, 279–289. doi:10.3233/IKS-2012-0197

Xie, Y. (2013). Population heterogeneity and causal inference. *Proceedings of the National Academy of Sciences, 110*, 6262–6268. doi:10.1073/pnas.1303102110

Xie, Y., Brand, J. E., & Jann, B. (2012). Estimating heterogeneous treatment effects with observational data. *Sociological Methodology, 42*, 314–347. doi:10.1177/0081175012452652

Chapter 5

Intersectionality in Transnational Education Policy Research

Sarah A. Robert ⓘD
University at Buffalo

Min Yu ⓘD
Wayne State University

This review assesses intersectionality as a theoretical and methodological approach to transnational education policy research. In particular, we are concerned with how the concept is translated and interpreted to interrogate globally circulating education policies and how that transformation might inform the concept within Western and Northern contexts. We acknowledge intersectionality's origins in U.S. Black feminist scholarship, but anticipate transformations as it travels to "Other" contexts and is translated to theorize systemic inequality in particular albeit interconnected spaces. Examining Eastern and Southern Hemisphere English-language, Chinese-language, and Spanish-language peer-reviewed publications, we ask how intersectionality translates to languages other than English and to Eastern and Southern contexts, and what analytic insights are gained from intersectionality's travel and translation that may contribute to its reconceptualization in Northern and Western contexts. Intersectionality coupled with transnationalism provides theoretical and methodological might toward understanding complex systems of inequality through/in which education policy travels, critiquing how inequality continues to flourish within nation-states and global-level hierarchies and privileging non-Western/Southern struggles for equity.

RESEARCH TOPIC AND GOALS

The purpose of this review is to assess intersectionality as a theoretical and methodological approach to transnational education policy research. In particular, we are concerned with how the concept is translated and interpreted to interrogate globally circulating education policies and how that transformation might inform the concept within Western and Northern contexts. We acknowledge intersectionality's origins in United States' Black feminist scholarship, but anticipate transformations as it travels to "Other" contexts and is translated to theorize systemic inequality in particular albeit interconnected spaces (Collins

Review of Research in Education
March 2018, Vol. 42, pp. 93–121
DOI: 10.3102/0091732X18759305
© 2018 AERA. http://rre.aera.net

& Bilge, 2016). "Translation is an integral element of transnational knowledge production" (Choo, 2012, p. 41), and so we wonder how intersectionality has been translated to examine education policy's travels through transnational spaces or networks (Ball, 2016; Ball & Junemann, 2012; Nagel, 2010). Intersectionality coupled with transnationalism, we hope, provides theoretical and methodological might toward understanding complex systems of inequality through/in which education policy travels, critiquing how inequality continues to flourish within nation-states and global-level hierarchies and privileging non-Western/Southern struggles for equity.

Questions

We will examine non-Western and Southern Hemisphere English-language, Chinese-language, and Spanish-language peer-reviewed education policy analyses. The questions guiding this review are the following:

1. How does intersectionality translate to languages other than English and to Eastern and Southern contexts?
2. What analytic insights are gained from intersectionality's travel and translation that may contribute to its reconceptualization in Northern and Western contexts?

Key Concepts and Argument

Initially, intersectionality was conceptualized as "a way of framing the various interactions of race and gender in the context of violence against women of color" in the United States (Crenshaw, 1991, p. 1296). The concept has traveled within the U.S. academy (e.g., Asher, 2007; Cho, Crenshaw, & McCall, 2013; Cole, 2009; Collins, 2000; Gillborn, 2015; Gonzalez, Tefera, & Artiles, 2015; Grant & Zwier, 2011; Patil, 2013; Pillow, 2017; Posey-Maddox, 2017) and has recently been translated. Transnationalism, we argue, creates an urgent need for multiscaled intersectional analyses because of the role the nation plays in the formation of differences and inequalities (Grzanka, 2014; Mohanty, 2013) and because of the changing role of the State in policymaking. Nation is "transmogrified into an independent variable, rather than a historical process that is produced within and by local and global gender, sexual, economic, and racial politics" (Grzanka 2014, p. 197). We build on what Patil (2013) and other scholars have argued to articulate a more complex understanding of nations, borders, and migrations in this review of research that applies intersectionality to analyze education policy in transnational context.

Specifically, we present Choo and Ferree's (2010) three practices[1] of intersectionality as both theoretical and methodological frameworks. Their three practices of intersectional analysis for sociology translate well to the interdisciplinary field of education policy analysis and the transnational policy context. They are group-centered or inclusive of multiply marginalized persons; process-centered or capturing analytic interactions of oppressive regimes; and systems-centered or institutional complexity. As a theoretical framework for this study, the practices imbue intersectionality with meaning, illuminating the complexity and the multiplicity of ways inequality is produced as identity, in relation to and with others, and institutionally.

The practices also serve as our methodological framework because it potentially provided the analytic view needed to understand policy at the multiple levels that it is enacted. In other words, we explore methodological approaches that are associated with the theoretical meaning of intersectionality and its analytic application. We do not force the practices on the literature but rather seek out how the authors have framed their analysis theoretically and methodologically. Our intention in understanding these practices of intersectionality is grounded in the importance of furthering transnational education policy analysis focused on challenging long-standing inequalities. In framing our review and discussion in this way, we advocate for envisioning intersectionality as methodology for transnational education policy analysis as it relates to conceptualizing social and educational inequalities not as segmented, but rather, as multiply determined and intertwined.

Organization of the Review

We begin by explaining how we understand and apply intersectionality in our review. We continue by elaborating our search process and selection criteria. Next are the findings from our analysis of 32 articles. The articles were first sorted into Choo and Ferree's (2010) three practices of intersectionality and short titled: group centered, process centered, and systems centered. This means we looked within the articles to find how the authors designed their study to examine education policy. Within these three main sections, we first explain how the articles reflect a group-, process-, or systems-centered approach. Next, we explain how the articles reveal the complex ways multiple forms of inequality intersect. In other words, what combinations of inequality are revealed by the analyses? And how do the multiple forms intersect? This is followed by a description of the ways inequality continues to flourish in the policy context. How, if at all, has policy addressed the complexity of inequality identified? Each section concludes with a discussion of what Western and Northern scholars might learn from the interpretation or translation of intersectionality in the "Other" context. What might be learned from the analyses to be applied to the U.S. context, specifically? The subsections are a restatement of our goals for this review and are short titled complex combinations, inequality flourishes, and interpretations beyond. In conclusion, we revisit the two guiding questions. Finally, we place our review in conversation with the special issue's focus.

INTERSECTIONALITY AS THEORY AND METHODOLOGY

Globally circulating education policies merit systematic analysis within and across transnational spaces (e.g., Fimyar, 2014; Powers, 2014; Robert, 2017) as an evolving global and local hierarchy. Thus, this review is concerned with the ways "multiply marginalized persons and groups" (Choo & Ferree, 2010) intertwined in a "matrix of domination" (Collins, 2000) are situated within multiple, larger institutional and geopolitical contexts and across spaces that we refer to as transnational. The spaces where intersectional analysis is needed are tangible and virtual, existing within and across nation-states (Purkayastha, 2012). Within them, ideologies, interactions, and institutions sustain and expand in new ways multiple axes of inequality and control of people.

[Patricia Hill Collins] . . . hoped [intersectionality] would travel beyond the U.S., not as yet another American export to the world, but part of the beginnings of a dialogue with similarly subordinated groups in a global context as well as those who wish to build vibrant multiethnic societies. (Choo, 2012, p. 40)

Intersectionality has moved well beyond the United States, as a fast-traveling theory, embraced by a global community of activists (Collins & Bilge, 2016; Hancock, 2016). Still there is a necessity for women of color theories within critical policy analysis (Pillow, 2017). Perhaps intersectionality can be applied to analyze different contexts and the paucity of "third-world women" in knowledge production (e.g., Ang, 2003; Bunjun, 2010; Mohanty, 2003; Mohanty, Russo, & Torres, 1991).[2]

Intersectionality is more than just an explanation for the manifestation of multiple forms of oppression; it is a way to examine the complex processes by which oppression is produced on multiple levels. Thus, when we sought out a means to understand the ongoing production of education inequality around the world, we also needed to find a means by which that production could be isolated in policy analyses that may be focused at the level of persons or groups, may be reflected in the interactional nature of policy enactment (Braun, Maguire, & Ball, 2010), or at the level of complex institutions or systems through which policy travels. We turned to Choo and Ferree's (2010) practices of intersectionality to facilitate our desired view of intersectional inequality resulting from education policy.

Three Ways to Practice Intersectionality

First Practice: Group-Centered or Inclusive of Multiply Marginalized Persons

The first practice is characterized as giving voice to perspectives of silenced persons. This practice brings individuals and the groups they "represent" to the fore though often fails to challenge hegemonic categories or capture how the categories work simultaneously and beyond the micro level. Moreover, the outcome is often an explanation of oppressive groups' experiences to the mainstream. There is often a failure to critique that very mainstream or advantaged position that exists as a result of disadvantage within society. Additionally, its methodological emphasis on inclusion sometimes "fetishizes study of 'difference' without necessarily giving sufficient attention to its relation to unmarked categories" (Choo & Ferree, 2010, p. 133). Thus, it is referred to as the less complicated (though not less complex) methodological approach to intersectional research and as such the most common in literature.

Second Practice: Process-Centered or Capturing Analytic Interactions of Oppressive Regimes

The second practice is typified by comparative and contextualized examinations of "relational" (Glenn, 2000) interactions that are sometimes inter- and at other times anticategorical (McCall, 2005). The emphasis is on the dynamic multilevel forces constructing inequality, or regimes and patterns in which we can identify a collusion of persons' agency and institutional constraints producing advantage/disadvantage. The challenge to its application—it is more complicated to apply to studies than the first practice—lies in methodological design. For example, where might a researcher "look for" or "find" this process? Also problematic for methodological application is the tendency to overemphasize abstract institutions or personify institutional tools such as policy at the expense of agency and persons.

Third Practice: System-Centered or Institutional Complexity

The third practice illuminates "how inequalities span and transform structures and activities at all levels and in all institutional contexts" (Choo & Ferree, 2010, p. 135). Differences exemplified by categories are jettisoned for relational and complex understandings. The challenge is to "identify the local and historically particular configurations of inequalities" (Choo & Ferree, 2010, p. 136). A limitation is the inability to disengage systems of inequality from a particular "level," for example, gender only explained as a personal attribute rather than a complex and transnational system of inequality or class as an economic "problem" part of a global economic system. There are no additions to analyses of inequality when this approach is pursued.

Our intent is not to critique or point out flaws when we apply the framework to the articles found. Like Choo and Ferree (2010), we "attempt to show how and when these three meanings become deployed" (p. 131). We speculate that by reading for the three approaches within the literature selected, we will be able to reveal how the concept is translated and interpreted to interrogate globally circulating education policies. In a sense, the adoption of the practices is an addition to the toolbox needed to theorize education policies in Latin America (e.g., Beech & Meo, 2016) and the many other locations included in this review.

Intersectionality has been theorized and retheorized into academic talk, used less for acting on inequality, a critique and a challenge we do not necessarily overcome with this review. We are wary of contributing to and participating in a process that perpetuates and extends a limited application of intersectionality as a "buzzword" (Davis, 2008) into education policy analysis, but acknowledge our location within the talkative academy, not within a social movement or grassroots organization. Thus, we set as our goal an honest, analytic one, pushing and pulling intersectionality toward clarity in its application in policy analyses and to learn from colleagues located beyond the U.S. academy.

RESEARCH DESIGN

Search Criteria

While Choo and Ferree's (2010) three practices of intersectionality did not require translation, the development of selection criteria entailed a complex process of translation between authors. We had to come to "terms" with transnational and intersectionality, both of which are a bit slippery. In the case of intersectionality, inequality or any number of systems of inequality from ability to xenophobia may be combined as focal concepts within a study selected for review. We initially limited our searches to the term *intersectionality* (more on this below).

Transnational education policy presented similar challenges to define. At times, it appeared as a signifier for globalization or even neoliberalism or just simply, global policy initiatives. We do not wish to conflate transnationalism-to-globalization-to-neoliberalism, nor do we aim to deflate the imagined nation at the behest of a "global." The literature included these various terms often with an explanation of traveling and/or adopted and adapted transnational education policies.

We limited our searches to peer-reviewed articles and to 2006 to 2017 to capture the significant changes in the transnational policy arena. The Millennium Development Goals emerged in 2000 with a goal of completion in 2015, representing significant commitments on global and national scales to address intersectional inequality in education. The delayed timeframe is an acknowledgment of publishing timelines for research and then the peer-reviewed articles produced afterward.

Searches in Multiple Databases and Multiple Languages

We first searched for literature in English, our shared language, using the following terms: *transnational education policy* and *intersectionality*. We used Google Scholar and U.S. academic databases (Academic Search Complete, ERIC, and Education Source). We repeated the search adding on *Southern Hemisphere*, *non-Western Hemisphere*, *Global South*, and *specific nations*. With each search, we sifted through the "hits" for peer-reviewed articles.

Next, we individually conducted searches in Google Scholar, academic databases, and regional or linguistic-specific databases for Chinese and Spanish. Robert conducted the search in Spanish and Yu conducted the search in Chinese. However, before conducting the actual searches, we referred to regional scholars to identify translations for the terms. Spivak (2000) warns against "'convenient' translations, produced without real understanding of the source materials and their cultural history . . . [The translations] signal the danger of generalizing about other cultures from one, powerful (in recent years, Anglo-American) perspective" (von Flotow, 2011, para 12). Meanwhile, K.-H. Chen (2010) argues that translation

gives us a way to conduct reinvestigations that allow the organic shape and characteristics of local society and modernity to surface . . . translation is not simply a linguistic exercise but a social linguistics, or an intersection of history, sociology, and politics. (p. 244)

Heeding these lessons, we consulted Latin American scholars and Chinese scholars for translations for intersectionality and transnational education policy. With the translations, we then conducted searches described below.

For Spanish-language literature, we did not limit the focus by nation, or region. We included articles in Spanish that focus on Latin American contexts and on Spain. The Spain-based studies were included because they also represented analyses of transnational populations, examining the movement of Latin Americans to Spain. We searched with the terms *interseccionalidad* [intersectionality] and *políticas educativas* [education policy] in Google Scholar, Education Source, ERIC, Academic Search Complete, and the Database of Research on International Education as a means of verifying our search results, using English and Spanish terms within them.[3] We also searched within the Scientific Electronic Library Online (SciELO), which is a regional Open Access repository.

For the Chinese literature, we focused on education research in mainland China. We searched China Academic Journals Full-text Database (CNKI) and National Social Sciences Database (NSSD), and looked within journals included in the Chinese Social Sciences Citation Index (CSSCI). It is worth noting that "intersectionality" [jiaochaxing 交叉性] is new to many scholars in mainland China (e.g., Su, 2016) and many Chinese articles do not necessarily use the term *intersectionality* when bringing, for example, class and ethnic inequality in conversation with gender. Thus, we selected articles with combinations of the following keywords: education policy [jiaoyu zhengce 教育政策], education equity [jiaoyu gongping 教育公平], education equality [jiaoyu pingdeng 教育平等], gender [xingbie 性别], female [nüxing 女性], ethnic minorities [shaoshu minzu 少数民族], and class [jieceng/jieji 阶层/阶级]. The search for English-language and Spanish-language studies was fruitful. However, the search for Chinese-language publications initially was not, which is why additional terms were combined to pull forth the studies reviewed.

A full account of addressing the anxiety of "representing Asia" and challenging a biased, circumscribed understanding of Asia via scholarship from mainland China is beyond the scope of this chapter. However, it is crucial to acknowledge the imbalances exacerbated by different colonial experiences and corresponding national tendencies (K.-H. Chen, 2010). We recognize the politics of location and identity shaped by contemporary Chinese society's similar but also unique historical power structure compared with other Asian societies. The educational and social experiences of different groups in China do not represent multiple inequalities that exist regionally. We aim instead to tease out historical transformations within the specific context of lived experiences of invisible groups and varied combinations of systemic inequalities.

The findings are subdivided by intersectional approach—group, process, and systems centered. The three approaches are subdivided to address our three goals—examine three different approaches to intersectional research, identify combinations of inequality, how inequality flourishes in the policy context, and insight from translations.

Selection Criteria

We searched each database using the same combinations of search terms. We then reviewed the hits, selecting articles that met the following criteria. First, we excluded hits that fell outside the 2006 to 2017 timeframe. Then, we selected non-Northern- and non-Western-based researchers, writing about non-Northern and non-Western locations. We actively sought to bring to the fore colleagues' research beyond the metropoles though must acknowledge that within the Southern Hemisphere there are power hierarchies and privilege too.

Then, we sifted through the hits again for peer-reviewed articles. Non–peer-reviewed papers such as those in newsletters and university or faculty bulletins were excluded though often found in the Latin American/Spanish searches. Also found though not included were nongovernmental organization reports and publications. Books and book chapters were excluded. They were catalogued in the databases unevenly. Taylor & Francis dominate but we were unable to ascertain if this is because

Taylor & Francis dominate publishing on related topics or because of the databases' inclusion criteria. We excluded theses, though acknowledge that like books and edited compilations, there is rigor and a review process. However, like books and book chapters, there is an unevenness to their cataloguing in databases. When theses were found in searches, we searched by title and author for peer-reviewed articles to try and include new scholars' work. Finally, we excluded articles that did not focus on an education policy or policies. Our searches and selection process yielded a total of 32 peer-reviewed articles. Each article is identified and summarized in the findings below according to the practice of intersectionality adopted by the authors.

Our analysis of how intersectionality is applied to examine transnational education policy was guided by four questions. First, we identified the intersectional approach employed: group centered, process centered, systems centered. (a) How do scholars attend to the complexity and specificity of intersectionality in relation to transnational education policy? Then, we read the articles for the three goals we alluded to in the review's first paragraph, reworded as questions here and in parentheses we include the shortened subtitle used to identify our responses to the questions in the findings: (b) How does intersectionality help advance our understanding of complex systems of oppression through/in which education policy travels? (Complex combinations), (c) How does the intersectional approach adopted critique whether and how inequality continues to flourish within nation-states and global-level hierarchies? (Inequality flourishes?), (d) How are non-Western/Southern struggles for equity privileged within the intersectional analysis of transnational education policies? (Interpretations beyond). Thus, in short, the findings are organized into three sections, titled as the three practices of intersectionality, and each section contains four subsections.

FINDINGS

Group Centered: Voicing Multiple Experiences of Transnational Education Policies

Three articles were found that applied the first practice of intersectionality to policy analysis: Dieltiens, Unterhalter, Letsatsi, and North (2009); Santamaria (2016); and Serrano Riobó (2014). From its inception, "part of the utility of an intersectional analysis . . . was to give voice to the particularity of the perspectives and needs of women of color who often remained invisible *as women*" (Choo & Ferree, 2010, p. 132, italics in original). Methodologically, the emphasis was on bringing multiply marginalized groups to the center, representing an oppressed position or standpoint that contrasted a mainstream or hegemonic one.

There is a strong tradition of testimonials [*testimonios*] in Latin America, which are first-person narrations of experiences and perspectives. The method has importantly brought the voices of women into the region's literature and historical narratives especially indigenous and politically active (radical) women. Surprisingly, there were only three studies found that applied the first intersectional practice to transnational education policy. Not surprising was the focus of Santamaria (2016) and Serrano Riobó (2014) on bringing the voices of indigenous women to bear on education policies. Santamaria (2016) shares the life trajectories of two Arahauco leaders, who are women, Ati Quigua and Luz Elena Izquierdo, as they negotiated a variety of education barriers from outright exclusion to epistemological dissonance. The article aims to understand how in the context of inclusive and indigenous education contexts the indigenous and women leaders navigated exclusionary Colombian and indigenous culture toward public leadership roles. Serrano Riobó (2014) introduces the educational trajectories of four indigenous women who rose to leadership positions within their communities and within the broader society: Rosa Manuela Montero, pueblo kankuamo leader; Mildred Patricia Montero, peublo kankuamo leader; Beatriz Saniceto, pueblo nasa; and Abigail Piñacué, pueblo nasa. Despite inclusive education policies—addressing ethnicity and gender—the pervasive constraints of intersectional inequality create significant barriers to education capital all the while that capital was crucial to their self-fulfilment and to leadership roles. Within testimonios and their analysis are insights on how indigenous and nonindigenous schools and education policies that create them continue a vicious cycle of oppression while at the same time also offering paths toward education capital.

Dieltiens et al. (2009) also reflected elements of the first practice (and the second and third) but not by bringing forth the voices of multiply marginalized local populations. Rather, the researchers bring to the literature the voices of South African policy actors who are differentially advantaged on a global scale of transnational policy flows. They reveal the limitations of abstract global ideals (in this case the Millennium Development Goals) when enacted as local gender equity policies in the national constitution and in the department of education, ignoring "legacies of gender, race, or location" (Dieltiens et al., 2009, p. 367).

Complex Combinations

There is a "coloniality of power" and "colonization of the mind" (Korol, 2007, as cited in Santamaria, 2016, p. 17) written into the studies in this grouping. Ethnicity and/or racism affect the Arhuaco, Nasa, and Kankuama women's struggles for educational capital despite 25 years of legal and policy acknowledgments (Santamaria, 2016). Naming gender, race, or locational inequality in laws and policies does not address ongoing oppressions within postcolonial contexts. Nations may adopt language and take simple measurements based on headcounts but that does not equate to equality and most certainly not equity. Histories of oppression are not erased by the erasure of exclusionary policies. How many U.S.-based quantitative and qualitative researchers would similarly count boys and girls to illuminate the success of a multitude of transnational educational policy ideals? This question is not meant to give the South African policy actors in Dieltiens et al. (2009) a "break" but to underline the lack of intersectional knowledge among transnational educational policy actors and to question simplistic notions of policy transfer and translation.

By postcolonial, the authors of all three articles in this group are referring to a continuation of a colonial project characterized by White, European, patriarchal hegemony. Within this ideological project, education continues to reproduce a racist and sexist society also layered with a classed/modern industrialized one. History is not so easily erased or smothered by a blanket of new language.

Education was still as Serrano Riobó (2014) titled it: A domination project the indigenous leaders struggled against gender and ethnic marginalization to enter and remain within indigenous and nonindigenous education institutions while also navigating the complex interplay of gender, ethnicity, poverty, and colonialism of everyday life. Education inclusion does not address broader societal exclusion that the women had to navigate to get to the school door.

Inequality Flourishing

Education is steeped in real and symbolic violence. In Santamaria (2016), Luz Elena Izquerdo and Ati Quigua, two Arhuaco women from Colombia, "fac[ed] education policies of latent homogenization from indigenous and educational institutions" (p. 17). For married women—and being married was the means to access education—a double burden is borne as she straddles community expectations and navigates institutional racism and exclusion. Serrano Riobó's (2014) participants, Rosa Manuela Montero and Mildred Patricia Montero (both from the Nasa Community) and Beatriz Saniceto and Abigail Piñacué (both from the Kankuama Community), insist that access to Indigenous educational institutions is quite limited; there is an important need, they explain, to acknowledge how limited access is for indigenous women and men to the few institutions meant to open up paths toward education and that rather than open up opportunities intersectional inequality is intensified based on gender, based on the indigenous community, based on location, based on poverty, and based on access to the colonizers language. Similar constraints to girls' access to education are not addressed by gender parity or gender equality policies in South Africa. What is overlooked is the marginalization in the nonschool arena that constrains access and opportunity within the school for girls.

Additionally accessing educational capital "costs" the women physically, psychologically, historically, and symbolically (Serrano Riobó, 2014). The women had to make difficult choices of divorcing so they might continue their journey of self-actualization and despite the dominant organization of society and women's place within it constrained to marriage and family. The women separated from their children for long periods of time to complete education while living in poverty. The indigenous women who shared their educational trajectories (Santamaria, 2016; Serrano Riobó, 2014) negotiated policy spaces that offered an elusive education capital, constrained by a lack of space within indigenous institutions already isolated and marginalized within the overall Colombian educational system. Attending nonindigenous institutions marginalized the women on a smaller, more personal level.

However, it also pays for access to new labor markets, political communities, and growth. Education also pays back to their families and communities as they return to be leaders or to support siblings and children. In the end, higher education is a prerequisite to self-actualization for women called to lead within the community (though not an expectation). The continued inequality experienced by the indigenous women is a negotiation of trade-offs and transactions, a transformation of historic systems of oppression layered with new ones.

Interpretations Beyond

Like Collins and Choo (e.g., Choo, 2012) desired, intersectionality can be interpreted into contexts beyond the United States to theorize the multiplicity of oppressions women experience. Both Serrano Riobó and Santamaria's studies combine Bourdieu (1997) and Bourdieu and Passeron's (2001) work with Latin American theorists Quijano (2000) and Segato (2010), specifically to theorize intersectionality within transnational, colonial, and postcolonial education projects. This suggests a move toward addressing imbalances in knowledge production necessary to recalibrate equitable transnational education policy knowledge. Unfortunately, Dieltiens et al. (2009) did not integrate other South African theorists or African Feminists, with Nancy Fraser's (1997) theory for recognition and redistribution of power for an emancipatory citizenship.

The three articles challenge inclusive educational discourses. Writing language of equity or equality does not make it appear in everyday educational experiences. Such ideals should be viewed with skepticism as to whether or not they alleviate *the White man's [and woman's] burden* that evolved from previous colonization projects into contemporary postcolonial and/or global ones. As educational policy researchers, do you know the history of the educational institutions and their role within the society that you study?

Intersectionality's travel beyond the United States is quite rich when the first practice is applied. Voices from local contexts are crucial for not only revealing marginalized experiences and perspectives, they are crucial to identifying local manifestations of and critiquing transnational education policy ideals. The three articles applied intersectionality theoretically and methodologically to understand the multiscaled power dynamics of transnational education policy without overlooking the historical legacies of oppression. The shortcomings of globally embraced language to address intersectional inequality is highlighted in each study. These studies reveal the diverging policy interpretations among global, national, and local education policy actors (and researchers for that matter) when transnational policies are interpreted into new contexts without critical and locally grounded reflection of what the ideal might mean in that context. Still, the three studies present policy researchers with the challenge of digging deeper into spaces to include and to learn from local actors' experiences of national and global policies and about local histories of education.

Process Centered: Comparing Interactions on Multiple Levels of Transnational Policies

Six articles were found that applied the second intersectional approach: Brandão and Hill (2014); Dieltiens et al. (2009); Olmos Alcaraz (2016); Balsera (2015); Song (2016); and Torres Corona (2014). The second practice of intersectionality is described as methodologically more complicated than that of the first. The reasons are that it requires comparison and multilevel views of inequality (Choo & Ferree, 2010). For example, Brandão and Hill (2014) situate their study of implementing intersectionality into higher education courses in Ecuador's adoption of the Millennium Development Goals and The Salamanca Declaration of Education for All (1994). How might educators engage in intersectional, not discriminatory, practices through self-reflection and interaction with students? Also, researchers who aim for this approach must move beyond voice to reveal the processes through which oppression is culturally constructed and institutionalized, for example, via policies, normative value systems, or *social imaginaries* (Castoriadis, 1975, 2005, as cited in Torres Corona, 2014). In the case of Torres Corona, it is the processes of parents choosing to send their children to an elementary indigenous school in Mexico that require confronting histories of educational marginalization and reimagining and building new relationships to indigenous culture and to schools. This last concept, social imaginaries, refers to the very process that such an approach "captures" methodologically and theoretically, a dynamic, relational construction, for example, of the school, by social actors in conversation with the "magma" of historical, politicoreligious, socioeconomic, and linguistic images of society (Torres Corona, 2014). The second practice, however, requires explanations of dynamic processes that are not abstracted away from persons. Balance between varied levels of sociocultural constructions is the demand. Song (2016) frames the global-to-national-to-local linkages through transnational policies of inclusion and the adoption of Universal Design for Learning, a Northern and Western–centric philosophy and method for supporting diverse learners and implementing inclusive education. Her study focuses on South African townships, specifically. Balsera (2015) and Olmos Alcaraz (2016) confront the relationships of the colonized and the colonizer. Both examine the case of Ecuadorians who have moved to Spain.

Complex Combinations

Song (2016) succinctly critiques the ongoing application of Universal Design for Learning in the absence of knowledge about disability in the Global South. Her study is designed to bring discourses of disability into conversation with the material and economic conditions in schools on the periphery of global power. What is brought to the fore is the ways that disabilities are embodied by inhabitants of lands that have a history of colonialism, bringing to our attention the domination of Northern and Western epistemologies without regard for context. Unfortunately, Song also finds that receptive South African township teachers (teachers teaching historically marginalized populations with less resources available) are cultivating their own versions of inclusive education that are context specific but not regarded by policymakers or by the teachers themselves as such, reflecting the hegemonic power of globally privileged perspectives.

The result of Song (2016) and of Dieltiens et al.'s (2009) studies is a "more methodologically appropriate and theoretically productive" study of equity and inclusion policies because their "assumptions about intersectionality were made explicit" (Choo & Ferree, 2010, p. 146). By making explicit the complex systems through which transnational education policy travels, the reader learns of policies relational intersectional qualities. At the same time, the authors, as well as Balsera and Olmos Alcaraz, reveal the symbolic violence of a continued "imposition of meanings that overtly legitimize power relations of historical colonial oppression" (Balsera, 2015, p. 159).

Gender is foregrounded by Dieltiens et al. (2009) somewhat reflecting segmented inclusion; however, it is not confined to "microlevel group[s] or individual social psychological-level processes" (Choo & Ferree, 2010, p. 135). Gender is not a simple headcount. Gender is an analytic tool for understanding education policy (Stambach & David, 2005). And gender equity is the connective policy tissue for illustrating the lack of attention to the intersectional legacies of gender–race–location within transnational education policy spaces. Both South African studies "critically interpret assumptions about free and equal citizens which do not consider such legacies" (Dieltiens et al., 2009, p. 367) and thus also bring in a critique of the ways that inequality continues to flourish.

Seeking a trifecta of intersecting inequalities was not the default methodological framework. While a multiplicity of constraining disadvantages was often mentioned, most studies critiqued the interplay of two such as perceived nationality and poverty (Balsera, 2015) or migrant and multilingualism (Olmos Alcaraz, 2016). Studies in this set beautifully illuminated the movement and interplay of complex combinations of oppression with transnational education policies of inclusion such as the relational qualities of antidiscriminatory education (Brandão & Hill, 2014); intercultural/multilingual education to immigration (Olmos Alcaraz, 2016); migrant education to economic and social integration (Balsera, 2015); and Universal Design Learning to disabilities (Song, 2016).

Inequality Flourishing

Legacies of colonialism emerged as a defining factor in the continued reproduction of inequality (Balsera, 2015; Dieltiens et al., 2009; Song, 2016; Torres Corona, 2014). With the demands of this intersectional approach for interactional explanations within local spaces, we are introduced to the enduring effects of colonization, for example, through Ecuadorian youth living in Spain (Balsera, 2015). While Ecuadorian youth share the same language with Spanish youth and teachers, they nevertheless experience marginalization and othering within their schools due to what the youth describe as visible (racial profiling) and less visible (curriculum) factors. A similar regime of othering overshadows the Mexican parents' decision whether or not to send their children to an indigenous elementary school (Torres Corona, 2014). Parents framed the nontraditional education as second class or "poor" compared with traditional schools. Still they send their child to indigenous school because of the better relationship with indigenous teachers or because as indigenous students themselves, the parents recalled the poor treatment at the nonindigenous school by nonindigenous teachers. In both instances, the parents are negotiating educational institutions in which they are marginalized and their own experiences of marginalization shape the schooling decision.

This set of six articles accomplish a difficult task, struggling to put multilevel data in conversation, to compare dynamic processes, and to avoid abstraction like Choo and Ferree (2010) warned. Dieltiens et al. (2009) and Song (2016) are situated in dynamic policy flows of global-to-national-to-practice levels. In both studies, the global is bridged to national level and policymaking is constructed through local practice. Dieltiens et al. (2009) frame the global level through the Millennium Development Goals for gender equity. At the national level, they point out that the "Constitution and the South African Schools Act promise to build a democratic, non-racist and non-sexist education system" (p. 365), adaptations of internal and external policy demands. At the practice level are South African policymakers translating policy for the education system. The authors critique all three levels for overlooking intertwined systems of uneven gender inequality. They urge an awareness that girls' experiences are different among girls: There is no one version of a "third world girl," to rephrase Mohanty (2003), and affirmative action measured by access or attainment does not equalize girls and boys struggles for education. Similarly, Song (2016) puts multilevel data in conversation to contextualize what is presumed to be natural, neutral, and applicable to all children around the world. She raises questions about the production of meaning in such terms as disability that often are overlooked or just ignored.

Brandão and Hill (2014) begin with a promising setup to process-oriented studies of intersectionality with a concern for disrupting the production of multiple inequalities within higher education. While offering strong, concise multileveled policy linkages and discussions of theoretical constructs, there were limited data and analysis of the micro-processes through which such policies are enacted (or not); there were no primary data. Historically and theoretically astute presentations of the polemic were not compared with or critiqued in conversation with the everyday production of intersectional educational inequality at the interstices of educator to student. How in everyday pedagogical engagements is discrimination constructed, or transformed, and practiced in spite of or in relation to the ideals of Education for All? It is clearly not enough to have national policies that embrace equality (as seen in all the cases); it is necessary to look within schools at talk, at curriculum, at practices to deconstruct and transform toward the new/alternative education model. Otherwise, the older framework remains.

Rather than finding only critiques of continued oppression, we also learned from the literature how to change pedagogical practices, support for teachers who wish to reflect on antidiscriminatory (Brandão & Hill, 2014) and intercultural–multilingual

(Olmos Alcaraz, 2016) education. Such contributions to the literature reflect the applied goals of intersectionality to bring change to systems of oppression.

Interpretations Beyond

Authors crafted intersectionality from globally situated, local contexts. In fact, gender–race–class is not the default trifecta/option in this set of articles. Torres Corona (2014), for example, elaborates the intersection of socioeconomic conditions, previous school experience or lack thereof, and indigeneity to understand how parents construct meaning for a Mexican primary indigenous school. This example, like those offered above under the subheading of complex combinations, vividly illustrates that not all transnational policy dynamics are gender-laden and perhaps not global. Torres Corona explains that the dual system of primary and indigenous primary schooling is a 20th-century creation in and of Mexico. Though links can be made with other contexts and globally shared concerns for brutal colonization of indigenous populations and limited education access, the author makes clear that the polemic of educating a culturally and linguistically diverse and unequal population and the challenge of overcoming the marginalization stemming from the very term *indigenous* should be confronted by Mexico, as a nation, a bound system.

Theoretical frameworks driving the studies were predominantly derived from Southern Hemisphere and nondominant locales. While some Northern/Western and White scholars were drawn on (e.g., Harding, Fraser, Foucault, Goffman), there was an epistemological depth and breadth. Freire (1970/2000) and Connell (2007, 2014) represented theorists whose work is embraced across the hemispheric divides. There was only one mention of Crenshaw, a founding mother of intersectionality (Olmos Alcaraz, 2016). This particular article's mention of intersectionality was as a conclusion too. Perhaps the demands of the second approach demand local theory and methodology to bring forth findings.

Systems Centered: Continuity of Complex Historically Bound Systems

Everything interacts and "societies are theorized as historically constructed, arbitrarily bounded systems" (Choo & Ferree, 2010, p. 136) whether the society in question is bound by nation or not. These were the dominant attributes of the third practice of intersectionality that we found in five studies: Chan de Avila, García Peter, and Zapata Galindo (2013); Dieltiens et al. (2009); Pazich and Teranishi (2014); Song (2016); and Torres Corona (2014).

Complex Combinations

These studies dislodged gender and race from persons (Dieltiens et al., 2009; Pazich & Teranishi, 2014) and class from the economy (Torres Corona, 2014), for example, and instead aimed to reveal and critique the complex system of intersectionality in which gender and race and location and ethnicity are "fundamentally embedded in, working through, and determining" (Choo & Ferree, 2010, p. 135) in this case educational opportunity. Some global-level comparative work is included (Pazich & Teranishi, 2014, explained below). However, systems-centered approaches are not always global. Global power is configured and reconfigured within national contexts such as is seen in Dieltiens et al. (2009) and Song (2016), discussed above. In both instances, researchers question the transnational education goals as a masked perpetuation of global hegemonies.

Transnational policies of inclusion also are questioned and examined through a systems-centered approach revealing further combinations of inequality. Torres Corona (2014) examines the impact on national education projects of such inclusive policies as indigenous education choices in Mexico, which are illuminated by the experiences of indigenous parents. Thus, we learn of the problematics of inclusion by looking across history and across the experience–institutional continuum.

While inclusion seems to encourage a dislodging of systems of inequalities at an institutional level and on a broader geographic scale, Chan de Avila et al. (2013) look at the translation of education inclusion and the expansion of educational opportunity on a regional level. They specifically examine new forms of exclusion produced within successful systems of higher education inclusion. What is revealed is, well, intersectionality: Systems of marginalization are tightly woven multithreaded fabrics. Pulling one thread does not necessarily unravel the piece of cloth. Instead, what is left is a new piece of cloth. In the case of Latin American higher education, ". . . one has to ask which Afro-descendants, which indigenous, which women, which men" (Chan de Avila et al., 2013, p. 133) are included (or excluded).

Inequality Flourishes

Policies for alleviating inequality do not always lead to transformation at global, national, or local levels of systemic oppression. The persistence of inequality despite justice-oriented policies was critiqued in higher education affirmative action in Brazil and India (Pazich & Teranishi, 2014) and throughout Latin America as a region (Chan de Avila et al., 2013), as well as in South African inclusion policies for gender (Dieltiens et al., 2009) and disability (Song, 2016).

Indeed, Pazich and Teranishi (2014) reveal how within bound national systems of racial/caste-based and economic inequality, underrepresented groups' access to higher education continues to be limited despite quotas. We, specifically, learned of the shortcomings of India's and Brazil's affirmative action programs in higher education. Higher education policies do not improve access to quality secondary education, which prepares multiply marginalized students for entrance exams and tertiary-level education. Thus, the heavily subsidized universities benefit those who need the subsidies least. Worse though, the policies are revealed to maintain privileged groups' access to this important socioeconomic lever. For example, advantaged groups have been able to manipulate affirmative action to maintain privilege through amendments to the policies, which "water down" the quotas, creating fewer seats for more students. In the case of Brazil, an intersectional "light" adjustment to the affirmative action policy created race- and class-based criteria. The authors explain that the result is less seats for students of color and poor students. The policies are manipulated by groups within power networks (financial, social, political, racial) who continue to attend university in greater percentages than multiply marginalized. This is but one example of many found in the literature detailing how dynamic forces of inequality operate through a "balanced combination of representational, social structural, and power dimensions" (Choo & Ferree, 2010, p. 145) to perpetuate advantaged positions and disadvantaged ones. And it is not just the power of policy/policymakers as in the case of Dieltiens et al. (2009). For example, the media played a significant role along with a national discourse of a "racial democracy" (a color inclusive society) promoting the amendment to the affirmative action policy such that students of color who would lose potential access cited a concern for being provided charity instead of gaining access due to merit.

Advantaged groups are able to mobilize systems of power to coopt policies (Pazich & Teranishi, 2014). The problem is found throughout Latin America leading to the development of a strategic program, Medidas para la Inclusión Social y la Equidad en Instituciones de Educación Superior de América Latina (MISEAL) [Measures for Social Inclusion and Equity in Higher Education Institutions of Latin America]. MISEAL aims to measure statistically, analyze theoretically, and share knowledge via a Latin American network to address the multidimensional nature of exclusion in universities (Chan de Avila et al., 2013).

Interpretations Beyond

We include the Chan de Avila et al. (2013) study less because of its nature as an empirical study and more for its aim to privilege the sharing of knowledge of programs and data collection that are less abstract and more grounded in the bound historical systems in which inclusion and access to a just life and full citizenship is the elusive goal. MISEAL thus represents "a complex intersectional approach that looks for multilevel systems and situates them in local relations of power to expose processes that create and transform inequalities over time" (Choo & Ferree, 2010, p. 145). This project report, published as an article, acknowledges the nature of national systems of higher education as contingent systems within local and historically particular configurations of inequalities but also nods at the macro-level region as an important system within which knowledge can and should be produced and shared.

Conditioning Possibilities of Intersectional Education Policy Research in China

To resist the "colonization of mind" and "coloniality of power" (Quijano, 2000), a growing number of Asian feminist scholars turn to various methodological and theoretical tools of intersectionality to address multiple axes of inequality within their nation-states (e.g., Choo, 2012; Su, 2016). For example, Choo (2012) and Su (2016) took the initial steps of introducing and translating intersectionality into Korean and

Chinese, respectively. In addition, Su (2016) provides an overview of the current trends of sociology and women's studies scholarship in mainland China to demonstrate the various applications of intersectional analysis even though the term *intersectionality* has yet been used in these texts. Such efforts echo a call from other postcolonial scholars in Asia for overcoming "unproductive anxieties" and developing "new paths of engagement," which propose "a means for self-transformation through shifting the points of reference toward Asia and the third world" (K.-H. Chen, 2010, p. 212).

Complex Combinations

China has a wealth of cultural knowledge and diverse forms (e.g., poetry and folklore) in history that resist mainstream education discourses including people from multiply marginalized positions who analyze the internal hierarchy of Chinese education (e.g., Han chauvinism and patriarchal dominance), discuss conflicting social and political culture, and confront education inequality. This tradition emphasizes individual resistance through personal narratives to critique the systems of oppression at micro and macro levels, echoing certain aspects of intersectionality. In addition, the imperialist invasion, semicolonization, and socialist transformation in China's modern history collide with the subsequent late-socialist and neoliberal ideologies in contemporary Chinese society, which implicate the need for a dynamic set of analytic tools to address multilevel forces constructing educational inequality.

Contemporary discussions of educational policies have shown a different path than cultural resources and concrete needs have revealed. For example, gender discourse in a large number of Chinese education studies have been caught up with a constrained version of a Western feminism focused on representing "her" as a pure victim of patriarchy (X. Li, 2002; Zheng, 2005). Such representations neglect the existence of agency and resistance. They also narrow inequality to gender without attending to intersections with class, age, region, and ethnicity (Duan & Yang, 2008; J. Wang, 2008; Zhou, 2007).

The same constraint exists in research concerning ethnic minority education. As a multiethnic country with 56 ethnic groups, there have been contentious struggles to maintain ethnic diversity within a framework of national integration and unity (H. Chen & Yuan, 2015). China's ethnic minority education policies have adapted Fei Xiaotong's framework of "a unified pluralist," with the Han ethnic group as the core (R. Ma, 2007, p. 17), and a limited multicultural education framework for ethnic minority groups (Wan & Bai, 2008). On the one hand, ethnic solidarity, plurality, and preferential policies are in place to provide education for ethnic minority students (J.-Y. Wang, 2006; Yuan, 2010); on the other hand, recognition of multiple axes of inequalities produced by interrelated identities such as gender, class, culture, language, and dis/ability are often subsumed by ethnic diversity into discourses of national unity and social stability. The goal being assimilation of ethnic minority groups into mainstream society (Cherng, Hannum, & Lu, 2014; Hong, 2010).

Inequality Flourishing

A growing number of Chinese education scholars started to pay attention to marginalized groups' different experiences in relation to the multilevel social processes that shape this discrepancy, and try to apply the experiences to address the macro-structures of inequality (Teng, 2009; Wu, 2006). Although these studies have not yet used the term *intersectionality*, many are situated in conversations of gender and class. New studies are emerging that construct dialogues among different categories, for instance, gender, class, ethnicity, migrant status, and so on. Many studies examine the impact of social and political changes in China, marked by the beginning of the reform era in early 1980s, and theorize how dimensions of identities co-construct one another in relation to state power in and symbolic violence of various education policies and practices (X. Chen, 2014; Lü, 2011). As K.-H. Chen (2010) further argues, "The object to be translated has to be subjected to existing social forces and must negotiate with dense local histories if it is to take root in foreign soil" (p. 244). Translation (e.g., Choo, 2012; Su, 2016) and comparison across publications with different foci such as gender–class or gender–ethnicity may allow us to understand intersectionality and to open up a different way of rethinking its characteristics in the Chinese context.

For example, articles by Gong and Luo (2013) and Zhang and Zheng (2016) show ethnic minority women teachers' career pathways and document how their diverse ethnic identities, gender, education background, and class status convey differential advantages and disadvantages "systematically decentering any one process as 'primary'" (Choo & Ferree, 2010, p. 135). Another article (Y. Li, 2010) shares life stories and education experiences of women teachers from Dongxiang ethnic group and analyzes their professional development trajectories from their perspectives. As one of the most economically and religiously marginalized ethnic minority groups in China, Dongxiang people, especially women and girls, are often the objects of stereotypical social and cultural discrimination. Y. Li (2010) focuses on the stories of one Dongxiang teacher living in remote mountainous areas to analyze how education equality and inequality can be understood through connections with a gendering process of ethnic identity. Yet the inclusion of the voices of marginalized groups is just the beginning step. For instance, Y. Li's (2010) article tells this teacher's education experiences as a Muslim girl enrolling in schools and her decisions of family planning for career advancement, while at the same time attending to larger social understandings of this teacher's life overall and the multiple factors affecting her access to education and career development. The data in these articles suggest that "intercategorical" analysis is in place to "highlight dynamic forces more than categories" that highlight "racialization rather than race, economic marginalization rather than class, gendering rather than gender" (Choo & Ferree, 2010, p. 134).

There are studies that analyze how marginalized individuals and groups at the micro-level become aware of the multistructures of power and hierarchies within education policies, representative of Choo and Ferree's (2010) first practice of intersectionality. Such studies pay attention to everyday experiences of power and policy, as well as explore possible ways to engage in conscious forms of resistance within the system (e.g., Lou, 2011; Y. Ma, 2016; Yu, 2015).

A crossover example between the first and the second practices, Lou's (2011) ethnographic study in a rural middle school explores how the lives of a group of rural youth in Northwest China are determined in part by economic and ideological hegemony on global and local scales. She documents the environmental pollution and societal corruption they have experienced due to multiple forms of marginalization, which also penetrate their everyday experiences in school. The discussions demonstrate the various ways they resist the social and educational inequalities reproduced by and in formal schooling.

A similar approach situating multilevel inequalities in local relations of power is evident in Yu (2015). The article concerns how a group of migrant teachers experience and react to their multiple marginalization in urban China but also shows how the mutually constitutive social, gendered, and economic factors inform one another to shape the work and identity of teachers in China's migrant children schools. This article illustrates the links between the patriarchal education system and the neoliberal state in the construction of a social space for women migrant teachers, and highlights the construction of these teachers' resistance and subjectivities in the context of profound personal and structural transformations in their lives. This last example may also blend elements of the second and third approach to intersectionality.

Interpretations Beyond

We see potential for applying the ideals of intersectionality for critical examination of educational issues produced within and by local and global gender, ethnic, economic, religious, and regional politics in China. Not only is there potential for exploring the voices of marginalized groups but also for transforming theory and praxis. Nevertheless, these articles also point to a crucial component necessary for intersectional analyses in China from China. Specifically, multiply marginalized groups are agents of neither the state, nor civil society, since these spaces are overwhelmingly occupied by social elites. Marginalized populations exist at the margins of politics. When they do appear in politics they are framed as out of place, challenging the existing modes of state control. Their resistances and struggles are considered to be illegal. Thus, researchers need to pay attention to the important role of the state and the different spatial relationship between the state and society.

Efforts to redefine the boundaries of intersectionality in Chinese contexts should not simply be regarded as an attempt to be included into knowledge production without complicating "the Eurocentric premises of social science knowledge" (Takayama, 2016, p. 81). Chinese, or Korean, or Japanese scholarship has long been treated as a separate development without possible interactions with the English-language scholarship (Takayama, Sriprakash, & Connell, 2017, p. S6). Rather, as Takayama et al. (2017) argue,

The challenge is to move away from "thin inclusion" or selective incorporation of "diverse" scholars and texts. Such additive models do little to challenge the prevailing hegemony. A "thick inclusion" of Southern, postcolonial theories and scholars in higher education, on the other hand, moves closer toward epistemic reflexivity, a focus on how things can be known. (p. S16)

This project thickens conversations on how intersectionality can be understood in Chinese contexts to facilitate a critical examination of educational issues produced within and by local and global gender, racial, ethnic, economic, religious, and regional politics.

CONCLUSIONS

This review applied Choo and Ferree's (2010) three practices of intersectional analysis to examine transnational educational policy research conducted in the Southern Hemisphere and China, published in English, Spanish, and Chinese. We now turn back to the questions we aimed to answer with this review.

How Does Intersectionality Translate to Languages Other Than English and to Eastern and Southern Contexts?

Intersectionality translated to the literature produced from and on the Southern Hemisphere whether written in English or Spanish but not as often as we had anticipated. We had expected to find many more articles in which the concept was applied to examine education policy. The lower number may be the result of search criteria that were too constrained. It also may be that researchers are conducting intersectional research by another name, or perhaps be calling out the multiple systems of oppression they find.

Our findings revealed a balance across the three practices for the literature in English and in Spanish, while the Chinese literature leans more on group- and process-centered practices. This is a finding considering that one of the reasons offered by the framework's authors (and the hunch of this literature review's authors) was that the first practice would be overrepresented. It is considered to be a bit easier theoretically and methodologically to accomplish. This was not the case. As for the Chinese research literature, the historical contexts of the development of intersectionality might be seen as differing in certain respects—Chinese scholars complicate practices by demonstrating how to bring multiple axes of inequalities into conversation with one another without using this relatively "new" term. Through the review, it is also important to keep in mind that rather than merely considering the complex political system as "an independent variable," one should pay attention to how state policies and politics actively shape the challenges and possibilities of engaging critical scholarships, in this case, intersectional analysis of systematic inequalities in different contexts.

What Analytic Insights Are Gained From Intersectionality's Travel and Translation That May Contribute to Its Reconceptualization in Northern and Western Contexts?

A large body of comparative education scholarship uncritically accepts Northern and Western epistemology "as a coherent, bounded entity that has given rise to special events, concepts, and paradigms that are now diffused throughout the world" (Takayama et al., 2017, pp. S4–S5). Scholars have proposed decentering the global North in knowledge production (Anzaldúa, 1987; Carney, Rappleye, & Silova, 2012; K.-H. Chen, 2010; Connell, 2007, 2014) to undermine the uneven power relations that naturalize the intellectual division of labor, provincialize the universalist ontology and epistemology that underpin official knowledge, and revalue knowledges that have been subjugated by global hegemony (e.g., Fischman & Gandin, 2016; Takayama, 2016). This review aimed to complicate the "framing and selling" of global education policy and its underlying logics and systems (Verger, 2012) that enhance inequality and introduce new forms of oppression simultaneously on multiple scales.

Analyzing for the three practices—group centered, relation centered, or systems centered—was quite difficult. Conducting rigorous intersectional analyses is a mighty difficult task as is a review of such analyses. Patricia Hill Collins, one of the scholars credited with coining the concept, suggested as much at the American Educational Research Association's annual conference (April 29, 2017). She confessed that bringing into focus the multiple axes of oppression is difficult and that often one axis is foregrounded while others are backgrounded.

Still this endeavor has reinforced our concern for conducting theoretically and methodologically rigorous research of transnational education policies. In fact, the literature review has proved to us that one does not just decide to take on intersectionality as a theoretical framework for looking at policy. Researchers must take on the methodological challenge of constructing education (policy) studies and critiquing data through an analytic lens attuned to the multiscalar production and experience of intersectional inequality.

How Have Scholars, Practitioners, and Activists Used Intersectional Approaches to Address Complex Educational and Social Problems and Promote Interventions That Foster Equity and Social Justice?

This review aimed to contribute insight to the issue's third key area, providing insight as to how scholars, practitioners, and activists in the Southern Hemisphere and China used intersectional approaches to address complex educational and social problems and promote interventions that foster equity and social justice.

Southern and Eastern contexts are transnational spaces of knowledge made invisible and colonized multiple times albeit under a different guise (e.g., Takayama et al., 2017). Colonization is layered and the colonization of indigenous groups continues into the 21st century. Within knowledge production arenas and public intellectual networks, the power dynamics between scholars is complicated too; it is not unidirectional. There are advantages and disadvantages at play within the institutional systems of academia and publishing and far too infrequently the system is questioned. We deploy intersectionality as a productive theoretical and methodological tool to examine transnational dynamics and to seek new forms of knowledge production.

With this project, we suggest that the North and West can learn much from Southern and Eastern contexts, but that learning endeavor requires three fundamental processes. First, from the North and West, it is necessary to look at the conditions of knowledge colonization that developed over the course of centuries (e.g., Connell, 2007; Said, 1978). That begins for us with an awareness that intersectionality is a theory from the North and West though with the purpose of pointing out the inequities within hegemonic contexts, specifically African American women's experiences to bear on legal systems, acknowledging that gender and race (and class, etc.) acted simultaneously to shape experiences, not separately. This calls into question essentializing systems that treat all women as equally unequal (e.g., Mohanty, 2003). Has intersectionality as theory been translated and transformed to understand the multiplicity of oppressions experienced within the transnational policy contexts we seek to learn from?

Second, from the South and East, there is a need for decolonization processes so as to cultivate regional knowledge without doing so in relation to the North and the West (e.g., de Sousa Santos, 2008; Mignolo & Escobar, 2010; A. L. Muñoz García, personal communication with Robert, May 4, 2017). How, if at all, has intersectionality been linked to or compared with knowledge from the South? Or within China? How have scholars beyond hegemonic locales transformed the theory for critiquing transnational education policy? Or what are the forms of intersectional theory within these contexts?

Third, it is important to acknowledge that theories are not simply reproduced in different contexts. There is always a process of appropriation, rereading, and modification. Still theories require a dialogue, not a monologue, in any transnational conversation. Theories must be thought through in terms of zones of privilege (who is privileged, where, when, why, by what/whom) not only in their site of origin but also in the temporal context in which they are interpreted and from whose pen they emerge and travel to a new transnational space. What zones of privilege are interpreted within and across transnational spaces and across the history of those spaces?

Not only is our deployment of the term *transnational* theorized, it is practiced. We, the authors, traveled to multiple continents, engaging in dialogues with scholars about this literature review, seeking feedback. We wish to be a part of a public intellectualism that is transnational and we wish to cultivate it collaboratively. Guzmán-Valenzuela and Muñoz García (2018) elaborate three current forms of academic partnerships: among advanced-economy countries in which every country has a similar role and position; another between advanced- and emerging-economy countries with a logic of "dominance of Western hegemonic research models to research dependent" (Naidoo, 2008, p. 258); and a third form involving learning and critiquing in "real time" and over time, creating and developing spaces to produce knowledge through encounters beyond hegemonic metropoles (see the work of the Inter-American Symposium on Ethnography and Education). For scholars located within advanced economies, this entails seeking out scholarship beyond our work locations and our research sites as we attempt to do in this literature review.

We found a broad range of social categories of inequality in the crosshairs of the policy research. This represents the multiple combinations of oppression globally. However, read another way, it also suggests that scholars, practitioners, and activists are attuned to the local conditions of oppression that globally circulating education policy is meant to address and may or may not be doing so. Thus, literature like what was reviewed here merits reading by a broader audience that includes policymakers and others in/with power to reform policy or formulate it to address inequity. In particular, our application of a framework that sought out the production of intersectional inequality on multiple scales (personal, interpersonal, and institutional) addresses the complexity of the contemporary education policy environment where local/national communities interpret and practice global policy idea(l)s. Rigorous intersectional analyses may prove to be invaluable tools for transnational policymaking and policy analyses.

NOTES

[1]We use the terms *practices* and *approaches* interchangeably in the article to refer to how we sought and analyzed intersectionality in the literature.

[2]We also keep in mind the danger of constructing third-world women monolithically and as victims, ignoring their agency and voice. Mohanty (2013) also reminds us of the "representational politics" characteristic of hegemonic feminist knowledge production within neoliberal landscapes. Our task is not to claim a voice for third-world women. Instead, this project allows us to learn from their work.

[3]Thank you to Christopher Hollister, education librarian, at the University at Buffalo Graduate School of Education, for search suggestions and for verifying search findings across multiple databases.

ORCID IDS

Sarah A. Robert 🆔 https://orcid.org/0000-0001-8151-2240
Min Yu 🆔 https://orcid.org/0000-0002-7614-0355

REFERENCES

Ang, I. (2003). I'm a feminist but . . . "other" women and postnational feminism. In R. Lewis & S. Mills (Eds.), *Feminist postcolonial theory: A reader* (pp. 190–206). New York, NY: Routledge.

Anzaldúa, G. (1987). *Borderlands/La Frontera: The New Mestiza*. San Francisco, CA: Aunt Lute Books.

Asher, N. (2007). Made in the (multicultural) USA: Unpacking tensions of race, culture, gender, and sexuality in education. *Educational Researcher, 36*(2), 65–73.

Ball, S. J. (2016). Following policy: Networks, network ethnography and education policy mobilities. *Journal of Education Policy, 31*, 549–566.

Ball, S. J., & Junemann, C. (2012). *Networks, new governance, and education*. Bristol, England: Policy Press.

Balsera, M. R. (2015). Are schools promoting social and economic integration of migrant and ethnic minorities? The experiences of some young people of Ecuadorian background in Spain. *Journal of Critical Education Policy Studies, 13*, 148–172.

Beech, J., & Meo, A. I. (2016). Explorando el uso de las herramientas teóricas de Stephen J. Ball en el estudio de las políticas educativas en América Latina [Exploring the use of Stephen J. Ball's theoretical tools to study education policies in Latin America]. *Archivos Analíticos de Políticas Educativas, 24*(23). doi:10.14507/epaa.24.2417

Bourdieu, P. (1997). *Razones prácticas. Sobre la teoría de la acción* [Practical reason: On the theory of action]. Barcelona, Spain: Anagrama.

Bourdieu, P., & Passeron, J. (2001). *La reproducción: Elementos para una teoría del sistema de enseñanza* [Reproduction in education, society, and culture]. Madrid, Spain: Popular.

Brandão, T., & Hill, D. (2014). Herramientas de transversalización de género en la educación superior: Una propuesta de pedagogía no discriminatoria en Ecuador [Gender mainstreaming tools in higher education: A proposal for nondiscriminatory pedagogy in Ecuador]. *Cuestiones de género: de la igualdad y la diferencia, 9*, 379–401.

Braun, A., Maguire, M., & Ball, S. J. (2010). Policy enactments in the UK secondary school: Examining policy, practice and school positioning. *Journal of Education Policy, 25*(4), 547–560.

Bunjun, B. (2010). Feminist organizations and intersectionality: Contesting hegemonic feminism. *Atlantis: Critical Studies in Gender, Culture & Social Justice, 34*, 115–126. Retrieved from http://journals.msvu.ca/index.php/atlantis/article/viewFile/338/319

Carney, S., Rappleye, J., & Silova, I. (2012). Between faith and science: World culture theory and comparative education. *Comparative Education Review, 56*, 366–393.

Chan de Avila, J., García Peter, S., & Zapata Galindo, M. (2013). Inclusion social y equidad en las institutiones de educacion superior de America Latina [Social inclusion and equity in Latin American higher education institutions]. *ISEES, 13*, 129–146.

Chen, H., & Yuan, T. (2015). Some theoretical orientations and development trends of studies of Chinese minority education based on documentary research. *Northwest Journal of Ethnology,* (2), 62–71. [In Chinese]

Chen, K.-H. (2010). *Asia as method: Toward deimperialization.* Durham, NC: Duke University Press.

Chen, X. (2014). The current research of anthropology of education in China: Content and focus. *Sociology Review of China, 2*(6), 78–89. [In Chinese]

Cherng, H. S., Hannum, E., & Lu, C. (2014). China. In P. A. J. Stevens & A. G. Dworkin (Eds.), *The Palgrave handbook of race and ethnic inequalities in education* (pp. 205–237). London, England: Palgrave Macmillan.

Cho, S., Crenshaw, K. W., & McCall, L. (2013). Toward a field of intersectionality studies: Theory, applications, and praxis. *Signs, 38*, 785–810.

Choo, H. Y. (2012). The transnational journey of intersectionality. *Gender & Society, 26*(1), 40–45.

Choo, H. Y., & Ferree, M. M. (2010). Practicing intersectionality in sociological research: A critical analysis of inclusions, interactions, and institutions in the study of inequalities. *Sociological Theory, 28*, 129–149.

Cole, B. A. (2009). Gender, narratives and intersectionality: Can personal experience approaches to research contribute to "undoing gender"? *International Review of Education, 55*, 561–578.

Collins, P. H. (2000). *Black feminist thought: Knowledge, consciousness, and the politics of empowerment.* New York, NY: Routledge.

Collins, P. H., & Bilge, S. (2016). *Intersectionality.* Cambridge, England: Polity.

Connell, R. (2007). *Southern theory: The global dynamics of knowledge in social science.* Cambridge, England: Polity.

Connell, R. (2014). Rethinking gender from the South. *Feminist Studies, 40*, 518–539.

Crenshaw, K. (1991). Mapping the margins: Intersectionality, identity politics, and violence against women of color. *Stanford Law Review, 43*, 1241–1299.

Davis, K. (2008). Intersectionality as a buzzword: A sociology of science perspective on what makes a feminist theory successful. *Feminist Theory, 9*(1), 67–85.

de Sousa Santos, B. (Ed.). (2008). *Another knowledge is possible. Beyond Northern epistemologies.* New York, NY: Verso.

Dieltiens, V., Unterhalter, E., Letsatsi, S., & North, A. (2009). Gender blind, gender-lite: A critique of gender equity approaches in the South African Department of Education. *Perspectives in Education, 27*, 365–374.

Duan, C., & Yang, G. (2008). Situations with rural girls who remain living in the countryside. *Collection of Women's Studies,* (6), 18–25. [In Chinese]

Fimyar, O. (2014). What is policy? In search of frameworks and definitions for non-Western contexts. *Educate, 14*(3), 6–21.

Fischman, G. E., & Gandin, L. A. (2016). The pedagogical and ethical legacy of a "successful" educational reform: The Citizen School Project. *International Review of Education, 62*(1), 63–89.

Fraser, N. (1997). *Justice interruptus: Critical reflections on the "postsocialist" condition.* London, England: Routledge.

Freire, P. (2000). *Pedagogy of the oppressed.* New York, NY: Continuum. (Original work published 1970)

Gillborn, D. (2015). Intersectionality, critical race theory, and the primacy of racism: Race, class, gender, and disability in education. *Qualitative Inquiry, 21*, 277–287.

Glenn, E. N. (2000). The social construction and institutionalization of gender and race. In M. M. Ferree, J. Lorber, & B. B. Hess (Eds.), *Revisioning gender* (pp. 3–43). Walnut Creek, CA: AltaMira Press.

Gong, T., & Luo, Z. (2013). Bottleneck restriction and route dependence in the development of rural minority female teachers in Guangxi Province. *Journal of Research on Education for Ethnic Minorities, 24*(2), 54–58. [In Chinese]

Gonzalez, T., Tefera, A., & Artiles, A. (2015). The intersection of language and disability: A narrative in action. In M. Bigelow & J. Ennser-Kananen (Eds.), *The Routledge handbook of educational linguistics* (pp. 145–157). New York, NY: Routledge.

Grant, C. A., & Zwier, E. (2011). Intersectionality and student outcomes: Sharpening the struggle against racism, sexism, classism, ableism, heterosexism, nationalism, and linguistic, religious, and geographical discrimination in teaching and learning. *Multicultural Perspectives, 13*, 181–188.

Grzanka, P. R. (2014). *Intersectionality: A foundations and frontiers reader.* Boulder, CO: Westview Press.

Guzmán-Valenzuela, C., & Muñoz García, A. L. (2018). Decolonizing international collaborative work: Creating new grammars for academic partnerships in Chile. In L. Gornall, B. Thomas, & L. Sweetman (Eds.), *Exploring consensual leadership in higher education: Co-operation, collaboration and partnership.* London, UK: Bloomsbury.

Hancock, A. M. (2016). *Intersectionality: An intellectual history.* New York, NY: Oxford University Press.

Hong, Y. (2010). Ethnic groups and educational inequalities: An empirical study of the educational attainment of the ethnic minorities in western China. *Chinese Journal of Sociology, 30*(2), 45–73. [In Chinese]

Li, X. (Ed.). (2002). *Culture, education and gender: Local experience and discipline construction.* Nanjing, Jiangsu, China: Jiangsu People's Press. [In Chinese]

Li, Y. (2010). Dual variation between inheritance and reform: A narrative study on career development of a female teacher of Dongxiang ethnic group. *Journal of Research on Education for Ethnic Minorities, 21*(2), 47–51. [In Chinese]

Lou, J. (2011). Transcending an urban–rural divide: Rural youth's resistance to townization and schooling, a case study of a middle school in Northwest China. *International Journal of Qualitative Studies in Education, 24*, 573–580.

Lü, X. (2011). *Gender perspective of hidden curriculum: An educational anthropology in Dongxiang primary and secondary schools.* Lanzhou, Gansu, China: Gansu Education Press. [In Chinese]

Ma, R. (2007). The subjects and approaches of current ethnic affairs study in China. *Journal of the Central University for Nationalities (Philosophy and Social Sciences Edition), 34*(3), 12–38. [In Chinese]

Ma, Y. (2016). School education, the development of urban minority migrants: Based on the study of children's education of Xinjiang migrant families in Keqiao. *Journal of South-Central University of Nationalities (Humanities and Social Sciences), 36*(6), 68–72. [In Chinese]

McCall, L. (2005). The complexity of intersectionality. *Signs, 30,* 1771–1800.

Mignolo, W., & Escobar, A. (Eds.). (2010). *Globalization and the de-colonial option.* London, England: Routledge.

Mohanty, C. T. (2003). *Feminism without borders: Decolonizing theory, practicing solidarity.* Durham, NC: Duke University Press.

Mohanty, C. T. (2013). Transnational feminist crossings: On neoliberalism and radical critique. *Signs, 38,* 967–991.

Mohanty, C. T., Russo, A., & Torres, L. (Eds.). (1991). *Third World women and the politics of feminism.* Bloomington: Indiana University Press.

Nagel, A.-K. (2010). Comparing education policy networks. In K. Martens, A.-K. Nagel, M. Windzio, & A. Weymann (Eds.), *Transformation of education policy* (pp. 199–226). New York, NY: Springer.

Naidoo, R. (2008). Higher education: A powerhouse for development in a neo-liberal age? In D. Epstein, R. Boden, R. Deem, F. Rizvi, & S. Wright (Eds.), *Geographies of knowledge, geometries of power: Framing the future of higher education* (pp. 248–265). New York, NY: Routledge.

Olmos Alcaraz, A. (2016). Diversidad lingüístico-cultural e interculturalismo en la escuela Andaluza: Un análisis de políticas educativas [Cultural-linguistic diversity and interculturalism in an Andaluzan school: An analysis of education policies]. *RELIEVE, 22*(2), 7.

Patil, V. (2013). From patriarchy to intersectionality: A transnational feminist assessment of how far we've really come. *Signs, 38,* 847–867.

Pazich, L. B., & Teranishi, R. T. (2014). Comparing access to higher education in Brazil and India using critical race theory. *Widening Participation and Lifelong Learning, 16*(1), 50–69.

Pillow, W. S. (2017). Policy studies debt: A feminist call to expand policy studies theory. In M. D. Young & S. Diem (Eds.), *Critical approaches to education policy analysis* (pp. 261–274). Cham, Switzerland: Springer International.

Posey-Maddox, L. (2017). Schooling in suburbia: The intersections of race, class, gender, and place in black fathers' engagement and family-school relationships. *Gender and Education, 29,* 577–593.

Powers, J. M. (2014). From segregation to school finance: The legal context for language rights in the United States. *Review of Research in Education, 38,* 81–105.

Purkayastha, B. (2012). Intersectionality in a transnational world. *Gender & Society, 26,* 55–66.

Quijano, A. (2000). Colonialidad del poder, eurocentrismo y América Latina [Coloniality of power, Eurocentrism, and Latin America]. In E. Langer (Ed.), *La colonialidad del saber: Eurocentrismo y ciencias sociales. Perspectivas Latinoamericanas* (pp. 122–151). Buenos Aires, Argentina: CLACSO.

Robert, S. A. (2017). US teachers as policy protagonists in digital public spaces? *Peabody Journal of Education, 92*(4), 521–536.

Said, E. (1978). *Orientalism.* London, England: Routledge & Kegan Paul.

Santamaria, A. (2016). Ethnicity, gender, and higher education. Trajectories of two Arhuaco women in Colombia. *Convergencia, 70*, 1–21.

Segato, R. (2010). Los causes profundos de la raza latinoamericana: Una relectura del mestizaje [The deep causes of Latin American race: A re-reading of *mestizaje*]. *Crítica y Emancipación*, (3), 11–44.

Serrano Riobó, Y. (2014). Itinerarios escolares y procesos políticos de cuatro mujeres indígenas nasa y kankuamo [School itineraries and political processes of four indigenous Nasa and Kankuamo women]. *Desafíos, 26*, 171–198. doi:10.12804/desafios26.1.2014.05

Song, Y. (2016). To what extent is Universal Design for Learning "universal"? A case study in township special needs schools in South Africa. *Disability and the Global South, 3*, 910–929.

Spivak, G. C. (2000). The politics of translation. In L. Venuti (Ed.), *The translation studies reader* (pp. 397–416). London, England: Routledge.

Stambach, A., & David, M. (2005). Feminist theory and educational policy: How gender has been "involved" in family school choice debates. *Signs, 30*, 1633–1658.

Su, Y. (2016). Intersectionality: A new perspective for Chinese sociology of gender. *Sociological Studies*, (4), 218–241. [In Chinese]

Takayama, K. (2016). Deploying the post-colonial predicaments of researching on/with "Asia" in education: A standpoint from a rich peripheral country. *Discourse: Studies in the Cultural Politics of Education, 37*(1), 70–88.

Takayama, K., Sriprakash, A., & Connell, R. (2017). Toward a postcolonial comparative and international education. *Comparative Education Review, 61*(Suppl. 1), S1–S24. doi:10.1086/690455

Teng, X. (2009). *Education for girls in a multicultural society: Introduction to China's ethnic minority education for girls*. Beijing, China: Publishing House of Minority Nationalities. [In Chinese]

Torres Corona, V. (2014). Imaginarios sociales sobre la primaria indigena en Puebla. Un estudio desde las elecciones escolares de los padres de familia [Social imaginaries of Puebla's indigenous elementary school. A study of parents' school choices]. *Revista Mexicana de Investigación Educativa, 19*, 1117–1139.

Verger, A. (2012). Framing and selling global education policy: The promotion of public–private partnerships for education in low-income contexts. *Journal of Education Policy, 27*, 109–130.

von Flotow, L. (2011, October 1). *Contested gender in translation: Intersectionality and metramorphics*. Retrieved from http://palimpsestes.revues.org/211

Wan, M., & Bai, L. (2008). A comparison between the Western multicultural education and Chinese ethnic education. *Ethno-National Studies*, (6), 32–41. [In Chinese]

Wang, J. (2008). A longitudinal study of the problem of school dropouts of adolescent girls in ethnic minority poverty-stricken areas. *Journal of Research on Education for Ethnic Minorities, 19*, 116–121. [In Chinese]

Wang, J.-Y. (2006). *Northwest ethnic minority basic education status and development strategy*. Beijing, China: Publishing House of Minority Nationalities. [In Chinese]

Wu, D. (2006). Reflections on issues of establishing an educational equity mechanism. *Educational Research, 27*(1), 38–41. [In Chinese]

Yu, M. (2015). Revisiting gender and class in urban China: Undervalued work of migrant teachers and their resistance. *Diaspora, Indigenous, and Minority Education, 9*(2), 124–139.

Yuan, T. (2010). Problems of schooling among ethnic minorities from the perspective of educational equality. *Journal of Yunnan Nationalities University, 27*(3), 138–143. [In Chinese]

Zhang, L., & Zheng, X. (2016). A study of the localized strategy of developing female school leadership in southwestern ethnic regions. *Journal of Research on Education for Ethnic Minorities, 27*(3), 49–56. [In Chinese]

Zheng, X. (2005). *Gender and education.* Beijing, China: Educational Science Publishing House. [In Chinese]

Zhou, X. (2007). Gender equity in education from a feminist perspective: Through analyzing three metaphors. *Journal of Huazhong Normal University (Humanities and Social Sciences), 46*(6), 125–130. [In Chinese]

Chapter 6

Intersectional Analysis in Critical Mathematics Education Research: A Response to Figure Hiding

Erika C. Bullock iD
University of Wisconsin-Madison

In this chapter, I use figure hiding as a metaphor representing the processes of exclusion and suppression that critical mathematics education (CME) seeks to address. Figure hiding renders identities and modes of thought in mathematics education and mathematics education research invisible. CME has a commitment to addressing figure hiding by making visible what has been obscured and bringing to the center what has been marginalized. While the tentacles of CME research address different analytical domains, much of this work can be connected to the social isms *that plague our world (e.g., sexism, racism, heterosexism, colonialism, capitalism, ableism, militarism, nationalism, religious sectarianism). However, the trend in CME research is to address these* isms *in silos, which does not reflect the compounded forms of oppression that many experience. I review CME studies that employ intersectionality as a way of analyzing the complexities of oppression. Intersectionality's limited use in CME research has been for identity-based analyses. I offer intersectional analysis as a strategy to extend intersectionality's power beyond identity toward more systemic analyses.*

It is a rare occasion when Hollywood and mathematics education converge. It happened in late 2016 as the Hollywood publicity machine prepared for *Hidden Figures* (Gigliotti et al., 2016), a film adaptation of Margot Lee Shetterley's 2016 book. The film depicts the stories of Mary Jackson, Katherine Johnson, and Dorothy Vaughan, Black women mathematicians who worked for NASA (National Aeronautics and Space Administration) and played key roles in support of John Glenn's 1962 orbit of the Earth. The film has prompted a surge in public discourse about girls and women in science, technology, engineering, and mathematics (STEM), as corporations and

Review of Research in Education
March 2018, Vol. 42, pp. 122–145
DOI: 10.3102/0091732X18759039

media have used the movie as a launching point to discuss broadening participation in STEM. *Hidden Figures* is part of a recent surge of efforts to amend the dominant historical record to include the unlikely and unsung contributors to developments in mathematics and science. This idea of hidden figures is central to much of the work of critical mathematics education (CME) research.

CME is neither a discrete domain of research nor a distinct political agenda. Rather, it represents a position that mathematics education can be used as a tool both to uncover and to prevent injustice (Alrø, Ravn, & Valero, 2010). If there were a unifying idea behind manifestations of CME, it would be that mathematics is a social, political, cultural, and economic product that "may provoke both exclusion and suppression" (Skovsmose, 2012, p. 343). Therefore, rather than having a shared sense of meaning, it can be said that CME has a shared sense of purpose. CME research takes on multiple characters, but all of them address, in some way, ideas of exclusion and suppression that render some invisible.

I offer figure hiding as a metaphor representing this invisibility. Often the hidden figures with which CME is concerned are everyday people who have been marginalized within or excluded from mathematics education (e.g., Henningsen, 2008; Heyd-Metzuyanim & Graven, 2016). Some CME researchers are concerned with how mathematics education hides identities (e.g., de Freitas, 2004; Gholson, 2016); some examine cultural forms of mathematics as hidden figures within academic mathematics discourse (e.g., D'Ambrosio, 1985; Greer & Mukhopadhyay, 2012); some consider how the politics of mathematics education requires certain modes of thought and exclude—or hide—others (e.g., Gutiérrez, 2008; Kollosche, 2014). Some examine specific practices, policies, and pedagogies (e.g., Gutstein, 2006; Larnell, 2016). Others use different theories and methodologies to urge the community toward a full rethinking of the enterprise of mathematics education (e.g., Stinson & Bullock, 2012; Thunder & Berry, 2016). Regardless of focus, CME has a commitment to addressing figure hiding by making visible what has been obscure and bringing to the center what has been marginalized.

While these tentacles of CME research address different analytical domains, much of this work can be connected to the social *isms* that plague our world (e.g., sexism, racism, heterosexism, colonialism, capitalism, ableism, militarism, nationalism, religious sectarianism, or extremism). Unfortunately, in the absence of a unifying sense of CME's commitments (Skovsmose, 2012), researchers operate most often in silos attached to these *isms*. While it is useful to focus on the singular analytical frame, isolating oneself within that frame can be dangerous as it limits the flow of ideas and limits what is visible. There is a distinct divide, for example, between Marxist CME research and race- or gender-based CME research. This separation is not unique to CME; there is a long-standing critique that Marxism ignores race and gender and that, likewise, race- and gender-based research do not acknowledge class (Hartmann, 1979; Leonardo, 2004). Race and gender scholars accuse Marxist scholars of reducing all inequalities to struggles against capital. It is also not new within social science to consider these *isms* together. However, mathematics education is emerging as a field prone to consider these *isms* (and others) separately, if at all.

This shift in the field of mathematics education is important because the siloed sensibility does not align with the way that most people experience these *isms* as sociopolitical forces. Attending to certain forms of domination while marginalizing others creates a false representation of how oppression works that reinstantiates some of the very divisions targeted for change. The response to oppression cannot be any less complex than oppression itself. Absent modes of analysis that confront this messiness head-on, there is a lingering question of how practices in CME reinscribe the distinctions and divisions that qualify some and disqualify others, thus undermining CME's goals of inclusion and justice. I envision intersectional analysis as a mechanism to address this issue. In this chapter, I review extant CME research that employs intersectionality and consider the possibilities that intersectional analysis offers for these and future studies in CME. The guiding questions for the review are the following: *How has intersectionality been applied in CME research? What methodological potential does intersectional analysis bring to CME research?*

CRITICAL MATHEMATICS EDUCATION RESEARCH

I envision CME research as encompassing two distinct, yet potentially related, modes of thought. First, there is critical research in mathematics education that applies critical theories to questions in mathematics education. This form of CME maintains an internal focus "concerned primarily with how mathematics is learned and taught" (Greer & Skovsmose, 2012, p. 3). Specifically, researchers in this manifestation concern themselves with how people who have been marginalized participate in mathematics education and how that participation can be improved. This internally focused approach uses critical theories to examine how figures are hidden within the structure of mathematics education (e.g., representation in mathematics courses).

The second mode of thought in CME focuses on the political nature of mathematics education and on the connection between mathematics education and critical education (Ernest, 2010; Skovsmose, 1985). The rise of critical education and Freirean thought catalyzed a movement within mathematics education research with an external focus on "how mathematics education might be stratifying, determining, and justifying inclusions and exclusions" (Skovsmose, 2014, p. 139). Freire declared that education is political and that the classroom should be politically engaged. Incorporating ideas from critical education into mathematics education shifted the focus from internal to external, "concerned with the embeddedness of mathematics education and mathematics within historical, cultural, social, and political contexts, and the implications and ramifications thereof" (Greer & Skovsmose, 2012, p. 3). For Fasheh (2012), the concern is with mathematics' ability to "contribute to protecting life or destroying it" (p. 93). In other words, this way of thinking about CME focuses externally on how mathematics education operates in the world. In this mode of thought, for example, hidden figures include the non-Eurocentric cultures and communities whose mathematics are not granted legitimacy within academic mathematics discourse (Joseph, 1987).

An important aspect of CME's "attempt to reconcile school mathematics as a site of political power, ethical contestation, and moral outrage" is a commitment to "confront[ing] the problems of access and opportunity according to skin color, gender, and class" (de Freitas, 2008, p. 48). Therefore, the internal and external approaches to CME are connected. These two ways of thinking reveal that CME is not the property of a group of researchers; rather, it is an orientation toward mathematics education research that "[criticizes] existing bodies of knowledge, theories, methodologies, and classroom practices, especially in relation to social inequality" (Collins & Bilge, 2016, p. 31). Therefore, while some may identify as CME researchers, the CME designation can be assigned to any work oriented in this way.

Mathematics education relies on the assumption that mathematics is devoid of ideological commitments and "bereft of ethical principles that might fuel moral outrage" (de Freitas, 2008, p. 47). CME, in its external focus, has a role in challenging these assumptions. One example of CME's critique of mathematics' assumptions is the idea of *mathematics identity*. Martin (2000) conceptualizes mathematics identity as a socially constructed identity akin to race, gender, or ability. Martin's mathematics identity is composed of four dimensions: "(a) [students'] ability to perform in mathematical contexts, (b) the instrumental importance of mathematical knowledge, (c) constraints and opportunities in mathematical contexts, and (d) the resulting motivations and strategies used to obtain mathematics knowledge" (p. 19). Research in mathematics identity is a way for CME to address the epistemic figure hiding implicit in perceptions of mathematics as a mode of thought that operates outside of social or political influence. If mathematics identity is constructed, then there exists an opportunity for it to be reconstructed, which opens different possibilities for analysis.

Solomon, Radovic, and Black (2015; also see Solomon, 2012) challenge the assumptions about mathematics' political neutrality by investigating how women who are successful in mathematics negotiated their participation and gender performances in the masculinized world of mathematics. This is a comment on mathematics as a discursive structure. The authors argue that Roz, the subject of this study, experiences a "contradiction between doing mathematics and enacting femininity."

Here, we can see that Roz views the other women as having resolved the contradiction between being female and being a mathematician by taking on masculine characteristics in order to fit into the world of mathematics, she has chosen to be different—to enact a different kind of mathematical identity, which retains simultaneously a strong and visible femininity (signalled by the use of the cultural tools of skirt and heels) alongside the mathematics. (p. 63)

Roz sees her feminine and mathematician identities as incommensurable. She chooses to perform traditional femininity through her dress as an act of resistance to the figure hiding of mathematics' masculine sensibility. This account speaks further to the exclusionary norms of mathematics.

Ernest (2010) proposes that those interested in CME should "question the state of mathematics education as a field of study" (p. 3). Skovsmose (2011) adds that CME, like any other critical project, should be characterized by a profound sense of uncertainty. In this review, I take up Ernest's proposal with the tentativeness that Skovsmose advises, asking, "What is the present state of the ideas, theories, research and publications in [mathematics education] and what should [or could] it be?" (Ernest, 2010, p. 3). However, as a perspective on mathematics education, CME is not itself exempt from critique (Ernest, 2010; Skovsmose, 2011). In this spirit of critique, I consider how intersectionality has been used in CME research and the potential that intersectionality offers CME to think differently about how forms of oppression operate within and through mathematics education.

INTERSECTIONALITY AND INTERSECTIONAL ANALYSIS

Legal scholar Kimberlé Crenshaw (1989, 1991, 2013) brought the term *intersectionality* into academe, and Black feminist scholars in the United States such as Zandria F. Robinson (2016), Brittney Cooper (2015), and Patricia Hill Collins (Collins, 1990/2009, 2015; Collins & Bilge, 2016) and abroad such as Nira Yuval-Davis (2006) have advanced this work to the point where it has become a significant concept in broader feminist scholarship (Davis, 2008). Crenshaw (1989) saw that the justice concerns of Black women were often subsumed in antiracist and feminist politics for Black people or women, broadly considered. However, a Black woman's experience is neither a *Black* experience nor a *woman's* experience, so "this single-axis framework erases Black women in the conceptualization, identification and remediation of race and sex discrimination by limiting inquiry to the experiences of otherwise-privileged members of the group" (Crenshaw, 1989, p. 140). Elsewhere she explains,

Racism as experienced by people of color who are of a particular gender—male—tends to determine the parameters of antiracist strategies, just as sexism is experienced by women who are of a particular race—white—tends to ground the women's movement. The problem is not simply that both discourses fail women of color by not acknowledging the "additional" issue of race or of patriarchy but that the discourses are often inadequate even to the discrete tasks of articulating the full dimensions of racism and sexism. Because women of color experience racism in ways not always the same as those experienced by men of color and sexism in ways not always parallel to experiences of white women, antiracism and feminism are limited, even on their own terms. (Crenshaw, 1991, p. 1252)

Here, Crenshaw points to the limits of both feminist and antiracist approaches as they relate to women of color. Each of these analytical axes, taken separately, hides the woman-of-color figure who experiences race different from men of color and gender different from White women.

Crenshaw (1989) proposes intersectionality to acknowledge "those who are multiply-burdened" (p. 140) by different modes of oppression—or different *isms*. The idea of multiple burdens speaks to intersectionality's key concern that racism, sexism, and other forms of oppression, when considered in parallel, appear additive, but those who experience these oppressions in combination endure multiplicative effects

(Choo & Ferree, 2010; Crenshaw, 1989; Robinson, 2016; Yuval-Davis, 2006). Collins (1990/2009) uses the term *matrix of domination* to refer to the "overall social organization within which intersecting oppressions originate, develop, and are contained" and the "historically specific organization of power in which social groups are embedded" (p. 246). The matrix of domination addresses how oppression is organized through social institutions such as government, health care, and (mathematics) education. Intersectionality creates the possibility for researchers to investigate oppression within a matrix of domination.

In recent years, intersectionality has garnered increased attention in academic and public circles as those who have been oppressed seek to articulate the multiple layers of subjugation that correspond to different identities. Intersectionality embraces a more postmodern approach to identity politics that particularizes the intersections of identity categories (Crenshaw, 1991). For example, a person who identifies as a queer Black woman experiences oppression in the name of racism, sexism, and heterosexism based on her racial, gender, and sexual identity, respectively. Intersectionality acknowledges that there is energy required to address each of these identities and that a person must sometimes make difficult decisions when those identity politics conflict.

Intersectionality's presence and proliferation in academic spaces represents a form of grassroots theorizing. A Black woman (Crenshaw) used her scholarly position as a vehicle to represent the practices and embodied knowledges that, historically, have characterized the lived experiences of her women-of-color foremothers who must simultaneously navigate the complexities of gender, race, language, and other identity politics (Collins & Bilge, 2016). Although the terminology is recent, there is a long history of intersectional analysis by both women-of-color scholars and lay scholars. Crenshaw's work rests on the shoulders of women like Sojourner Truth, Anna Julia Cooper, Gloria Anzaldúa, Ida B. Wells-Barnett, Paula Gunn Allen, The Combahee River Collective, and countless other known and unknown women who have shaped the consciousness of women of color through the verbal and written articulation of their lived experiences (Gines, 2011). Like Crenshaw, Cooper (2015) identifies her mother's and grandmother's teachings as more than just simple life lessons:

Because of Black feminism, I understand the *theorizing* that my mother and grandmother taught me to do as being critical and crucial to my survival as a Black woman of Southern [United States], semi-rural, working-class origins now navigating a middle class, urban, academic life. (p. 10, emphasis in original)

The theorizing that Cooper's mother and grandmother taught her—and that my mother and grandmothers taught me—is not considered "appropriate" or "rigorous" enough for academic discourse based on academe's tendency toward figure hiding through elitist and exclusionary practices of legitimizing knowledge (Gines, 2011). Naming these articulations as Crenshaw did is a form of scholarly legitimization that makes them "more compatible with academic norms of discovery, authorship, and ownership" (Collins & Bilge, 2016, p. 80).

One significant characteristic of intersectionality is its commitment to praxis (Cho, Crenshaw, & McCall, 2013; Collins & Bilge, 2016).[1] The women of color who have embraced intersectionality as both an intellectual and practical approach to the world throughout history have not had the luxury of separating their intellectual work from their efforts to survive the matrix of domination (Cooper, 2015). Therefore, the women who have advanced intersectionality within academe have retained praxis as a significant part of that conceptualization. Given this legacy, it is not enough to think through the multiple ways in which oppression weighs on various identities, but it is the scholar's responsibility to use her or his power to do something in response. This focus on praxis also validates the knowledges that lay scholars who do not share our academic credentials bring to this work and promotes collaboration within and outside of academe.

It is also noteworthy that, although intersectionality is best known and most often articulated as a means of considering domination, oppression is not necessarily its focus. Rather, intersectionality considers the operations and intersections of social structures (which often are oppressive).

It is worth emphasizing that intersectionality is *not* the opposite of privilege or advantage: it is possible to be intersectionally advantaged or privileged as well as intersectionally marginalized, dominated or oppressed. . . . The idea of intersectionality also points out that social structures not only disadvantage particular groups (as the language of burdens [or oppression] suggests); they also privilege certain groups, again, in ways unique to particular gender-race-class groupings. Every person is marked by multiple social structures. So the idea of intersectionality criticizes, improves on, and moves beyond the language of double or triple burdens as well as the concept of "dual systems." (Weldon, 2008, pp. 196, 197, emphasis in original)

In this excerpt, Weldon dispels a myth that intersectionality is only a way to comment on oppression by raising the idea that intersectional advantage and disadvantage are not mutually exclusive. For example, while an able-bodied Latinx girl and a Latinx girl with a physical disability may experience similar racial and gender oppression, the able-bodied girl has relative privilege related to ability. Intersectionality allows the researcher to examine how these two girls would experience situations differently based on this relative privilege. There is also an opportunity to use intersectionality to examine how these girls' experiences reflect the interaction of systems characterized by racism, sexism, and ableism. For example, discourses of health and physical fitness in schools may disparage foods that Latinx families eat or can access, which is an example of racism within these discourses. Additionally, proposing walking as a way to promote health at no cost marginalizes the child who is unable to walk freely. This point underscores the messiness of intersectional analyses and the need to continue to think deeply about how intersectional analyses can capture these nuances.

Models for Intersectional Analysis

Collins and Bilge (2016) propose a distinction between *intersectionality* and *intersectional analysis* to capitalize on the theory's potential beyond identity. Once understood only as a theory of identity, intersectionality has taken on broader meaning over time, and intersectional analysis has become a way to engage intersectionality in critical inquiry. Intersectional analysis represents a move in critical *ism*-focused scholarship "from parallelism to simultaneity and multiplicity" (Robinson, 2016, p. 491). As "oppressions must work together to produce injustice" (Collins, 1990/2009, p. 21), intersectional analyses interrogate both the individual modes of oppression and the entanglements that the matrix of domination produces. Weldon (2008) articulates intersectional analysis' potential beyond intersectionality's identity focus: "It refers to a form of relationship between social structures, specifically one in which social structure combine to create social categories to which certain experiences and forms of oppression are unique" (pp. 195–196). Scholars have taken this shift from identity-focused to structural thinking as an opportunity to create analytical frameworks that encourage broader thinking about intersectionality.

Crenshaw (1991) establishes three forms of intersectionality: structural intersectionality, representational intersectionality, and political intersectionality. Choo and Ferree (2010) provide a similar three-part framework—group-centered approach, process-centered approach, and institution-centered approach. These ways of thinking about intersectional analysis make apparent the broad potential that this theory offers for reading the world. They each investigate figure hiding in different ways, taking an "intersectionality-only" or "intersectionality-plus" approach (Weldon, 2008). Weldon (2008) adopts the mathematical vocabulary of matrices to explain the difference:

> Drawing on the idea of a "matrix of domination," I suggest that the concept of intersectionality directs our analytical attention to the possibility that there are effects or experiences that are unique to each cell, not shared by other groups in the same "row" or "column." The *intersectionality-only* approach demands that we focus on each cell individually, eschewing a broader analysis of each social structure . . . the *intersectionality-plus* approach admits that there might be "row and/or column" effects as well as cell-specific effects or experiences. (p. 217)

The intersectionality-only approach considers the domains represented in the matrix of domination (e.g., race, gender, ability) as elements that combine equally to create a cell-specific form of subjection. Like Collins and Bilge's (2016) intersectionality, this model assumes a unity among intersectional identities that occupy the same cell (e.g., Native American women). The intersectionality-plus approach—like Collins and Bilge's intersectional analysis—resists this unification by acknowledging that different *isms* (i.e., different rows or columns) operate in different ways in different contexts. Said differently, the relevance of social structures varies across sociopolitical and sociohistorical contexts. Therefore, the intersectionality-plus model is "more elastic" and "it *travels* better" (Weldon, 2008, p. 218).

Choo and Ferree's (2010) typology maps, in part, onto Crenshaw's (1991). This mapping creates the analytical framework that I use for the review of literature later in this chapter. At the risk of introducing undue complexity, I created a new set of names for the four approaches to intersectional analysis (i.e., identity, conflict, institutional, and discourse models). These names reflect more clearly the focus of each model (e.g., "identity model" reflects structural intersectionality and the group-centered approach's

TABLE 1
Framework for Four Models of Intersectional Analysis Based on Crenshaw (1991) and Choo and Ferree (2010)

Model	Weldon (2008)	Crenshaw (1991)	Choo and Ferree (2010)
Identity model	Intersectionality-only	Structural intersectionality	Group-centered approach
Conflict model	Intersectionality-plus	Political intersectionality	—
Institutional model	Intersectionality-plus	—	Institution-centered approach
Discourse model	Intersectionality-plus	Representational intersectionality	Process-centered approach

focus on identity). Table 1 shows the four models of intersectional analysis that I propose and the elements from Crenshaw and Choo and Ferree that each represents. The table also indicates which of Weldon's (2008) approaches corresponds with each model. The conflict and institutional models map onto only Crenshaw and Choo and Ferree, respectively. Below, I describe each of these models.

Identity Model

Structural intersectionality (Crenshaw, 1991) and the group-centered approach (Choo & Ferree, 2010) constitute the identity model. This intersection-only model addresses how intersections of identity categories create different life experiences. One's location within the matrix of domination affects the ways that they experience all aspects of life. The identity model is the most familiar appropriation of intersectionality as it is concerned with "giving voice to the oppressed" (Choo & Ferree, 2010, p. 130) by explicitly acknowledging the complexity of identities—or the different cells in the matrix of domination. This approach to intersectionality relies on the idea that figure hiding occurs when analytical focus is on only one dimension of identity (i.e., one row or one column) or when identities are considered as composite rather than compounded. In these situations, those who are multiply marginalized can be excluded, at worst, or included with limited understanding, at best.

Domestic violence is an issue that transcends race, gender, and class, but strategies to support people who experience domestic violence often do not take experiences of the multiply marginalized into account (Crenshaw, 1991). For example, women who do not speak English have limited access to domestic violence support services. When materials advertising support resources are in English and shelters do not have translation services, how do these women get support? They are hidden figures. Failure to consider language in designing domestic violence support services creates a situation that may appear supportive to women but leaves one group without recourse. An identity model approach to intersectionality requires domestic violence service providers to consider how identities in different cells of the matrix of domination experience their services and adjust accordingly.

Conflict Model

The conflict model is an intersectionality-plus approach that encompasses Crenshaw's (1991) political intersectionality. Crenshaw concentrates on women of color whose experiences align with at least two dimensions of oppression based on race and gender. Political intersectionality acknowledges that these women must distribute their political energy among different agendas that may conflict because each is designed based on those who have privilege within that category. Antiracist and feminist projects center on race and gender, respectively. In the interest of furthering justice for women, feminist projects can perpetuate racism because they center on White women. Likewise, antiracist efforts can perpetuate patriarchy while working for racial justice by centering on men. Figure hiding occurs in these blind spots. The woman-of-color figure is hidden as she negotiates an interest in justice based on both race and gender. Aligning with feminist politics means enduring racial subjugation, while aligning with antiracist politics means turning a blind eye toward misogyny. In either case, the woman of color cannot trust these efforts to represent her fully.

Crenshaw (1991) uses rape as an issue that exemplifies the conflict model. When a woman accuses a man of rape, her race largely determines what follows. If the woman is White and the man is Black, the accused will likely be presumed guilty and treated harshly. In the case where a Black woman accuses a White man, there will not likely be a resumption of guilt and any prosecution. This differential response to an interracial rape accusation creates a dual sense of injustice. Black men accused of raping White women are less likely to receive due process, so advocacy related to these men focuses on the idea that there is a long-standing practice of punishing them for rape without substantiation. Similarly, there is a long-standing precedent of White men raping Black women with impunity and of using narratives of Black women's sexual promiscuity to negate sexual assault claims. Policies that support victims' rights and the aggressive prosecution of sexual assault do so in the interest of "all women" with White women as the icon of a rape victim. Antiracist advocates oppose strong sexual assault laws because of the disproportionate effect on Black men. In this case, Black women victims "fall into the void between concerns about women's issues and concerns about racism" (p. 1282).

Institutional Model

Choo and Ferree's (2010) institution-centered approach constitutes the institutional model. This intersectionality-plus model applies intersectional thinking to institutions. Often, we connect certain *isms* with certain institutions (Choo & Ferree, 2010; Weldon, 2008). Class or capitalism are often central to discussion of economic institutions such as the World Bank, the mortgage industry, or the labor market. The idea of the economy relies on economic theory. Therefore, economic theory (e.g., capitalism) will likely be central, and class will appear to be the only element of oppression at issue in economic discussions. In this case, it is not possible to take an intersectionality-only approach because it is not possible to consider all modes of power equally when there is a sense of primacy of class. Thus, the focus on class hides how other *isms* operate through economic institutions. The institution-centered approach to intersectional analysis permits *isms* to have *primacy* within institutions but not *exclusivity*. Figure hiding occurs in this case when the central concern eclipses any other systems that may be in operation. Choo and Ferree (2010) argue that the institution-centered approach to intersectionality forces us to view systems as complex structures:

> The account of intersectionality as a complex system sees gender and race are fundamentally embedded in, working through, and determining the organization of ownership, profit, and commodification of labor, for example, by fixing which types of work and types of people enter the market at all. (p. 135)

The authors argue that issues of labor are issues of class, race, *and* gender, so it is not enough to lump labor issues under a label of capitalism or class without attending to how capitalism "uses race and gender to support itself" (p. 135).

Another ready example of the institutional model is the family. When discussing family, the analysis is more commonly related to gender or sexism (Choo & Ferree, 2010). The example of family presents a more reasonable possibility that the primary focus on gender could eventually shift from its place of primacy as the sociohistorical constructs of family and marriage face political challenge. However, the dominant Western discourse of the family remains gendered and heteronormative. Considering sexuality in conversations about the family reveals the inequities in policies that do not allow for families formed outside of state-sanctioned means. Same-sex partnerships, even if legally recognized, face increased scrutiny or outright discrimination in adoption proceedings. Adding an intersectional analysis based on heterosexism to the gender-primary domain of the family reveals complexity in family discourse that is not plain.

Discourse Model

Representational intersectionality (Crenshaw, 1991) is an intersectionality-plus approach related to the production of cultural images and how racial and gender metanarratives shape these images and perpetuate the marginalization of women of color. Similarly, Choo and Ferree's (2010) process-centered approach takes a wide-angle perspective on how structures organize power. These two approaches contribute to the discourse model and are about hidden systems. Here, figure hiding is the myopic focus on one *ism* at the exclusion of others in a way that limits the scope of analysis. Figure hiding can also occur in a failure to acknowledge the dynamic nature of systems—"racialization rather than races, economic exploitation rather than classes, gendering and gender performance rather than genders" (p. 134).

One can consider reactions to the Black Lives Matter (BLM) movement in the United States as an example of the discourse model of intersectional analysis. BLM formed in direct response to a discourse that repeatedly articulates through actions that Black lives have no value. As BLM has emerged as a political force, the response from the mainstream political structure has placed BLM in the crosshairs of militarism and terrorism. Public officials have deployed tanks, riot gear, and extreme police force in response to BLM protests. Narratives in the media frame those who exclaim "Black lives matter!" as domestic terrorists without acknowledging the racial terror that prompts the protests. By enacting discourses of militarism and terrorism, the political establishment creates a discursive image of BLM activists as threats to the public peace, thus reinforcing the matrix of domination (Hooker, 2016; Taylor, 2016).

REVIEW METHOD

I selected the sample of literature for this analysis through two initial searches using the terms *intersectionality mathematics education* and *intersectionality math education* in Google Scholar. These searches yielded 742 unique results. From the results, I pulled only the peer-reviewed journal articles and eliminated articles that were clearly not mathematics education research based on the title, abstract, and/or keywords (e.g., STEM education studies, studies in mathematics addressing intersectional algebras), leaving 39 articles. These articles were all published between 2008 and 2016. After reading each article, I put it into one of three categories: mention (for articles in which the authors used the words "intersectional" or "intersectionality" in passing; 20 articles), recommendation (for articles in which the authors recommend intersectionality as a limitation of their work or as a means to expand the analysis but do not conduct an intersectional analysis; 11 articles), application (for articles in which the authors use intersectionality as the central analytical framework; 5 articles), and conceptual (for conceptual articles and reviews; 3 articles). The articles in this review come from the application category. I chose to focus on empirical articles that use intersectionality as a core part of their theoretical framework to best address the following research questions: *How has intersectionality been applied in CME research? What methodological potential does intersectional analysis bring to CME research?*

To address the first research question, I turned to Bowleg's (2008) recommendations for intersectionality research based on her experience researching Black lesbians. Bowleg argues that intersectionality research requires effort beyond traditional qualitative narrative analysis and proposes two additional phases to honor the complexity of intersectionality. First, researchers who use intersectionality must commit to a transdisciplinary approach to research that allows them to understand the broader sociohistorical discourses that are at work. They must take up a broad scope of analysis that requires a sophisticated sociohistorical understanding. The second additional phase of analysis that Bowleg suggests entails the explicit examination of tensions with respect to the intersections of identities. In this phase, the researcher should pay attention to how tension and contradiction manifest in their analysis and spend time interrogating those spaces. In this review, I looked for evidence of Bowleg's recommendations by asking the following questions: Does the author address broader sociohistorical discourses? Does the author engage the tensions inherent in the intersections of identities?

TABLE 2
Description of Each Model of Intersectional Analysis

Model	Description
Identity model	Intersections of identity categories create different life experiences and these different experiences must be considered.
Conflict model	Those who are multiply marginalized must negotiate often conflicting political commitments.
Institutional model	In situations where certain *isms* have primacy, they are not exclusive.
Discourse model	Structures organize power in ways that perpetuate and maintain the matrix of domination.

For the first and second research questions, I use the framework that I created based on Crenshaw (1991) and Choo and Ferree's (2010) typologies of intersectionality (Table 1). In Table 2, I describe each element of this framework based on the comparison detailed in the previous section. In the next section, I describe each of the five studies and its findings. Then, I use Bowleg's two criteria and the intersectionality models from Table 2 to analyze how intersectionality is applied in the study. Finally, I return to the intersectionality models to propose a way that the researchers could approach the study differently through another model. For the sake of space, I choose one model on which to base an alternative framing that demonstrates additional methodological potential for intersectional analysis (i.e., Research Question 2).

INTERSECTIONALITY IN MATHEMATICS EDUCATION RESEARCH

There are few mathematics education researchers who employ intersectionality as a theoretical framework. However, it is common for mathematics education researchers to recommend intersectionality as a potential means to further their analyses of race or gender. Damarin and Erchick (2010) call on intersectionality's most common use in race–gender analysis to assert that "attention to the intersection of clearly defined constructs, including gender" is required to address issue of equity in mathematics for girls and women (p. 312). Although it is most common for intersectionality to surface in gender- and race-related studies in mathematics education, some mathematics education researchers suggest this theory for analysis related to other identities. Lambert (2015), for example, argues that intersectionality is useful for considering how disability intersects with race. Scholars such as Berry (2008) and McGee (2015) position intersectionality as a way of thinking about how mathematics identity operates with racial identity. For those mathematics education researchers who center on intersectionality in their work, there are varying modes of engagement. The five studies that emerged from the review as applications of intersectionality theory represent the present scope of intersectionality research in mathematics education.

Esmonde, Brodie, Dookie, and Takeuchi (2009)

Esmonde et al. (2009) investigated how students' identities affect their cooperative group work in an urban secondary mathematics classroom. Operating from the premise that "*who students are* influences what and how they learn together" (p. 19, emphasis in original), Esmonde and colleagues focus on students' articulations of their own identities and how they matter in the mathematics classroom. The authors take up intersectionality as an approach to acknowledge the multiplicity of identity and use sociocultural learning theories to understand these identities in practice. They also used critical race theory (CRT) to analyze race, stereotype threat to analyze how identity impacts individual performance, and expectation states theory[2] to understand how identities operate in group work. However, they employed intersectionality to acknowledge a limiting assumption in expectation states theory. While expectation states theory treats identities as additive, the authors assert that "multiple status characteristics can qualitatively influence one another" (p. 23). To capture identities in practice, Esmonde and colleagues analyzed the classroom as a single case, but to ensure that they acknowledged the particularities of student identity, they conducted a second level of analysis with each student. The researchers coded student interviews for explicit and implicit references to identities such as race, gender, and grade level.

In their presentation of results, Esmonde et al. (2009) outline two phases of analysis. In the first phase, they used the whole class as the unit of analysis and coded the data for themes related to group work. In the second analytical phase, they chose a sample of students to analyze individually. This student-level approach allowed the authors to look more deeply into participants' comments to see how their identities affected their experiences of group work. They observed that students engaged in group work according to the identities that they claimed and that they made decisions about their classmates based on identities that they imposed on them. For example, the boys assumed leadership positions more frequently than girls. In interracial groups of boys, White boys led more than boys of color. Likewise, White girls led in interracial groups of girls. However, in heterogeneous gender groups of the same race, girls did not lead. The authors also observed that identity affects the benefits of group work for students. Although teachers use cooperative learning as a means of support for students who struggle, the authors noted that a White student did not slow the pace to support a Black girl in the group who needed help.

I classify this study in the identity model of intersectional analysis because Esmonde et al.'s (2009) multiphase analysis highlights both the implicit and the explicit effects of identities on cooperative group work in secondary mathematics. They address intersectionality as a concept that characterizes the student participants' identities and reveals the limitations of an established theory. A limitation of the study with respect to intersectionality is that the authors do not present theories of gender, socioeconomic status, urbanism, or other social categories represented in the participants' identities, which limits the analysis with respect to Bowleg's (2008) recommendation for incorporating transdisciplinary literatures. This also limits the potential for an intersectional analysis of the identities themselves. In their data reporting, Esmonde and colleagues acknowledge intersectional identities by referring to participants in multiple-identity terms (e.g., White girl, Latinx boy), but they largely report results in terms of single dimensions of identity (e.g., race, gender, grade level) and combined identity categories (e.g., students of color). Although they allude to shifting privilege for some students (i.e., the White girl who would lead only in groups with students of color), they do not dig into the tensions of intersectional identities as Bowleg recommends, nor do they consider what issues like the inability to assume a leadership role mean for students at the bottom of the intersectional hierarchy (i.e., girls of color).

By engaging in two analytical phases, Esmonde et al. (2009) address the figure hiding that occurs when mathematics education researchers do not look deeper into the data for less obvious social meanings. However, the study also perpetuates figure hiding in that the discussion of differential experiences and opportunities in group work is done only at the level of identity; the discursive structure of mathematics education that creates and maintains these differences remains hidden. The discourse model of intersectional analysis offers another way to consider Esmonde et al.'s (2009) study results at this discursive level. The exclusion that they noted relative to leadership responsibilities and benefits of group work occurs within the mathematics classroom, a space that has been identified as masculinized (Solomon et al., 2015) and as an institutional space of whiteness (Martin, 2011). Therefore, the experiences of these students are not idiosyncratic; they are the result of the way in which mathematics education has organized itself through patriarchy and White supremacy.

Riegle-Crumb and Humphries (2012)

Riegle-Crumb and Humphries (2012) explore how tracking in high school mathematics courses creates different contexts in which students experience stereotypes. The authors argue that mathematics teachers are gatekeepers for students' mathematics trajectories. They perform a quantitative analysis on national course-taking data from high school transcripts in the Education Longitudinal Study of 2012. They were looking for evidence of teacher bias in course assignment based on gender and race using White males as the comparison group. Riegle-Crumb and Humphries use intersectionality to move beyond prior studies that address gender and race separately. The study's findings suggest that after taking achievement differences into account, "teachers do not perceive male and female minority students as having lower math ability than their white male peers" (p. 312). In fact, the data show that teachers have more confidence in Black female students in advanced classes than White male students because of the figure hiding that they have overcome to get there.

Riegle-Crumb and Humphries (2012) ground their use of intersectionality in general feminist literature instead of the core literature from Black feminism (apart from one citation of Patricia Hill Collins). This observation introduces an important issue relative to intersectional analysis. Cho et al. (2013) argue that intersectional analysis is bigger than a particular genealogy and that a work is intersectional based on "its adoption of an intersectional way of thinking about the problem of sameness and difference and its relation to power" (p. 795). Although the absence of Black women in citations does not undermine the application of intersectionality in this study, it does signal a form of figure hiding. As mentioned in earlier sections, intersectionality is a recent instantiation of a long-standing epistemic practice among women of color who remain nameless and without credit. Crenshaw (1989, 1991) named intersectionality as a direct response to marginalization of Black women from mainstream feminism. Neglecting to credit Black women in discussions of intersectionality connotes a similar dysconscious marginalization.

The identity model is the most appropriate representation of Riegle-Crumb and Humphries' (2012) study. Their intent was to move beyond separate analyses of mathematics course-taking based on race or gender to consider these factors together. The study did not take up the broader sociohistorical discourses that affect course-taking decisions. Student test data were a contributing factor to the disparities that the authors address, and they did account for it in the analysis. However, they do not engage with how students experience the "long structure of testing and prerequisites extending back to middle and elementary school" (p. 295) in racialized and gendered ways that limit their possibilities in high school. The nature of this large-scale study did not lend itself to the depth of analysis related to the intersectional tensions that Bowleg recommends.

Riegle-Crumb and Humphries' (2012) study demonstrates the potential power for a national-level intersectional analysis in the discourse model. Looking at students longitudinally can help show how race/gender patterns in mathematics emerge, shift, and are maintained over time. It would also be valuable to include data such as socioeconomic status, parent education, food access, and teacher experience to see how these factors contribute to racial and gender disparities in mathematics achievement.

Gholson and Martin (2014)

In their study of a group of Black girls in third grade, Gholson and Martin (2014) used intersectionality "to highlight the constructed nature of studying age, race, and gender" (p. 19). They argue that childhood, itself, is an identity marker, so research about Black girls requires that the researcher consider these girls not only as Black and female but also as children who are "forming and maintaining complicated, history-rich interpersonal relationships with each other" (p. 19). With this analysis, Gholson and Martin's goals were not only to investigate Black girls' positions within Collins's (1990/2009) matrix of domination but to go a step further and "acknowledge Black girlhood as a context for nurturance, support, and competence" (Gholson & Martin, 2014, p. 20).

Gholson and Martin (2014) focus the analysis on two Black girl students—Shawna and Mia—and characterize their experiences and relationships in the mathematics classroom as moving between social network positions as "bullies, smart girls, mean girls, and Black girls" (p. 24). Both Shawna and Mia were coded as bullies. Shawna got into physical altercations with peers, and her larger stature encouraged this classification from her peers. Mia's peers described her as verbally aggressive. However, both girls' mathematical competence earned them labels as smart girls. Shawna expressed a self-confidence in mathematics that did not translate to her social life where she was isolated. Mia, on the other hand, was a key part of a social group that included other girls who were mathematically successful. The authors coded Mia's group of popular girls as mean girls because they used their social power to maintain exclusion even in the mathematics class. The Black girls label related to the girls' self-identification as Black or African American. Shawna described her racial identification with certainty, while Mia's understanding of race allows for a broader sense of what blackness is. In spite of their identification as Black, both girls expressed a desire to fit into more Eurocentric ideas of beauty. Mia's proximity to these standards—her lighter skin, long hair, and thinner body—afforded her privilege from others that Shawna did not experience due to her darker skin, shorter hair, and heavier body.

With respect to Bowleg's (2008) recommendations for intersectionality research, Gholson and Martin's (2014) emic approach creates a narrative of the hidden Black-girl-child figure that counters dominant sociohistorical narratives of children as nonagentic or Black girls as invisible "'background noise' in a larger view of urban life that prioritizes men and boys" (Morris, 2016, p. 18). Putting Black girlhood in a positive light helps reframe perceptions of Black girls as defiant, loud, and more mature than their age indicates (Morris, 2016). The authors also outline an analytical process that confronts the tensions and complexities inherent in the intersectional analysis of three identity categories (i.e., Black, girl, and child). Their large corpus of data combined with the extended ethnographic engagement in the classroom—multiple times per week for the school year—promoted a rich, multilayered analysis.[3] By engaging in analytical separation (Gholson & Martin, 2014), they could analyze the data through single-identity lenses and bring those analyses together to negotiate the conflicts among them.

Gholson and Martin's (2014) study largely falls within the identity model of intersectional analysis as its greatest contribution is to explore the complexity of the Black-girl-child identity category. They also entertain the conflict and discourse models through their analysis of differentiated intraracial privilege. To extend the analysis into the discourse model, the authors could zoom in on the issues of colorism raised in the Shawna and Mia's identification as Black girls. Martin (2011) argues that mathematics education is White institutional space, and Stinson (2013) further charges that mathematics is governed by a "white male math myth." Under these conditions, the Black-girl-child is invisible at the bottom of the racial and gender hierarchies of mathematics (Gholson, 2016). Colorism assigns privilege to people of color based on their physical proximity to whiteness. Further intersectional analysis can explore how this proximity to whiteness affects students' mathematics experiences.

Zavala (2014)

In her study of Latinx high school students' accounts of learning mathematics, Zavala (2014) argues that prior analyses of Latinx students in mathematics education research have focused on linguistic identity with little attention to racialized identity, noting that "the issues of race and language terms to be compartmentalized in the literature: an either-or (race or language) approach rather than a both-and (both race and language) approach" (p. 56). Therefore, Latinx students are hidden as figures with *both* racialized and linguistic identities. The author argues that this omission renders the picture of Latinx students' experiences in mathematics incomplete. Zavala draws on literature that highlights how race and language separately affect mathematics identity and uses Latino critical race theory (LatCrit) to navigate the "multiple constructs specific to the experiences of Latinas/or in the United States, such as language, culture, ethnicity, immigration status, phenotype, and sexuality" (p. 62). In addition to a theoretical framework, LatCrit also provided Zavala with a methodological approach to narrative analysis, testimonio. The narratives came from individual and focus group interviews.

Zavala (2014) presents three sets of findings: the utility of mathematics, the role of race, and the role of language. She argues that the participants envisioned mathematics as important for their long-term goals. The participants had a color-blind perspective on what creates mathematical success: individual motivation. The author reports that the immigrant students used meritocratic language, "charging those who did not finish [high school in Mexico] with not wanting it enough" (p. 68). The participants who were born in the United States expressed a connection between their racial and mathematical identities, particularly as it relates to dehumanizing stereotypes of Latinx as illegal or violent. With respect to the role of language, Zavala spotlights Julieta, an emergent bilingual immigrant Latina. Instruction in Spanish was critical to Julieta's success in mathematics. She pointed to the privilege that English-speaking students have in mathematics classes to have ready access to the curriculum materials and the ability to communicate with the teacher. Julieta perceived English-speaking students to be squandering these advantages that she wished she had. Her strategy to address this disadvantage was to do mathematics in Spanish and to partner with another student who could also do the work in Spanish. Zavala attributes Julieta's agency in the classroom to "the intersectionality of multiple layers of [her] identity . . . , how she liked mathematics, how she connected mathematics to a broader sense of self, her linguistic identity, as well as her initiative" (p. 77).

While Zavala (2014) does not explicitly cite intersectionality literature from Black feminist theory, she engages intersectionality as a core tenet of both CRT and LatCrit.[4] She uses the language in addressing identity as intersectional and honors this idea in her theoretical and methodological choices. Using LatCrit required that Zavala address identity intersections, but she acknowledges that presenting the analysis in written form limited her to a more discrete presentation that may make it appear that these identities "do not subsume, overlap, or influence each other" (p. 65). The traditionally linear approach to academic writing can limit opportunities for the researcher to fully explore the conflicts that Bowleg (2008) urges researchers to confront. However, Zavala does address the complexities of racial and linguistic identities separately in detail. She also suggests that further research is needed to address how larger discourses about immigration and stereotypes of Latinx youth as illegal or violent affect mathematics learning, but she does not step into these issues as Bowleg would require.

While Zavala's (2014) study falls squarely within the identity model of intersectional analysis due to its focus on combined identities, Julieta's case represents a step toward the conflict model. Julieta was negotiating a solid mathematical identity with her identities as an immigrant, a girl, and an emergent bilingual. She developed a detailed strategy for success that included initiating a friendship that support her to do mathematics in Spanish and to have access to the capital that English-speaking students held in the classroom. By stepping fully into the conflict model of intersectional analysis, Zavala could bring attention to the demand for hidden work that U.S. school mathematics places on students who negotiate *isms* such as those Julieta faced. It would also be pertinent to the conflict model to expand on the intersectional privilege that Julieta assigned to her English-dominant Latinx classmates and any conflicts that she experienced between her identity as a Latina and her immigrant or linguistic identities.

Leyva (2016)

Leyva (2016) uses intersectionality grounded in Black feminist theory as the central theoretical framework in his analysis of Latinx college women's mathematics experiences as STEM majors. He argues, "Research that focuses on a single dimension of identity, however, risks homogenizing group experiences and overlooking within-group differences for negotiating discourses in mathematics and society at large" (p. 81). To capture these different dimensions of the participants' identities, Leyva included poststructural theory as part of his theoretical framework. He presented the findings by constructing a case for each participant based on data gathered from individual and focus group interviews and written mathematical autobiographies. The counterstories focused on Lauren and Tracy's intersectional experiences as Latinx women from both an interpersonal and an institutional perspective.

In the cross-case analysis of Lauren and Tracey's counterstories, Leyva (2016) focused on four discourses: "(a) mathematics ability is innate, (b) women and Latin@s are not good at mathematics, (c) Latin@ women are underrepresented in STEM, and (d) Latin@ women become young mothers and wives instead of college students" (p. 109). When Lauren and Tracey faced challenges to their confidence in their natural mathematics ability, they learned that mathematics is a discipline whose racialized and gendered nature cannot be mitigated by talent alone. The racial and gender identification with their teachers caused them to name pedagogy and teacher–student relationship as critical to supporting women and Latinx students in mathematics. Lauren and Tracey were aware that, as Latinx women, they were part of an underrepresented group. They each valued the encouragement that came from peers, teachers, and family. They also saw themselves as role models to younger family and community members. Tracey used her connection to other Latinx college women to navigate cultural expectations to marry and have children instead of going to college.

In this study, intersectionality directs the analysis in that Leyva (2016) analyzes the data for both its text (i.e., explicit evidence of participants negotiating intersectional identities) and for its subtext (i.e., implicit evidence of participants negotiating intersectional identities). This consideration of subtext connects to Bowleg's (2008) call for intersectional analysts to use sociohistorical consciousness to see more in the data than what is immediately evident. Leyva (2016) presents detailed case studies of the two focal participants, which allows for a more nuanced understanding of their experiences and honors their complex identities. In these cases, the reader gets a sense of how the participants negotiate their identities within mathematics and the inherent tensions in the process. Although Leyva cites Bowleg in support of his choice to focus on subtext, there are few moments where he takes the transdisciplinary step to analyze the cases through broader sociohistorical realities that Bowleg identifies as an essential phase of intersectionality research. One such moment is when he discusses the participants' pursuit of a mathematics-intensive major as an act of resistance against dominant cultural narratives that Latinx women are destined to be little more than wives and mothers. Leyva describes this sense of family commitment as *familismo* "or sense of loyalty and responsibility to the Latin@ family unit" (p. 113). This discourse has the potential to be both limiting and empowering as it "played a critical role in [the participants'] motivations to excel in mathematics while negotiating STEM higher education with family expectations" (p. 113). While the participants described feeling limited by *familismo*, it also fueled their sense of resistance to create new possibilities for the family through education.

I classify Leyva's (2016) study as following the identity model by focusing on the racial and gender intersections of Lauren and Tracey's identities. However, Leyva also connects these identity intersections to larger sociocultural discourses about mathematics, women, Latinx students, and Latinx women, which moves toward the discourse model. The institutional model of intersectional analysis provides additional analytical opportunity in this study through the idea of *familismo*, which hides the figure of the Latinx child who does not want to follow its cultural norms. As outlined earlier, the family is a discourse determined largely by gender. *Familismo* dictates male and female roles in the family, but these roles can also be mediated by other issues such as class, immigration status, and ethnicity. Exploring these added intersections may illuminate why, for example, Lauren's family was willing to support her to defy cultural norms about young Latinx women while Tracey had to rely on a group of peers to "not fall victim to discourses that steer them away from applying their mathematics ability and interest" (p. 113).

CONCLUSION

Extant CME research has taken up the identity model and made some steps toward broader applications of intersectional analysis, but there is a power in the theory that is yet untapped. The four categories of intersectional analysis that I have presented represent opportunities to address figure hiding in CME by complexifying and enriching research into the social and political aspects of mathematics education. Limiting the use of intersectionality in CME research to the identity model forfeits the opportunities that intersectional analysis makes possible related to ideological and institutional analysis. Failing to employ the full power of intersectionality also limits CME's potential for praxis toward justice. According to Rawls (1971), justice is the first virtue of any social institution and "laws and institutions . . . must be reformed or abolished if they are unjust" (p. 3). I envision CME's role within mathematics education writ large as pushing justice to the center of conversations about all parts of the "network of mathematics education practices" (Valero, 2010, p. 374).

In this review, I have proposed intersectional analysis as a methodology for those who engage in either internally or externally focused CME research to address the complexities of social and political realities and to identify ways that current approaches to research unintentionally participate in figure hiding. If CME researchers take on Rawls' (1971) charge to place justice as the first virtue and to dismantle or reform any social institution that is unjust, they also agree to assume all risk associated with this commitment. Given that CME consistently operates on the fringes of the mathematics education research landscape, this risk is not unfamiliar. Embracing intersectional analysis as a way of thinking about CME has the potential to work against figure hiding by breaking down analytical silos.

Embracing intersectional analysis also has the potential to encourage a sense of community and cohesion among CME scholars because turning an intersectional analytic eye on CME cannot be done in isolation. It is not possible for any one scholar or any one *ism* group to fully interrogate the matrix of domination; there are always things that one cannot see or commitments under which one cannot not operate. Therefore, the pursuit of justice through inquiry is a necessarily collaborative and strategic partnership in which scholars come together across *ism* groups with the intention of pooling their intellectual resources in the service of justice. These collaborative justice communities can gather around identities (e.g., the mathematics education of trans youth), issues (e.g., Islamophobia and mathematics education), places (e.g., mathematics education in rural China), or spaces (e.g., urban mathematics education). A justice community has one aim: to move toward justice by directly confronting the multiplicative effects of injustice and oppression.

Intersectional justice communities encourage a different form of accountability. As scholars, we are most often accountable to the theories we use, the participants and institutions we study, to our colleagues via blind review, and the discipline to which we belong. When different scholarly interests come together holding a common value, there is a different form of accountability. Each *ism* group becomes accountable to the others and, more important, to justice itself. While this situation makes us each vulnerable, that vulnerability creates the opportunity for less figure hiding, more critical self-reflection, stronger interpersonal relationships, and more effective coalitions. It is in this space that, I believe, the critical scholar's justice mandate can be fulfilled.

NOTES

[1]Praxis is the idea that the scholar and activist are connected because theory and practice necessarily inform each other (Crenshaw, 1991).

[2]Expectation states theory asserts that "members of a group will act as if higher status people are more competent members than lower status people, regardless of the demands of the activity" (Esmonde et al., 2009, p. 23).

[3]The data for this study included classroom observations, student work, classroom artifacts, interviews, teacher reflections, community artifacts, and assessment results.

[4]Kimberlé Crenshaw is one of the critical legal scholars who originated CRT and

established intersectionality as one of its core tenets. LatCrit, an outgrowth of CRT, also has a commitment to intersectionality (Crenshaw, 2011).

ORCID ID

Erika C. Bullock (iD) https://orcid.org/0000-0002-4785-9408

REFERENCES

Alrø, H., Ravn, O., & Valero, P. (2010). Inter-viewing critical mathematics education. In H. Alrø, O. Ravn, & P. Valero (Eds.), *Critical mathematics education: Past, present and future, Festschrift for Ole Skovsmose* (pp. 1–10). Rotterdam, Netherlands: Sense.

Berry, R. Q. III. (2008). Access to upper-level mathematics: The stories of successful African American middle school boys. *Journal for Research in Mathematics Education, 39,* 464–488.

Bowleg, L. (2008). When black + lesbian + woman ≠ black lesbian woman: The methodological challenges of qualitative and quantitative intersectionality research. *Sex Roles, 59,* 312–325.

Cho, S., Crenshaw, K. W., & McCall, L. (2013). Toward a field of intersectionality studies: Theory, applications, and praxis. *Signs: Journal of Women in Culture and Society, 38,* 785–810.

Choo, H. Y., & Ferree, M. M. (2010). Practicing intersectionality in sociological research: A critical analysis of inclusions, interactions, and institutions in the study of inequalities. *Sociological Theory, 28,* 129–149.

Collins, P. H. (2009). *Black feminist thought: Knowledge, consciousness, and the politics of empowerment.* New York, NY: Routledge. (Original work published 1990)

Collins, P. H. (2015). Intersectionality's definitional dilemmas. *Annual Review of Sociology, 41,* 1–20.

Collins, P. H., & Bilge, S. (2016). *Intersectionality.* Malden, MA: Polity Press.

Cooper, B. C. (2015). Love no limit: Towards a black feminist future (in theory). *The Black Scholar, 45*(4), 7–21.

Crenshaw, K. W. (1989). Demarginalizing the intersection of race and sex: A black feminist critique of antidiscrimination doctrine, feminist theory and antiracist politics. *University of Chicago Legal Forum, 1989,* 139–167.

Crenshaw, K. W. (1991). Mapping the margins: Intersectionality, identity politics and violence against women of color. *Stanford Law Review, 43,* 1241–1299.

Crenshaw, K. W. (2011). Twenty years of critical race theory: Looking back to move forward. *Connecticut Law Review, 43,* 1255–1352.

Crenshaw, K. W. (2013). From private violence to mass incarceration: Thinking intersectionally about women, race, and social control. *Journal of Scholarly Perspectives, 9*(1), 21–50.

Damarin, S. K., & Erchick, D. B. (2010). Toward clarifying the meanings of "gender" in mathematics education research. *Journal for Research in Mathematics Education, 41,* 310–323.

D'Ambrosio, U. (1985). Ethnomathematics and its place in the history and pedagogy of mathematics. *For the Learning of Mathematics, 5*(1), 44–47.

Davis, K. (2008). Intersectionality as buzzword: A sociology of science perspective on what makes a feminist theory successful. *Feminist Theory, 9,* 67–85.

de Freitas, E. (2004). Plotting intersections along the political axis: The interior voice of dissenting mathematics teachers. *Educational Studies in Mathematics, 55,* 259–274.

de Freitas, E. (2008). Critical mathematics education: Recognizing the ethical dimension of problem solving. *Counterpoints, 326,* 47–63.

Ernest, P. (2010). The scope and limits of critical mathematics education. *Philosophy of Mathematics Education Journal, 25,* 1–21.

Esmonde, I., Brodie, K., Dookie, L., & Takeuchi, M. (2009). Social identities and opportunities to learn: Student perspectives on group work in an urban mathematics classroom. *Journal of Urban Mathematics Education, 2*(2), 18–45. Retrieved from http://ed-osprey.gsu.edu/ojs/index.php/JUME/article/view/46/35

Fasheh, M. J. (2012). The role of mathematics in the destruction of communities, and what we can do to reverse this process, including using mathematics. In O. Skovsmose & B. Greer (Eds.), *Opening the cage: Critique and politics of mathematics education* (pp. 93–106). Rotterdam, Netherlands: Sense.

Gholson, M. L. (2016). Clean corners and algebra: A critical examination of the constructed invisibility of black girls and women in mathematics. *Journal of Negro Education, 85,* 290–301.

Gholson, M., & Martin, D. B. (2014). Smart girls, black girls, mean girls, and bullies: At the intersection of identities and the mediating role of young girls' social network in mathematical communities of practice. *Journal of Education, 194*(1), 19–33.

Gigliotti, D., Chernin, P., Topping, J., Williams, P., & Melfi, T. (Producers), & Melfi, T. (Director). (2016). *Hidden figures* [Motion picture]. Los Angeles, CA: 20th Century Fox.

Gines, K. T. (2011). Black feminism and intersectional analyses: A defense of intersectionality. *Philosophy Today, 55,* 275–284.

Greer, B., & Mukhopadhyay, S. (2012). The hegemony of mathematics. In O. Skovsmose & B. Greer (Eds.), *Opening the cage: Critique and politics of mathematics education* (pp. 229–248). Rotterdam, Netherlands: Sense.

Greer, B., & Skovsmose, O. (2012). Seeing the cage? The emergence of critical mathematics education. In O. Skovsmose & B. Greer (Eds.), *Opening the cage: Critique and politics of mathematics education* (pp. 1–20). Rotterdam, Netherlands: Sense.

Gutiérrez, R. (2008). A "gap-gazing" fetish in mathematics education? Problematizing research on the achievement gap. *Journal for Research in Mathematics Education, 39,* 357–364.

Gutstein, E. (2006). *Reading and writing the world with mathematics: Toward a pedagogy for social justice.* New York, NY: Routledge.

Hartmann, H. I. (1979). The unhappy marriage of Marxism and feminism: Towards a more progressive union. *Capital & Class, 3*(2), 1–33.

Henningsen, I. (2008). Gender mainstreaming of adult mathematics education: Opportunities and challenges. *Adults Learning Mathematics, 3*(1), 32–40.

Heyd-Metzuyanim, E., & Graven, M. (2016). Between people-pleasing and mathematizing: South African learners' struggle for numeracy. *Educational Studies in Mathematics, 91,* 349–373.

Hooker, J. (2016). Black Lives Matter and the paradoxes of U.S. black politics: From democratic sacrifice to democratic repair. *Political Theory, 44,* 448–469.

Joseph, G. G. (1987). Foundations of eurocentrism in mathematics. *Race & Class, 28*(3), 13–28.

Kollosche, D. (2014). Mathematics and power: An alliance in the foundations of mathematics and its teaching. *ZDM, 46,* 1061–1072.

Lambert, R. (2015). Constructing and resisting disability in mathematics classrooms: A case study exploring the impact of different pedagogies. *Educational Studies in Mathematics, 89,* 1–18.

Larnell, G. V. (2016). More than just skill: Examining mathematics identities, racialized narratives, and remediation among black undergraduates. *Journal for Research in Mathematics Education, 47,* 233–269.

Leonardo, Z. (2004). The color of supremacy: Beyond the discourse of "white privilege." *Educational Philosophy and Theory, 36,* 137–152.

Leyva, L. A. (2016). An intersectional analysis of Latin@ college women's counter-stories in mathematics. *Journal of Urban Mathematics Education, 9,* 81–121.

Martin, D. B. (2000). *Mathematics success and failure among African-American youth: The roles of sociohistorical context, community forces, school influence, and individual agency.* Mahwah, NJ: Erlbaum.

Martin, D. B. (2011). What does quality mean in the context of white institutional space? In B. Atweh, M. Graven, W. Secada, & P. Valero (Eds.), *Mapping equity and quality in mathematics education* (pp. 437–450). Dordrecht, Germany: Springer.

McGee, E. (2015). Robust and fragile mathematical identities: A framework for exploring racialized experiences and high achievement among black college students. *Journal for Research in Mathematics Education, 46,* 599–625.

Morris, M. W. (2016). *Pushout: The criminalization of Black girls in schools.* New York, NY: New Press.

Rawls, J. (1971). *A theory of justice.* Cambridge, MA: Oxford University Press.

Riegle-Crumb, C., & Humphries, M. (2012). Exploring bias in math teachers' perceptions of students' ability by gender and race/ethnicity. *Gender & Society, 26,* 290–322.

Robinson, Z. F. (2016). Intersectionality. In S. Abrutyn (Ed.), *Handbook of contemporary sociological theory* (pp. 477–499). Dordrecht, Netherlands: Springer.

Shetterley, M. L. (2016). *Hidden figures: The American dream and the untold story of the black women mathematicians who helped with the space race.* New York, NY: HarperCollins.

Skovsmose, O. (1985). Mathematical education versus critical education. *Educational Studies in Mathematics, 16,* 337–354.

Skovsmose, O. (2011). *An invitation to critical mathematics education.* Rotterdam, Netherlands: Sense.

Skovsmose, O. (2012). Towards a critical mathematics education research programme? In O. Skovsmose & B. Geer (Eds.), *Opening the cage: Critique and politics of mathematics education* (pp. 343–368). Rotterdam, Netherlands: Sense.

Skovsmose, O. (2014). *Critique as uncertainty.* Charlotte, NC: Information Age.

Solomon, Y. (2012). Finding a voice? Narrating the female self in mathematics. *Educational Studies in Mathematics, 80,* 171–183.

Solomon, Y., Radovic, D., & Black, L. (2015). "I can actually be very feminine here": Contradiction and hybridity in becoming a female mathematician. *Educational Studies in Mathematics, 91,* 55–71.

Stinson, D. W. (2013). Negotiating the "white male math myth": African American male students and success in school mathematics. *Journal for Research in Mathematics Education, 44,* 69–99.

Stinson, D. W., & Bullock, E. C. (2012). Critical postmodern theory in mathematics education research: A praxis of uncertainty. *Educational Studies in Mathematics, 80,* 41–55.

Taylor, K.-Y. (2016). *From #blacklivesmatter to black liberation.* Chicago, IL: Haymarket Books.

Thunder, K., & Berry, R. Q. III. (2016). The promise of qualitative metasynthesis for mathematics education. *Journal for Research in Mathematics Education, 47,* 318–337.

Valero, P. (2010). A socio-political look at equity in the school organization of mathematics education. In B. Sriraman & L. D. English (Eds.), *Theories of mathematics education: Seeking new frontiers* (pp. 225–233). Dordrecht, Germany: Springer.

Weldon, S. L. (2008). Intersectionality. In G. Goertz & A. G. Mazur (Eds.), *Politics, gender, and concepts: Theory and methodology* (pp. 193–218). Cambridge, England: Cambridge University Press.

Yuval-Davis, N. (2006). Intersectionality and feminist politics. *European Journal of Women's Studies, 13,* 193–209.

Zavala, M., & del, R. (2014). Latina/o youth's perspectives on race, language, and learning mathematics. *Journal of Urban Mathematics Education, 7*(1), 55–87.

Chapter 7

Is the "First-Generation Student" Term Useful for Understanding Inequality? The Role of Intersectionality in Illuminating the Implications of an Accepted—Yet Unchallenged—Term

THAI-HUY NGUYEN
Seattle University

BACH MAI DOLLY NGUYEN
Lewis & Clark College

First-generation students (FGSs) have received a great deal of attention in education research, practice, and policy. The difficulty of understanding and subsequently addressing the various and persistent configurations of inequality associated with FGSs lies with the complicated yet obscure state of the FGS term itself. Leaving the term unquestioned limits the capacity to grasp how these students' backgrounds and identities shape their decisions and relationships to others and to institutions, and risks reproducing the very inequality that education researchers wish to mitigate. This chapter begins to resolve these conflicts by offering a critical analysis and discussion—grounded by the concept of intersectionality—of the empirical literature on FGSs. We identify and discuss the dominant and problematic manner in which the FGS term has been operationalized in research and discuss the implications of their findings. We end with a discussion on emerging topics that extends the consideration of research on FGSs beyond the imaginary, traditional boundaries of college campuses.

Google "first-generation students." The result is 74,400 news articles.[1] American higher education as well as the American public have been fascinated with this population of students—broadly conceived as those first in their family to attend college—in part because they symbolize the social inequality that colleges and universities are perceived to help stamp out. But, in fact, institutions have been accused for doing the exact opposite. As of late, major news outlets like the *New York Times* (Harris, 2017;

Review of Research in Education
March 2018, Vol. 42, pp. 146–176
DOI: 10.3102/0091732X18759280
© 2018 AERA. http://rre.aera.net

Pappano, 2015), *The Washington Post* (Banks-Santilli, 2015; Cardoza, 2016), *The Boston Globe* (Foster, 2015), and *The Atlantic* (Kahlenberg, 2016; Young, 2016) have pointed out this wrongdoing by featuring the plight of first-generation college students (FGSs)[2] and the challenges and conflicts they encounter and contend with as they seek a life beyond their current status. From feelings of alienation as they transition to an unfamiliar space, including the uncertainty of navigating accepted social decorum, to the persistent fear of homelessness and starvation between academic terms, the status of being an FGS reveals policies, norms, and cultural processes of institutions that privilege the experiences and knowledge of "traditional" students, whose parents attended college (Dumais & Ward, 2010; London, 1989). As such, institutions reinforce the inequality of opportunity that facilitate "the unequal distribution of desirable life outcomes" (Carter & Reardon, 2014, p. 3; see also Stevens, Armstrong, & Arum, 2008). The difficulty, however, of understanding and subsequently addressing the various, and persistent, configurations of inequality associated with FGSs lies with the complicated, yet obscure state of the FGS term itself, a term used superfluously and without question.

First-generation students can make up 22% to 77% of the undergraduate enrollment and their 6-year graduation rates can range from 10.9% to 50.2% (DeAngelo, Franke, Hurtado, Pryor, & Tran, 2011; Núñez & Cuccaro-Alamin, 1998; Pell Institute for the Study of Opportunity in Higher Education, 2011; Toutkoushian, Stollberg, & Slaton, in press; U.S. Department of Education, 2014). Why such drastic ranges? Since the term was originally defined by Fuji Adachi in 1979 to refer to students who do not have at least one parent with a bachelor's degree, researchers have shifted the criteria for inclusion up and down a wide spectrum of parental educational attainment (Auclair et al., 2008; Toutkoushian et al., in press). Today, the FGS term can include students whose parents have a high school diploma or less, or parents with some postsecondary experience, but without a 4-year degree (Toutkoushian et al., in press). Toutkoushian et al. (in press) argued that how FGSs are counted is largely determined by how they are defined. Using the Educational Longitudinal Study of 2002, they demonstrated how differences in definition, or levels of parental education, significantly affected student behavior (i.e., taking the Scholastic Assessment Test/American College Testing) and enrollment in 2- or 4-year institutions. This critical distinction, however, is rarely made in research or popular media, which opens up claims about the FGS population to significant critique, as differences in its definition have theoretical, empirical, and policy implications. Assumptions undergirding the term are linked to their parents' level of education, where the "effect"—the type, amount, and quality of resources imparted on students by their parents' education—of being an FGS shapes their level of confidence, degree of comfort in college, and possession of privileged knowledge. Given that this may lead to hugely diverse realities for students who are grouped together into a single FGS category, it begs the following questions: Are the experiences and outcomes of students with parents with only a high school diploma similar to students with one college-educated parent? Are the resources and knowledge similarly passed on? When the definition is inconsistent, as is evident by drastic ranges in enrollment and graduation, how we make sense of this effect is problematic and leads to a muddled understanding of the actualized inequality facing FGSs.

The FGS term, then, simultaneously seeks *and* fails to capture the richness and complexity of students' lives. This point is affirmed by the wide demographic variation within this population. FGSs, depending on the inclusion criteria, are more likely to be female (60.2%) and to come from homes with a family income of less than $25,000 (50.3%; Chen & Carroll, 2005; Pascarella, Pierson, Wolniak & Terenzini, 2004). Within racial groups, Hispanic[3] students are more likely to be an FGS (53% at 2-year institutions, 38.2% at 4-year institutions) than their peers, with Black and Native American students following closely behind (40% to 45% at 2-year institutions, 16% to 23% at 4-year institutions; Nomi, 2005; Saenz, Hurtado, Barrera, Wolf, & Yeung, 2007). Despite these characteristics, studies often use the FGS term to lay claim to students' challenges and educational outcomes, ignoring the possibility that other dimensions of their lives and identities may overlap or play a larger role than the FGS status alone (Billson & Terry, 1982). Studies also assume that being an FGS has an effect that is unique from gender, race, social class, and other salient categories of analysis, and thus, dismiss the fact that parental education (i.e., how the FGS term is defined) is already an outcome of structural circumstances related to those same social forces. Moving beyond parental education "invites us to characterize as fully as possible the conditions and circumstances of early life" (Hout, 2015, p. 28). Efforts to better understand students who are considered first-generation, however, are challenged by the confounding nature and use of the FGS term, for it masks their differences across multiple dimensions of social life. And because those dimensions cannot be precisely identified, how we make sense of the mechanisms that maintain our highly stratified system of education is hindered. The FGS term is a conceptual conundrum. Leaving it unquestioned limits the capacity to grasp how students' backgrounds and identities shape their decisions and relationships to others and to institutions, and risks reproducing the very inequality that education researchers wish to mitigate. This chapter begins to resolve these conflicts by offering a critical analysis and discussion—grounded by the concept of intersectionality—of the empirical literature on FGSs (Collins, 2015; Crenshaw, 1989, 1991).

Intersectionality captures "the critical insight that race, class, gender, sexuality, ethnicity, nation, ability, and age operate not as unitary, mutually exclusive entities, but as reciprocally constructing phenomena that in turn shape complex social inequalities" (Collins, 2015, p. 2). Because of its intent to complicate the characterization of individuals and reveal sources of power and oppression, intersectionality offers a path to critique the manner in which categories of analysis, such as the FGS status, are operationalized in broad strokes without recognizing the granular dynamics between a student's background, their institution, and their experience and outcomes. In this chapter, we suggest that FGS status must be understood by their relationships to other identities and to institutions and that those associations cannot be captured by their marginalized status alone. Instead, an intersectional approach pushes us to examine who FGSs are *underneath* this broad term and, thus, uncover the structural forces attached to categorization that drives unequal relationships. An excerpt from *The Atlantic* (Young, 2016) captures the essence of this idea:

. . . labels that assume first-generation always correlates with low-income may get in the way of the more important conversation of how individuals relate to their college community. . . . Does it matter if first-generation students are also low-income? What about a first-generation student of color who comes from a family of means? How many labels are necessary to understand first-generation students' needs?

In this chapter, we do not offer a definitive response to "how many labels are necessary to understand first-generation students' needs," but we contend that it is more than the single and simple dominant narrative that the FGS term currently offers. By employing intersectionality to guide the analysis, this review of research makes two primary contributions. First, we demonstrate the quandary of using the FGS term so profusely without the distinct acknowledgment of the inconsistent nature of the category, and thus highlight the obscure state of our understanding of this undefined population. Second, we bring attention to the limited capacity of the FGS term to demonstrate differential outcomes and experiences of students, which are conditional on who these students are and the extent by which they are valued by their institutions. In utilizing intersectionality, we point out that the effect and influence of the FGS category is exceptionally difficult to isolate, and contend that the explicit examination of relationships between categories of analysis can better disentangle the education field's ambiguous conceptualizations of FGSs. In short, we seek to answer the following question: Should the FGS term continue to be used as a category for understanding and addressing inequality in higher education? We argue, yes. The FGS term brings consequential attention to many students who struggle. However, to ensure that attention is translated to effective practice and scholarship, the process of how the FGS term is used—the capacity to unveil the who, what, and where—must be discussed and evaluated. Refraining from doing so promotes misunderstanding, casting a wide shadow that blinds us from the forces that maintain inequality.

We organize this review of research into three main sections. First, we discuss our strategy in securing and organizing the literature and introduce our theoretical approach, arguing its significance in peeling back the layers of the FGS term and clarifying the power dynamics undergirding the unequal relationship between student and institution. We draw on McCall's (2005) and Núñez's (2014) conceptualizations of intersectionality to guide our analysis of the literature. Second, we review and discuss the dominant and problematic manners in which the FGS term has been operationalized in research for the past 30 years and discuss the implications of their findings. Third, we provide a discussion of the effectiveness of how the FGS term has been used, highlighting its theoretical and methodological strengths and shortcomings. Additionally, we discuss emerging topics that extend this discussion beyond the imaginary, traditional boundaries and understandings of college campuses.

INTERSECTIONALITY AND LOCATIONS OF INEQUALITY

We maintain that mitigating inequality for FGSs requires that we render the term and how it is used suspect. This means that we must take an insular look at the term by refraining from merely establishing differences between FGSs and non-FGSs and using the term in ways that obscure how individuals are multiply disadvantaged. To achieve this goal, we conceive intersectionality as an analytic strategy, a "theory of marginalized subjectivity" as this allows us to seize and center the locations where colleges and universities *differentially* influence FGSs' lives, as opposed to reinforcing the category as a mere analytic additive to student identities (Nash, 2008, p. 10). These locations of inequality, however, are often difficult to find and acknowledge when dominant institutions have a narrow view of students that precludes seeing individuals as multiply disadvantaged.

In 1989, Kimberlé Crenshaw presented the concept of intersectionality by citing a legal case, *DeGraffenreid v General Motors*, where the court refused to acknowledge the plaintiff's—five Black women—claim of discrimination in hiring practices. In the court's eyes, General Motors did not violate the law because it hired Black men *and* White women, albeit not Black women. According to Crenshaw (1989),

Under this view, Black women are protected only to the extent that their experiences coincide with those of either of the two groups. Where their experiences are distinct, Black women can expect little protection as long as approaches, such as that in *DeGraffenreid*, which completely obscure problems of intersectionality prevail. (p. 143)

Twenty-seven years later at a TED (Technology, Entertainment and Design) talk, Crenshaw (2016) made the same argument about society's refusal to acknowledge the disproportionate killings of and violence against Black women by police, "These women's names have slipped through our consciousness because there are no frames for us to see them." Intersectionality then is a frame to acknowledge the ways multiple social realities, structured by the dominant norms and values of institutions, converge to produce distinct, overlapping moments and experiences of disadvantage that are often rendered invisible by the majority (Crenshaw, 1989). This acknowledgment is not immediate, nor always clear. In the case of students categorized as an FGS, we draw on McCall's (2005) and Núñez's (2014) approaches to the study of intersectionality, which expound Crenshaw's main premise and offer a path and direction to guide our analysis and help demonstrate the limitations of how the FGS term is used. Whereas McCall (2005) focuses on the deconstruction of categories and the relationships between categories, Núñez (2014) looks outward to consider how multiple layers of systems shape the individuals captured in those categories. Together, they allow us to critique who the FGS term captures and how it is used to explain students' relationships with their postsecondary institutions.

McCall (2005) advances three methodological approaches to intersectionality of which we use two—anticategorical complexity and intercategorical complexity—to undermine the assumptions of the FGS term and begin complicating the differences that have been established between FGSs and their peers, which have confounded, rather than clarified, locations of inequality. The anticategorical complexity argues for the deconstruction of analytical categories, augmenting the "skepticism about the possibility of using categories in anything but a simplistic way" (McCall, 2005, p. 1773), which offers the opportunity to problematize the many variations of the FGS term. McCall contends that no single category can capture the complexities of human life; thus, we can speculate about the relative usefulness of the term even if the inclusion criteria shifts from one study to the next. For the past 30 some years, research on FGSs has steadily increased, with exceptional growth of "606% between 1999 and 2013" (Wildhagen, 2015, p. 287). We have collected and organized this literature and were struck by how studies (with some rare exceptions discussed in our next section) reinforced the power of this category by reducing the complexity of self and self's relations to others and to systems of inequality. Research and institutions are at fault for discursively constructing the FGS term by comparing these students against those with college-educated parents, thereby creating a dominant narrative that is wrought with overly vague assumptions in which to base their decisions. We have chosen to deconstruct this binary and, in doing so, deconstruct the power that maintains this narrative because "any research that is based on such categorization . . . inevitably leads to demarcation, and demarcation to exclusion, and exclusion to inequality" (McCall, 2005, p. 1777). We then draw from the notion of intercategorical complexity, in which we "provisionally adopt existing analytical categories to document relationships of inequality among social groups" (McCall, 2005, p. 1773). Although these categories alone are inclined to minimize the complexity of lives, it is the evolving and shifting nature of their relationships to each other that lie at the heart of our analysis (Crenshaw, 1989). McCall's approaches allow us a path to critique how the FGS term is operationalized in research, thereby questioning the power of this category to obscure and confound the social forces that shape students' lives.

We would be remiss, however, to ignore the social, political, and economic context of student marginality. Students' marginality is not simply a point in which identities intersect but a space where "dynamics of identity, power, and history play out to shape educational experiences and outcomes in differential ways" (Núñez, 2014, p. 87). To this point, Núñez (2014) advances a three-level approach that accounts for "micro-, meso-, and macro-levels of analysis" (p. 87). The first level examines how social categories are defined and related to each other. The second level situates the individual across "domains of power" (p. 88), including the following: "(a) organizational (e.g., positions in structures of society such as work, family, and education), (b) representational (e.g., discursive processes), and (c) intersubjective (e.g., relationships between individuals and members of groups), and (d) experiential (e.g., narrative sensemaking)" (p. 88). Both levels are then contextualized "within a broader temporal and spatial context," or the third level, which is called historicity. Therefore, making sense of students' experiences from this framework helps delineate—make visible—overlapping forces and contexts, bringing to light how colleges and other systems reward or penalize students by their identities and backgrounds at various moments and across various contexts. By leaning on McCall (2005) and Núñez (2014), we demonstrate and explicate limitations to how the FGS term is used. This is a first step toward providing alternative narratives that highlight the way systems of dominance manifest and endure over time.

Methodology

Using EBSCOhost and Google Scholar, we conducted a detailed search of literature on FGSs. Key words included "First-Generation Students," "First-Generation
College Students," and "First in Family." A total of 450 items were located, representing published research—peer-reviewed journal articles, book chapters, books,
dissertations, policy reports, newspaper articles, and magazine articles—between
1986 and 2017. We established several criteria to narrow our focus for this review.
We focused on studies that centered FGSs in their primary questions and analyses.
Items that mentioned FGSs tangentially were excluded. We excluded any books,
book chapters, and policy reports that did not discuss empirical data and analysis on
FGSs. Some of these items, however, were used to help contextualize the purpose of
our inquiry, especially if they offered key descriptive data. Non–peer-reviewed
sources such as dissertations and some books and book chapters were also excluded
since the peer-review process provides legitimacy to the significance of the FGS term
(Lamont, 2009), which undergirds the process of classification and, ultimately, supports the claim that the complex lives of students fit neatly "into a single 'master'
category" (McCall, 2005, p. 1777). Given that the peer-review process reinforces
and legitimizes the knowledge that is put forth, we wanted to only include items
that have gone through such a process since this chapter keys in on the discursive
construction and use of the FGS term (Lamont, 2009). Peer-reviewed articles were
excluded to the extent that they were conceptual syntheses or only offered a summary of best practices and recommendations, which typically do not require empirical data. And last, we also excluded peer-reviewed articles on FGSs that stood outside
the American context. Because systems of postsecondary education vary drastically
around the world, it would be beyond the scope of our inquiry to discuss and
account for those differences in analyzing the FGS term (Shavit, Arum, & Gamoran,
2007). The remaining 77 peer-reviewed sources that make up our selective review
were primarily made up of journal articles and a handful of books. Although all 77
sources were reviewed and included in our references, our in-text citations only
feature 74 sources. The remaining three sources were excluded because they did not
further illustrate our argument and points (Byrd & MacDonald, 2005; Bui, 2005;
Núñez, 2005).

RENDERING THE FGS TERM SUSPECT AND LOOKING WITHIN

Intersectionality channels our attention to how institutions are constructed to
"shape the multiple dimensions" of students' experiences (Crenshaw, 1991, p. 1241).
For those considered an FGS, we struggle to understand and identify how this phenomenon occurs and where it takes place. This problem emerges from the power of
the FGS term, so narrowly and inconsistently defined, to transpose a single narrative
of inequality on a heterogeneous population of students—a process that is reified by
the very scholarship aimed to clarify students' experiences and outcomes. We

contend, that left unaddressed, how the FGS term is currently used in research can lead to precarious implications for both theory and practice. In this section, McCall's (2005) and Núñez's (2014) approaches to intersectionality guide our review and analytical critique of how the FGS term is used in research. These insights are organized around two points, in which we call attention to the issues with how the term is currently operationalized, discuss the consequences of that operationalization, and offer promising model(s) as alternatives. In doing so, the organization of literature also fell along unintended methodological lines. Nonetheless, this emergence allowed us to illustrate the multiple implications of the FGS term in research. In the section, "Masking Social Realities," we review quantitative research on FGSs to discuss how the term informs or how it hides the inequality of student outcomes when used as a variable of analysis. In "Locations of Inequality," we question how the use of the FGS term in primarily qualitative studies anchors our capacity to more precisely understand how institutions are structured to differentially shape the experiences of students. As a result of this inquiry, intersectionality allows us to pose critical questions and to highlight conflicting views, a fundamental step to developing a wider frame, one "that allows us to see how social problems impact all the members of a targeted group," (Crenshaw, 2016) for students considered first-generation.

Masking Social Realities

The FGS term is equally simple and complex—the former because current usage of the term has conflated an entire population under a single category and the latter because beneath that category is a wide diversity of individuals representing a spectrum of experiences, histories, and contexts. Given the dichotomous disposition of the term, it is useful to examine research on the FGS population through McCall's (2005) approach to intersectionality, which offers a lens to both "render suspect" (p. 1777) simplicity, and uncover social realities within complexity. Influenced by McCall's anticategorical and intercategorical approaches, this section begins with an analysis of quantitative research on FGSs, pointing out two primary concerns with how the FGS term has been utilized—inconsistent and unrepresentative study samples, and failure to acknowledge that FGS status is a circumstance born from other social forces. We then discuss why these matters have implications for both understanding FGSs' social realities and also for addressing the persistent forms of inequality that are masked by these methodological practices. We conclude this section with promising examples for how quantitative scholars may examine this population of students more comprehensively.

Ironically, we use the singular phrase "the FGS term" when in our review, 18 different definitions of FGSs were used by researchers to determine their sample of students. In fact, articles published in one single journal—selected as an example—offered four different variations of how FGS is defined (Fischer, 2007; Ishitani, 2006; Pascarella et al., 2004; Pike & Kuh, 2005). Although the variation in definition is not an issue, nor is the fact that the populations may fluctuate, the concern is that the population of FGSs is considered the same, and the narrative about their experiences is singular, when, in fact, they are different. This approach confounds who the FGS population actually includes and, at other times, excludes. Thus, the issue of study samples is our first methodological concern. The lack of clarity in defining who is counted is not only problematic because it can misrepresent the population, it also inhibits our ability to make sense of the comparison between FGSs against non-FGSs, which is the prevalent approach for distilling the academic barriers of FGSs. In other words, the group contrast that research on FGSs relies on is a false binary, as it is rooted in an inconsistently defined sample population. Analyzing seven different studies (Dumais & Ward, 2010; Hahs-Vaughn, 2004; Inman & Mayes, 1999; Lombardi, Murray, & Gerdes, 2012; Palbusa & Gauvain, 2017; Strayhorn, 2006; Vuong, Brown-Welty, & Tracz, 2010) on the disparity between FGSs and non-FGSs in grade point average (GPA), for example, seven different variations of who counted as an FGS were defined ranging as widely as neither parent earned a bachelor's degree (Strayhorn, 2006) to "no immediate family member could have attended any college, two-year or four-year, with or without having earned a degree" (Inman & Mayes, 1999, p. 6). In the former study, Strayhorn (2006) found that FGS status had an effect on cumulative GPA, accounting for 22% of the variance between FGSs and non-FGSs. Counter to that conclusion, other studies found that there were no significant differences in the GPA of FGSs and non-FGSs, and that FGS status had no effect on GPA (Dumais & Ward, 2010; Hahs-Vaughn, 2004). Compared with Strayhorn's use of bachelor's degrees as the distinction for FGS status, the latter studies relied on samples based on neither parent attending schooling past high school and neither parent earning more than a high school diploma, respectively. Recognizing that differing results may be a by-product of the unique parameters of each study or the methodology employed, the inconsistent definitions call attention to the problematic way in which study samples for research on FGSs is being determined to understand disparities in academic performance. The bifurcated understanding of FGSs versus non-FGSs, then, is only as valuable as the line that separates those two groups, which is one that remains considerably blurry given the operationalization of the FGS term in existing research.

In addition to the issue of inconsistency in defining FGSs, there is also concern regarding the representativeness of sample populations used in research. Despite the fluctuating boundaries for constructing this student population, it is collectively affirmed by scholars that FGSs are more likely to be low-income, racial/ethnic minorities, female, and older (Chen & Carroll, 2005; Choy, 2001; Pascarella et al., 2004; Toutkoushian et al., in press). Even so, a number of studies proceed with samples that are exceedingly unrepresentative, with many samples that are made up of between 50% and 90% White students and almost entirely between 18 and 24 years of age (Francis & Miller, 2007; Hahs-Vaughn, 2004; Ishitani, 2003, 2006; Martinez, Sher, Krull, & Wood, 2009; McCarron & Inkelas, 2006; Seay, Lifton, Wuensch, Bradshaw, & McDowelle, 2008; W. Smith & Zhang, 2010; Soria & Stebleton, 2012; Stebleton, Soria, & Huesman, 2014). In a study on the unique characteristics of FGSs in community colleges, for example, the sample is 91.6% White and the median age is 19 years (Inman & Mayes, 1999). In the context of community college students, in particular, this presents a considerable drawback to the study, as it severely counters the characterizations of both FGSs and of community college students, who are even more likely than their 4-year counterparts to be racial and ethnic minorities and older (American Association of Community Colleges, 2016). In this way, while the demographics in the study provide a general overview of the FGS community college population, it can conclude little with regard to outcomes because the sample is unrepresentative of FGSs. What makes this problematic is the proclivity of these studies to draw conclusions about a widely heterogeneous population (Choy, 2001) based on samples that are unrepresentative of that heterogeneity.

McCall's anticategorical approach was helpful in identifying concerns related to study samples in quantitative research on FGSs because it offered the opportunity to be skeptical of the category of FGS itself. In critiquing how the term is defined and operationalized, we could uncover that the decisions made to construct the category are a mechanism to mark difference and disparity, and yet the uncritical attention to that construction have perpetuated, rather than addressed those disparities. Insofar as quantitative research on FGSs goes, there are a number of remaining questions regarding who FGSs are, what barriers they face, and how to address those obstacles, which are left unanswered when using inconsistent and unrepresentative approaches for representing the population.

A second, and compounded methodological, concern with the FGS term is in how it is currently utilized in quantitative studies as a category independent of other social forces. Although sample populations include some characteristics—primarily race, gender, and social class—the explicit examination of how those categories interact with FGS status is not a methodological approach that has been undertaken in most studies (Dennis, Phinney, & Chuateco, 2005; Dumais & Ward, 2010; Giancola, Munz, & Trares, 2008; Hahs-Vaughn, 2004; Ishitani, 2003; Majer, 2009; Próspero & Vohra-Gupta, 2007; Ramos-Sanchez & Nichols, 2007; Vuong et al., 2010; Westbrook & Scott, 2012). This point is affirmed when reviewing the results of Ishitani's (2006) study on FGS persistence and graduation, which provides reports of students by FGS status, race, gender, and income in isolation from one another. As such, while Ishitani concludes that there is variance between groups when it comes to each of these categories separately, it falls short in investigating how these factors may interweave to result in the inequitable outcomes of FGSs who represent a spectrum of those social realities. Likewise, Soria and Stebleton's (2012) study, which found lower odds of FGSs' persistence, academic engagement, and sense of belonging, used gender and race as control variables. However, those categories were not included in the discussion, failing to acknowledge that FGS status is a circumstance born from the social forces related to gender and race.

McCall's (2005) intercategorical approach pushes researchers to observe relationships of inequality across social groups and to center these relationships in their analyses. To this point, several studies do call attention to this very issue; however, it has been relegated to limitations sections or concluding thoughts for future research. For instance, Hahs-Vaughn (2004) closes the article on differences between FGSs and non-FGSs by stating, "Continued future research in this line of study is needed as are studies that further delve into background characteristics (e.g., minority vs. nonminority first generation students" (p. 498). Similarly, Dumais and Ward's (2010) study on cultural capital and FGS success suggests, "Dummy variables for sex and race/ethnicity were included in the analyses, but future research should consider how sex and race/ethnicity interact with first-generation status and cultural capital for the different educational outcomes" (p. 263). Although the acknowledgment of the need to investigate the relationships between social categories is an important first step, there are too few examples of such practices to confirm that future research on FGSs is committed to this important methodological endeavor. As McCall (2005) theorizes, "Relationships of inequality among social groups do not enter as background or contextual or discursive or ideological factors, [. . .], but as the focus of the analysis itself" (pp. 1785–1786), which is particularly relevant for research on FGSs who embody interwoven forms of inequality, given their multiple marginal identities.

Taking the intercategorical approach to examine quantitative studies, it becomes apparent that there must be greater intentionality in how the FGS term is used methodologically to uncover the precise social realities students in this population face, unique from the inequalities defined by other social forces alone. As McCall states, "It is not the intersection of race, class, and gender in a single social group that is of interest but the relationships among the social groups defined by the entire set of groups constituting each category" (p. 1787). Put together with anticategorical intersectionality, then, research must be more cognizant to avoid inconsistent and unrepresentative constructions of the FGS population and more aware of how to account for relationships of inequality. As it stands now, the heart of the issue is that quantitative research on this population relies on broad generalizations without careful attention to precisely identifying the mechanisms that actually produce disparities.

As recommendations for how to mitigate these issues, we offer a few promising examples for how quantitative research may be more comprehensively approached. For the issue of inconsistent definitions of the FGS population, we highlight the foundational study on cognitive development of FGSs by Terenzini, Springer, Yaeger, Pascarella, and Nora (1996) and the follow-up study by Padgett, Johnson, and Pascarella (2012). Both studies found that FGSs are significantly disadvantaged in cognitive and psychosocial measures as compared with non-FGSs and point to factors that benefit FGSs' development, such as experiencing academically challenging interactions with peers (Padgett et al., 2012) and studying more hours (Terenzini et al., 1996). Most important, both studies used models with the same varying levels of parental education defined as neither parent has any college experience, parents with some college experience, one parent has a bachelor's degree, both parents have bachelor's degrees, and one parent has master's degree or above. These studies present a compelling example for consistency in defining the FGS population and demonstrate how findings are more useful for affirming or contradicting former studies when definitions are matched (see also Lee, Sax, Kim, & Hagedorn, 2004). To the second sampling concern, we urge scholars to be more mindful of their study populations, as Gibbons and Borders (2010) were in their research on college-going expectations of FGS and non-FGS middle schoolers. In their methods, they point out the careful selection of schools based on high proportions of low-income and minority student populations, as they are characteristics of FGSs. Intentionality and a commitment to accurate representation are central to addressing the current issues with FGS samples.

Regarding the use of FGS status independent from other social forces, we highlight a few examples. First, a study on the influence of psychological, personal, and institutional factors on college choice process of FGSs (Cho, Hudley, Lee, Barry, & Kelly, 2008) used omnibus interaction effects in their multivariate analysis to examine the relationships between social categories. In so doing, the authors were able to make explicit conclusions about which of those categories functioned together to generate disparities such as "Latino first-generation students perceived [campus racial/ethnic climate] as significantly more important than their nonfirst-generation peers and all Asian and White students" (Cho et al., 2008, p. 100). Furthermore, the scholars advanced three-way interactions that allowed for an even deeper investigation of relationships between categorized identities, which produced findings such as "Compared to other groups, first-generation females, African American in particular, considered the academic scale more important in their choice of college" (Cho et al., 2008, p. 101). Taking a slightly different approach, but with equal attention to relationships, Lohfink and Paulsen's (2005) study on persistence of FGSs used composite variables in logistic regressions, grouping background characteristics such as gender, race, income, and marital status together. Using this approach, the scholars could conclude that "being a Hispanic, first-generation student, a lower income first-generation student, or a female first-generation student, made first-to-second year persistence more problematic" (Lohfink & Paulsen, 2005, p. 418). These approaches and other examples are further highlighted in Schudde's (2018) chapter in this volume titled "Heterogeneous Effects in Education: The Promise and Challenge of Incorporating Intersectionality Into Quantitative Methodological Approaches," which further addresses how to insert intersectionality into quantitative methodologies (see also Próspero, Russell, & Vohra-Gupta, 2012). In taking an intersectional approach, whether it is through interaction terms or another statistical measure, future quantitative research on FGSs must supersede the notion that FGS status, alone, explains disparities in education. Instead, research should methodologically affirm FGSs' standing at the crossroads of several marginalized identities to unmask their social realities, which perpetuate inequality.

Locations of Inequality

In Crenshaw's (1991) seminal article, "Mapping the Margins: Intersectionality, Identity Politics, and Violence against Women of Color," she argued that oppression of Black women does not come from being Black women, but from the extent in which institutions are structured to acknowledge and value these mutually constitutive identities. Núñez (2014) explicates this point by advancing a framework that accommodates and explains how various levels across space and time shape the experiences of students. It is challenging, however, to locate the points in which inequality occurs because the FGS term is often conflated with another category of analysis, dismissing the ways in which institutions are mutually constructed from all dominant forms of capital, including race, gender, social class, or others markers of inequality to marginalize students. Moreover, when research uses the FGS term, it is remiss in considering how an institution's influence on a student's perceptions and experiences is conditioned by their unique background that often cannot be captured by quantitative measures. To address the challenges associated with students included in this population, those issues must be taken into account. In this section, by drawing on Núñez's (2014) multilevel intersectionality, we analyze and critique primarily qualitative studies that characterize student successes and challenges along a single dimension of inequality, as well as discuss the consequences of doing so. Given multilevel intersectionality's focus on the locations of inequality as they emerge between student and institutional context, the studies explored in this section highlight students' experiences in college as they relate to the concept of belongingness or cultural match, which explicates FGSs' relationships with college campuses (Stephens, Fryberg, Markus, Johnson, & Covarrubias, 2012; Stephens, Townsend, Hamedani, Destin, & Manzo, 2015; Strayhorn, 2012). We then move on to discuss studies that exemplifies Núñez's (2014) framework in which multiple and mutually reinforcing social forces and layers are shown to shape moments of oppression.

Student belongingness captures the extent to which students find a fit or match with their institution, where they are recognized, valued, and embraced by their institution (Strayhorn, 2012). The process of this match is far from linear and is contingent on who students are, the culture of the institution, and the context of both space and time (Núñez, 2014; Orbe, 2004). Studies in our review aimed to highlight and explain this process, but their focus lead to tapered explanations of "the systems of power and oppression that shape those experiences" (Núñez, 2014, p. 85). Take, for instance, a recently developed framework by social psychologists, Stephens, Fryberg, et al. (2012) and Stephens, Townsend, Markus, and Phillips (2012)—cultural mismatch theory. This theory makes three claims to explain the (mis)match phenomenon (Stephens, Fryberg, et al., 2012). First, American higher education is structured by independent values that encourage students "to separate and distinguish themselves from their parents and to realize their individual potential" (p. 1179). These values, the authors premise, are most commonly upheld by middle- to upper-class families. This stands in contrast to interdependent values—"adjusting and responding to others' needs, connecting to others, and being part of the community" (p. 1179)—which Stephens, Fryberg, et al. (2012) found are more commonly privileged by working-class communities. Second, the extent of a university culture's influence is contingent on a student's disposition to independent values. Therefore, students that find their university climate to be an extension of their home life, experience a cultural match "between their own norms and the norms represented in the university culture" (p. 1181). For others, the experience of college is a cultural mismatch. And third, a cultural match or mismatch can encourage or discourage, respectively, students' performance in school. Cultural mismatch theory, therefore, is an attempt to explain achievement gaps between FGSs and non-FGSs solely on the basis of social class values and norms. This is shortsighted when institutional culture is a product of "norms, values, and practices and the historical and social circumstances in which the institutions were developed and in which they exist" related to race, gender, and social class, among others (D. Smith, 2012, p. 233). From the viewpoint of intersectionality, promoting a match along a single category of analysis only paints a partial image of how institutions, which are structured by mutually constructing dominant forms of capital and external, yet connected, "interlocking systems of power" produce, rather than eliminate, barriers (Núñez, 2014, p. 89; see also Armstrong & Hamilton, 2013; Emirbayer & Desmond, 2015; Sarcedo, Matias, Montoya, & Nishi, 2015). Continuing to characterize students by a single category misses the mark in clarifying how institutional structure and culture are products of multiple forms of social dominance and in understanding students' struggles, especially as the FGS population is more likely to be female and working-class and proportionately more likely to be people of color.

Several studies on FGSs have explored how students experience a match or mismatch with their institutions while only focusing solely on generation status or conflating the FGS term with another category of analysis without explicating their relationship to each other. This phenomenon has occurred along several dimensions of social life, such as race and ethnicity (Benmayor, 2002; Núñez & Sansone, 2016; Orbe, 2003; Parks-Yancy, 2012), social class (Collier & Morgan, 2008; Hinz, 2016; Longwell-Grice & Longwell-Grice, 2008), origin of upbringing (Bradbury & Mather, 2009; Bryan & Simmons, 2009), and faith (Rood, 2009). Through their findings, these studies reveal little about how institutions are structured to advantage or disadvantage FGSs because they fall short in fleshing out the diversity within this category or the relationship between the FGS status and other categories of analysis and the institution. We discuss two examples to illustrate this point.

Collier and Morgan (2008) sought to explore how differences in faculty and student expectations, by generation status, explain differences in educational outcomes. They conducted eight focus groups, which included 63 FGSs and students "from more traditional, highly educated backgrounds (students with at least one college graduate parent)" (p. 431). They attributed the differences between FGSs and non-FGSs to the former's "lack of cultural capital and background information about higher education [which] may limit their awareness of how to 'do the college student role'" (p. 441). Collier and Morgan's (2008) findings reinforce a narrative by which the FGS category holds explanatory power without regard to how race, as an example, may also shape the development of cultural capital that bears on the relationships between faculty, students, and space (Carter, 2003; Guiffrida, 2005). Because Collier and Morgan's (2008) study leaned on a *unidimensional* conceptualization of FGSs (i.e., neither parent is a college graduate), it is challenging to explain the mismatched expectations between students and faculty that could be rooted in inequalities related to social identities other than, or in relation to, the FGS status.

Núñez's (2011) study pushes the conversation further by exploring the influence of Chicano Studies on 19 Latino, FGSs' transition to college. She argued, "Chicano Studies coursework supports students in several tasks identified as being important in Latino college student development, including those of handling racism and building a support network of peers, family, and community (Torres & Hernandez, 2007; Yosso, 2006)" (p. 649). Although critical in providing insight to how curriculum can promote a student's belongingness, her findings did not clarify how students' challenges are related to being both an FGS and Latino, as well as the relationship between the two. In fact, her discussion conflates the two categories and ties the findings, primarily, to students' Latino identity. Students expressed the significance of Chicano Studies to their experiences in college, demonstrating that when institutions provide curriculum that centers and reflects students' background, students may be more likely to succeed. But what about their identity as FGSs as it relates to the institution? What does Chicano Studies have to do with the quality of FGSs' experiences in college? We do not argue nor believe that the categories of generation status and of race be mutually exclusive, in that they have separate, direct influence on students' experiences and outcomes. We take issue with the lack of discussion about the relationship between the two and the extent to which institutions acknowledge this intersection. This leads us to question what the FGS category is expected to capture, further confounding how we identify and make sense of inequality in higher education.

Each study (Collier & Morgan, 2008; Núñez, 2011) is a contribution to our understanding of FGSs, and yet, the narrative of the students in these studies remains incomplete because they either look at how institutions discourage students along a single dimension of social life or do not explain how generation status and other categories of analysis interact to shape students' experiences within their given context. Collier and Morgan (2008) offered no details beyond the generation status of their student participants and a single statement describing their FGSs as diverse: "Some were returning to college as older adults while others came from immigrant backgrounds with English as a second language" (p. 431). There is no further acknowledgment of the heterogeneity within the population. Núñez's (2011) claims are based on a sample of 19 FGS, Latino students. To note, she did collect their gender, ethnicity, and immigrant status, but they too did not play a role in clarifying students' perceptions as an FGS. Both studies would benefit from identifying and allowing other mutually constitutive identities an opportunity to explain the phenomenon of interest (Collier & Morgan, 2008; Núñez, 2011). Without this level of information, our ability to identify and address where and how students struggle is minimized. How can we be certain that a student's challenges are not attributed to another identity or multiple identities, differentially shaped by context and time, as claimed by intersectionality? By tending to a wider vision of the FGS term and its relationship to other, overlapping social realities, we come closer to understanding the quality of relationships that students have with their institutions.

Developing clearer insight in how institutions influence students' belonging and achievement requires that we move away from seeing FGSs as a single status, unique or void of influences from other categories of analysis. Altering the class conditions, for instance, of institutional culture, as suggested by cultural mismatch theory, does little but promote "blanket programming aimed at helping lower-income undergraduates adjust to college" (Jack, 2014, p. 471). This can also be said about efforts solely addressing issues of race or gender. Given that American higher education was built for and by elite, White, and heteronormative men, and that institutions continue to be steeped and wrapped in dominant values (DiAngelo, 2006; Karabel, 2005), research on FGSs must reflect that history because, together, they shape and influence how students behave, including their choices and how they present themselves on campus. In our review, there were studies among a few scholars on FGSs that exemplify this viewpoint across multiple categories of analysis (Armstrong & Hamilton, 2013; Kouyoumdjian, Guzmán, Garcia, & Talavera-Bustillos, 2017; Orbe, 2004; Sarcedo et al., 2015; Stuber, 2011b) and contexts, such as the transition to college (Wilkins, 2014), participation in a TRiO program (Jehangir, Williams, & Jeske, 2012), doctoral education (Holley & Gardner, 2012), and elite universities (Jack, 2014, 2016; Stuber, 2011a). We describe three of these studies in length to best illustrate how overlapping social categories are shaped by their location across several domains of relationships with institutions, others and themselves, and ultimately influenced by the context of time and space (Núñez, 2014). We contend that pursuing this line of inquiry—to take a multilevel intersectionality approach to the study of FGSs—keeps the obscurity, which emerges from how the FGS term is used, at bay.

Stuber (2011b) sought out to explore the diverse experiences of White FGSs, and, rare among studies on this population, grounded her inquiry and analysis in intersectionality. Setting aside dominant narratives that so often homogenize White students, Stuber's (2011b) findings help render the FGS term suspect:

[. . .] generalizations have been made about students who are on the margins not just in terms of social class and parental education but also in terms of race and ethnicity, age, and enrollment status (full-part-time). Little effort has been made to disentangle the ways in which social class, parental education, and race differently impact students' adjustment to college. (p. 120)

Drawing on interview data from 28 White, FGSs (15 females and 13 males) between a private and a public 4-year institution, Stuber found that a little more than half of the students adjusted relatively well to social life on campus, while others expressed feelings of marginality. Findings demonstrated how race and social class interacted to explain these differences in student experiences. One male participant considered his college, "home," even going as far as sharing his preference for college over life at home. These experiences of seamless navigation may be partly due to their racial identity, where Whiteness operates "as an asset for their collegiate adjustment" (Stuber, 2011b, p. 125). Given that both campuses in her study are predominately White, students' Whiteness discouraged feelings of alienation, in part because Whiteness becomes the default in which middle- and upper-class values are defined (DiAngelo, 2006). As many of her participants stem from racially homogenous communities, the racial similarity between home life and campus life "drown[ed] out the 'noise' of social class" (Stuber, 2011b, p. 132). For another White male student, the majority White student body and the emphasis on the Greek system affected him unfavorably, promoting a sense of loneliness and alienation. He found it difficult to engage with other students and "framed his struggles in terms of race (even though he is white), urbanicity, and family background" (Stuber, 2011b, p. 127). In this case, being White was a liability because it concealed how social class shaped his perceptions and circumstances on campus. When studies demonstrate how mutually constitutive forces across different domains shape students' experience, they offer institutions an opportunity to question their own logic about FGSs and gain knowledge that is possibly situated beyond their purview. Stuber's study is evidence that not all students considered FGSs' struggle and achieve equally, a narrative that can be hard to come by when the FGS term is used to cast such a wide net.

In "Paying for the Party: How College Maintains Inequality," Armstrong and Hamilton (2013) conducted a 5-year case study where they interviewed and observed several White women from various social class backgrounds, including six FGSs from working-class families, at a single, public 4-year university. Broadly speaking, they argued that the institution maintains inequality among students because it privileges social activities and spaces—the Party Pathway, structured by the large, Greek system—for which mainly upper-class students are able to fully participate in without risk to their success during and after college. The price of admission into the Greek system is quite high and tends to exclude those students without the economic and cultural resources to meet its inextricably tied classed and gendered standards. For those women from working-class and lower-middle-class backgrounds who chose to engage with the Greek system, Armstrong and Hamilton observed how they were continually disadvantaged because they were unaware of the standards of femininity that regulated the stratified system, nor did they have the financial resources to achieve or maintain physical appearances (i.e., clothes, makeup) that would mark them as respectable, dateable women. In this case, femininity is defined by the dispositions and tastes of the elite. This in turn weakened their ability to develop quality social ties for which women from upper-class backgrounds were able to fully take advantage of after college. Parents, at times, intervened with messages of encouragement and support (Wang, 2012), but their unequal knowledge of navigating campus social settings made it further unlikely that their daughters would be the beneficiaries of the dominant culture (Hamilton, 2016). In other words, the institution's emphasis on the Greek system meant that it endorsed values, norms, and standards for which women from working-class or lower middle-class backgrounds would then struggle to acknowledge or meet, leading them to disengage or to leave college altogether. These findings offer a rare glimpse into how institutions are complicit in maintaining systems and practices that regulate and sort students by the quality of capital they possess, marginalizing them in multiple and overlapping ways. Marginalization then is not a product of being working-class or a woman, but it is a process by which an individual is devalued to the extent that their whole being violates or remains hidden to the standards and values defined by the spaces and the relationships they may wish to occupy and develop, respectively. It is those standards and values and the practices and individuals that enforce and maintain them that are of ultimate interest to those taking an intersectionality approach to addressing inequality.

To further demonstrate the degree in which students are marginalized, Núñez (2014) points out that we must locate "social categories, associated concrete relations, and arenas of practice within a broader temporal and spatial context" (p. 89). Research on FGSs must also look to their histories and backgrounds that can help inform students' relationship to their institutions in order to more accurately map out locations of inequality on campus. Jack (2014) argued that "class marginality and culture shock are contingent on the social and cultural dissimilarity between an individual's life before college and her life therein" (p. 455). Interviewing 35 Black FGSs (13 male and 22 female), he captured their experiences at a single, elite institution, grouping them into one of two categories: Privileged Poor and Doubly Disadvantaged. Although they are similar in demographics and came from poor neighborhoods, each group experienced the transition to college differently. The former reported a more seamless transition to the institution because they possessed a higher stock of cultural capital that they cultivated early on in their elite secondary education, whereas the latter expressed uncertainty around the cultural norms of the institution and difficulty in finding a sense of community (Carter, 2003). These extremes are attributed to differences in educational background in which the Privileged Poor had a head start in acclimating to elite spaces by attending highly selective boarding academies and cultivating forms of cultural capital that are valued by their university. The Doubly Disadvantaged attended poor, local high schools, making their adjustment to college a greater challenge. While race played a role across both groups, their initial responses to racist interactions were conditioned by their precollege experiences. Whereas a Doubly Disadvantaged student had to hold back her "aggressive demeanor, a dominant form of capital back home," the Privileged Poor student saw these events as "manageable moments" in which public displays of anger were left behind in high school. Indeed, "Not all lower-income, black undergraduates experience the strangeness, unfamiliarity, and isolation that entering elite colleges bring" (Jack, 2014, p. 470). Jack's findings advance our stance in problematizing how we study FGSs, for prior research fails in capturing the differential consequences of social inequality in higher education that are contingent on students' prior experiences. These prior experiences are an outcome of broader economic, political, and social challenges and opportunities that in turn reveals more about how FGSs will experience college than their identities alone. According to Jack (2014),

Grouping lower-income undergraduates together biases estimates of the effect of class background on college outcomes given that the social inequalities manifesting themselves in everyday experiences in neighborhoods and schools do not fall evenly on all lower-income students. (p. 472)

Marginality of FGSs is not a singular experience, but it is a function of a much deeper relationship of students' histories that either strengthen or weaken their capacity to succeed in higher education.

Locating inequality is the first step toward addressing it. Mapping the margins, to echo Crenshaw's (1991) language, requires that we not only acknowledge the unequal relationship between students and institutions, but that we pry it open to understand the underlying mechanisms that shape FGSs' diverse experiences. Núñez's (2014) multilevel approach to intersectionality holds research accountable to these efforts, to maintain fidelity to the process of drawing out how individuals' relationships to others, institutions, and systems work in tandem to create spaces and moments of oppression that can often go hidden if we choose to see social categories as one dimensional and mutually exclusive. Studies by Stuber (2011b), Armstrong and Hamilton (2013), and Jack (2014) are examples of how a multilevel intersectional approach offers a wider frame to locating inequality for FGSs. The design of their studies allowed them to compare differences between and among students and institutions, thereby bringing to light the interlocking relationships between race, social class, and/or gender.

In the end, reimagining a frame—so that fewer students are left behind and more students are understood—requires that we question how the FGS term is defined and used in order to gain clearer insight on how institutions of higher education are constructed to shape those spaces and moments where students experience anything less than acceptance. We offer three points, then, that researchers must address to improve how we study and make sense of FGSs: (a) who we include in the FGS term matters, as it fashions what we look for and compare with in addressing inequality; (b) the FGS term is used to capture inequality, but its explanatory power is limited when studies do not account for other social realities and, to that point; (c) for any one student, the degree of mismatch they experience with their institution can occur along several and overlapping dimensions of social life. Using the FGS term as a proxy for social class or conflating it with another category of analysis not only diminishes the complicated nature of social inequality (Wildhagen, 2015), it also wipes away the multiple, intricately tied paths of other categories of analysis that operate across time and space, hindering the opportunity to effectively address students' challenges. Furthermore, given that many samples are derived from institutions with whom researchers have partnerships or access, we urge scholars to consider opportunities for collecting categories of analysis that better capture dimensions of students' lives that can more clearly reveal relationships and locations of inequality.

BEYOND THE IMAGINARY, TRADITIONAL
BOUNDARIES OF FGS RESEARCH

Higher education research expresses a desire to improve the conditions of colleges and universities that will facilitate the achievement of all students, especially those living at the margins. The details behind the extent, circumstances, and effect of those margins remains largely at bay because institutions and researchers continue to utilize and rely on labels and categories to accomplish more than they, in practice, actually can. Reified by popular media, research, and institutional policies and practices, the FGS term represents this ambiguous, shifting cluster that has made it hard to understand who students are, what students need, and what institutions can do to provide for them. Problematizing how the FGS term is used through the concept of intersectionality, we were able to take pause and reflect critically on its purpose and implications for social inequality. In doing so, we see intersectionality—the ability to render categories suspect, to deconstruct categories, to further uncover the power and oppression that emerge from unequal relations between provisional categories of analysis, and to contextualize intersecting points of marginalization—as a critical tool to assess a term, as well as the research behind it, that has no theoretical basis, and yet, has gained undue legitimacy and popularity within the discourse on higher education (McCall, 2005; Núñez, 2014; Wildhagen, 2015). By critiquing how FGS has been conceptualized and used in research, we offer researchers, practitioners, and educators the opportunity to reimagine a frame—to echo Crenshaw's call—that more precisely identifies how students struggle and achieve in college.

In this critical review, we demonstrated multiple ways that the FGS term has been conceptualized and used to make claims about the experiences and outcomes of students. We have highlighted examples of research that limit, instead of expand, and confuse, instead of clarify, how students should be conceived in respect to the institutions and systems in which they find themselves. To be clear, our critique is not against the FGS term itself, but with its canon of research that showcase inconsistency in criteria, poses questions of representation in sampling, and does not take into account the many, overlapping ways students are influenced by their institutions. Given the issues raised in the current operationalization of the FGS term, we call on scholars to be more critical of and attentive to the construction and representativeness of study samples, the use of the category in statistical methods, and the consideration of its overlapping realities in qualitative research within the unique contexts of students' lives and histories.

Intersectionality: Strengths and Possibilities

For the purposes of discussing the strengths of intersectionality and the possibilities it holds for monitoring and understanding trends and patterns in student experiences and outcomes, we will remark specifically on the approaches employed by McCall (2005) and Núñez (2014). The strengths, which we have commented on extensively throughout this chapter, emerge in the "new" knowledge that comes forth when examining the intersections of identity, or in the case of FGSs, the heterogeneity of marginality. McCall's (2005) anticategorical approach to intersectionality challenges us to rethink and reframe our understanding of individuals by pushing us to be skeptical of taken-for-granted categorizations of identity. It reminds us that there is more beneath the surface. Furthermore, intercategorical complexity anchors research within complex realities by centralizing the multiple marginalized identities that many students face, disallowing studies to ignore the diversity of experiences that exist on college campuses. McCall's approaches allows us to be critical of current conceptualizations of inequality, in order to seek more accurate depictions of real and lived inequality endured by students through more intentional quantitative methodologies (see Schudde, 2018, this volume).

Intersectionality can also help pry open the importance of understanding the role of colleges and university in hindering their students. As Núñez (2014) critically asserts, there must be less focus "on the 'additive' (Collins, 2007) descriptions of how individuals experience holding multiple social identities and to focus more on the constitutive dynamics of power in institutions that perpetuate social reproduction of inequalities (Anthias, 2013; Collins, 2007, 2009)" (p. 86). In our review, it becomes apparent that organizations, through its independent culture or unspoken rules of engagement (Yee, 2016), are differentiated sources of oppression and inequality. Grounding our analysis in the concept of intersectionality increases our resolve for future lines of inquiry to design qualitative studies that center the relationships between students and institutions, for they are far more revealing of the heterogeneity within the FGS population and the hidden and overlapping mechanisms that facilitate "power relations and social inequalities" (Collins, 2015, p. 3). For our purpose, the concept of intersectionality unveiled the hidden aspects—social forces, forms of inequality, and unclear boundaries—of the FGS population that would continue to be obscured when not viewed through this conceptual lens.

Our review of the literature showcases the inability of, mainly quantitative, studies to theorize the assumptions undergirding their research design, thereby discouraging their findings from offering points of clarity about students grouped under the FGS category. While research presently may include varying markers of identity in a regression model, or choose to control for particular identities to isolate the effect of the FGS status, there are still questions regarding what is the best, or the most appropriate, way to capture the broader contextual factors that Núñez (2014) offers are important for identifying locations of inequality. Although intersectionality offers a useful framing for considering research design, how to achieve both detailed and multilevel studies on FGSs is unresolved and demands further exploration. We offer that the inquiry should begin with (a) greater attention and partnerships with institutions to collect data categories that represent a multilevel design or (b) merge cohorts of data (e.g., county or district) to create a statewide sample that may provide a response to small sample size concerns. In taking an intersectional approach to designing studies, researchers will be able to achieve a fuller construction of the multiple, overlapping identities that produce inequality and the locations where that inequality emerges. This will allow for conclusions about FGSs to be drawn based on more authentic recognition of their complex lives, pushing findings outside singular categories that reveal too little about FGSs' struggles. We also urge researchers to review Schudde's (2018) chapter in this volume for additional strategies.

Future Research on First-Generation College Students

Research on students considered an FGS remains highly limited to the 4-year, undergraduate experience, with little attention to community colleges and graduate studies (Gardner & Holley, 2011; Holley & Gardner, 2012; Inman & Mayes, 1999). While future research should remain attuned to shifts and changes on campus, it should also expand the scope of these boundaries in order to see how changes in demographics along the educational pipeline, immigration policies under a new administration, or the workforce offer new insights to student challenges. These insights, however, must be foreshadowed by a *heightened sense of the heterogeneity that exists within the FGS population to the extent that inequality is contingent on the intersecting identities that dominant institutions do or do not embrace.*

Feliciano and Lanuza (2017) puts into question how research in education has conceived of the effect of parental education. With a focus on explaining the overachievement of children of immigrant parents relative to their White peers of native-born parents, they argue that "parental contextual attainment . . . captures hidden dimensions of class background that matter for the intergenerational transmission of advantage or disadvantage" (p. 232). In other words, differences in school structure and, thus, differences in educational opportunities reflect variation in social class structure. As such, earning a high school diploma in one country can be considered upper class if the majority complete only elementary school, offering similar dispositions and aspirations as someone earning a baccalaureate degree in the United States. Indeed, "U.S. immigrants originated from higher social class locations, providing them with a particular set of class-specific resources . . . that buttresses their children's achievement" (p. 233). Their findings confirm the need to complicate the notion of parental education, to look beyond differences in attainment to their contexts (Hout, 2015). These findings also push against the notions of parental education that are traditionally tied to current conceptions of FGSs. Instead, they point out that depending on their parents' country of origin, being the "first" to attend or earn a postsecondary degree in their family may not characterize the FGS experience we have come to know. Future studies should consider how various contexts shape the assumptions institutions—such as those related to immigration and social class—use to understand and make choices about how best to support students considered first-generation.

In a similar vein, we must also look to other contextual aspects of students' lives that may influence how we understand their educational realities. FGSs who are undocumented, for example, occupy an ambiguous, and sometimes invisible, space in which their pathway to degree is complicated, and in some instances hindered, by federal and state policies and the growing xenophobia among the U.S. populace

(Gildersleeve & Hernandez, 2012; Gonzales, 2016; Muñoz, 2013; Pyne & Means, 2013). As such, the matter of citizenship and/or immigration status is of significance for understanding this population. As institutions continue to struggle to rearrange themselves to fully support nontraditional students, so too do they struggle to care for their undocumented students (Southern, 2016). There are institutions that have publicly championed the educational opportunity of undocumented students, but few are ready to address the challenges that emerge from this sociopolitical space. Growing concerns with undocumented students' sense safety and of belongingness underscores the importance for studies and theories on FGSs to account for how changes in immigration policy, as well as a growing nativism across the United States, refashions the capacity of institutions to address new locations of inequality for these students.

As campuses shore up their resources to support FGSs, some institutions are also witnessing a growing, collective social movement by these very students. We are concerned that these coalitions—Alliance for Low-Income First-Generation Narrative, First-Generation Student Union, 1vyG, to name a few—may elevate the struggles of some, while hiding the struggles of others. Within these organizations, students have reconstructed the FGS identity to symbolize empowerment and community (Foster, 2015; Pappano, 2015; Young, 2016), offering the possibility of disempowering a dominant narrative of disadvantage to resemble one of resilience, in which the FGS status is seen more as an asset, than a liability (1vyG, 2017; Jehangir et al., 2012; Stephens et al., 2015). However, in the same way that Crenshaw questioned the capacity of "dominated antidiscrimination regimes and anti-racist and feminist discourses" (Carbado, Crenshaw, Mays, & Tomlinson, 2013, p. 311) to acknowledge the plight of Black women, we ask, who remains hidden as the FGS narrative is reified by formal social organizing? We contend that future work seeking to understand this phenomenon see intersectionality as a point of departure in order to sensitize inquiries and analyses to the group conditions "of solidarity that are presumed but not realized" (Carbado et al., 2013).

Various structural barriers tied to students' identities can continue to manifest and transverse the boundaries of their undergraduate years. Although we know little about FGSs pursuing advanced education, and the differences within, existing research aligns with the narrative on FGSs broadly—this population is more likely to delay matriculation into graduate education, to be enrolled part-time, and to be working full-time while enrolled than their non-FGS peers (Seay et al., 2008). Like the FGS population in undergraduate education, those in graduate school expressed their challenging position between home and college life, including a decline in support from family and the unfamiliarity of norms and values regulating graduate education (Gardner & Holley, 2011). In order to complicate this narrative and move beyond the limiting FGS and non-FGS dichotomy, future research should look to how graduate education is structured—by dominant forms of capital—to differentially regulate the achievement of students. Research on their pathways to graduate education, as broad as professional degrees like the masters of business administration to research degrees like the doctor of philosophy, offers a rich opportunity to further identify new locations of inequality or observe how older locations of inequality endure overtime (Posselt & Grodsky, 2017).

For those foregoing advanced education, examining the differential relationship between those considered first-generation and their place of work can offer institutions of higher education insight into how they can better support students as they transition from student to college graduate. Disadvantage may continue into the workforce, as "there appears to be a distinct gap between the understanding of [first-generation and non-first-generation] students about the world of work they wish to enter and its actual expectations, demands, and what it takes to enter and survive there" (Hirudayaraj, 2011, p. 6). A fruitful area of research would include examining this cumulative disadvantage as upwardly mobile FGSs navigate new dominant systems (or spaces within those systems), in particular those areas that often require more nuanced cultural knowledge and experiences limited to the ruling class (Rivera, 2015; Stuber, 2005). In other words, examining how students are multiply disadvantaged across different systems in society offers new insight in how higher education and the occupational structure do not operate in a vacuum, but influence and support each other in maintaining inequality.

Disadvantage for students beyond their college years also lies in the material outcome of educational debt. FGSs borrow more frequently than their non-FGS peers, borrow in larger amounts, and have higher levels of student debt (Furquim, Glasener, Oster, McCall, & DesJardins, 2017). "Students with college-educated parents may have a distinct advantage over FG students in accessing knowledge about the financial aid process and financing college" (Furquim et al., 2017, p. 87), and thus students considered FGSs may be less informed of the financial consequences of earning a college degree. Future research on educational debt must move away from framing and explaining student outcomes by the "FGS" versus "non-FGS" dichotomy for it tells us little about who financial aid systems are precisely disadvantaging. The inequality that emerges from this framing represents a vague gap that does not offer sufficient capacity to identify the overlapping mechanisms that affect student constraints and choices.

Final Thoughts

Inequality can manifest, morph, and operate in the most inconspicuous manner, as it is often hidden among the intertwining shifts in our social, economic, and political terrains (Shapiro, 2017). As we continue to witness the expansion of a stratified system of higher education, critiquing our conceptual and methodological tools remains key to sensitizing us to new student challenges that are veiled behind our failure to see the complexity of their lives. We conclude that it is not about keeping the FGS term or not, it is about how the FGS term is used. It must always be advanced with a careful eye to how students are grouped, what intersections exist, and what relationships it holds with institutions and power structures.

NOTES

[1]This search was conducted on June 12, 2017.

[2]We use the broad term "first generation student" (FGS) to reflect the current operationalization of the category to represent this group of students.

[3]The Hispanic term encompasses a broad range of Spanish-speaking communities, thereby overestimating those who identify as Latino/a. For consistency, we use this term only when the source we are citing has chosen to use it.

REFERENCES

1vyG. (2017). *Who we are*. Retrieved from http://www.1vyg.org/about/

American Association of Community Colleges. (2016). *Fast facts*. Washington, DC: Author.

Anthias, F. (2013). Intersectional what? Social divisions, intersectionality, and levels of analysis. *Ethnicities, 13*, 3–19.

Armstrong, E. A., & Hamilton, L. T. (2013). *Paying for the party*. Cambridge, MA: Harvard University Press.

Auclair, R., Bélanger, P., Doray, P., Gallien, M., Groleau, A., Mason, L., & Mercier, P. (2008). *First-generation students: A promising concept* (Transitions Research Paper 2). Retrieved from https://qspace.library.queensu.ca/handle/1974/5809

Banks-Santilli, L. (2015, June 3). Guilt is one of the biggest struggles first-generation college students face. *The Washington Post*. Retrieved from https://www.washingtonpost.com/posteverything/wp/2015/06/03/guilt-is-one-of-the-biggest-struggles-first-generation-college-students-face/

Benmayor, R. (2002). Narrating cultural citizenship: Oral histories of first-generation college students of Mexican origin. *Social Justice, 4*(90), 96–121.

Billson, J. M., & Terry, M. B. (1982). In search of the silken purse: Factors in attrition among first-generation students. *College University, 58*, 57–75.

Bradbury, B. L., & Mather, P. C. (2009). The integration of first-year, first-generation college students from Ohio Appalachia. *Journal of Students Affairs Research and Practice, 46*, 388–411.

Bryan, E., & Simmons, L. A. (2009). Family involvement: Impacts on post-secondary educational success for first-generation Appalachian college students. *Journal of College Student Development, 50*, 391–406.

Byrd, K. L., & MacDonald, G. (2005). Defining college readiness from the inside out: First-generation college student perspectives. *Community College Review, 33*(1), 22–37.

Bui, K. T. (2005). Middle school variables that predict college attendance for first-generation students. *Education, 126*, 203–221.

Carbado, D. W., Crenshaw, K. W., Mays, V. M., & Tomlinson, B. (2013). Intersectionality: Mapping the movements of a theory. *Du Bois Review, 10*, 303–312.

Cardoza, K. (2016, January 20). First-generation college students are not succeeding in college, and money isn't the problem. *The Washington Post*. Retrieved from https://www.washingtonpost.com/posteverything/wp/2016/01/20/first-generation-college-students-are-not-succeeding-in-college-and-money-isnt-the-problem/?utm_term=.f5b807fc489b

Carter, P. L. (2003). "Black" cultural capital, status positioning, and schooling conflicts for low income African American youth. *Social Problems, 50*, 136–155.

Carter, P. L., & Reardon, S. F. (2014). *Inequality matters*. New York, NY: William T. Grant Foundation. Retrieved from http://wtgrantfoundation.org/library/uploads/2015/09/Inequality-Matters.pdf

Chen, X., & Carroll, C. D. (2005). *First-generation students in postsecondary education: A look at their college transcripts* (NCES 2005-171). Washington, DC: National Center for Education Statistics.

Cho, S. J., Hudley, C., Lee, S., Barry, L., & Kelly, M. (2008). Roles of gender, race, and SES in the college choice process among first-generation and nonfirst-generation students. *Journal of Diversity in Higher Education, 1*, 95–107.

Choy, S. (2001). *Students whose parents did not go to college: Postsecondary access, persistence, and attainment: Findings from the condition of education.* Washington, DC: National for Education Statistics.

Collier, P. J., & Morgan, D. L. (2008). "Is that paper really due today?" Differences in first generation and traditional college students' understandings of faculty expectations. *Higher Education, 55*, 425–446.

Collins, P. H. (2007). Pushing the boundaries or business as usual? Race, class, and gender studies in sociological inquiry. In C. Calhoun (Ed.), *Sociology in America: A history* (pp. 572–604). Chicago, IL: University of Chicago Press.

Collins, P. H. (2015). Intersectionality's definitional dilemmas. *Annual Review of Sociology, 41*, 1–20.

Crenshaw, K. (1989). Demarginalizing the intersection of race and sex: A black feminist critique of antidiscrimination doctrine, feminist theory and antiracist politics. *University of Chicago Legal Forum, 1*, 139–167.

Crenshaw, K. (1991). Mapping the margins: Intersectionality, identity politics, and violence against women of color. *Stanford Law Review, 43*, 1241–1299.

Crenshaw, K. (2016, October). *The urgency of intersectionality* [Video file]. Retrieved from https://www.ted.com/talks/kimberle_crenshaw_the_urgency_of_intersectionality

DeAngelo, L., Franke, R., Hurtado, S., Pryor, J. H., & Tran, S. (2011). *Completing college: Assessing graduation rates at four-year institutions.* Los Angeles: Higher Education Research Institute, UCLA.

Dennis, J. M., Phinney, J. S., & Chuateco, L. I. (2005). The role of motivation, parental support, and peer support in the academic success of ethnic minority first-generation college students. *Journal of College Student Development, 46*, 223–236.

DiAngelo, R. J. (2006). The production of whiteness in education: Asian international students in a college classroom. *Teachers College Record, 108*, 1983–2000.

Dumais, S. A., & Ward, A. (2010). Cultural capital and first-generation college success. *Poetics, 38*, 245–265.

Emirbayer, M., & Desmond, M. (2015). *The racial order.* Chicago, IL: University of Chicago Press.

Feliciano, C., & Lanuza, Y. R. (2017). An immigrant paradox? Contextual attainment and intergenerational educational mobility. *American Sociological Review, 82*, 211–241.

Fischer, M. J. (2007). Settling into campus life: Differences by race/ethnicity in college involvement and outcomes. *Journal of Higher Education, 78*, 125–161.

Foster, B. L. (2015, April 9). What is it like to be poor at an Ivy League school? *The Boston Globe.* Retrieved from https://www.bostonglobe.com/magazine/2015/04/09/what-like-poor-ivy-league-school/xPtql5uzDb6r9AUFER8R0O/story.html

Francis, T. A., & Miller, M. T. (2007). Communication apprehension: Levels of first-generation college students at 2-year institutions. *Community College Journal of Research and Practice, 32*(1), 38–55.

Furquim, F., Glasener, K. M., Oster, M., McCall, B. P., & DesJardins, S. L. (2017). Navigating the financial aid process: Borrowing outcomes among first-generation and non-first generation students. *Annals of the American Academy of Political and Social Science, 671*(1), 69–91.

Gardner, S. K., & Holley, K. A. (2011). "Those invisible barriers are real": The progression of first-generation students through doctoral education. *Equity & Excellence in Education, 44*(1), 77–92.

Giancola, J. K., Munz, D. C., & Trares, S. (2008). First- versus continuing-generation adult students on college perceptions: Are differences actually because of demographic variance? *Adult Educational Quarterly, 58*, 214–228.

Gibbons, M. M., & Borders, L. D. (2010). Prospective first-generation college students: A social-cognitive perspective. *Career Development Quarterly, 58*, 194–208.

Gildersleeve, R. E., & Hernandez, S. (2012). *Undocumented students in American higher education*. Retrieved from https://www.hacu.net/images/hacu/OPAI/H3ERC/2012_papers/Gildersleeve%20%20hernandez%20-%20undocumented%20students.pdf

Gonzales, R. (2016). *Lives in limbo: Undocumented and coming of age in America*. Oakland: University of California Press.

Guiffrida, D. (2005). Othermothering as a framework for understanding African American students' definitions of student-centered faculty. *Journal of Higher Education, 76*, 701–723.

Hahs-Vaughn, D. (2004). The impact of parents' education level on college students: An analysis using the beginning postsecondary students longitudinal study 1990–92/94. *Journal of College Student Development, 45*, 483–500.

Hamilton, L. T. (2016). *Parenting to a degree: How family matters for college women's success*. Chicago, IL: University of Chicago Press.

Harris, E. A. (2017, May 30). "I won't give up": How first-generation students see college. *The New York Times*. Retrieved from https://www.nytimes.com/interactive/2017/05/30/us/07firstgen-listy.html?_r=0

Hinz, S. E. (2016). Upwardly mobile: Attitudes toward the class transition among first-generation college students. *Journal of College Student Development, 57*, 285–299.

Hirudayaraj, M. (2011). First-generation students in higher education: Issues of employability in a knowledge based economy. *Online Journal for Workforce Education and Development, 5*(3), 2. Retrieved from http://opensiuc.lib.siu.edu/cgi/viewcontent.cgi?article=1098&context=ojwed

Holley, K. A., & Gardner, S. (2012). Navigating the pipeline: How socio-cultural influences impact first-generation doctoral students. *Journal of Diversity in Higher Education, 5*, 112–121.

Hout, M. (2015). A summary of what we know about social mobility. *Annals of the American Academy of Political and Social Science, 657*(1), 27–36.

Inman, W. E., & Mayes, L. (1999). The importance of being first: Unique characteristics of first generation community college students. *Community College Review, 26*(4), 3–22.

Ishitani, T. T. (2003). A longitudinal approach to assessing attrition behavior among first-generation students: Time-varying effects of pre-college characteristics. *Research in Higher Education, 44*, 433–449.

Ishitani, T. T. (2006). Studying attrition and degree completion behavior among first-generation college students in the United States. *Journal of Higher Education, 77*, 861–885.

Jack, A. A. (2014). Culture shock revisited: The social and cultural contingencies to class marginality. *Sociological Forum, 24*, 453–475.

Jack, A. A. (2016). (No) harm in asking class, acquired cultural capital, and academic engagement at an elite university. *Sociology of Education, 89*(1), 1–19.

Jehangir, R., Williams, R., & Jeske, J. (2012). The influence of multicultural learning communities on the intrapersonal development of first-generation college students. *Journal of College Student Development, 53*, 267–284.

Kahlenberg, R. D. (2016, February 24). How low-income students are fitting in an elite colleges. *The Atlantic*. Retrieved from https://www.theatlantic.com/education/archive/2016/02/the-rise-of-firstgeneration-college-students/470664/

Karabel, J. (2005). *The chosen: The hidden history of admission and exclusion at Harvard, Yale, and Princeton*. New York, NY: Houghton Mifflin Harcourt.

Kouyoumdjian, C., Guzmán, B. L., Garcia, N. M., & Talavera-Bustillos, V. (2017). A community cultural wealth examination of sources of support and challenges among Latino first-and second-generation college students at a Hispanic serving institution. *Journal of Hispanic Higher Education, 16*(1), 61–76.

Lamont, M. (2009). *How professors think.* Cambridge, MA: Harvard University Press.

Lee, J. J., Sax, L. J., Kim, K. A., & Hagedorn, L. S. (2004). Understanding students' parental education beyond first-generation status. *Community College Review, 32*(1), 1–20.

Lohfink, M. M., & Paulsen, M. B. (2005). Comparing the determinants of persistence for first-generation and continuing-generation students. *Journal of College Student Development, 46,* 409–428.

Lombardi, A. R., Murray, C., & Gerdes, H. (2012). Academic performance of first-generation college students with disabilities. *Journal of College Student Development, 53,* 811–826.

London, H. B. (1989). Breaking away: A study of first-generation college students and their families. *American Journal of Education, 97,* 144–170.

Longwell-Grice, R., & Longwell-Grice, H. (2008). Testing Tinto: How do retention theories work for first-generation, working-class students? *Journal of College Student Retention, 9,* 407–420.

Majer, J. M. (2009). Self-efficacy and academic success among ethnically diverse first-generation community college students. *Journal of Diversity in Higher Education, 2,* 243–250.

Martinez, J. A., Sher, K. J., Krull, J. L., & Wood, P. K. (2009). Blue-collar scholars? Mediators and moderators of university attrition in first-generation college students. *Journal of College Student Development, 50,* 87–103.

McCall, L. (2005). The complexity of intersectionality. *Signs, 30,* 1771–1800.

McCarron, G. P., & Inkelas, K. K. (2006). The gap between educational aspirations and attainment for first-generation college students and the role of parental involvement. *Journal of College Student Development, 47,* 534–549.

Muñoz, S. M. (2013). "I just can't stand being like this anymore": Dilemmas, stressors, and motivators for undocumented Mexican women in higher education. *Journal of Student Affairs Research and Practice, 50,* 233–249.

Nash, J. C. (2008). Re-thinking intersectionality. *Feminist Review, 89,* 1–15.

Nomi, T. (2005). *Faces of the future: A portrait of first-generation community college students.* Washington, DC: American Association of Community Colleges.

Núñez, A. M. (2005). Negotiating ties: A qualitative study for first-generation female students' transitions to college. *Journal of the First-Year Experience, 17,* 87–118.

Núñez, A. M. (2011). Counterspaces and connections in college transitions: First-generation Latino students' perspectives on Chicano Studies. *Journal of College Student Development, 52,* 639–655.

Núñez, A. M. (2014). Employing multilevel intersectionality in educational research Latino identities, contexts, and college access. *Educational Researcher, 43*(2), 85–92.

Núñez, A. M., & Cuccaro-Alamin, S. (1998). *First-generation students: Undergraduates whose parents never enrolled in postsecondary education.* Washington, DC: National Center for Educational Statistics.

Núñez, A. M., & Sansone, V. A. (2016). Earning and learning: Exploring the meaning of work in the experiences of first-generation Latino college students. *Review of Higher Education, 40,* 91–116.

Orbe, M. P. (2003). African American first generation college student communicative experiences. *Electronic Journal of Communication/La Revue Electronique de Communication, 13*(2/3). Retrieved from http://www.cios.org/EJCPUBLIC/013/2/01322.html

Orbe, M. P. (2004). Negotiating multiple identities within multiple frames: An analysis of first generation college students. *Communication Education, 53,* 131–149.

Padgett, R. D., Johnson, M. P., & Pascarella, E. T. (2012). First-generation undergraduate students and the impacts of the first year of college: Additional evidence. *Journal of College Student Development*, *53*, 243–266.

Palbusa, J. A., & Gauvain, M. (2017). Parent–student communication about college and freshman grades in first-generation and non–first-generation students. *Journal of College Student Development*, *58*, 107–112.

Pappano, L. (2015, April 8). First-generation students unite. *The New York Times*. Retrieved from https://www.nytimes.com/2015/04/12/education/edlife/first-generation-student-sunite.html?_r=0

Parks-Yancy, R. (2012). Interactions into opportunities: Career management for low-income, first-generation African American college students. *Journal of College Student Development*, *53*, 510–523.

Pascarella, E. T., Pierson, C. T., Wolniak, G. C., & Terenzini, P. T. (2004). First-generation college students: Additional evidence on college experiences and outcomes. *Journal of Higher Education*, *75*, 249–284.

Pell Institute for the Study of Opportunity in Higher Education. (2011). *Fact Sheet: 6-Year degree attainment rates for students enrolled in a post-secondary institution*. Washington, DC: Author. Retrieved from www.pellinstitute.org/downloads/fact_sheets-6-Year_DAR_for_Students_Post-Secondary_Institution_121411.pdf

Pike, G. R., & Kuh, G. D. (2005). First-and second-generation college students: A comparison of their engagement and intellectual development. *Journal of Higher Education*, *76*, 276–300.

Posselt, J. R., & Grodsky, E. (2017). Graduate education and social stratification. *Annual Review of Sociology*, *43*, 1–26.

Próspero, M., Russell, A. C., & Vohra-Gupta, S. (2012). Effects of motivation on educational attainment: Ethnic and developmental differences among first-generation students. *Journal of Hispanic Higher Education*, *11*, 100–119.

Próspero, M., & Vohra-Gupta, S. (2007). First-generation college students: Motivation, integration, and academic achievement. *Community College Journal of Research and Practice*, *31*, 963–975.

Pyne, K. B., & Means, D. R. (2013). Underrepresented and in/visible: A Hispanic first generation student's narratives of college. *Journal of Diversity in Higher Education*, *6*, 186–198.

Ramos-Sánchez, L., & Nichols, L. (2007). Self-efficacy of first-generation and non-first-generation college students: The relationship with academic performance and college adjustment. *Journal of College Counseling, 10*(1), 6–18.

Rivera, L. A. (2015). *Pedigree: How elite students get elite jobs*. Princeton, NJ: Princeton University Press.

Rood, R. E. (2009). Driven to achieve: First-generation students' narrated experience at a private Christian college. *Christian Higher Education*, *8*, 225–254.

Saenz, V. B., Hurtado, S., Barrera, D., Wolf, D., & Yeung, F. (2007). *First in my family: A profile of first-generation college students at four-year institutions since 1971*. Los Angeles: Higher Education Research Institute, UCLA.

Sarcedo, G. L., Matias, C. E., Montoya, R., & Nishi, N. W. (2015). Dirty dancing with race and class: Microaggressions toward first-generation and low-income college students of color. *Journal of Critical Scholarship on Higher Education and Student Affairs*, *2*(1), 1–17.

Schudde, L. (2018). Heterogeneous effects in education: The promise and challenge of incorporating intersectionality into quantitative methodological approaches. *Review of Research in Education*, *42*, 72–92.

Seay, S. E., Lifton, D. E., Wuensch, K. L., Bradshaw, L. K., & McDowelle, J. O. (2008). First-generation graduate students and attrition risks. *Journal of Continuing Higher Education*, *56*(1), 11–25.

Shapiro, T. M. (2017). *Toxic inequality: How America's wealth gap destroys mobility, deepens the racial divide, and threatens our future.* New York, NY: Basic Books.

Shavit, Y., Arum, R., & Gamoran, A. (Eds.). (2007). *Stratification in higher education: A comparative study.* Stanford, CA: Stanford University Press.

Smith, D. (2012). Diversity: *A bridge to the future?* In M. N. Bastedo (Ed.), *The organization of higher education* (pp. 225–255). Baltimore, MD: Johns Hopkins University Press.

Smith, W., & Zhang, P. (2010). The impact of key factors on the transition from high school to college among first-and second-generation students. *Journal of the First-Year Experience & Students in Transition, 22*(2), 49–70.

Soria, K. M., & Stebleton, M. J. (2012). First-generation students' academic engagement and retention. *Teaching in Higher Education, 17,* 673–685.

Southern, K. G. (2016). Institutionalizing support services for undocumented students at four year colleges and universities. *Journal of Student Affairs Research and Practice, 53,* 305–318.

Stebleton, M. J., Soria, K. M., & Huesman, R. L. (2014). First-generation students' sense of belonging, mental health, and use of counseling services at public research universities. *Journal of College Counseling, 17*(1), 6–20.

Stevens, M. L., Armstrong, E. A., & Arum, R. (2008). Sieve, incubator, temple, hub: Empirical and theoretical advances in the sociology of higher education. *Annual Review of Sociology, 34,* 127–151.

Stephens, N. M., Fryberg, S. A., Markus, H. R., Johnson, C. S., & Covarrubias, R. (2012). Unseen disadvantage: How American universities' focus on independence undermines the academic performance of first-generation college students. *Journal of Personality and Social Psychology, 102,* 1178–1197.

Stephens, N. M., Townsend, S. S., Hamedani, M. G., Destin, M., & Manzo, V. (2015). A difference-education intervention equips first-generation college students to thrive in the face of stressful college situations. *Psychological Science, 26,* 1556–1566.

Stephens, N. M., Townsend, S. S., Markus, H. R., & Phillips, L. T. (2012). A cultural mismatch: Independent cultural norms produce greater increases in cortisol and more negative emotions among first-generation college students. *Journal of Experimental Social Psychology, 48,* 1389–1393.

Strayhorn, T. L. (2006). Factors influencing the academic achievement of first-generation college students. *NASPA Journal, 43*(4), 82–111.

Strayhorn, T. L. (2012). *College students' sense of belonging: A key to educational success for all students.* New York, NY: Routledge.

Stuber, J. M. (2005). Asset and liability? The importance of context in the occupational experiences of upwardly mobile white adults. *Sociological Forum, 20,* 139–166.

Stuber, J. M. (2011a). *Inside the college gates.* Lanham, MD: Lexington.

Stuber, J. M. (2011b). Integrated, marginal, and resilient: Race, class, and the diverse experiences of white first-generation college students. *International Journal of Qualitative Studies in Education, 24,* 117–136.

Terenzini, P. T., Springer, L., Yaeger, P. M., Pascarella, E. T., & Nora, A. (1996). First-generation college students: Characteristics, experiences, and cognitive development. *Research in Higher Education, 37*(1), 1–22.

Torres, V., & Hernandez, E. (2007). The influence of ethnic identity on self-authorship: A longitudinal study of Latino/a students. *Journal of College Student Development, 48,* 558–573.

Toutkoushian, R. K., Stollberg, R. A., & Slaton, K. A. (in press). Talking 'bout my generation: Defining 'First-Generation Students' in higher education research. *Teachers College Record.*

U.S. Department of Education. (2014). *Profile of undergraduate students: 2011–2012.* Washington, DC: Author. Retrieved from https://nces.ed.gov/pubsearch/pubsinfo. asp?pubid=2015167

Vuong, M., Brown-Welty, S., & Tracz, S. (2010). The effects of self-efficacy on academic success of first-generation college sophomore students. *Journal of College Student Development, 51*(1), 50–64.

Wang, T. R. (2012). "I'm the only person from where I'm from to go to college": Understanding the memorable messages first-generation college students receive from on-campus mentors. *Communication Education, 61*, 335–357.

Westbrook, S. B., & Scott, J. A. (2012). The influence of parents on the persistence decisions of first-generation college students. *Focus on Colleges, Universities & Schools, 6*(1), 1–9.

Wildhagen, T. (2015). "Not your typical student": The social construction of the "first generation" college student. *Qualitative Sociology, 38*, 285–303.

Wilkins, A. C. (2014). Race, age, and identity transformations in the transition from high school to college for Black and first-generation White men. *Sociology of Education, 87*, 171–187.

Yee, A. (2016). The unwritten rules of engagement: Social class differences in undergraduate academic strategies. *Journal of Higher Education, 87*, 831–858.

Yosso, T. J. (2006). *Critical race counterstories along the Chicana/Chicano pipeline.* New York, NY: Routledge.

Young, M. S. (2016, October 16). The cost of being first. *The Atlantic.* Retrieved from https://www.theatlantic.com/education/archive/2016/10/the-cost-of-being-first/504155/

Chapter 8

Mapping Intersectionality and Latina/o and Chicana/o Students Along Educational Frameworks of Power

SONYA M. ALEMÁN

University of Texas at San Antonio

This chapter reviews scholarship using intersectional analyses to assess how Latina/o and Chicana/o youth navigate imbricated systems of privilege and oppression in their educational trajectories. Scholars have explored the navigational tactics Latina/o and Chicana/o students use to negotiate their intersectional identities and the institutional practices that amplify or negate experiences of privilege or disenfranchisement. Others have articulated distinct forms of overlapping oppression, such as racist nativism, gendered familism, privilege paradox, and citizenship continuum. Researchers have also developed a methodology for intersectional analysis that combines both quantitative and qualitative elements, as well as a conceptual model that maps out the micro, meso, and macro levels of intersectionality to account for both structure and agency within multifaceted dynamics of power. This chapter notes the reliance on race- and gender-based frameworks, on interviews and focus groups, and on college-age or graduate students for intersectional analysis on Latina/o and Chicana/o students. Together, the chapter reveals the complexity of capturing the multitiered planes of privilege and power that intersect in dynamic ways to disenfranchise and empower Latina/o and Chicana/o students.

Multiple forms of systemic and hierarchical oppression have made Latina/o and Chicana/o[1] youth one of the most disenfranchised groups of students in America's educational system (Covarrubias, 2011; Núñez, 2014b; Ramirez, 2011). Latina/os are part of the largest, youngest, and fastest growing demographic group in the United States[2] and have been the second largest group of school-aged children since 2014, at nearly 13 million (Hussar & Bailey, 2013; Krogstad & Fry, 2014). Regrettably, educational attainment of these groups has not maintained parity with

Review of Research in Education
March 2018, Vol. 42, pp. 177–202
DOI: 10.3102/0091732X18763339

their increasing presence, buying power, and political clout, necessitating attention to persistent imbalances in the quality of schooling for Latina/o and Chicana/o communities, particularly compared to their White counterparts.

Scholars have documented the disparities in retention, achievement, funding, teacher quality, college preparation, and graduation rates for Latina/o and Chicana/o students that serve as pitfalls along the educational pipeline, often by delineating these inequities along the single dimension of race (Contreras, 2011; De Jesús, 2005; Delgado Bernal & Alemán, 2017; Gándara & Contreras, 2009; Gándara, Larson, Rumberger, & Mehan, 1998; Yosso, 2006). However, a growing number of researchers have begun to employ intersectionality, a theoretical framework that allows them to identify the processes, actions, and impact of concurrent forms of marginalization and empowerment on Latina/o and Chicana/o students.

This chapter reviews scholarship that employs intersectional analysis to assess how Latina/o and Chicana/o youth navigate the imbricating systems of privilege and oppression that manifest in their educational trajectories. Within this corpus, scholars have primarily explored the tactics that Latina/o and Chicana/o students use to navigate their intersectional identities, as well as the ways institutions function to amplify or negate experiences of intersectional oppression (Abrica & Martinez, 2016; Cabrera, Rashwan-Soto, & Valencia, 2016; Castro & Cortez, 2017; Knight, Dixon, Norton, & Bentley, 2006; Leyva, 2016; Muñoz & Maldonado, 2012; Pérez, Rodríguez, & Guadarrama, 2015; Ramirez, 2011, 2014; Urrieta & Villenas, 2013; Zavala, 2014). A few have used this approach to develop constructs such as *racist nativism* (Pérez Huber, 2010), *gendered familism* (Ovink, 2013), *privilege paradox* (Rashwan-Soto & Cabrera, 2011), and *citizenship continuum* (Covarrubias & Lara, 2014) to classify the distinct forms of intersectional oppression experienced by Latina/o and Chicana/o students that are fueled by one or more axes of power. Other scholars have developed a quantitative intersectional analysis methodology to disaggregate educational attainment data for various Latina/o subgroups along the educational pipeline (Covarrubias, 2011; Covarrubias & Lara, 2014; Sólorzano, Villalpando, & Oseguera, 2005), to challenge unidimensional understandings of this trajectory. Lastly, researchers have proposed methodological or conceptual models that seek to discern the impact of and relationships between the multiple systems of power affecting the academic pathways of Latina/o and Chicana/o students (Covarrubias & Veléz, 2013; Núñez, 2014a, 2014b). Together, this body of work uncovers the complexity of capturing the multitiered planes of privilege and power that intersect in dynamic ways to disenfranchise and empower Latina/o and Chicana/o students.

This chapter comprises five sections. The first section will highlight the injustices and inequities that plague the educational experiences of Latina/o and Chicana/o youth, reiterating the impetus for much of the scholarship reviewed here. The second will summarize the characteristics of intersectionality as engaged by scholars within the education field. The next section will detail the parameters used to identify and delimit the literature reviewed here. The fourth section fleshes out how intersectional analysis can inform understandings of how overlapping socially constructed categories of identity and compounding matrices of marginalization affect the ways Latina/o and Chicana/o students experience the policies, practices, pedagogy, and procedures used by educators and administrators. While there are a few points of alignment with a previous literature review of intersectional scholarship in education conducted by Núñez (2014a; included in this chapter), this analysis identified three foci that contour the intersectional scholarship about Latina/o students: (1) the multiple responses Latina/o students engage to traverse the complex power relations that shape their educational experiences, (2) the institutional practices by schools and their stakeholders that foster advantages or disadvantages for Latina/o or Chicana/o students, and (3) the structural, historical, and ideological relations of power at play that concurrently actualize the experiences of Latina/o and Chicana/o students. Importantly, these focal areas are not discrete categories, as much of the research addressed more than one of these spheres simultaneously. Findings also include a discussion of the topics and groups studied and the theoretical and methodological frameworks used. Two contributions of this intersectional research are the development of a methodological approach for intersectional analysis that fuses quantitative and qualitative elements, and the advancement of a conceptual model for intersectional analysis. The concluding section highlights the strengths and opportunities intersectional analysis offers to scholars committed to transforming the unfavorable educational conditions that many Latina/o and Chicana/o students endure.

EDUCATIONAL INEQUITIES FACED BY LATINA/O AND CHICANA/O STUDENTS

According to the U.S. Department of Education, Latina/o and Chicana/o students comprised about 27% of the 50 million students in the nation's public schools in 2016 (Hussar & Bailey, 2013), a growing population that has transformed the nation's K–12 public school students into "majority-minority" (Hussar & Bailey, 2013). In 2014, Latina/o and Chicana/o students also became the largest non-White population enrolled in U.S. 4-year colleges and universities, totaling 2.3 million and representing about 16.5% of college enrollment overall (Fry & Lopez, 2012).

The increasing numbers of Latina/o and Chicana/o students in the K–16 educational pipeline, however, have not yet resulted in educational attainment rates that remedy the inequities plaguing these communities. For instance, while the high school dropout rates in this group have been decreasing, dropping from 32% in 2000 to 12% in 2014 for 18- to 24-year-olds, the latter figure was twice the dropout rate of Black students, and 2½ times the rate of White students (Krogstad, 2016a). College enrollment is on the rise, but 48% of those 2.3 million Latina/o and Chicana/o college students attend community colleges rather than 4-year universities, compared to 36% of Black students and 30% of White students. Latinas/os and Chicanas/os make up more than a quarter of the community college student population. The low transfer rate between community colleges and universities (NCES, 2003; Yosso & Solórzano, 2006) may be one reason why only 15% of Latinas/os or Chicanas/os between the ages of 25 and 29 have at least a bachelor's degree (Krogstad, 2016a). In contrast, about 41% of Whites in this age group have a college degree, as do 22% of Blacks (2016a). Finally, Latina/o and Chicana/o students remain exceedingly underrepresented in graduate education, earning only 6% of all doctorates awarded in 2011, compared to the 74% earned by Whites (National Science Foundation & National Center for Science and Engineering Statistics, 2012). Because Latina/o and Chicana/o communities make up such an instrumental segment of this nation's citizenry, educators and researchers should better understand and redress these staggering disparities in educational attainment, as they have repercussions for the entire nation. These youth are a promising resource that can contribute to the U.S. economy and civic life that is not being developed. Intersectional analysis is a tool that can offer both clarity and remedy.

INTERSECTIONALITY AND INTERSECTIONAL ANALYSIS DEFINED

An intersectional analysis illuminates related and interdependent phenomena. The first concerns identity politics. For scholars who employ intersectional analysis to study Latina/o and Chicana/o students, this means acknowledging the heterogeneity within Latina/o and Chicana/o communities (or any marginal group) as a way to challenge essentialist, monolithic, and undifferentiated representations of this community, while also accounting for the strategic, coalitional, collective, and transformational affiliations that members of disenfranchised groups often adopt as an instrument for social justice (Cho, Crenshaw, & McCall, 2013; Collins & Bilge, 2016; McCall, 2005). A second phenomenon examined by researchers engaged in intersectional analysis are the oscillating experiences of privilege and oppression that result from the complex and interconnected domains of power relations within which those heterogeneous subjectivities are situated (Cho et al., 2013; Collins & Bilge, 2016). Specifically, because transecting conditions of power negatively and positively constitute and affect the lives and identities of Latina/o and Chicana/o students, an intersectional analysis situates the myriad Latina/o and Chicana/o subjectivities within larger systems of privilege and oppression, contending that these complex, contingent, and interlocking relationships must be made visible and analyzed primarily to upend structural inequalities. The goal of an intersectional analysis is not to chart out a hierarchy of oppression among the subgroups of Latinas/os and Chicanas/os or between them and other ethnoracial[3] groups (Carbado, 2013) but, instead, to map out the array of subjectivities that result from multiple domains of power Latinas/os and Chicanas/os experience to fashion interventions that strive for social justice and capitalize on their agency, resiliency, and resistance.

Educational sites in the United States function as a microcosm of these transecting power dynamics, often disenfranchising Latina/o and Chicana/o students through a reinscription and flattening of various power differentials. In essence, because educational institutions tend to unequally disseminate resources, status, and power along racial, gender, and class axes, the educational trajectories of Latina/o and Chicana/o students are irrevocably shaped by these forces, which delimit access and opportunities for many Latina/o and Chicana/o youth (Alemán, Delgado Bernal, & Cortez, 2015; Alemán, Delgado Bernal, McKinney, & Freire, 2017; Auerbach, 2002; Ladson-Billings, 2006; Solórzano & Ornelas, 2004). Schools, therefore, are important sites for intersectional analysis as this research reveals the unjust manifestations of marginalization endemically endured by the growing number of Latina/o and Chicana/o students in U.S. schools.

LITERATURE REVIEW METHODOLOGY

Unlike Nuñez's (2014a) broader research synthesis of education literature that explores how multiple social identities and societal contexts shape Latino college access and success, this review narrows the range of scholarship to work that explicitly applied an intersectional analysis to study this particular ethnoracial student population. For this survey, several academic research databases were searched using the keywords "intersectionality" or "intersectional analysis" in combination with variations on the labels used to identify Latina/o communities: "Latina," "Latinas," "Latina/o," "Chicano," "Chicanas," "Chicana/o," "Hispanic," "Mexican," "Mexican American," and "undocumented." The targeted databases included those that primarily feature education research like EBSCO/ERIC, as well as other collections that contain research from all disciplines, such as JSTOR, Google Scholar, and Academic Search Premier. To narrow the results of these queries, which yielded an initial sample of over 300 articles, the following parameters were used to identify peer-reviewed, published research for review: (1) the research explicitly used an intersectional analysis to make sense of the data under study; (2) the research focused on P–20 students who identified as Latina/o, Chicana/o, Hispanic, Mexican American, Mexican immigrant, or undocumented; (3) the research primarily engaged the education field and literature to ground its research; and (4) the scholarship was published after 2000, in order to look at the most recent scholarship.

In other words, scholars had to do more than mention the word *intersectionality* and had to also actively employ an intersectional analysis to make sense of how Latina/o and Chicana/o students with positionalities predicated along various social markers such as race, gender, class, sexuality, or religion navigate the interlocking and hierarchical systems of oppression that fashion their educational experiences. For instance, a significant amount of scholarship using critical race theory or Chicana feminism allude to their respective theoretical precepts that acknowledge that racism and sexism occur along the intersection of identities, privilege, and marginalization, but studies that did not specifically analyze the contingent and compound conditions of intersectional subjectivities or untangle the web of advantages and disadvantages Latina/o or Chicana/o students face were excluded from the set reviewed here. Moreover, the conversation the scholars sought to contribute to had to be rooted in the field of education for this review.

The search yielded 19 sources. These include 14 articles published in education journals and 5 book chapters, listed in Table 1. One article, although published in *Gender & Society*, was included in this chapter because it met the research parameters stated above. Together, this scholarship represents how intersectional analysis has been employed to understand the educational experiences of Latina/o and Chicana/o students.

The computer-aided qualitative coding software NVivo was used to help analyze the body of work. Two guiding questions were used to shape the initial coding categories:

1. How have intersectional analyses produced knowledge about the ways Latina/o and Chicana/o students experience educational sites, trajectories, policies, and practices?
2. What are the theoretical and methodological implications of the concept of intersectionality when used to study the educational experiences and realities for Latina/o and Chicana/o students' education?

For the first round of coding, excerpts from every article or chapter that corresponded to these two categories were flagged, creating two broad sets of data: knowledge produced and theory/method. These initial groupings were then further refined. All the excerpts identifying the knowledge produced about Latina/o and Chicana/o students were reexamined to discern patterns that would help categorize the findings and focus of each article. NVivo was once again used for this second level of coding. Items categorized included findings about the day-to-day challenges Latina/o or Chicana/o students navigate, the coping strategies they engaged, and the matrices of power at play engendering the circumstances under study. This grounded theory approach resulted in the three aforementioned focal areas: individual coping strategies, institutional practices, and structural causes. The second set of codes flagged the theoretical frameworks used and the methods employed, revealing commonalities in these approaches. It also identified items such as the particular population studied (Latina females, Latino males, undocumented, high school youth, working class, etc.), the educational site scrutinized (high school, community college, university), purpose of study, and distinct educational issue (college going, college access, college choice, educational attainment, community college transfer, etc.) to help better understand the purview of intersectional analysis regarding Latina/o and Chicana/o students. The section below outlines these findings.

FOCI OF INTERSECTIONAL ANALYSIS: INDIVIDUAL, INSTITUTIONAL, STRUCTURAL

Several insights emerged from the extant research applying an intersectional analysis. These are discussed below in four sections. The first section discusses the ways scholars have documented the various strategies Latina/o and Chicana/o students use

TABLE 1
List of Literature Reviewed

Author(s)	Year	Title	Journals
Abrica and Martinez	2016	Strategies for Navigating Financial Challenges Among Latino Male Community College Students: Centralizing Race, Gender, and Immigrant Generation	*Journal of Applied Research in the Community College*
Castro and Cortez	2017	Exploring the Lived Experiences and Intersectionalities of Mexican Community College Transfer Students: Qualitative Insights Toward Expanding a Transfer Receptive Culture	*Community College Journal of Research and Practice*
Covarrubias	2011	Quantitative Intersectionality: A Critical Race Analysis of the Chicana/o Educational Pipeline	*Journal of Latinos in Education*
Covarrubias and Lara	2014	The Undocumented (Im)migrant Educational Pipeline: The Influence of Citizenship Status on Educational Attainment for People of Mexican Origin	*Urban Education*
Muñoz and Maldonado	2012	Counterstories of College Persistence by Undocumented Mexicana Students: Navigating Race, Class, Gender, and Legal Status	*International Journal of Qualitative Studies in Education*
Leyva	2016	An Intersectional Analysis of Latin@ College Women's Counter-Stories in Mathematics	*Journal of Urban Mathematics Education*
Núñez	2014	Employing Multilevel Intersectionality in Education Research: Latino Identities, Contexts, and College Access	*Educational Researcher*
Ovink	2013	"They Always Call Me an Investment": Gendered Familism and Latino/a College Pathways	*Gender & Society*
Pérez Huber	2010	Using Latina/o Critical Race Theory (LatCrit)and Racist Nativism to Explore Intersectionality in the Educational Experiences of Undocumented Chicana College Students	*Educational Foundations*
Ramirez	2011	"No One Taught Me the Steps": Latinos' Experiences Applying to Graduate School	*Journal of Latinos in Education*
Ramirez	2014	"¿Qué estoy haciendo aquí? (What Am I Doing Here?)": Chicanos/Latinos(as) Navigating Challenges and Inequalities During Their First Year of Graduate School	*Equity & Excellence in Education*
Sólorzano, Villalpando, and Oseguera	2005	Educational Inequities and Latina/o Undergraduate Students in the United States: A Critical Race Analysis of Their Educational Progress	*Journal of Hispanic Higher Education*
Urrieta and Villenas	2013	The Legacy of Derrick Bell and Latino/a Education: A Critical Race Testimonio	*Race, Ethnicity, and Education*
Zavala	2014	Latina/o Youth's Perspectives on Race, Language, and Learning Mathematics	*Journal of Urban Mathematics Education*

(continued)

TABLE 1 (CONTINUED)

Author(s)	Year	Chapter	Book
Cabrera, Rashwan-Soto, and Valencia	2016	An Intersectionality Analysis of Latino Men in Higher Education and Their Help-Seeking Behaviors	*Ensuring the Success of Latino Males in Higher Education: A National Imperative*
Covarrubias and Veléz	2013	Critical Race Quantitative Intersectionality: An Anti-Racist Research Paradigm That Refuses to "Let the Numbers Speak for Themselves"	*Handbook of Critical Race Theory in Education*
Knight, Dixon, Norton, and Bentley	2006	Contextualizing Latina Youth's Constructions of Their College-Bound Identities	*Chicana/Latina Education in Everyday Life: Feminista Perspectives on Pedagogy and Epistemology*
Núñez	2014	Advancing an Intersectionality Framework in Higher Education: Power and Latino Postsecondary Opportunity	*Higher Education: Handbook of Theory and Research* (Vol. 29)
Pérez, Rodríguez, and Guadarrama	2015	Rising Voices: College Opportunity and Choice Among Latina/o Undocumented	*Higher Education Access and Choice for Latino Students: Critical Findings and Theoretical Perspectives*

to negotiate the ebb and flow of power that can both privilege and subjugate. The second section highlights research that attempts to make visible the institutional machinations that can benefit or harm Latina/o or Chicana/o students depending on context and positionality. A third section examines scholarship that deconstructs the structural, historical, and ideological components of the imbricating matrices of power that scaffold both the layered identities and the educational opportunities of Latina/o and Chicana/o students. The final section reviews the methodologies and theoretical frameworks informing and driving the intersectional analysis reviewed here, underscoring the development of a methodological framework drawing from quantitative and qualitative approaches, and a conceptual framework as distinct approaches for intersectional analysis of Latinas/os, Chicanas/os, and other students of color.

Coping Strategies

A significant amount of the current research using intersectional analysis maps out the navigational or coping strategies Latina/o and Chicana/o students engage to mitigate experiences of disenfranchisement and/or capitalize on instances of privilege via their educational journeys. Together, these studies reveal the contradictions in the array of tactics used by Latina/o and Chicana/o students to navigate these conditions, as not all students countered intersectional forms of oppression in an antihegemonic manner, even when they intuit the injustices they endure. For example, Knight et al. (2006) analyzed a bricolage of texts produced by three young girls for the dominant ideologies about their identities and educational capabilities, as well as the ways the girls acquiesce or challenge them. The authors found that the girls exhibited a multitude of identities that are fashioned and repositioned among overlapping oppressive structures—which include sexist interpretations of their bodies, capitalist expectations about their labor, and nativist understandings about their Latinidades.[4] Muñoz and Maldonado (2012) examined narratives of resistance shared by undocumented Latinas, noting the ways these strategic discourses allow them to develop positive self-images that allow "them to hang on to their academic aspirations, to persist in college, and to envision and pursue the possibility of success" (p. 293) but also at times reinscribe dominant narratives. For instance, the authors found that many undocumented students take pride in knowing Mexican history and traditions, challenging how this knowledge is discounted in the United States. Nonetheless, their participants echoed their Anglo U.S. peers in minimizing racism as merely resulting from an individual's ignorance rather than being institutional and systemic.

In studying the ways Latino college students overcome financial difficulties, Abrica and Martinez (2016) plotted three different persistence strategies—conditional, meritocratic, and transformational—based on the level of critique against racial oppression or meritocracy. For example, participants who invested in developing business plans and acquiring financial capital to solve their money woes "expressed limited racial understanding and emphasized the need to be associated with Whiteness," whereas those who identified campus resources as a way to offset these financial challenged more readily offered "a critique of racial oppression and deeper racial understanding," (p. 66). Leyva (2016) found that Latina STEM majors often held success-oriented beliefs that both marginalized and empowered their understanding of themselves as capable math students. In her quest to understand "the mathematical agency of Latina/o students," Zavala (2014, p. 62) found that both Spanish-dominant and English-dominant high school–aged Latina/o students "most-often adopted a colorblind stance" (p. 66) about their own mathematics identity, stating that race did not matter in their own learning but drew from racialized narratives to make sense of the overachievement of Asian students in math. However, at times, they recognized that their immigrant status and years in the United States affected their mathematics experiences, revealing a contradictory and uncritical assessment of the power dynamics in a math classroom.

A couple of studies suggest that some coping strategies used by Latino/a students can be fueled by a critical consciousness. Ramirez (2014) used the notion of transformational resistance (Solórzano & Delgado Bernal, 2001) to describe the ways Latina/o and Chicana/o graduate students circumvent overlapping instances of racism, sexism, ghettoization, and classism they encountered during their first years. Ramirez paid particular attention to the struggle students with working-class Latino backgrounds faced socializing to the middle-class White milieu of graduate school—as initially both race and class markers made them feel as if they did not belong in a graduate school program. To counter these feelings of isolation and alienation, students formed "peer support networks," accessed "faculty mentorship and support," established "academic counterspaces" (Yosso, 2006), joined "Chicano/Latino(a) and women's organizations on campus," and/or avoided "interactions on campus with individuals perceived as hostile and toxic" (Ramirez, 2014, p. 179). Lastly, professors Urrieta and Villenas (2013) reflected on the intersectional forms of power they faced during their respective educational journeys, as well as the privilege and marginalization they face as a result of their faculty positions. For instance, as students, Urrieta and Villenas both experienced racism against their indigeneities and Latinidades, classism as a result of their working-class origins, and Eurocentrism and colonialism as products of whitestream educational institutions. As professors, they now leverage their multiple identities in ways unavailable to them before, but they are not impermeable from various forms of subjugation. For example, Villenas had to learn to balance being a middle-class professional with a newborn child at a conservative institution with no parental leave, while Urrieta battled racial micro aggressions as a result of the privileged White students who challenged his authority, abilities, and antiracist pedagogy and curriculum. Given the range of coping strategies Latina/o and Chicana/o students employ revealed by intersectional analysis, educators could use these finding to imagine pedagogical interventions that teach Latina/o and Chicana/o students socially conscious and self-preserving coping strategies for navigating the structures of power that shape their educational trajectories.

Institutional Practices

A second major theme in the intersectional research reviewed here is a focus on the educational practices, policies, curricula, or pedagogy that marginalize or empower Latina/o or Chicana/o students. In particular, these include the types of academic preparation, resources, or campus climate that Latina/o and Chicana/o students navigate as they pursue higher education. Intersectional analysis with this particular focus makes visible the ways institutional practices can either enfranchise or disenfranchise Latina/o and Chicana/o students, allowing scholars to draft recommendations that institutions can adopt to enable Latina/o and Chicana/o students to succeed.

For example, in her work with Latina/o and Chicana/o graduate students, Ramirez (2011) identified the institutional barriers hampering Latina/o and Chicana/o student success that result from the transections of racism, patriarchy, classism, ethnocentrism, and nativism. These include a lack of information about graduate school, the biased GRE entrance exam, and the absence of mentoring from counselors and faculty. As an implication of her research, she advocated that institutions design supportive programs that account for the "multidimensionality of Latino college choice process" (p. 220) to mitigate these constraints. When analyzing the college decision-making process for undocumented Latina/o students, Pérez et al. (2015) found that

Latina/o students often lack college-going preparation because a lack of citizenship channels their parents into the low-wage labor market and relegates them to under-funded and underresourced schools. The underresourced schools many Latina/o and Chicana/o students attend function to limit college-going options for undocumented students, but, Pérez noted, these conditions can also serve to positively motivate undocumented students to pursue college as a way to give back and better the quality of life for their family members and larger community. Moreover, the authors noted that undocumented students seek affordable options for college that allow them to remain close to familial support. As members of families who endure the convergence of racism, classism, nativism, linguicism, and xenophobia in their daily lives, a close-knit support system is a survival mechanism to navigate these conditions, and a key consideration for Latina/o and Chicana/o students who are encouraged to pursue higher education. Lastly, Castro and Cortez (2017) interviewed Mexican-origin com-munity college transfer students to shed light on how the transfer-receptive culture—that is, "the collective practices and norms of an institutional environment as well as the discursive habits and narrative logics that drive institutional thinking" (p. 89)—of the receiving university hinders the acculturation process for this group of stu-dents. The authors argue that the onus should be on the institution—not on the student—to change by tailoring a transfer-receptive culture unique to its needs.

Structural Forms of Oppression

A third focus of the intersectional analyses reviewed here specified the forms of intersectional oppression frequently experienced by Latina/o and Chicana/o stu-dents. One of the contributions of this research is the vernacular scholars have pro-posed to distinguish the ways larger hierarchies of power shape Latina/o and Chicana/o students' experiences: the *privilege paradox*, the *citizenship continuum, gen-dered familism, racist nativism*, and *internalized racist nativism*. These concepts are fleshed out below.

Cabrera et al. (2016) investigated the structural causes for the increasing under-representation of men of color in higher education. Because this issue lies along the fault lines of both advantage and disadvantage, intersectional analysis allowed the authors to interrogate Latino masculinity as a power dynamic balanced on both colo-nization and patriarchy, problematizing the benefits Latino men may derive through this gendered identity. The term *privilege paradox* refers to the contradiction that Latino students would be "systemically marginalized via their racial/ethnic identity, much like all other non-White racial/ethnic groups" yet synchronously "systemically privileged relative to women in terms of their gendered identity" (Cabrera et al., 2016, p. 75). This study elucidated the intersectional tension that men of color expe-rience as a result of their ethnoracial identities and hegemonic Western and colonial ideas of masculinity, pressures that work in tandem to impede Latino males from seeking help to navigate hostile campus climates, resulting in the decreased numbers of Latino males pursuing higher education.

In their work disaggregating the educational attainment rates of undocumented Latina/o students from documented (U.S.-born or naturalized) Latinas/os (a study and methodology more fully discussed in the next section), Covarrubias and Lara (2014) found that the closer Latina/o students are to idealized notions of U.S. citizens, that is, "American-born, English-speaking, Christian, mostly White" (p. 98), the more likely they are to graduate from high school, enroll in college, graduate from college, and pursue graduate or professional degrees. They advance the idea that a *citizenship continuum* operates systemically to "wield[s] its own power and exert[s] its own impact" (p. 97), privileging some Latinas/os and disadvantaging others. They argue that the notion of citizenship operates concurrently with the hierarchical systems of race, gender, religion, sexuality, and so on and requires more theorizing to better account for the challenges it holds for those students.

Ovink (2013) tracked the college-going behaviors of Latina/o high school youth and found that gender and racial/ethnic cultural beliefs intersected to influence the respondents' attitudes, behaviors, and college-going pathways. She found that many Latina/o students trust that a college education will lead to social mobility for themselves and their family members. However, Latinas desired greater economic means for their current family unit (parents, siblings, cousins, grandparents, etc.), while Latinos hoped to achieve mobility for their future families (wife, children). Moreover, for Latinas, a college degree ensured autonomy and independence, preventing financial dependence on men, whereas Latinos already assumed a sense of independence and freedom as college-going students. In addition, Latinas indicated that romantic relationships distracted from educational success, but for Latinos, romantic relationships often kept them persisting toward their degree. According to Ovink, these differences "revealed the intersectional influence of Latino/a and gender beliefs—or gendered familism—on life course decisions and college pathways," (p. 271). Ovink's concept—*gendered familism*—complicates familism, or "a social pattern that privileges family interests above those of the individual" (p. 267), often associated with Latino/a groups, as a factor affecting the college-going choices of Latina/o and Chicana/o students. With her intersectional analysis, Ovink differentiated the effects of a Latino cultural norm, systemic patriarchy, and Eurocentric ideals of educational attainment for Latinas/os and Chicanas/os.

Lastly, two additional conceptualizations of interlocking forms of oppression are the constructs of *racist nativism* and *internalized racist nativism* (Pérez Huber, Benavides Lopez, Malagon, Velez, & Solorzano, 2008). Racist nativism names the convergence of these two interrelated ideologies of power to assign

values to real or imagined differences, in order to justify the superiority of the native, who is to be perceived white, over that of the non-native, who is perceived to be People and Immigrants of Color, and thereby defend the right of whites, or the natives, to dominance. (Pérez Huber et al., 2008, p. 43)

Pérez Huber (2010) applied an intersectional analysis to discover how racist nativism becomes "layered with class and gender at particular moments in" the educational trajectories of undocumented Latina college students (p. 82). She offered examples of racist nativism—such as when her participants recalled particular painful moments when they felt unsafe, outnumbered, frightened, and/or targeted as a result of anti-immigrant discourses espoused by authority figures in school settings. When this rhetoric is infused with commentary about Latina women purposely seeking to have "anchor babies" and draw on social services, it exemplifies they ways racist nativism traverses with gender and sexism. Furthermore, Pérez Huber argued that a "racist nativist class structure" relegates the college-educated parents of these undocumented women to low-wage labor market, erasing the "educational capital" the women's parents attained and consigning their children to schools that lacked "educational resources and quality teachers, decaying school facilities and limited college access" (p. 87). Also, because undocumented Latinas often have work to pay their college tuition, they are often unable to participate in programming on campus that could aid in their persistence, a systemic disadvantage Pérez Huber claims is rooted in the convergence of class and racist nativism.

Lastly, Pérez Huber theorizes *internalized racist nativism* to account for the ways members of Latina/o communities adopt racist nativist logics. She argued that the normalization of a racial hierarchy predicated on White supremacy in both mainstream media content and the U.S. educational curriculum results in many Latina/o and Chicana/o students internalizing these beliefs and perpetuating them by repeating racist nativist language or ideas—such as calling other classmates "beaners," teasing about the arrival of *la migra* (Immigration and Customs Enforcement or border patrol), and mocking accented English.

In this set of intersectional analyses, attention to the structural power dynamics seek to name multilayered forms of marginalization. Together, these concepts— *privilege paradox, citizenship continuum, gendered familism, racist nativism,* and *internalized racist nativism*—offer a specificity to the experiences of subjugation and empowerment that result from these interconnecting sources of power, arming Latina/o and Chicana/o students with a language that allows them to identify, understand, and, if necessary, subvert these circumstances. This scholarship also points to other cultural forces that have yet to be fully explored, namely, colorism, transnationalism, postcoloniality, diaspora, neoliberalism, capitalism, globalism, and imperialism. For instance, many waves of immigration from Mexico and Latin America are the result of neoliberal and imperialist policies (Gonzalez, 2011). Also, many generations of Chicanas/os have suffered displacement in a land that was once their homeland, as a result of continued colonization (Gonzalez, 2011). As these repressive conditions and doctrines have shaped and continue to shape the experiences of Latina/o communities across the North American continent, it is only appropriate to begin unmasking the ways in which they intersect in the lives of Latina/o and Chicana/o students.

Highlighting these three nodes individually allows an efficient means to expose the primary contours of intersectional analysis regarding Latina/o and Chicana/o students, but it does not intend to create rigid boundaries or divisions within this corpus of research. Additionally, by paying attention to the theoretical and methodological frameworks employed by scholars applying this approach, additional findings are revealed. The next section attends to these characteristics.

Theoretical and Methodological Frameworks

Assessing the characteristics of the 19 articles and 5 book chapters synthesized here revealed patterns in this scholarly work, as well as opportunities for additional applications of intersectional analysis. These patterns reveal the following: (1) that the diversity, or intracatergorical intersectionality (McCall, 2005), that comprises the Latina/o community has yet to be represented in this sample; (2) that the entirety of the P–20 educational trajectory has yet to be studied through this lens, as most studies focus on high school (Knight et al., 2006; Leyva, 2016; Ovink, 2013; Pérez et al., 2015; Zavala, 2014), college (Abrica & Martinez, 2016; Cabrera et al., 2016; Castro & Cortez, 2017; Muñoz & Maldonado, 2012; Pérez Huber, 2010), or graduate students (Ramirez, 2011, 2014); (3) that the theoretical frameworks have remained rooted to a race-based or gender-based orientations; and (4) that qualitative methods—primarily interviews—are the most frequent methods for this work. Indeed, two different frameworks—a methodological approach called CRQI, or critical race quantitative intersectionality (Covarrubias, 2011; Covarrubias & Lara, 2014; Covarrubias & Veléz, 2013) and a conceptual model named the multilevel model of intersectionality (Nuñez, 2014a, 2014b)—have been proposed to help broaden the methods and research designs used in intersectional analysis. These frameworks and the insights they offer will be discussed below.

Although intersectionality is often critiqued as research that merely subdivides marginal groups rather than transforming unjust social conditions (Carbado, 2011; Cho et al., 2013), the particular groups studied in this corpus of work instead illustrate the value of this nuanced analysis and, in fact, leave room for additional gradations for study. In particular, three articles focused exclusively on undocumented Latina/o students (Muñoz & Maldonado, 2012; Pérez et al., 2015; Pérez Huber, 2010), four studied only Latinos (Abrica & Martinez, 2016; Cabrera et al., 2016), and another three only examined the educational experiences of Latinas (Knight et al., 2006; Leyva, 2016; Zavala, 2014). The intersectional analysis Covarrubias developed to disaggregate educational pipeline data (Covarrubias, 2011; Covarrubias & Lara, 2014; Covarrubias & Veléz, 2013) exemplified the ways Latinas/os and Chicanas/os can be subdivided into groups that account for their generational status, citizenship, income level, and gender, yet few other scholars examined groups along additional axes, including sexuality, phenotype, or language abilities. In addition, very few other Latinidades (beyond Mexican, Mexican Americans) have been studied along class, language, gender, or sexual orientation. Given the common application of intersectional analysis to recognize how all these aspects of identity affect educational experiences, it seems warranted for there to be additional work along these key identity markers. Intersectional analysis would also be a useful tool to examine the experiences of other types of Latina/o or Chicana/o students, such as elementary or middle school Latino students, English-language learners, students who have been pushed out of high school or into alternative tracks, or high-achieving high schoolers.

The limited number of issues studied through an intersectional lens also points to prospective areas to research. Only one article focused on the experiences of Spanish-speaking Latina/o high school youth in their mathematics classrooms (Zavala, 2014). The rest of this research was focused on higher education. For example, this work examined either the college selection process (Knight et al., 2006; Ovink, 2013; Pérez et al., 2015; Ramirez, 2011) or Latina/o and Chicana/o students' various experiences navigating a college environment (Abrica & Martinez, 2016; Cabrera et al., 2016; Muñoz & Maldonado, 2012; Ramirez, 2014) or college math courses (Leyva, 2016). Another article examined the transfer process from community college to a 4-year university (Castro & Cortez, 2017), and one investigated the intersecting layers of power structures shaping the K–20 educational trajectories of its participants (Pérez Huber, 2010). A final article applied intersectionality to understand how two scholars of color experienced, learned about, researched, and navigated being both marginalized and privileged as first-generation college students, graduate students, junior faculty, and tenured professors (Urrieta & Villenas, 2013). College-going and persistence have been most often studied, but many other possibilities remain: inquiries regarding how Latina/o or Chicana/o students of all ages might come to understand and/or use the tool of intersectionality toward increased educational success, whether colorblind ideologies in K–8 public school curricula allow for students to embrace multiple identities, whether working-class third- or fourth-generation Chicanas/os who are not fluent Spanish speakers and do not have strong ties to Mexico or Latin America find saliency between their identity and educational achievements, or how queer Latina/o or Chicana/o students navigate both racist and heteronormative educational policies.

Fittingly, critical race—or gendered—theoretical frameworks were often combined with intersectional analysis in this body of work. Twelve of the articles evoked critical race theory (Covarrubias, 2011; Covarrubias & Lara, 2014; Covarrubias & Veléz, 2013; Leyva, 2016; Muñoz & Maldonado, 2012; Pérez Huber, 2010; Urrieta & Villenas, 2013; Zavala, 2014) or critical race theoretical constructs like social capital or community cultural wealth (Abrica & Martinez, 2016; Pérez et al., 2015; Ramirez, 2011), counterstories (Leyva, 2016; Zavala, 2014), transformational resistance (Ramirez, 2014), micro agressions and racial battle fatigue (Cabrera et al., 2016), and a transfer-receptive culture (Castro & Cortez, 2017) guided by the tenets of critical race theory (Jain, Herrera, Bernal, & Sólorzano, 2011). A few also coupled intersectionality with Latino critical race theory (Leyva, 2016; Muñoz & Maldonado, 2012; Pérez Huber, 2010; Urrieta & Villenas, 2013; Zavala, 2014), Chicana feminist epistemologies (Knight et al., 2006; Pérez Huber, 2010; Urrieta & Villenas, 2013), or other multiracial or multicultural feminist theories (Knight et al., 2006; Ramirez,

2011). Leyva (2016) drew on poststructural theory and its conceptualizations of discourse and power to help him analyze the counterstories he collected. Clearly, there is an opportunity to draw on queer theory, class theories, or disability theories as additional pivot points for intersectional analyses of the educational experiences of Chicana/o and Latina/o students.

Similarly, the methodologies employed for intersectional analysis are primarily qualitative in nature. Twelve out of the 19 articles analyzed for this section relied on interviews (Abrica & Martinez, 2016; Cabrera et al., 2016; Castro & Cortez, 2017; Leyva, 2016; Muñoz & Maldonado, 2012; Ovink, 2013; Pérez et al., 2015; Pérez Huber, 2010; Ramirez, 2011, 2014; Zavala, 2014). Some of the interviews were conducted over a period of time—revisiting the same participants at different points along their trajectories (Abrica & Martinez, 2016; Ovink, 2013; Pérez et al., 2015; Zavala, 2014)—while the rest were only interviewed once. Two incorporated testimonio methodology[5] as part of their data collection and analysis (Pérez Huber, 2010; Urrieta & Villenas, 2013). A few interviews were coupled with focus groups (Abrica & Martinez, 2016; Leyva, 2016; Muñoz & Maldonado, 2012; Pérez et al., 2015; Zavala, 2014) and a written questionnaire or reflections (Leyva, 2016; Ramirez, 2014). One analyzed a mélange of student-produced text and data to understand the various critical literacies Latina youth engage to make sense of their college-aspirant identities (Knight et al., 2006). Given the overreliance on interview data, it is likely that other forms of qualitative and quantitative approaches—such as ethnographies, textual analysis, or even survey data—might provide additional approaches to intersectional analysis of the experiences of Latina/o and Chicana/o students.

Notably, several scholars employing an intersectional analysis advanced a distinctive quantitative methodology as a way to expand the scope and breadth of intersectional scholarship (Covarrubias, 2011; Covarrubias & Lara, 2014; Covarrubias & Veléz, 2013; Sólorzano et al., 2005). The next section provides an overview of these efforts.

A Quantitative Approach to Intersectionality

Scholars have sought to construct a comprehensive picture of the ways various Latina/o and Chicana/o subpopulations navigate schooling to earn high school, college, and graduate degrees. Driving this strand of scholarship is an emerging quantitative intersectional analysis methodology that functions to disaggregate data initially used to craft an educational pipeline of U.S.-based Latina/o and Chicana/o communities (Sólorzano et al., 2005; Yosso & Solórzano, 2006).

Sólorzano et al. (2005) first proposed the educational pipeline based on an analysis of Census data used to visually illustrate the points along the K–20 academic trajectory that push out Latina/o students, and result in lower retention and persistence rates in comparison to the educational achievement of other racial and ethnic groups. The initial project delineated separate pathways for Chicana and Chicano students in addition to mapping out the pathway for both male and female Chicano students—suggesting an intersectional analysis—and it proved to be a critical cornerstone for scholarship critiquing the practices and policies within educational institutions that adversely affect the educational attainment rates of Latina/o and Chicana/o communities.

Covarrubias (2011) and others (Covarrubias & Lara, 2014, Covarrubias & Veléz, 2013) have built on this pivotal work to launch a thread of intersectional analysis that problematizes the Census umbrella terms for Latina/o and Chicana/o communities because of the way these labels conflate third-generation U.S.-born Chicanas, first-generation working-class Latina/o immigrants, middle-class naturalized Mexican American citizens, and undocumented Mexican male students into a skewed and homogenized depiction of these communities. Instead, Covarrubias and his collaborators (Covarrubias, 2011; Covarrubias & Lara, 2014; Covarrubias & Veléz, 2013) have developed CRQI, a framework and methodology to disaggregate Census data and identify academic pathways that are contingent on the unique intermingling of race, gender, class, and citizenship for people of Mexican origin. Informed by the tenets of critical race theory, its working definition is the following:

An explanatory framework and methodological approach that utilizes quantitative methods to account for the material impact of race and racism at its intersection with other forms of subordination and works toward identifying and challenging oppression at this intersection in hopes of achieving social justice for students of color, their families, and their communities. (Covarrubias & Veléz, 2013, p. 276)

The goal of this approach is to heighten the understanding that while Latina/o and Chicana/o communities have been burdened by a "racial tax" (Carbado, 2011, pp. 1608–1609) that underwrites the privileges afforded to Whites, other forms of oppression—such as class, citizenship status, colorism, or linguicism—acting in conjunction with endemic racism affect different segments of Latina/o and Chicana/o communities distinctly. In their explication, Covarrubias and Vélez (2013) lay out five principles for conducting CRQI. The first premise is that intersectionality is a tangible, measurable element constituted through the confluence of socially constructed identity categories "by which society and its institutions disseminate resources, status, and power, often privileging one group over all others, but arranging all in existing interlocking hierarchies" (p. 277). CRQI, then, seeks to quantify the condition created by these mechanisms.

The second tenet is rooted in work by Zuberi (2001) and Zuberi and Bonilla-Silva (2008) that problematizes the origin and trustworthiness of statistical methods in the social sciences. Specifically, Zuberi (2001) argues that

. . . the white supremacist, Eugenicist movement in the U.S. after emancipation led to the development of the modern fields of statistics, genetics, demography and psychology, in order to affirm and rank racial categories. The data, its analysis, methods, and dissemination were flawed and biased from the beginning. (p. 277)

Therefore, transparency and a mindfulness about these histories should guide the "collection, computation, analyses, and reporting of" numerical data and statistics (p. 277).

Third, the experiential knowledge of the researcher conducting CRQI should help ground the analysis of the numerical or statistical data at hand. Whether it is channeled as a form of cultural intuition[6] (Delgado Bernal, 1998) or resulting from experiences of activism, these memories and ways of knowing should guide the analytical process. This principle aligns with the critical race theory tenet that asks scholars to center the experiences of those at the bottom (Matsuda, 1995); however, Covarrubias and Vélez (2013) urge that when studying intersectionality, scholars remain cognizant that "the bottom" does not pivot on a single axis of domination, like race, but rather is a fluctuating and relative space depending on the context, history, and power relations at play.

The fourth and fifth tenets replicate core precepts of critical race theory, such as the call for praxis and inter- and transdisciplinary work. As such, CRQI scholarship similarly aims to improve the educational conditions of the Latina/o and Chicana/o students it studies. Lastly, scholars should draw from a multitude of disciplinary traditions to shore up the transformative and explanatory value of CRQI findings.

CRQI framework proposed above seeks to add an additional tool for intersectional analysis in order to map out undulations of various hierarchical and systemic power structures. While still an emerging framework, it seeks to bridge the qualitative work that comprises the majority of critical race theory scholarship with quantitative research, in a way that aligns with critical race theory's core tenets and critical stance on objectivity, yet resists a reliance on race, racialization, or racism as the single factor engendering subordination. For instance, while the original pipeline (Sólorzano et al., 2005; Yosso & Solórzano, 2006) indicated that overall, about 56 out of 100 Chicanas/os graduate high school each year, Covarrubias's (2011) found that annually, only one third of noncitizens earn a high school diploma and one half of Mexican-born naturalized citizens graduate from high school, while over three fourths of U.S.-born Mexican-origin students do. Thus, Covarrubias was able to quantify how the intersecting dimensions of race and citizenship status create distinct educational pathways for documented, naturalized, and undocumented Latinas/os.

This analysis (Covarrubias, 2011) also revealed the interplay of gender and class, with race and citizenship status and college degree completion. As a whole, more Chicanas enroll in college and earn college degrees than Chicanos, but when disaggregated by citizenship status, naturalized Chicanas and Chicanos enroll and complete college at the same rates. When controlled for class, Covarrubias's (2011) intersectional analysis revealed that for all Mexican-origin students, educational attainment increases as class status increases. For example, 40% of Latina/o and Chicana/o students in the lowest income quartile graduate from high school compared with 84% of Latinas/os and Chicanas/os from the highest income quartile. Sadly, only 3 out of every 100 Latina/o and Chicana/o students in the lowest income quartile will earn a bachelor's degree, while 30 out of every 100 Latina/o students in the highest income quartile will graduate from college.

In a follow-up study, Covarrubias and Lara (2014) used the same data set to take a more nuanced look at the educational achievement rates for the undocumented Latina/o and Chicana/o student population. They used the five existing Census citizenship categories to more accurately identify what portion of the Mexican-origin sample comprised undocumented Latina/o and Chicana/o students. Since four of the categories account for formalized citizenship (born in the United States, born in Puerto Rico, born abroad to U.S. citizen parents, and naturalized citizens), Covarrubias and Lara focused on the noncitizen category. They found that "U.S.-born Mexicans show significantly higher high school, college, and graduate school attainment rates, and higher enrollment rates in higher education than foreign-born and noncitizen" Latinas/os and Chicanas/os (p. 87). For Latina/o students who have citizen as a birthright and for those who are able to earn it through naturalization, reaching key educational transitions such as graduating high school was much more probable.

These findings also complicate the dominant narrative of the DREAMers, high-achieving undocumented Latina/o students who have proved their worth by excelling in school (Abrego & Gonzales, 2010). Certainly, highly educated undocumented students have effectively mobilized to claim a voice and space in the current sociopolitical discourse about immigration, and consequently have become idealized in mainstream discourse. However, Covarrubias and Lara (2014) illustrate that though DREAMers embody a small percentage of the undocumented student population (15 out of every 100) their dominant presence in the public discourse might inadvertently obscure the needs of the majority of the undocumented Latina/o student population.

These contributions to the literature using intersectional analyses are predicated on an understanding of "the complexity of intersectionality" and caution scholars that they need to avoid uncritically essentializing the Latina/o and Chicana/o experience, and instead consider how they might "expose more multifaceted relationships" (Covarrubias, 2011, p. 101) of power and privilege that simultaneously allow and limit access to education for this diverse ethno/racial community. Moreover, this methodology has also been employed for an intersectional analysis of Asian American students (Covarrubias & Liou, 2014), which holds promise for continued contributions from this model.

Multilevel Model of Intersectionality

The conceptual model proposed by Nuñez (2014a, 2014b), the multilevel model of intersectionality, attempts to capture the micro, meso, and macro levels of intersectionality to counter critiques that this "buzzword" merely heightens attention to difference and experiences across different social identities, "rather than [analyzing] the systems of power and oppression that shape these experiences" (Nuñez, 2014b, p. 85). Advocating the potential of intersectionality to both account for the "role of structure" and to capture individual experiences within multifaceted dynamics of power, Nuñez fashioned a template for such a task. Informed by Anthias (2013), Nuñez's model has three nested levels, depicted as three concentric circles, with the first level at the core, the second encircling the core, and the third subsuming the other two. The first level of the multilevel model of intersectionality expresses multiple dimensions of identity salient to Latina/o and Chicana/o students, including immigrant status, class, and gender. Nuñez classified most intersectional research as typifying this level of analysis. None of the scholarship for this review would have been placed in this category.

The second level is divided into four quadrants—organizational, representational, intersubjective, and experiential—that represent the institutions, discourse, relationships, and sense-making that one's multiple identities engage with. Organizational, for example, encompasses governmental laws and initiatives, school district– or school-level educational policies and practices, or procedures that regulate and track the mobility, access, and opportunities for Latina/o students. The representational quadrant refers to mass-mediated discourses that frame and perpetuate stereotypical and discriminatory narratives and imagery about the educability of Latina/o and Chicana/o communities that influence decision making about their educational paths. The intersubjective quadrant signifies the individual level judgements about Latina/o and Chicana/o students by teachers, administrators, classmates, and staff that fashion particular educational trajectories. The experiential quadrant refers to the ways Latina/o students process, reconcile, and/or internalize both positive and negative messages about their academic abilities. This last two quadrants correspond with two foci identified by this review: the focus on student coping strategies align with the experiential quadrant Nuñez describes, while the institutional practices that engender occurrences of intersectionality coincide with her intersubjective quadrant. Nuñez (2014a) posits that these four quadrants are meant to serve as departure points for analysis, and encourages researchers to "conceptualize these arenas differently, or identify other domains" (p. 90). She casts studies that engage this plane of analysis as resulting in a deeper understanding of "how individuals make meaning and perceive power structures in shaping educational experiences according to their multiple identities" (p. 50).

Lastly, the third level of this model denotes the historical and sociopolitical contexts that constitute the current conditions Latina/o and Chicana/o students endure, such as the "broader interlocking systems of economic, legal, political, media, and social power and classification that evolve over time in specific places, as well as social movements to challenge these systems" (Nuñez, 2014b, p. 89). Attention to this level allows researchers to note the social processes that engender the often fluid social categories of identity, such as the term we now understand as *Latina/o*; the role economic fluctuations have played in influencing the lived experiences of Latina/o and Chicana/o students, including their educational opportunities; or the legacy of the Chicano Civil Rights Movement that resulted in the formation and challenge of a Chicano Studies curriculum for Latina/o and Chicana/o students. The set of intersectional analysis reviewed here that contributed the concepts such as privilege paradox, gendered familism, and racist nativism best relate to this level in Nuñez's model.

Nuñez (2014a) acknowledged that this model is "what sociologist Max Weber would call an ideal type," and thus, unrealistic to enact singlehandedly. Nonetheless, she hopes that even if researchers do "not address all of the levels empirically" in their individual projects, "they can draw on literature that addresses other levels to help contextualize and interpret results" (p. 49), or that the model might inspire scholars "to attend simultaneously to social identities and contextual power structures" (p. 53). As of this review, no scholar had adopted this model for his or her research. However, the multilevel model of intersectionality illuminates the intricacies highlighted by intersectionality analysis by visually charting the processes that constitute interlaced positionalities and power structures that Latina/o and Chicana/o students weather in educational systems. While navigating the map Nuñez offers may require technologies and an acuity that have yet to materialize, this model is a useful guidepost for expanding the niche of intersectional research, and useful for bearing in mind the full spectrum of intersectional analysis.

DISCUSSION/CONCLUSION

Several important contributions surfaced from the intersectional analyses reviewed here. This research revealed important focal points of interlocking oppression and privilege: at the level of the individual, at the level of institutional policy and practice, and at a structural level. Studies at the individual level disclosed contradictions in the coping strategies Latina/o and Chicana/o students used to manage the varied power relations they experience. Findings from research grouped at the institutional level detected barriers—such as financial aid policies limited to citizens—that are created by institutional policies and practices that disproportionately affect the educational trajectories of Latina/o and Chicana/o students because they are implemented within stratified systems of privilege. Findings from the set of intersectional analyses that examined the larger network of power dynamics resulted in a more precise understanding of these imbricated forces, with concepts such as *racist nativism, internalized racist nativism, gendered familism, citizenship continuum,* and *privilege paradox.* Researchers wishing to employ intersectional analysis should be careful to avoid homogenizing ethno/racial communities, and avoid assuming that all Latina/o and Chicana/o students are equipped with the critical awareness to navigate the barriers resulting from intersectional oppression. They can also rely on this literature to document the legacies of hierarchical ideologies like racism, sexism, and classism.

Revelations about educational pathways that are unique to Latina/o and Chicana/o subgroups resulted from a specialized quantitative methodological approach, CRQI, for disaggregating data. A second conceptual intervention, the multilevel model of intersectionality, illuminated the full spectrum of study available through intersectional analysis, and suggests a wide-scale approach to better assess these constitutive and interconnected processes. Moreover, this chapter uncovered the lack of diversity in the various Latina/o and Chicana/o populations studied with this framework. There was a concentration of intersectional analysis aimed at studying higher education but very little examining Latina/o and Chicana/o students in elementary and junior high or middle school. Race-based or gender-based theoretical frameworks are most often coupled with an intersectional analysis, leaving opportunities for other critical theories to ground such analyses. Lastly, the predominance of qualitative methods—primarily interviews—leaves room for other methods to be explored. As such, the groups studied, the issues addressed, the theories engaged, and the methods employed are indicative of an emerging field of work with considerable untapped potential.

NOTES

[1]The terms *Latina/o* and *Chicana/o* will be used in tandem throughout this chapter. These labels reflect the terms engaged by the research reviewed here. *Latina/o* is an umbrella term for individuals with ties to Mexico, South America, or Central America, who share a tenuous ethnic, cultural, and linguistic history tied to Spain or Spanish colonization. A term of self-determination, *Chicana/o* emerged during the Civil Rights Movement to counter the second-class citizenship experienced by Mexican Americans in the Southwest, and while it originally referred to people of Mexican ancestry who were born in the United States, it has evolved to characterize a decolonial and critical political sensibility. Importantly, using these understandings, all Chicanos/as would also be considered Latinas/os but not all Latinas/os ascribe to the political philosophies of Chicanismo and would not necessarily identify as Chicanas/os. As noted by Castañeda, Anguiano, and Alemán (2017), the "a/o" configuration counters the patriarchy embedded in the Spanish language that privileges the male identity in mixed-gender plural constructions. Chicanx and Latinx have since evolved to include any person with geographic, cultural, ethnic, or linguistic ties to Mexico, Latin American, and the Caribbean who wish to deconstruct patriarchy and gender binaries and better reflect intersectional identities, particularly gender-fluid and gender-nonconforming individuals by composing these words with an "x." While the use of Latinx and Chicanx is on the rise in various academic and activist circles as a way to deconstruct gender binaries, it has yet to gain universal acceptance as its evolution and use warrants greater critical reflection. For instance, these terms can be critiqued for the ways they obscure the historical struggles of Latinas and Chicanas to assert their voices in the academy by fighting for the a/o construction, their inability to be pronounced in Spanish, and the focus on the word "Latin," which continues to elide the indigenous roots of many Latino ethnic groups. These important conversations over these terms highlight how language constitutes reality, the role grammatical norms play in the fight for social justice, and the difficulty in articulating the complexities of the Latina/o and Chicana/o experience. At the time of writing this chapter, I am continuing to reflect and follow the conversation regarding these terms but opt to continue to use Chicana/o and Latina/o for now.

[2]According to Pew Research Center, there were 58.6 million Latinos in 2017 (Krogstad, 2017), comprising 18% of the total U.S. population (Krogstad, 2016a) but expecting to grow to 29% of the nation's population by 2060 (Colby & Ortman, 2015). With a median age of 28, Latinos are the youngest of all racial and ethnic groups, with about a quarter of them aged 18 to 33 (Krogstad, 2016b). In addition, U.S.-born Latinos have a median age of 19 (Krogstad, 2016b), while Latino children make up 20% of the nation's kindergarten population in 17 states (Krogstad & Fry, 2014).

[3]*Ethnoracial* is a term that attempts to articulate the experiences of an ethnic group—or a group that is defined by practices or customs that are the result of culture, history, and

geography—that experiences racialization, or being treated as a racial group, that is, a group that is defined by identifiable physical and visible characteristics. For example, while Latinos are classified as White in the U.S. Census, their daily experiences are unlike those of White European Americans', and so this term helps in understanding how this ethnic group is racialized.

[4]*Latinidad* is a Spanish-language term used to signal the shared cultural and experiential attributes of Latin American people, primarily as a way to build a pan-ethnic community and identity among Latino/a communities who reside outside Latin America and therefore supersede geography or place.

[5]*Testimonio* has a rich tradition in Chicana/Latina studies as an important theoretical and empirical framework. Chicana feminist scholars have utilized *testimonio* as a method to reflect on their experiences as well as the experiences of other marginalized communities.

[6]Cultural intuition is an evolving and dynamic construct that reimagines Strauss and Corbin's (1990) notion of theoretical sensitivity that draws from Chicana scholars' ways of knowing and informs their research. These include (1) personal experience, including community memory and collective experience; (2) professional experience; (3) the existing literature on a topic; and (4) the analytic research process itself. Importantly, this analytical lens must be cultivated to be enacted, as it is not inherent based on one's racialized identity.

REFERENCES

Abrego, L. J., & Gonzales, R. G. (2010). Blocked paths, uncertain futures: The postsecondary education and labor market prospects of undocumented Latino students. *Journal of Education for Students Placed At-Risk, 15*, 144–157.

Abrica, E. J., & Martinez, E., Jr. (2016). Strategies for navigating financial challenges among Latino male community college students: Centralizing race, gender, and immigrant generation. *Journal of Applied Research in the Community College, 23*(2), 59–72.

Alemán, E., Jr., Delgado Bernal, D., & Cortez, E. (2015). A Chican@ pathways model of acción: Affirming the racial, cultural and academic assets of students, families and communities. *Association of Mexican American Educators Journal, 9*, 13–27.

Alemán, E., Jr., Delgado Bernal, D., McKinney, A., & Freire, J. (2017). Community-based pathways to higher education: A snapshot of teacher perceptions, school culture and partnership building. *Urban Education, 49*, 852–873.

Anthias, F. (2013). Intersectional what? Social divisions, intersectionality, and levels of analysis. *Ethnicities, 13*(1), 3–19.

Auerbach, S. (2002). "Why do they give the good classes to some and not to others?" Latino parent narratives of struggle in a college access program. *Teachers College Record, 104*, 1369–1392.

Cabrera, N. L., Rashwan-Soto, F. D, & Valencia, B. G. (2016). An intersectionality analysis of Latino men in higher education and their help-seeking behaviors. In V. B. Sáenz, L. Ponjuán, & J. L. Figueroa (Eds.), *Ensuring the success of Latino males in higher education: A national imperative* (pp. 75–92). Sterling, VA: Stylus.

Carbado, D. W. (2011). Afterword: Critical what what? *Connecticut Law Review, 43*, 1593–1643.

Carbado, D. W. (2013). Colorblind intersectionality. *Signs, 38*, 811–845.

Castañeda, M., Anguiano, C., & Alemán, S. M. (2017). Voicing for space in academia: Testimonios of Chicana communication professors. *Chicana/Latina Studies, 16*(2).

Castro, E. L., & Cortez, E. (2017). Exploring the lived experiences and intersectionalities of Mexican community college transfer students: Qualitative insights toward expanding a transfer receptive culture. *Community College Journal of Research and Practice, 41*(2), 77–92.

Cho, S., Crenshaw, K. W., & McCall, L. (2013). Toward a field of intersectionality studies: Theory, applications, and praxis. *Signs, 38*, 785–810.

Colby, S. L., & Ortman, J. (2015, March). *Projections of the size and composition of the U.S. population: 2014 to 2060.* Washington, DC: U.S. Census Bureau. Retrieved from https://www.census.gov/content/dam/Census/library/publications/2015/demo/p25-1143.pdf

Collins, P. H., & Bilge, S. (2016). *Intersectionality.* Cambridge, England: Polity Press.

Contreras, F. (2011). *Achieving equity for Latino students: Expanding the pathway to higher education through public policy.* New York, NY: Teachers College Press.

Covarrubias, A. (2011). Quantitative intersectionality: A critical race analysis of the Chicana/o educational pipeline. *Journal of Latinos in Education, 1*, 86–105.

Covarrubias, A., & Lara, A. (2014). The undocumented (im)migrant educational pipeline: The influence of citizenship status on educational attainment for people of Mexican origin. *Urban Education, 49*, 75–110.

Covarrubias, A., & Liou, D. (2014). Asian American education and income attainment in the era of post-racial America. *Teachers College Record, 116*(6), 1–38.

Covarrubias, A., & Veléz, V. (2013). Critical race quantitative intersectionality: An anti-racist research paradigm that refuses to "let the numbers speak for themselves." In M. Lynn & A. Dixon (Eds.), *Handbook of critical race theory in education* (pp. 270–285). New York, NY: Routledge.

De Jesús, A. (2005). Theoretical perspectives on the underachievement of Latino/a students in U.S. schools: Toward a framework for culturally additive schooling. In P. Pedraza & M. Rivera (Eds.), *Latino education: An agenda for community action research* (pp. 343–371). Mahwah, NJ: Lawrence Erlbaum.

Delgado Bernal, D., & Alemán, E., Jr. (2017). *Transforming educational pathways for Chicana/o students: A critical race feminista praxis.* New York, NY: Teachers College Press.

Fry, R., & Lopez, M. H. (2012). *Now largest minority group on four-year college campuses: Hispanic student enrollments reach new highs in 2011.* Washington, DC: Pew Research Center.

Gándara, P., & Contreras, F. (2009). *The Latino crisis: The consequences of failed social policies.* Cambridge, MA: Harvard University Press.

Gándara, P., Larson, K., Rumberger, R., & Mehan, H. (1998). Capturing Latino students in the academic pipeline (CLPP Policy Report). Retrieved from https://escholarship.org/content/qt84h2j4qs/qt84h2j4qs.pdf

Gonzalez, J. (2011). *Harvest of empire: A history of Latinos in America.* New York, NY: Penguin Books.

Hussar, W. J., & Bailey, T. M. (2013). *Projections of education statistics to 2022* (NCES 2014-051). Washington, DC: U.S. Government Printing Office. Retrieved from https://nces.ed.gov/pubs2014/2014051.pdf

Jain, D., Herrera, A., Bernal, S., & Sólorzano, D. (2011). Critical race theory and the transfer function: Introducing a transfer receptive culture. *Community College Journal of Research and Practice, 35*, 252–266.

Knight, M. G., Dixon, I. R., Norton, N. E., & Bentley, C. C. (2006). Contextualizing Latina youth's constructions of their college-bound identities. In D. Delgado Bernal, F. E. Godinez, S. Villenas, & C. A. Elenes (Eds.), *Chicana/Latina education in everyday life: Feminista perspectives on pedagogy and epistemology* (pp. 39–58). Albany: State University of New York Press.

Krogstad, J. M. (2016a, July 28). *5 facts about Latinos and education.* Washington, DC: Pew Internet & American Life Project. Retrieved from http://www.pewresearch.org/fact-tank/2016/07/28/5-facts-about-latinos-and-education/

Krogstad, J. M. (2016b, September 15). *10 facts for National Hispanic Heritage Month.* Washington, DC: Pew Internet & American Life Project. Retrieved from http://www.pewresearch.org/fact-tank/2016/09/15/facts-for-national-hispanic-heritage-month/

Krogstad, J. M. (2017, August 3). U.S. Hispanic population growth has leveled off. Washington, DC: Pew Internet & American Life Project. Retrieved from http://www. pewresearch.org/fact-tank/2017/08/03/u-s-hispanic-population-growth-has-leveled-off/

Krogstad, J. M., & Fry, R. (2014, August 18). *Department of Education projects public schools will be "majority-minority" this fall.* Washington, DC: Pew Internet & American Life Project. Retrieved from http://www.pewresearch.org/fact-tank/2014/08/18/u-s-public-schools-expected-to-be-majority-minority-starting-this-fall/

Ladson-Billings, G. (2006). From the achievement gap to the educational debt: Understanding achievement in the U.S. schools. *Educational Researcher, 35*(7), 3–12.

Leyva, L. A. (2016). An intersectional analysis of Latin@ college women's counter-stories in mathematics. *Journal of Urban Mathematics Education, 9*, 81–121.

Matsuda, M. (1995). Looking to the bottom: Critical legal studies and reparations. In K. Crenshaw, N. Gotanda, & G. Peller (Eds.), *Critical race theory: The key writings that formed the movement* (pp. 63–79), New York, NY: The New Press.

McCall, L. (2005). The complexity of intersectionality. *Signs, 30*, 1771–1800.

Muñoz, S. M., & Maldonado, M. M. (2012). Counterstories of college persistence by undocumented Mexicana students: Navigating race, class, gender, and legal status. *International Journal of Qualitative Studies in Education, 25*, 293–315.

National Center for Education Statistics. (2003). *Community college students goals, academic preparation, and outcomes* (Postsecondary Educational Descriptive Analysis Reports, NCES 2003-164). Washington, DC: U.S. Department of Education.

National Science Foundation & National Center for Science and Engineering Statistics. (2012). *Doctorate recipients from U.S. universities: 2011* (Special Report NSF 13-301). Arlington, VA: Author. Retrieved from http://www.nsf.gov/statistics/sed/.

Núñez, A. (2014a). Advancing an intersectionality framework in higher education: Power and Latino postsecondary opportunity. In M. B. Paulsen (Ed.), *Higher education: Handbook of theory and research* (Vol. 2, pp. 33–92). New York, NY: Springer.

Núñez, A. (2014b). Employing multilevel intersectionality in educational research: Latino identities, contexts, and college access. *Educational Researcher, 43*, 85–92.

Ovink, S. M. (2013). "They always call me an investment": Gendered familism and Latino/a college oathways. *Gender & Society, 28*, 265–288.

Pérez, P. A., Rodríguez, J. L., & Guadarrama, J. (2015). Rising voices: College opportunity and choice among Latina/o undocumented. In P. A. Pérez & M. Ceja (Eds.), *Higher education access and choice for Latino students: Critical findings and theoretical perspectives* (pp. 84–93). New York, NY: Routledge.

Pérez Huber, L. (2010). Using Latina/o critical race theory (LatCrit) and racist nativism to explore intersectionality in the educational experiences of undocumented Chicana college students. *Educational Foundations, 24*, 77–96.

Pérez Huber, L., Benavides Lopez, C., Malagon, M. C., Velez, V., & Solorzano, D. (2008). Getting beyond the "symptom," acknowledging the "disease": Theorizing racist nativism. *Contemporary Justice Review, 11*, 39–51.

Ramirez, E. (2011). "No one taught me the steps": Latinos' experiences applying to graduate school. *Journal of Latinos in Education, 10*, 204–222.

Ramirez, E. (2014). "Qué estoy haciendo aquí? (What am I doing here?)": Chicanos/Latinos(as) navigating challenges and inequalities during their first year of graduate school. *Equity & Excellence in Education, 47*, 167–186.

Rashwan-Soto, F. D., & Cabrera, N. L. (2011, March). *The privilege paradox: Latino masculinity and educational underachievement in higher education.* Paper presented at the annual meeting of the National Association of Chicana and Chicano Studies, Pasadena, CA.

Solórzano, D., & Delgado Bernal, D. (2001). Examining transformational resistance through a critical race and Latcrit theory framework: Chicana and Chicano students in an urban context. *Urban Education, 36*, 308–342.

Solórzano, D. G., & Ornelas, A. (2004). A critical race analysis of Latina/o and African American advanced placement enrollment in public high schools. *High School Journal, February/March*, 15–26.

Sólorzano, D., Villalpando, O., & Oseguera, L. (2005). Educational inequities and Latina/o undergraduate students in the United States: A critical race analysis of their educational progress. *Journal of Hispanic Higher Education, 4*, 272–294.

Strauss, A., & Corbin, J. (1990). *Basics of qualitative research: Grounded theory procedures and techniques*. Thousand Oaks, CA: Sage.

Urrieta, L., Jr., & Villenas, S. A. (2013). The legacy of Derrick Bell and Latino/a education: A critical race testimonio. *Race, Ethnicity, and Education, 16*, 514–535.

Yosso, T. (2006). *Critical race counterstories along the Chicana/Chicano educational pipeline*. New York, NY: Routledge.

Yosso, T. J., & Solórzano, D. G. (2006). *Leaks in the Chicana and Chicano educational pipeline* (Latino Policy & Issues Brief No. 13). Retrieved from http://www.chicano.ucla.edu/files/LPIB_13March2006.pdf

Zavala, M. D. R. (2014). Latina/o youth's perspectives on race, language, and learning mathematics. *Journal of Urban Mathematics Education, 7*, 55–87.

Zuberi, T. (2001). *Thicker than blood: An essay on how racial statistics lie*. Minneapolis: University of Minnesota Press.

Zuberi, T., & Bonilla-Silva, E. (2008). *White logic, white methods: Race and methodology*. New York, NY: Rowman & Littlefield.

Chapter 9

(Re)Centering Quality in Early Childhood Education: Toward Intersectional Justice for Minoritized Children

Mariana Souto-Manning
Ayesha Rabadi-Raol
Teachers College, Columbia University

In this chapter, we offer a critical intersectional analysis of quality in early childhood education with the aim of moving away from a singular understanding of "best practice," thereby interrupting the inequities such a concept fosters. While acknowledging how injustices are intersectionally constructed, we specifically identified critical race theory as a counterstory to White supremacy, culturally relevant and sustaining pedagogies as counterstories to monocultural teaching practices grounded in deficit and inferiority paradigms, and translanguaging as a counterstory to the (over)privileging of dominant American English monolingualism. While each of these counterstories forefronts one particular dimension of oppression, together they account for multiple, intersecting systems of oppressions; combined, they expand the cartography of early childhood education and serve to (re)center the definition of quality on the lives, experiences, voices, and values of multiply minoritized young children, families, and communities. Rejecting oppressive and reductionist notions of quality, through the use of re-mediation, this article offers design principles for intersectionally just early childhood education with the potential to transform the architecture of quality.

Young children from multiply minoritized[1] backgrounds are the fastest growing demographic group in the United States (Pew Research Center, 2016). Despite this demographic diversity, the field of early childhood education continues to promote the concept of developmentally appropriate practice (DAP) defined by the National Association for the Education of Young Children (NAEYC) as signifying quality (Connors & Morris, 2015; NAEYC, 2009), without adequately acknowledging or including the experiences, practices, and identities of children from multiply minoritized backgrounds (Goodwin, Cheruvu, & Genishi, 2008; Mallory & New, 1994; Pérez & Saavedra, 2017). The purpose of this chapter is to offer a critical

Review of Research in Education
March 2018, Vol. 42, pp. 203–225
DOI: 10.3102/0091732X18759550
© 2018 AERA. http://rre.aera.net

intersectional analysis of quality in early childhood education with the aim of moving away from a singular understanding of "best practice," thereby interrupting the inequities such a concept fosters.

We employ intersectionality as "a way of understanding and analyzing the complexity in the world, in people, and in human experiences" (Hill Collins & Bilge, 2016, p. 2). From such a perspective, the field of early childhood education's definition of quality is socially, historically, culturally, and racially constructed. We reject the acultural and colonialist normative aims of a single "best practice" defining quality in early education and refute the notion that DAP is "at the core of being an excellent early childhood teacher" (Copple & Bredekamp, 2009, p. 33). Herewith, we engage with intersectionalities in doing, redoing, and transforming (Hill Collins & Bilge, 2016).

We highlight how traditional notions of quality in early childhood education are exclusionary, rooted in White monolingual and monocultural values and experiences, and apply deficit paradigms to frame the developmental trajectories of multiply minoritized children. We then engage with the theoretical tool of re-mediation (Cole & Griffin, 1983; Gutiérrez, Morales, & Martinez, 2009) to (re)center the concept of quality. In contrast to remediation, which blames individuals for the results of systemic injustices,[2] Griffin and Cole (1984) proposed the notion of re-mediation to put forth the idea that perhaps it is the tools and artifacts, and/or the learning environments that must be reorganized in ways to encourage deep learning. We define the term *(re)center* as both centering and recentering. The term accounts for the reorientations that place people of color's ontologies and epistemologies foundationally to interrupt the Eurocentric notion of quality defined by DAP (Copple & Bredekamp, 2009). We employ (re)center here to explain the purposeful and intentional positioning of practices, knowledges, values, and experiences of multiply minoritized young children, families, and communities as essential to redefining quality in early childhood education.

We also make visible how the positioning of multiply minoritized children, families, and communities in this normative definition of quality is damaging and stands in stark contrast to NAEYC's own *Code of Ethical Conduct* (NAEYC, 2011), as illustrated by the following principles:

P-1.1: Above all, we shall not harm children. We shall not participate in practices that are emotionally damaging, physically harmful, disrespectful, degrading, dangerous, exploitative, or intimidating to children. This principle has precedence over all others in this Code.

P-1.2: We shall care for and educate children in positive emotional and social environments that are cognitively stimulating and that support each child's culture, language, ethnicity, and family structure.

MAPPING QUALITY IN EARLY CHILDHOOD EDUCATION

To develop the cartography of quality in early childhood education, we first conducted a Google Scholar search for the terms "quality" and "early childhood education." This literature search yielded over 177,000 results. To confirm the prevalence of DAP as defining quality in early childhood education, we read the 20 most-cited publications and verified the overwhelming presence of the term "developmentally appropriate practice" in 18 out of 20 of these, or 90%. We then drew on our knowledge of the field and on findings from our analysis of the earlier search, adding the term "developmentally appropriate practice" and delimiting results to the past 30 years, the period since NAEYC published the first DAP guide (Bredekamp, 1987). This new search produced 7,690 results. To map from the margins, we specifically used terms associated with the major paradigms that have historically positioned children from multiply minoritized communities and backgrounds (Goodwin et al., 2008): "deficit," "diversity," "inferiority" (in their plural and singular forms). This resulted in 188 publications inclusive of articles, books, and chapters. Our review and analysis were then guided by the following questions:

1. In what ways—if any—has the NAEYC concept of developmentally appropriate practice (vis-à-vis "best practice") in early childhood education fostered intersectional injustice?
2. What frameworks and fields of study can afford intersectional understandings of quality in early childhood education that are just and honor the ontologies and epistemologies of multiply minoritized children, their families, and communities?

We provide a critical review of quality in early childhood education over the past 30 years. The aim of our review of research is not to establish a chronology of the field but to identify the ways in which the normative definition of "best practice" in early childhood education defined by the NAEYC's *Developmentally Appropriate Practice* guide (Bredekamp, 1987; Bredekamp & Copple, 1997; Copple & Bredekamp, 2009) positions and affects children from multiply minoritized backgrounds, their families, and communities, and to offer design principles for authoring counterstories[3] to quality, (re)centering their values, experiences, and practices.

DAP AS "BEST PRACTICE" IN EARLY CHILDHOOD EDUCATION

Three paradigms have punctuated the landscape of early childhood education in the United States over time: inferiority, deficit, and cultural difference (Bloch, 1987; Genishi & Goodwin, 2008; Goodwin et al., 2008; Valdés, 1996). They rest on the following assumptions:

*   *Inferiority:* Children from multiply minoritized backgrounds have been seen as biologically inferior—as having smaller brains and lower IQs than White children, who have been seen as racially superior.
*   *Deficit:* Children from multiply minoritized backgrounds have been seen as experiencing poor upbringings in their homes and communities and developing a deficit—whether linguistic or cultural—for example, as having a word gap, as being "at risk," as needing a head start to succeed in schools and schooling (grounded in the desirability of colonial monocultural, monolingual norms imposed ethnocentrically and violently onto them).

- *Cultural Difference*: Children from multiply minoritized backgrounds have been seen as different from the colonial monocultural, White, monolingual norm.

These paradigms historically trace the development of early childhood education as a field and continue to function today, upholding "deep-seated, uninterrogated assumptions, values and beliefs of cultural normativity that perpetuate coloniality" (Dominguez, 2017, p. 227) and undergird DAP.

DAP was first defined by the NAEYC, one of the largest education professional organizations in the world, as "a framework of principles and guidelines for best practice in the care and education of young children, birth through age 8" (NAEYC, 2009). It was conceptualized in the 1980s, when NAEYC developed a system to accredit early childhood education programs, which included guidelines requiring programs to provide DAP and learning opportunities for young children (NAEYC, 2009). Because DAP was linked to the assessment and rating of early childhood education programs, NAEYC defined and exemplified DAP in a self-published guide (Bredekamp, 1987), now in its third edition (Copple & Bredekamp, 2009). Since then, DAP has been widely used to assess quality in early childhood education and "best practice" for the care and education of young children (Connors & Morris, 2015; NAEYC, 2009).

Developmentally Appropriate Practice in Early Childhood Programs Serving Children from Birth through Age 8 (Bredekamp, 1987; Bredekamp & Copple, 1997; Copple & Bredekamp, 2009) was first published in 1986 (Lally, Provence, Szanton, & Weissbourd, 1996, as cited in Bredekamp, 1987), expanded in 1987, revised in 1997, and updated in 2009 (the current edition). Although the guide has been revised twice, each new iteration remained centered on defining developmental appropriateness according to colonial White monolingual and monocultural norms. Even the most recent version of the DAP guide acknowledges its Eurocentrism: "It is necessary to acknowledge that developmentally appropriate practice (as defined by NAEYC) reflects the individualistic, independence-oriented culture prevalent in many Western societies (in contrast to the emphasis on interdependence that characterizes many non-Western societies)" (Copple & Bredekamp, 2009, p. 332). DAP scales and rates multiply minoritized young children's learning and development against a Eurocentric norm. From such a colonialist perspective,[4] multiply minoritized children "may be allowed to participate in" early education, but their values, voices, experiences, and perspectives—and those of their families and communities—"are far from welcome; something oppressive, colonial, survives in how" they, their families, and communities are positioned, treated, and de/valued (Dominguez, 2017, p. 227).

As we analyzed the three editions of *Developmentally Appropriate Practice in Early Childhood Programs Serving Children from Birth through Age 8* (Bredekamp, 1987; Bredekamp & Copple, 1997; Copple & Bredekamp, 2009), we considered the critical race theory (CRT) concept of interest convergence (Bell, 1980). Interest convergence helped us understand how any changes in conceptualizations, evaluations, definitions, and policies "for racial integration and equity will occur only insofar as the interests of dominant and minoritized groups converge, specifically, when White citizens perceive that such policies will benefit them" (Cervantes-Soon et al., 2017, p. 408). It helped us understand how albeit there have been shifts in terminology, DAP has remained centered on Whiteness and continued to privilege the interests of dominant groups, perpetuating colonialism.

Across editions (Bredekamp, 1987; Bredekamp & Copple, 1997; Copple & Bredekamp, 2009), the text moved to labeling behaviors not deemed to be "developmentally appropriate" from "developmentally inappropriate" (Bredekamp, 1987; Bredekamp & Copple, 1997) to "in contrast" (Copple & Bredekamp, 2009). When multiply minoritized children and families' cultural practices are considered in each of these DAP guides (Bredekamp & Copple, 1997; Copple & Bredekamp, 2009), they are positioned in opposition to, or in the margins of, what counts as DAP. This results in multiply minoritized children being positioned as "the figure[s] of colonial otherness" (Bhabha, 1994, p. 45).

Within the most recent edition of the text, when the cultural diversity of families is addressed, readers are directed to the box "Bridging Cultural Differences" (Gonzalez-Mena, 2009, p. 46). Questions about children from multiply minoritized backgrounds are largely addressed in a section titled "FAQs about Developmentally Appropriate Practice" (Copple & Bredekamp, 2009). Upholding the White gaze of coloniality, DAP defines cultural differences in ways that sustain the centrality and superiority of Whiteness; difference means difference *from* Whiteness, monolingual, middle-class identities, values, and practices. For example, when such families are included in *Developmentally Appropriate Practice in Early Childhood Programs Serving Children from Birth through Age 8* (Copple & Bredekamp, 2009), they are described by their perceived deficits—for example, "parents who do not speak English" (p. 183). Such descriptors signal the coloniality framing multiply minoritized children and their families' experiences, values, and voices in marginal and deficit-ridden ways—even in the most recent version of the guide.

Early childhood education scholars have pinpointed how DAP marginalizes and exerts control over multiply minoritized children and their families and how the intersectional injustices perpetuated by DAP are symptoms of coloniality, propagated through the overvaluing of White, middle-class, monolingual norms and aligning with White supremacist ontologies[5] (Cannella, 1997; Goodwin et al., 2008; Hatch, 1988; Long, Souto-Manning, & Vasquez, 2016; Lubeck, 1998; Mallory & New, 1994; Soto & Swadener, 2002; Souto-Manning, 2010, 2013; E. B. Swadener, 1990). Although they highlight different facets of systems of oppression, taken together, these studies highlight how DAP fosters and upholds intersectional injustices.

While examples are present throughout the DAP guide, across its three iterations, here we present a few examples as representations of a larger trend. For example, DAP privileges Eurocentric practices such as self-feeding at an early age, a practice absent in many Latinx households (Souto-Manning, 2009). In doing so, not only does it enact a White gaze but it also promotes assimilation as a goal of early learning and child development. It uses subtractive and deficit descriptions of children and families (e.g., "do not speak English"—Copple & Bredekamp, 2009, p. 183, and "[b]y 36 months of age, substantial socioeconomic disparities already exist in vocabulary knowledge," p. 2).

In addition, the NAEYC (2009) position statement *Developmentally Appropriate Practice in Early Childhood Programs Serving Children From Birth Through Age 8* cites problematic research: "On average, children growing up in low-income families have dramatically less rich experience with language in their homes than do middle-class children. They hear far fewer words and are engaged in fewer extended conversations" (p. 2). Such a statement embraces the rhetoric of the "word gap." The notion of the word gap was drawn from a study involving a very small number of families in the Midwestern United States, which suggested that children from minoritized backgrounds have a 30–million word gap (Hart & Risley, 1995, 2003). The latest DAP guide (Copple & Bredekamp, 2009) propagates the findings of this widely critiqued study (Hart & Risley, 1995). Researchers such as Dudley-Marling and Lucas (2009), Michaels (2013), and Orellana (2016) have analyzed the ways in which the Hart and Risley (1995) study frames multiply minoritized children of color as needing remediation, from deficit perspectives. This is visible in the DAP guide—for example, equating professional families with White families, and families receiving public assistance as families of color in essentialist ways such as: "A child in a professional family hears an average of 11 million words a year, while a child receiving public assistance hears an average of just 3 million" (Copple & Bredekamp, 2009, p. 332). In doing so, it characterizes multiply minoritized families of color by their perceived deficits and calls on early childhood education programs to remediate or fix such perceived deficits in ways that align with the colonialist logic of assimilation: "Clearly, programs serving low-income children and English language learners need to give special attention to building children's oral language and vocabulary . . . [which are] important for school success" (Copple & Bredekamp, 2009, p. 332).

A final example comes from the NAEYC (2009) position statement, which contains an abundance of claims such as the following: "Most disturbing, low-income and African American and Hispanic students lag significantly behind their peers on standardized comparisons of academic achievement throughout the school years, and they experience more difficulties while in the school setting" (p. 2). These claims are void of critiques of the historical and contemporary racial inequities inherent in many standardized tests (Fish, 1994). Furthermore, these examples illustrate a framework that ignores systemic racism, linguicism, and historically sedimented socioeconomic inequities (Gutiérrez et al., 2009) in deeply colonial ways (Dominguez, 2017). Children who are developing bilingually or multilingually are positioned as not having language (from an inferiority paradigm) or as having limited language (from a deficit paradigm). DAP ascribes problematic identities to multiply minoritized children without an acknowledgment of how they were constructed as problems, deficits, or "at risk" by a history of oppression and systemic racism.

To interrupt such paradigmatic positionings which undergird DAP, we adopt an intersectional framework, honing in on race, language, and cultural practices and values. With the understanding that inequities never result from single factors but are produced by interconnecting social locations, power relations, and experiences (Hankivsky, 2014), we problematize NAEYC's (2009) discursive construction and framing of diversities and multiply minoritized identities of entire groups of people—that is, "low-income and African American and Hispanic students" (NAEYC, 2009)—stereotypically and problematically as liabilities. DAP upholds colonialist values and has privileged Whiteness, dominant American English, economically advantaged individuals and communities, and has cloaked these inequities under the guise of a purportedly neutral measure of quality. Yet as Scribner (1970) unveiled, "'neutrality' often masks support of dominant interest groups" (p. 40). DAP excludes the rich practices and varied developmental timelines of children and families from multiply minoritized backgrounds (Genishi & Dyson, 2009, 2012). It "not only disaffirms diversity but also stigmatizes children of color through discourses of underdevelopment and underachievement" (Pérez and Saavedra, 2017, p. 6), serving as a tool for the enactment of intersectional structural oppressions.

In this critical review, we reject the "ideology of pathology" (Gutiérrez et al., 2009, p. 227), which aims to remediate children who do not fit the narrow, monocultural, and monolingual parameters established by the dominant and colonialist definition of quality sponsored by DAP (Goodwin et al., 2008; New & Mallory, 1994; Pérez & Saavedra, 2017). We engage in an intersectional analysis (Crenshaw, 1993) of DAP and use re-mediation (Cole & Griffin, 1983; Gutiérrez et al., 2009) as a theoretical tool for reorganizing the relationship between the experiences, values, and knowledges of children, families, and communities from multiply minoritized backgrounds and what counts as quality in early childhood education. Unlike the traditional notion of remediation, instead of blaming individual children and families for perceived gaps or problems (e.g., Copple & Bredekamp, 2009) and seeking to fix or remedy them as if they were broken or behind, the concept of "re-mediation involves a reorganization of the entire ecology for learning" (Gutiérrez et al., 2009, p. 227). Re-mediation has the power and potential to foster more expansive and robust definitions of quality learning environments and experiences through "a shift in the way that mediating devices regulate coordination with the environment" (Cole & Griffin, 1983, p. 70). Through the use of re-mediation, we offer architectural principles for building intersectional counterstories to the dominant master-narrative of quality in the field of early childhood education.

RE-MEDIATING QUALITY IN EARLY EDUCATION

As our review reveals, DAP is a colonialist and White supremacist construct, which inflicts harm on children, families, and communities from culturally, linguistically, and racially minoritized backgrounds. To interrupt such harm, we address our second guiding question: What frameworks and fields of study can afford intersectional understandings of quality in early childhood education that are just and honor the ontologies and epistemologies of multiply minoritized children, their families, and communities?

Epistemologically, race, culture, and language (as prioritized in our review) intersect with each other and are informed by power in society. They "cannot be tagged on to each other mechanically for, as concrete social relations, they are enmeshed in each other" (Anthias & Yuval-Davis, 1983, pp. 62–63). Isolating them delegitimizes multiply minoritized individuals' and communities' practices and ways of being (Artiles, Dorn, & Bal, 2016). With this recognition, we worked to identify oppositional pedagogies and theories that refuted dominant narratives as ways of engaging in reparations and stopping the violence enacted by DAP, a conceptualization of quality that fosters assimilation, promotes erasure, and furthers society's endemic racist and colonialist aims (Ladson-Billings & Tate, 1995; Pérez & Saavedra, 2017). We did so by drawing on our professional knowledge, consulting with nine experts (three in each of the following fields: race, culture, and language education), and finally confirming them via Google Scholar searches.[6] This led us to CRT, culturally relevant and sustaining pedagogies,[7] and translanguaging.

While acknowledging how injustices are intersectionally constructed, we specifically identified CRT as a counterstory to White supremacy, culturally relevant and sustaining pedagogies as counterstories to monocultural teaching practices grounded in cultural deficit and inferiority paradigms, and translanguaging as a counterstory to the privileging of dominant American English monolingualism. We did so to re-mediate quality in early childhood education in ways that essentially honor and value the practices of young children of color who are multilingual and of families and communities whose cultures do not mirror the culture of power (Delpit, 1988). While each of these counterstories forefronts one particular dimension of oppression (race, culture, language), together they account for multiple, overlapping systems of oppressions. We conclude with a brief discussion of the need to move from oppressive and reductionist notions of quality and offer design principles for intersectionally just early childhood education. Before engaging in re-mediation to (re)center quality in early childhood education, we employ intersectionality to ask: Whose knowledges, practices, and identities are privileged in current notions of quality in early childhood education? How are these related to social categories and power structures? How can intersectional frameworks help us move toward (re)centering notions of quality?

Intersectionality

Intersectionality has been employed in research across fields of study (e.g., sociology, women's studies, legal studies) to support the analysis of policy and practice in ways that attend to multiple locations and identities across axes of oppression related to social identifiers including, but not limited to, class, race, ethnicity, language, culture, dis/ability, gender, and sexuality (Dhamoon, 2009; Hankivsky & Cormier, 2011; Hankivsky et al., 2010; Taefi, 2009; Taylor, Hines, & Casey, 2010). Intersectionality foregrounds a richer and more complex ontology than approaches that attempt to reduce people to one category at a time. It also points to the need for "multiplex epistemologies" (Phoenix & Pattynama, 2006). In particular, the concept indicates that fruitful knowledge production must treat social positions as relational. Intersectionality " . . . aims to make visible the multiple positioning that constitutes everyday life and the power relations that are central to it" (Phoenix & Pattynama, 2006, p. 187).

As a framework, intersectionality helps us understand the layered and multidimensional nature of injustice and inequity—not as individual issues but as systemic problems (Crenshaw, 1989). As early childhood educators who developed at the crossroads, as immigrant women of color who grew up speaking languages other than dominant American English, throughout our careers we have navigated complex social inequalities legitimized by normative concepts of quality. We thus operate on standpoints that allow us to unveil the oppressive and damaging nature of a singular and colonialist normative definition of quality. Employing intersectionality as a framework affords sophisticated understandings of power and inequalities in early childhood education in general and DAP in particular. It is from such a perspective that we engage in the concurrent analyses of multiple, overlapping sources of oppression and subordination (Denis, 2008) affecting multiply minoritized young children, families, and communities.

We also engage with intersectionality as activism, after all, "from its inception, intersectionality has been a political strategy as much as it has been a theoretical lens" (Luft & Ward, 2009, p. 10). Reading and rereading intersectional oppressions enacted by the dominant conceptualization of quality in early childhood education—namely, DAP—we sought to complicate narrow and exclusivist definitions of quality. Thus, we subscribe to a strengths-based approach and adopt the term *global majority*,

to represent many populations variously characterized in the United States as minority, at risk, underserved, non-white, of color, urban, of low socioeconomic status and poor—all terms that are used to mask the hegemony of European American populations and the numeric and political reality of black, brown and lower-income people worldwide. We use the term "global majority" to reflect a more affirming and accurate sense of the vast diversity of individuals represented in the United States. (Croft, Roberts, & Stenhouse, 2015, p. 87)

To disrupt interconnected systems of oppressions and foster intersectional justice, we draw on CRT, culturally relevant and sustaining pedagogies, and translanguaging as counterstories to DAP. Combined, these counterstories expand the cartography of early childhood education and (re)center the dominant definition of quality in the field. Thus, critically rereading historically sedimented, problematic positionings of multiply minoritized young children, families, and communities in DAP allows us to reclaim the multiple assets of language repertoires, racial identities, and cultural practices that belong to the global majority.

SEEKING TO AUTHOR INTERSECTIONALLY JUST COUNTERSTORIES OF QUALITY IN EARLY EDUCATION

To center the practices, expertise, and values of young children, families, and communities who are members of the global majority, we engage in the critical study of DAP's proposed beliefs about reality and in the problematization of "how certain categories of reality and existence are apprehended and defined" (Ellis, 2010, p. 112). Departing from Eurocentric definitions of epistemology, we keenly understand "that the concept of epistemology is more than a "way of knowing." An epistemology is a "system of knowing . . . intimately linked to worldview" (Ladson-Billings, 2000, pp. 257–258). We engage in this epistemological rereading with the understanding that

developing a worldview that differs from the dominant worldview requires active intellectual work on the part of the knower, because schools, society, and the structure and the production of knowledge are designed to create individuals who internalize the dominant worldview". (Ladson-Billings, 2000, p. 258)

This informs our engagement with CRT, culturally relevant and sustaining pedagogies, and translanguaging as counterstories to DAP.

A Critical Race Theorizing of DAP

Critical race theory, as a form of oppositional scholarship, serves as a counterstory to White supremacy and thus helps us (re)center quality by offering the theoretical tools to move toward intersectional justice. We are aware of critiques of CRT resulting from its analytical focus on race, "seemingly to the detriment of gendered and class-based analyses" (Gillborn, 2006, p. 320). Yet CRT does not exclude interconnected and overlapping factors shaping oppression. Instead, it unapologetically focuses on denouncing, theorizing, understanding, and interrupting racism.

Emanating from critical legal studies and radical feminism (Delgado & Stefancic, 2017), CRT helps us understand how racism is endemic in American society (Ladson-Billings & Tate, 1995), undergirding everyday life. We find that CRT helps us understand how "white supremacy is conceived as a comprehensive condition whereby the interests and perceptions of white subjects are continually placed centre stage and assumed as 'normal'" (Gillborn, 2006, p. 318). This comes to life in DAP, as it is a racialized notion of development, which seeks to normalize Whiteness while ignoring and/or silencing structures of colonialism and racism.

As applied to education, CRT highlights how Whiteness, a design feature of American society, comes to define what is "normal" and "acceptable" in (pre)schools[8] and what is instantiated in curriculum, teaching, and assessments. CRT makes visible how White supremacist ontologies disempower people of color and advance the interests of White elites (Delgado & Stefancic, 2017; Ladson-Billings & Tate, 1995). CRT thus urges us to unpack claims of neutrality and objectivity in notions of quality and achievement in education (Dixson & Rousseau, 2006).

Critical race theory helps us unveil how framing DAP neutrally effectively serves to reinforce the practices of White, middle-class, and dominant American English-speaking families. CRT's clear commitment to social transformation (Delgado & Stefancic, 2017) urges us to center transformation on a critical race-consciousness, on the knowledge of the intertwined nature of race and power. CRT focuses on the interruption of racial oppression through the "naming [of] one's own reality" (Delgado & Stefancic, 2013, p. 61). We draw on CRT to name problematic realities represented by DAP as it defines quality grounded in a White superiority ontology and not on the ontologies and epistemologies of people of color who experience multiple intersecting oppressions. Furthermore, we seek to disrupt the essentialism, the imposition of White ways of being, behaving, and communicating onto children of color as if they applied to the entire universe of young children in today's (pre)school classrooms, thereby marginalizing and pathologizing those who are members of the global majority in early childhood education and beyond. Thus, DAP cloaks dominant cultural practices as "normal" (Delgado & Stefancic, 2017; Dixson & Rousseau, 2006; Gillborn, 2006). It effectively defines quality as White and as a property only Whites possess and can display (Ladson-Billings,

1998; Ladson-Billings & Tate, 1995). As a result, NAEYC's DAP sponsors racism and racial oppression and as such harms young children, families, and communities who are members of the global majority—those who navigate multiple interconnected systems of oppression. Ultimately, as DAP affects the structures, policies, and practices of early childhood education classrooms and (pre)schools, it serves as a tool for institutionalized racism (Dowd & Bensimon, 2015; Jones, 2002).

Culturally Relevant and Sustaining Pedagogies: Rejecting One-Size-Fits-All Approaches

Culturally relevant and sustaining pedagogies (Ladson-Billings, 1995; Paris, 2012; Paris & Alim, 2017) are counterstories to the myth of acultural teaching promoted by dominant pedagogies. They serve as sites of struggle against the violence and oppression enacted by paradigms, practices, and standards, which marginalize young children, families, and communities who are part of the global majority (Ball & Pence, 1999; Brown & Mowry, 2016; McKeough et al., 2008; Meier, 2000; Novick, 1996). Culturally relevant educators and students develop not just cultural competence but also critical consciousness—or "critical meta-awareness"—of oppressive conditions linked to White privilege and superiority. In addition, culturally relevant educators must have (a) high expectations for all children, believing in their infinite capacity and potential, and (b) a critical understanding of the monocultural nature of mainstream curricula, teaching, and assessments.

Building on culturally relevant teaching (Ladson-Billings, 1995), Paris and Alim (2017) called for culturally sustaining pedagogies, which

extend the previous visions of asset pedagogies by demanding explicit pluralist outcomes that are not centered on White middle-class, monolingual/monocultural norms and notions of educational achievement—and that call out the imposition of these norms as harmful to and discriminatory against our communities. (p. 12)

This stands in stark contrast to the concept of quality proposed by DAP, which views such languages and cultural practices through a deficit lens.

Instead of framing members of the global majority as incapable or flawed, culturally relevant and sustaining pedagogies propose that the pedagogies, curriculum, and practices in place are impoverishing and need to be transformed (Ladson-Billings, 2014; Paris, 2012; Souto-Manning & Martell, 2016). Such pedagogies reject the language of academic, developmental, or linguistic gaps, which blame individuals and families for their academic failure. Instead, they acknowledge that there is an education debt (Ladson-Billings, 2006), which has historically, morally, economically, and sociopolitically disempowered individuals and communities of color—and imposed multiple systems of overlapping oppressions.

Culturally relevant and sustaining pedagogies require openly naming, questioning, and rejecting inferiority and cultural deficit paradigms by demanding that educators have high expectations. That is, they demand that educators acknowledge, honor, leverage, and sustain the infinite capacity of young children of color, instead of feeling sorry for them before ever meeting them (Delpit, 2012). This requires not only transforming teaching, but reframing the way educators see children from the global majority, moving from seeing them as being "at risk" to seeing them as being "at promise" (B. B. Swadener, 2010; E. B. Swadener, 1990). This also means imagining powerful futures for children of color, acknowledging that a future Toni Morrison or Cesar Chavez is likely in a (pre)school classroom—"you just never know" (Ladson-Billings, 2012). Instead of regarding the cultural practices of multiply minoritized children of color, their families, and communities as comparatively inferior, or in contrast to the "developmentally appropriate" dominant practices typically displayed by White middle-class families—for example, oral storytelling versus bedtime book reading; call-and-response versus initiation–response–evaluation speech patterns—these pedagogies demand that the rich practices of children, families, and communities who are members of the global majority be identified, honored, cultivated, and sustained.

Instead of measuring the varied, rich, and sophisticated cultural practices of all children against a monocultural norm, defined by those who have power in society, these oppositional pedagogies propose that every student needs to become culturally competent—in their own cultures as well as in at least one other culture (Ladson-Billings, 2012). These pedagogies are not only for children deemed to be disprivileged; they are "good teaching" for everyone (Ladson-Billings, 1995) because they work to undo intersectional injustices in schooling and in society by troubling restrictive notions of what counts as legitimate knowledge in schools and schooling and unveiling multiple interconnected injustices in and through pedagogies. They urge educators to (re)center their teaching on the genius of the child who is a member of the global majority. Finally, these pedagogies are not about conforming; they are about transforming. As such, they seek to foment critical consciousness, to develop young children as active civic participants who critically read the injustices that characterize their lives and worlds, and actively work to problematize, challenge, and change them. This fosters a process whereby children who are members of the global majority act as agents individually and collectively, troubling injustices and promoting justice.

These foundational principles of culturally relevant and sustaining pedagogies—which reject the simplicity of one-size-fits-all practices—seek to confront, interrupt, and delink pedagogy "from the colonial matrix of power" (Mignolo, 2009, p. 20), decolonizing notions of quality. These principles also seek to acknowledge, cultivate, foster, leverage, and sustain linguistic and cultural pluralism—not as marginally positioned, but as central design features of quality teaching and learning. Taken together, these principles comprise pedagogical antidotes to paradigms that disempower children from the global majority and to conceptions of quality teaching practice, which continue to oppress and marginalize them.

Translanguaging: Interrupting Monolingualism as the Norm

We also draw on translanguaging as a counterstory to the inferiority and deficit master narratives that define multilingual children as not having language or as having limited language. Instead of regarding language as "a simple system of structures that is independent from human activity" (García & Wei, 2014, p. 8) and can be assessed by the number of words a child knows (e.g., Copple & Bredekamp, 2009), we engage with the concept of languaging, which accounts for the "ongoing process that is always being created as we interact with the world lingually. To learn a new way of languaging is not just to learn a new code" (García & Wei, 2014, p. 8). According to Swain (2006), languaging is "the process of making meaning and shaping knowledge and experience through language" (p. 98). To recognize and account for how multilingual children language within and across systems, we take up the García and Wei (2014) definition of translanguaging as "an approach . . . that considers the language practices of bilinguals not as two autonomous language systems . . . but as one linguistic repertoire with features that have been societally constructed as belonging to two separate languages" (p. 2). We reject paradigms that frame multilingual children—often and problematically labeled "language learners"—as biologically or genetically inferior and reject notions of deprivation and limited language.

Through her scholarship on translanguaging, García (2014) offers us a counterstory of hope, a way of reconceptualizing language as a verb and of moving from understanding languages as discrete and hierarchical to translanguaging practices. That is, "speakers select language features from one integrated system and 'soft-assemble' their language practices in ways that fit their communicative situations" (García, 2014, p. 150). This perspective positions multilingualism and translanguaging as global norms. After all, multilingualism and translanguaging "are only rendered problematic by school systems that insist on monolingualism in the dominant language as the only acceptable goal of education" (García, 2014, p. 157). This insistence on dominant language practices and norms pervades DAP (Cannella, 1997; Rhedding-Jones, 2003; Souto-Manning, 2010; Viruru, 2001).

To understand the intersection between racism and other forms of oppression in how supposedly deficient languages and language practices are framed in DAP, we draw on the work of critical language researchers and raciolinguistics to unveil the connections between race and language (Alim, Rickford, & Ball, 2016; Flores, 2016; Flores & Rosa, 2015; García & Wei, 2014). While multilingualism is positioned as an asset for White people (Valdés, 1997), it is often framed as a deficit for students of color, who "inhabit a shared racial positioning that frames their linguistic practices as deficient regardless of how closely they follow supposed rules of appropriateness" (Flores & Rosa, 2015, p. 149). We draw on raciolinguistics to theorize and analyze "how language shapes our ideas about race" (Alim et al., 2016) and how we language in racially specific ways. Denouncing how dominant populations define what counts as a language and define legitimate languaging practices, Flores and Rosa (2015) propose that "discourses of appropriateness . . . involve the conceptualization of standardized linguistic practices as objective sets of linguistic forms" (p. 150). Thus, we situate dominant American English and the very notion of Standard English as "raciolinguistic project[s] that sought to discursively produce the American bourgeoisie in opposition to the racialized Other" (Flores, 2016, p. 16). We also recognize how the language practices of children who speak dominant American English, the language of power, are overvalued by DAP, whereas the sophisticated language practices of the global majority tend to be marginalized due to the hegemony of Whiteness (Cervantes-Soon et al., 2017; Flores, 2016; Hughey, 2012).

The construction of languages as separate is a historically sedimented artifact of White hegemonic and colonialist "ideologies through which racialized bodies come to be constructed as engaging in appropriately academic linguistic practices" (Flores & Rosa, 2015, p. 149). After all, language practices are often racialized, comodified, and marginalized in ways that lead to and uphold injustice through inequitable educational opportunities. Children and families who are members of the global majority are often positioned as lagging behind—e.g., as not having a robust enough vocabulary, as learning English—instead of being positioned by the assets they have—e.g., their translanguaging practices and multilingual repertoires. They are authored pathologically. Thus, we seek to (re)center quality on the experiences and practices of young children who belong to the global majority and who navigate within and across multiple and complex ways of languaging.

Critical Race Theory, Culturally Relevant/Sustaining Pedagogies, and Translanguaging

As we considered counterstories to Whiteness, monoculturalism, and monolingualism—pervasive and ingrained features of DAP across time—we deepened our understandings of the overlapping systems of oppression and injustice experienced by young children who are members of the global majority in the name of quality. The absence of linguistically, culturally, and racially empowering practices, pedagogies, and principles in DAP reinforces an invisible "matrix of domination characterized by intersecting oppressions" (Hill Collins, 2009, p. 26). From such a perspective, not only does DAP marginalize, but it effectively harms children who are members of the global majority.

In response, we propose intersectionally just design principles for quality in early childhood education. These design principles emanate from our counterhegemonic intersectional review of the affordances offered by CRT, culturally relevant and sustaining pedagogies, and translanguaging in (re)centering quality in early childhood education. Such counterhegemonic work resulted from a purposeful and deliberate move away from damaging Eurocentric epistemologies and ontologies (Ladson-Billings, 2000; Pérez & Saavedra, 2017), which have framed members of the global majority in disempowering and oppressive ways. We understand that this is the beginning of a much longer journey to shift the architecture of what defines quality in early childhood education.

LOOKING BACK, MOVING FORWARD: TOWARD INTERSECTIONALLY JUST DESIGN PRINCIPLES

As multilingual women of color who grew up in the margins (hooks, 1984), navigating overlapping systems of oppression, we engaged our "intersectional sensibility" (Crenshaw, 1991, p. 1475) to imagine ways to (re)center quality away from dominant norms established by DAP. We encoded some of these ways into design principles, which purposefully reject Eurocentric positionings (Ladson-Billings, 2000) and build on theories, ideologies, and epistemologies emanating from scholarship grounded in the rich values, experiences, and practices of the global majority. "We call them design principles to signal the sort of architectural change that is required to achieve successful outcomes for all our children" (Teacher Education Exchange, 2017, p. 11).

We believe that the four design principles outlined below can help us—as a field—get started working toward redefining quality in intersectionally just ways:

1. Children's development is social, cultural, and historical; it will not follow discrete trajectories or certain timelines.

From an intersectionally just perspective, quality early childhood education positions teachers as learning from young children, families, and communities who are members of the global majority, identifying, leveraging, and supporting their rich cultural and linguistic repertoires of practice in and through curriculum and teaching. Instead of imposing normative definitions, timelines, and trajectories onto children's development, this principle proposes that quality early childhood education must recognize and honor diversities, paying special attention to the centrality of knowledges emanating from the global majority. This principle rejects Eurocentric measures of development and learning. That is, quality early childhood education must wrestle with and reject the intersectional injustices inherent in deficit-informed diagnostic tools, standardized developmental timelines, and high-stakes assessments (Fish, 1994; Steele & Aronson, 1995).

2. All children, families, and communities have rich cultural and linguistic assets and are "at promise."

Quality early childhood education recognizes and accounts for the richness, power, and sophistication of young children's cultural repertoires and translanguaging practices. It is grounded in high expectations and aspirations for children who are members of the global majority. It demands supporting these high expectations and aspirations by centrally engaging in identifying, supporting, leveraging, and sustaining such cultural and linguistic assets, thereby unleashing their power and potential. Rejecting normative definitions of language practices, such as the notions of children having "no language" or "limited English proficiency," quality early childhood education positions young children as multilinguals "at promise." Furthermore, it commits to cultivating and leveraging children's translanguaging resources. This requires interrupting the racialization of multilingualism and the ingrained racism in early education programs—even those that seek to promote bilingualism and/or multilingualism. Thus, quality early education is predicated on the commitment to recognizing, developing, and sustaining sophisticated cultural and linguistic repertoires.

3. Quality early childhood education must positively engage intersectional identities.

This principle requires recognizing that social categories, power structures, and relations privilege specific racial, cultural, and linguistic identities. "The hegemony of the dominant paradigm makes it more than just another way to view the world—it claims to be the only legitimate way to view the world" (Ladson-Billings, 2000, p. 258). This design principle seeks to foster quality in early childhood education that is paradigmatically in contrast to DAP, which positions multiply minoritized identities as deficient or different *from* the norm. Instead of attempting "to find legitimacy in the dominant paradigm" (Ladson-Billings, 2000, p. 260), to foster intersectional justice, quality must be redefined according to an epistemological frame that can account for and "describe the experiences and knowledge systems of peoples outside the dominant paradigm" (Ladson-Billings, 2000, p. 260). This transformation requires engaging with paradigms informed by epistemological stances centered on the assets of the global majority such as CRT, culturally relevant and sustaining pedagogies, and raciolinguistic approaches to translanguaging.

4. Quality early childhood education must center the voices, values, practices, and experiences of the global majority.

Rejecting Eurocentric, Whiteified, monocultural, and monolingual definitions of quality, this principle demands that curriculum, teaching, and learning experiences be redesigned to align with the values and practices of the global majority, naming, problematizing, and disrupting (a) the pervasiveness of racism in early education and in society and (b) the rights historically afforded by Whiteness (Ladson-Billings & Tate, 1995). It also moves to problematize the cultural and racial features of material and theoretical tools for teaching and learning and to interrupt how members of the global majority have not only been invisiblized in curriculum (Au, Brown, & Calderón, 2016; Woodson, 1933), but deliberately "educated away from their own culture and traditions and attached to the fringes of European culture" (Asante, 1991, p. 170) in harmful ways. Ultimately, as this design principle seeks to (re)center quality early childhood education on the values, experiences, and practices of the global majority, it also moves to redefine it in intersectionally just and ethical ways.

CONCLUSION

We believe that the design principles we outline are central to the enactment of an intersectionally just framework for quality in early childhood education, although we recognize that they are likely not the only ones. The design principles we proposed are grounded in the understanding that to achieve sustainable, positive transformation in quality as it pertains to early childhood education, we must commit to constantly challenge existing structures that reify hegemonic values, make visible what is normalized, and interrupt the power relations that are central to it. We propose that together these four design principles can help us—as a field—respond to prevalent and persistent injustices in early childhood education. They have the potential to inform re-mediations of quality in early childhood education, building more robust and intersectionally just notions of quality in early childhood education, which unapologetically center on the multiple values, experiences, and practices of the global majority. This requires interrupting and dismantling systems of oppression that perpetuate colonialism and racism from the earliest years.

The analysis presented in this chapter makes visible how the normative definition of quality in early childhood education is at once colonialist and racist. In doing so, it urges us to commit to dismantling these systems of oppression by design and to interrupt the harm being done to the majority of young children in the United States in the name of quality. Just as these oppressive systems were intentionally and deliberately created—they must be purposefully taken down. We can no longer afford to limit ourselves to tweaks or minor revisions of quality as defined by the DAP, which focuses on "advancing the goals of the dominant group, while benefits for minoritized students may be rendered only as a by-product of such efforts" (Cervantes-Soon et al., 2017, p. 409). Instead, quality must fundamentally originate from the values, voices, experiences, and practices of the young children, families, and communities who belong to the global majority. This can only happen when we recognize that it is our ethical responsibility as a profession to recognize and value the power, possibility, and promise of children who are members of the global majority in our efforts to redefine quality in early childhood education. The design principles we identified have the potential to transform the architecture of quality in early childhood education. (Re)centering quality in the ways proposed in this chapter is not a choice or a privilege. It is a matter of justice.

NOTES

[1]McCarty (2002) proposes: "'Minority' is stigmatizing and often numerically inaccurate . . . 'Minoritized' more accurately conveys the power relations and processes by which certain groups are socially, economically, and politically marginalized within the larger society" (p. xv).

[2]As Rose (1989) observed, remediation positions multiply minoritized individuals and communities as being "substandard, inadequate, and, because of the origins of the term, the inadequacy is metaphorically connected to disease and mental defect" (p. 171).

[3]Counterstories are "the stories of those people whose experiences are not often told (i.e., those on the margins of society)" (Solórzano & Yosso, 2002, p. 26). They serve to expose,

analyze, and challenge dominant stories, which oppress and disempower. Counterstories are the very stories on which we seek to (re)center quality in early childhood education, moving toward intersectional justice.

[4]Critical early childhood education researchers have highlighted the racist and colonialist roots of DAP (e.g., Bloch, 1992; Cannella, 1997; Goodwin et al., 2008; Mallory & New, 1994; Pérez & Saavedra, 2017; Soto & Swadener, 2002; Souto-Manning, 2010). Their critiques have made visible the ways in which DAP represents "long standing patterns of power that emerged as a result of colonialism . . . that define culture . . . and knowledge production well beyond the strict limits of [explicit] colonial administrations" (Maldonado-Torres, 2010, p. 97).

[5]According to Solórzano and Vélez (2017), "White supremacy is defined as the set of beliefs or ideologies that guides a system of racial domination and exploitation where power and resources are unequally distributed to privilege whites and oppress People of Color" (p. 93).

[6]Seeking to confirm the prevalence and importance of such fields of oppositional scholarship, we conducted Google Scholar searches. We took high numbers to signify prevalence and importance. Our search for "critical race theory" and "Whiteness" yielded 18,300 results. "Culturally relevant teaching" and "culturally sustaining pedagogy" combined with (mono) cultural yielded 13,288 results. "Translanguaging" and "monolingual" yielded 25,311 results. These searches confirmed that the oppositional theories and pedagogies identified were widely known and used.

[7]Given the intricately connected nature of "culturally relevant pedagogy" and "culturally sustaining pedagogy," which Ladson-Billings (2012) called a remix of "culturally relevant pedagogy," we combined these two terms under a single category.

[8]The term *(pre)schools* encompasses preschools and/or schools. It accounts for the places of most formal early childhood education programs.

REFERENCES

Alim, H. S., Rickford, J. R., & Ball, A. (Eds.). (2016). *Raciolinguistics: How language shapes our ideas about race*. New York, NY: Oxford University Press.

Anthias, F., & Yuval-Davis, N. (1983). Contextualizing feminism: Gender, ethnic and class divisions. *Feminist Review, 15*, 62–75.

Artiles, A., Dorn, S., & Bal, A. (2016). Objects of protection, enduring nodes of difference: Disability intersections with "other" differences, 1916–2016. *Review of Research in Education, 40*, 777–820.

Asante, M. K. (1991). The Afrocentric idea in education. *Journal of Negro Education, 60*, 170–180.

Au, W., Brown, A., & Calderón, D. (2016). *Reclaiming the multicultural roots of U.S. curriculum: Communities of color and official knowledge in education*. New York, NY: Teachers College Press.

Ball, J., & Pence, A. R. (1999). Beyond developmentally appropriate practice: Developing community and culturally appropriate practice. *Young Children, 54*(2), 46–50.

Bell, D. (1980). *Brown v. Board of Education* and the interest-convergence dilemma. *Harvard Law Review, 93*, 518–533.

Bhabha, H. (1994). *The location of culture*. Abington, England: Routledge.

Bloch, M. (1987). Becoming scientific and professional: A historical perspective on the aims and effects of early education. In T. Popkewitz (Ed.), *The formation of school subjects: The struggle for creating an American institution* (pp. 25–62). London, England: Falmer Press.

Bloch, M. (1992). Critical perspectives on the historical relationship between child development and early childhood education research. In S. Kessler & E. B. Swadener (Eds.), *Reconceptualizing the early childhood curriculum: Beginning the dialogue* (pp. 3–20). New York, NY: Teachers College Press.

Bredekamp, S. (Ed.). (1987). *Developmentally appropriate practice in early childhood programs serving children from birth through age 8*. Washington, DC: National Association for the Education of Young Children.

Bredekamp, S., & Copple, C. (Eds.). (1997). *Developmentally appropriate practice in early childhood programs serving children from birth through age 8* (2nd ed.). Washington, DC: National Association for the Education of Young Children.

Brown, C., & Mowry, B. (2016). Using testimonio to bring children's worlds into a standardized teaching context: An example of culturally relevant teaching in early childhood education. *Childhood Education, 92*, 281–289.

Cannella, G. S. (1997). *Deconstructing early childhood education: Social justice and revolution*. New York, NY: Peter Lang.

Cervantes-Soon, C., Dorner, L., Palmer, D., Heiman, D., Schwedtfeger, R., & Choi, J. (2017). Combating inequalities in two-way language immersion programs: Toward critical consciousness in bilingual education spaces. *Review of Research in Education, 41*, 403–427.

Cole, M., & Griffin, P. (1983). A socio-historical approach to re-mediation. *Quarterly Newsletter of the Laboratory of Comparative Human Cognition, 5*(4), 69–74.

Connors, M. C., & Morris, P. A. (2015). Comparing state policy approaches to early care and education quality: A multidimensional assessment of quality rating and improvement systems and child care licensing regulations. *Early Childhood Research Quarterly, 30*, 266–279.

Copple, C., & Bredekamp, S. (2009). *Developmentally appropriate practice in early childhood programs serving children from birth through age 8* (3rd ed.). Washington, DC: National Association for the Education of Young Children.

Crenshaw, K. (1989). Demarginalizing the intersection of race and sex: A Black feminist critique of antidiscrimination doctrine, feminist theory and antiracist politics. *University of Chicago Legal Forum, 1*, 139–167.

Crenshaw, K. (1991). Race, gender, and sexual harassment. *Southern California Law Review, 65*, 1467–1476.

Crenshaw, K. (1993). Beyond racism and misogyny. In M. Matsuda, C. Lawrence, R. Delgado, & K. W. Crenshaw (Eds.), *Words that wound: Critical race theory, assaultive speech, and the first amendment* (pp. 113–132). Boulder, CO: Westview Press.

Croft, S. J., Roberts, M., & Stenhouse, V. L. (2015). The perfect storm of education reform: High-stakes testing and teacher evaluation. *Social Justice, 42*(1), 70–92.

Delgado, R., & Stefancic, J. (Eds.). (2013). *Critical race theory: The cutting edge*. Philadelphia: Temple University Press.

Delgado, R., & Stefancic, J. (2017). *Critical race theory: An introduction* (3rd ed.). New York: New York University Press.

Delpit, L. (1988). The silenced dialogue: Power and pedagogy in educating other people's children. *Harvard Educational Review, 58*, 280–298.

Delpit, L. (2012). *"Multiplication is for white people": Raising the expectations for other people's children*. New York, NY: New Press.

Denis, A. (2008). Intersectional analysis: A contribution of feminism to sociology. *International Sociology, 23*, 677–694.

Dhamoon, R. (2009). *Identity/difference politics: How difference is produced and why it matters*. Vancouver, British Columbia, Canada: University of British Columbia Press.

Dixson, A., & Rousseau, C. (2006). *Critical race theory in education: All god's children got a song*. New York, NY: Routledge.

Dominguez, M. (2017). "Se hace puentes al andar": Decolonial teacher education as a needed bridge to culturally sustaining and revitalizing pedagogies. In D. Paris & S. Alim (Eds.), *Culturally sustaining pedagogies: Teaching and learning for justice in a changing world* (pp. 225–246). New York, NY: Teachers College Press.

Dowd, A., & Bensimon, E. (2015). *Engaging the "race question": Accountability and equity in U.S. higher education.* New York, NY: Teachers College Press.

Dudley-Marling, C., & Lucas, K. (2009). Pathologizing the language and culture of poor children. *Language Arts, 86,* 362–370.

Ellis, V. (2010). Impoverishing experience: The problem of teacher education in England. *Journal of Education for Teaching, 36,* 105–120.

Fish, S. (1994). Affirmative action and the SAT. *Journal of Blacks in Higher Education, 2,* 83.

Flores, N. (2016). A tale of two visions: Hegemonic whiteness and bilingual education. *Educational Policy, 30,* 13–38.

Flores, N., & Rosa, J. (2015). Undoing appropriateness: Raciolinguistic ideologies and language diversity in education. *Harvard Educational Review, 85,* 149–171.

García, O. (2014). Becoming bilingual and biliterate: Sociolinguistic and sociopolitical considerations. In C. Stone, E. Silliman, B. Ehren, & G. Wallach (Eds.), *Handbook of language & literacy: Development disorders* (2nd ed., pp. 145–160). New York, NY: Guilford Press.

García, O., & Wei, L. (2014). *Translanguaging: Language, bilingualism and education.* New York, NY: Palgrave Macmillan.

Genishi, C., & Dyson, A. H. (2009). *Children, language, and literacy: Diverse learners in diverse times.* New York, NY: Teachers College Press.

Genishi, C., & Dyson, A. H. (2012). Racing to the top: Who's accounting for the children? *Bank Street Occasional Papers, 27,* 18–20.

Genishi, C., & Goodwin, A. L. (Eds.). (2008). *Diversities in early childhood education: Rethinking and doing.* New York, NY: Routledge.

Gillborn, D. (2006). Rethinking white supremacy: Who counts in "WhiteWorld." *Ethnicities, 6,* 318–340.

Gonzalez-Mena, J. (2009). Bridging cultural differences. In C. Copple & S. Bredekamp (Eds.), *Developmentally appropriate practice in early childhood programs serving children from birth through age 8* (3rd ed., p. 46). Washington, DC: National Association for the Education of Young Children.

Goodwin, A. L., Cheruvu, R., & Genishi, C. (2008). Responding to multiple diversities in early childhood education. In C. Genishi & A. L. Goodwin (Eds.), *Diversities in early childhood education: Rethinking and doing* (pp. 3–10). New York, NY: Routledge.

Griffin, P., & Cole, M. (1984). Current activity for the future: The zo-ped. In B. Rogoff & J. Wertsch (Eds.), *Children's learning in the "zone of proximal development."* (pp. 45–63). San Francisco, CA: Jossey-Bass.

Gutiérrez, K., Morales, P., & Martinez, D. (2009). Re-mediating literacy: Culture, difference, and learning for students from nondominant communities. *Review of Research in Education, 33,* 212–245.

Hankivsky, O. (2014). *Intersectionality.* Vancouver, British Columbia, Canada: Institute for Intersectionality Research and Policy.

Hankivsky, O., & Cormier, R. (2011). Intersectionality and public policy: Some lessons from existing models. *Political Research Quarterly, 64,* 217–229.

Hankivsky, O., Reid, C., Cormier, R., Varcoe, C., Clark, N., Benoit, C., & Brotman, S. (2010). Exploring the promises of intersectionality for advancing women's health research. *International Journal for Equity in Health, 9*(5). Retrieved from https://equity-healthj.biomedcentral.com/articles/10.1186/1475-9276-9-5

Hart, B., & Risley, T. R. (1995). *Meaningful differences in the early experience of young American children.* Baltimore, MD: Paul H. Brookes.

Hart, B., & Risley, T. R. (2003). The early catastrophe: The 30 million word gap by age 3. *American Educator, Spring,* 4–9.

Hatch, J. A. (1988). Kindergarten philosophies and practices: Perspectives of teachers, principals, and supervisors. *Early Childhood Research Quarterly, 3,* 151–166.

Hill Collins, P. (2009). *Black feminist thought: Knowledge, consciousness, and the politics of empowerment.* New York, NY: Routledge.

Hill Collins, P., & Bilge, S. (2016). *Intersectionality.* Cambridge, England: Polity Press.

hooks, b. (1984). *Feminist theory: From margin to center.* Boston, MA: South End Press.

Hughey, M. (2012). *White bound: Nationalists, antiracists, and the shared meaning of race.* Stanford, CA: Stanford University Press.

Jones, C. P. (2002). Confronting institutionalized racism. *Phylon, 50*(1/2), 7–22.

Ladson-Billings, G. (1995). But that's just good teaching! The case for culturally relevant pedagogy. *Theory Into Practice, 34,* 159–165.

Ladson-Billings, G. (1998). Just what is critical race theory and what's it doing in a nice field like education? *International Journal of Qualitative Studies in Education, 11*(1), 7–24.

Ladson-Billings, G. (2000). Racialized discourses and ethnic epistemologies. In N. Denzin & Y. S. Lincoln (Eds.), *The SAGE handbook of qualitative research* (2nd ed., pp. 257–277). Thousand Oaks, CA: Sage.

Ladson-Billings, G. (2006). From the achievement gap to the education debt: Understanding achievement in U.S. schools. *Educational Researcher, 35*(7), 3–12.

Ladson-Billings, G. (2012). *Cultural competency* [Video file]. Retrieved from https://www.youtube.com/watch?v=XSE8nxxZN5s

Ladson-Billings, G. (2014). Culturally relevant pedagogy 2.0: a.k.a. the remix. *Harvard Educational Review, 84*(1), 74–84.

Ladson-Billings, G., & Tate, W. (1995). Toward a critical race theory of education. *Teachers College Record, 97,* 47–68.

Lally, J. R., Provence, S., Szanton, E., & Weissbourd, B. (1996). Developmentally appropriate care for children from birth to age 3. In S. Bredekamp (Ed.), *Developmentally appropriate practice in early childhood programs serving children from birth through age 8* (Expanded ed., pp. 17–33). Washington, DC: National Association for the Education of Young Children.

Long, S., Souto-Manning, M., & Vasquez, V. (2016). *Courageous leadership in early childhood education: Taking a stand for social justice.* New York, NY: Teachers College Press.

Lubeck, S. (1998). Is developmentally appropriate practice for everyone? *Childhood Education, 74,* 283–292.

Luft, R., & Ward, J. (2009). Toward an intersectionality just out of reach: Confronting challenges to intersectional practice. In V. Demos & M. T. Segal (Eds.), *Perceiving gender locally, globally, and intersectionally* (pp. 9–37). Bingley, England: Emerald.

Maldonado-Torres, N. (2010). On the coloniality of being: Contributions to the development of a concept. In W. Mignolo & A. Escobar (Eds.), *Globalization and the colonial option* (pp. 94–124). New York, NY: Routledge.

Mallory, B., & New, R. (Eds.). (1994). *Diversity and developmentally appropriate practices: Challenges for early childhood curriculum.* New York, NY: Teachers College Press.

McCarty, T. (2002). *A place to be Navajo: Rough Rock and the struggle for self-determination in Indigenous schooling.* New York, NY: Routledge.

McKeough, A., Bird, S., Tourigny, E., Romaine, A., Graham, S., Ottman, J., & Jeary, J. (2008). Storytelling as a foundation to literacy development for aboriginal children: Culturally and developmentally appropriate practices. *Canadian Psychology, 49,* 148–154.

Meier, D. (2000). *Scribble scrabble—Learning to read and write: Success with diverse teachers, children, and families.* New York, NY: Teachers College Press.

Michaels, S. (2013). Déjà vu all over again: What's wrong with Hart & Risley and a "linguistic deficit" framework in early childhood education? *LEARNing Landscapes, 7*(1), 23–41.

Mignolo, W. D. (2009). Epistemic disobedience, independent thought and de-colonial freedom. *Theory, Culture & Society, 26*(7–8), 1–23.

National Association for the Education of Young Children. (2009). *Developmentally appropriate practice in early childhood programs serving children from birth through age 8.* Retrieved from https://www.naeyc.org/files/naeyc/file/positions/position%20statement%20Web.pdf

National Association for the Education of Young Children. (2011). *NAEYC code of ethical conduct and statement of commitment.* Retrieved from https://www.naeyc.org/files/naeyc/image/public_policy/Ethics%20Position%20Statement2011_09202013update.pdf

New, R. S., & Mallory, B. L. (1994). Introduction: The ethics of inclusion. In B. Mallory & R. New (Eds.), *Diversity and developmentally appropriate practices: Challenges for early childhood curriculum* (pp. 1–13). New York, NY: Teachers College Press.

Novick, R. (1996). *Developmentally appropriate and culturally responsive education: Theory in practice.* Portland, OR: Northwest Regional Educational Lab.

Orellana, M. F. (2016, 19 May). A different kind of word gap. *The Huffington Post.* Retrieved from http://www.huffingtonpost.com/marjorie-faulstich-orellana/a-different-kind-of-word-_b_10030876.html?

Paris, D. (2012). Culturally sustaining pedagogy: A needed change in stance, terminology, and practice. *Educational Researcher, 41*(3), 93–97.

Paris, D., & Alim, H. S. (Eds.). (2017). *Culturally sustaining pedagogies: Teaching and learning for justice in a changing world.* New York, NY: Teachers College Press.

Pérez, M. S., & Saavedra, C. (2017). A call for onto-epistemological diversity in early childhood education and care: Centering global South conceptualizations of childhood/s. *Review of Research in Education, 41,* 1–29.

Pew Research Center. (2016). *Among newborns, minorities slightly surpass non-Hispanic whites.* Retrieved from http://www.pewresearch.org/fact-tank/2016/06/23/its-official-minority-babies-are-the-majority-among-the-nations-infants-but-only-just/ft_16-06-23_census-majorityminority_trend/

Phoenix, A., & Pattynama, P. (2006). Intersectionality. *European Journal of Women's Studies, 13,* 187–192.

Rhedding-Jones, J. (2003). Questioning play and work, early childhood, and pedagogy. In D. E. Lytle (Ed.), *Play and educational theory and practice* (pp. 243–254). Westport, CT: Praeger.

Rose, M. (1989). *Lives on the boundary: The struggles and achievements of America's underprepared.* New York, NY: Simon & Schuster.

Scribner, S. (1970). Which agenda for advocacy? *Social Policy, 1,* 40.

Solórzano, D., & Vélez, V. (2017). Using critical race spatial analysis to examine redlining in Southern California communities of color, circa 1939. In D. Morrison, S. Annamma, & D. Jackson (Eds.), *Critical race spatial analysis: Mapping to understand and address educational inequity* (pp. 91–108). Sterling, VA: Stylus.

Solórzano, D., & Yosso, T. (2002). Critical race methodology: Counter-storytelling as an analytical framework for education research. *Qualitative Inquiry, 8*(1), 23–44.

Soto, L. D., & Swadener, B. B. (2002). Toward liberatory early childhood theory, research and praxis: Decolonizing a field. *Contemporary Issues in Early Childhood, 3*(1), 38–66.

Souto-Manning, M. (2009). Educating Latino children: International perspectives & values in early education. *Childhood Education, 85,* 182–186.

Souto-Manning, M. (2010). Challenging ethnocentric literacy practices: (Re)Positioning home literacies in a Head Start classroom. *Research in the Teaching of English, 45,* 150–178.

Souto-Manning, M. (2013). Teaching young children from immigrant and diverse families. *Young Children, 68*(4), 72–80.

Souto-Manning, M., & Martell, J. (2016). *Reading, writing, and talk: Inclusive teaching strategies for diverse learners, K–2.* New York, NY: Teachers College Press.

Steele, C. M., & Aronson, J. (1995). Stereotype threat and the intellectual test performance of African Americans. *Journal of Personality and Social Psychology, 69,* 797–811.

Swadener, B. B. (2010). "At risk" or "at promise"? From deficit constructions of the "other childhood" to possibilities for authentic alliances with children and families. *International Critical Childhood Policy Studies Journal, 3*(1), 7–29.

Swadener, E. B. (1990). Children and families "at risk": Etiology, critique, and alternative paradigms. *Journal of Educational Foundations, 4,* 17–39.

Swain, M. (2006). Languaging, agency and collaboration in advanced second language proficiency. In H. Byrnes (Eds.), *Advanced language learning: The contribution of Halliday and Vygotsky* (pp. 95–108). London, England: Continuum.

Taefi, N. (2009). The synthesis of age and gender: Intersectionality, international human rights law and the marginalisation of the girl-child. *International Journal of Child Rights, 17,* 345–376.

Taylor, Y., Hines, S., & Casey, M. (Eds.). (2010). *Theorizing intersectionality and sexuality.* London, England: Palgrave Macmillan.

Teacher Education Exchange. (2017). *Teacher development 3.0: How we can transform the professional education of teachers.* Retrieved from https://teachereducationexchange.files. wordpress.com/2017/01/tedx-teacher-development-threepointzero.pdf

Valdés, G. (1996). *Con respeto: Bridging the distances between culturally diverse families and schools.* New York, NY: Teachers College Press.

Valdés, G. (1997). Dual-language immersion programs: A cautionary note concerning the education of language-minority students. *Harvard Educational Review, 67,* 391–430.

Viruru, R. (2001). Colonized through language: The case of early childhood education. *Contemporary Issues of Early Childhood, 2*(1), 31–47.

Woodson, C. G. (1933). *The mis-education of the Negro.* Philadelphia, PA: Hakim's.

Chapter 10

(Un)Hidden Figures: A Synthesis of Research Examining the Intersectional Experiences of Black Women and Girls in STEM Education

Danyelle T. Ireland
University of Maryland, Baltimore County

Kimberley Edelin Freeman
Cynthia E. Winston-Proctor
Kendra D. DeLaine
Stacey McDonald Lowe
Kamilah M. Woodson
Howard University

In this chapter, we argue that intersectionality is a theoretical and methodological framework by which education researchers can critically examine why and how students in STEM fields who are members of intersecting marginalized groups have distinctive experiences related to their social identities, other psychological processes, and educational outcomes. Taken separately, the bodies of education research focused on the experiences of Black students and female students in STEM fields often render Black women and girls "hidden figures" in that they have not sufficiently addressed their simultaneous racialized and gendered experiences in educational contexts. Additionally, we find that the current discourse on intersectionality is limited in that it does not attend to key psychological processes associated with identity and the intersectional experience in STEM education. We take a theoretical and methodological approach to examining intersectionality in STEM education and provide a new interpretation of the literature on Black women and girls in this social context. A synthesis of (N = 60) research studies revealed that (1) identity; (2) STEM interest, confidence, and persistence; (3) achievement, ability perceptions, and attributions; and (4) socializers and support systems are key themes within the experiences of Black women and girls in STEM education. Our analysis also highlights the ways that researchers have employed intersectionality to make the experiences of Black women and girls in STEM education more visible, or "unhidden." We discuss these findings

Review of Research in Education
March 2018, Vol. 42, pp. 226–254
DOI: 10.3102/0091732X18759072
© 2018 AERA. http://rre.aera.net

from a psychological perspective and provide insights to guide future research and practice directions in STEM education.

Margo Lee Shetterly's non-fiction book, *Hidden Figures: The American Dream and the Untold Story of the Black Women Who Helped Win the Space Race*, was released in 2016 and met with critical acclaim. Set in 1967, *Hidden Figures* tells the story of three African American[1] women, Katherine Johnson, Mary Jackson, and Dorothy Vaughn, who worked as "human computers" for the National Aeronautics and Space Administration performing highly complex calculations to support pivotal space launches from the United States. The book details not only the persistent gender and racial discrimination the women faced professionally but also their extraordinary intellectual aptitude in mathematics and engineering, and the full lives they led as daughters, wives, mothers, teachers, and members of their community. *Hidden Figures* rose to first place on the *New York Times* bestseller list, and a motion picture film of the same name was released the same year, earning three Academy Awards nominations including Best Film. Despite the recent popularity of these stories and decades of research studies and educational interventions aimed at increasing the participation of "women and minorities" in science, technology, engineering, and mathematics (STEM), policymakers, researchers, and educators still contend with ways to explain and address the gender and racial disparity in these fields (National Science and Technology Council, Committee on STEM Education, 2013).

There are three prominent reasons for the attention placed on the status of women and racial ethnic minorities in STEM: the current demand for professionals to fill the STEM workforce, the benefit of diverse perspectives and ideas to promote STEM innovation and discovery, and the social justice imperative to ensure equity in STEM access and literacy as our society advances technologically. However, the rhetorical focus on "women and minorities" in STEM risks treating these two groups as mutually exclusive and obscuring the particular experiences of individuals who exist as members of both groups. Furthermore, education research and practice efforts to address diversity issues in STEM have failed to adequately contend with the ways U.S. institutions have historically marginalized students of color while educationally privileging both whiteness and maleness (Collins & Bilge, 2016; Ladson-Billings & Tate, 1995). *Intersectionality*, a term that has been used to describe the meaning and consequences of multiple categories of group membership (Cole, 2009), is a concept that can facilitate a critical examination of educational experiences of students in STEM fields across and within groups, and consider the multidimensional co-constructing factors that may promote or preclude the participation of underrepresented students in STEM fields.

Black women represent approximately 7% of the United States (noninstitutionalized) population, yet they remain underrepresented in the majority of STEM fields. As of 2014, the proportion of Black women earning degrees in biological sciences (4.23%), computer sciences (2.61%), physical sciences (2.83%), mathematics and statistics (2.35%), and engineering (0.99%) remain disproportionately low (National Science Foundation, National Center for Science and Engineering Statistics, 2017). In the context of national efforts to promote diversity and inclusion within STEM fields, the *double bind* is cited as a hindrance for Black women throughout the educational and professional pipeline (Charleston, Adserias, Lang, & Jackson, 2014; Hanson, 2008; Malcom, Hall, & Brown, 1976; Ong, Wright, Espinosa, & Orfield, 2011). The *double bind* refers to the exclusion of women of color in STEM and the undermining of their career pursuits because of both racism and sexism. Notwithstanding its conceptual ambiguity in the research literature, we assert that the concept of intersectionality, rooted in Black feminist theory (Crenshaw,1989), has particular utility for advancing discourse on Black women and girls beyond the initial framing of the *double bind* and examining their complex and multidimensional experiences within STEM education.

In our discussion of STEM education, we focus on core subjects across the academic pipeline as well as STEM fields in which Black women are significantly underrepresented. Therefore, we do not address research on Black women and girls in psychological science or other social sciences. We also do not address training in allied health professions such as medicine, dentistry, or nursing; however, we acknowledge that preparatory educational experiences in core academic subjects such as biology and chemistry will encompass the students who are positioning themselves to enter those professional fields. We also acknowledge the variance in degree of underrepresentation for Black women and girls across the various STEM fields, the unique cultural and historical contexts of each discipline, and thus the need for differentiated interventions and approaches to understanding the way students are educated in these areas.

Taken separately, the bodies of education research focused on the experiences of Black students and female[2] students in STEM fields often render Black women and girls hidden figures in that they have not sufficiently addressed their simultaneous racialized and gendered experiences in educational contexts. When the unique experiences of Black women and girls are hidden in aggregate results, their intersectional experiences are largely ignored. Recently, notable reviews of education research on women and girls of color in STEM across the educational pipeline have provided insights on the personal and institutional factors that influence their participation and success in STEM fields (see Espinosa, 2011; Joseph, Hailu, & Boston, 2017; Ong et al., 2011), and authors have discussed the invisibility of Black women and girls in discourse on participation and achievement in particular STEM fields (see Gholson, 2016). These works are enriched by their nuanced interpretations of the literature and their use of critical frameworks such as critical race theory and intersectionality.

Collins and Bilge (2016) argue that "much is at stake for getting the relationship between identity and intersectionality right" (p. 115) and present an extensive discussion on this topic, including the implications of identity politics in the context of hip hop culture and the limits of essentialized or "fixed" perceptions of identity in intersectionality discourse. However, we also find limitations in the literature on intersectionality in that it has not consistently conceptualized identity (i.e., the internalized and evolving narrative of self; see McAdams, 2001) and has not addressed the multidimensional psychological nature of social identity (e.g., salience, centrality, regard, and ideology; see Sellers, Smith, Shelton, Rowley, & Chavous, 1998) or attended to other key psychological constructs and dynamics related to the intersectional experience, such as identity interference (i.e., experience of difficulty enacting multiple identities; see Settles, 2006), stereotype threat (i.e., risk of conforming to stereotypes about one's social group; see Bowe, Desjardins, Covington Clarkson, & Lawrenz, 2017), and self-efficacy (i.e., belief in one's ability to succeed in a given situation or accomplish a given task; see MacPhee, Farro, & Canetto, 2013). We believe it is important to attend to the psychological meaning and experience (i.e., mental processes and behaviors) associated with being a Black woman or girl in STEM education because these factors influence students' choices and ultimate success in STEM fields.

We argue that intersectionality is a theoretical and methodological framework by which education researchers can critically examine why, how, and in what situations students in STEM fields who are members of intersecting marginalized groups have distinctive experiences related to their social identities, psychological processes, and educational outcomes. This framework can also be used to evaluate the extent to which research methods facilitate the illumination or obfuscation of student experiences across multiple axes of power and privilege within STEM education. We also argue that Black women and girls exist at the intersection of two primarily underrepresented social identity groups in STEM education and that intersectionality is an essential lens through which Black women and girls emerge as unhidden figures and by which education researchers and practitioners can enhance our understanding of this particular population in the literature. We consider how the construct of the *psychology of intersectionality in education* adds value to theoretical and methodological approaches to understanding Black women and girls' experiences in STEM education.

In this chapter we (1) describe ways intersectional approaches have produced new knowledge about the education of Black women and girls in STEM and identify common themes throughout this body of work with a focus on psychological processes and educational outcomes and (2) evaluate the various ways in which researchers of Black women and girls in STEM education have employed intersectionality as both a theoretical and a methodological framework, including opportunities for intersectionality to advance education research in this area. First, we present the theories and perspectives that frame our analysis and discussion of intersectionality among Black women and girls in STEM education. Next, we detail the methodological approach we took for this review, including our literature search process and analytic framework. We then present the findings of our analysis with respect to themes within the literature and intersectional approaches. We conclude with a discussion on how scholars and practitioners can advance knowledge about intersectionality among Black women and girls in STEM education.

THEORETICAL FRAMING

The Evolution of "Intersectionality"

The context of Crenshaw's (1989, 1991) discussion of intersectionality was to confront the inadequacy of one-dimensional antiracist and antidiscriminatory discourse in addressing the sociopolitical concerns of Black women. Over time, scholars from multiple disciplines have wrestled with how to conceptualize the term *intersectionality* (see Cho, Crenshaw, & McCall, 2013; Cole, 2009; Collins, 2015; Collins & Bilge, 2016). Is intersectionality an experience, an analytic framework for conceptualizing problems, or a method of inquiry for scholarship and practical application? Scholars have also grappled with how to best characterize its origins (e.g., expressions of it in writing, naming of the term). Should the origins of "intersectionality" be credited to early activists who asserted in various ways within their movements that race, gender, and class are simultaneously experienced (e.g., Combahee River Collective, 1977/1995; hooks, 1981) or should its origins be attributed to the explicit coining of the term *intersectionality* and its legal application (see Crenshaw, 1989, 1991; J. A. Winston, 1991)?

Also, scholars have contended with how best to apply the core tenets of common conceptualizations to contexts outside of the law (see Cole, 2009; Collins, 2015). These challenges notwithstanding, scholars from the fields of psychology, sociology, and legal studies have produced seminal syntheses of the knowledge and frameworks that consider how to conceptualize and analyze the implications and meanings of multiple social statuses (e.g., Cho et al., 2013; Cole, 2009; Collins, 2015). Collins's (2015) discussion of intersectionality's definitional dilemmas confronts urgent questions regarding how the concept is operationalized, including its development as a field of study, an analytic strategy, and a form of critical praxis.

We conceptually define intersectionality as a theoretical and methodological approach to understanding the meaning and consequences of holding multiple co-constructing categories of social group membership. This approach is centered on an examination of power and privilege (within and across groups) as well as attention to the personal, interpersonal, and structural significance of simultaneous social group membership. In a recent keynote speech, Crenshaw (2016) rightly clarifies that her original articulation of intersectionality was a theory not of multiple identities but of how holding certain identities makes one vulnerable to discrimination and exclusion. We define identity as a person's internal and evolving sense of self (both as an individual and as a member of various social groups). Our present discussion is concerned with social identity (e.g., racial identity, gender identity, occupational identity) and is informed by well-established psychological research on the multidimensional nature of social identity (e.g., racial salience, racial centrality, public/private racial regard, and racial ideology in the case of racial identity; see Sellers et al., 1998). Consistent with Crenshaw, our understanding of intersectionality as it relates to identity is not simply as a matter of group membership (which we all have) but as the psychological meaning of membership in oppressed groups, for example, how important is membership in one's racial or gender group to one's personal sense of self? What is one's assessment of how their racial or gender group is viewed by broader society and what consequences does this assessment have for one's personal sense of self? These considerations include the personal, interpersonal, and structural implications associated with group membership (all of which vary by group and intersection).

The Psychology of Intersectionality in STEM Education

Within education research on student outcomes, race and gender are often analyzed simply as social categories. This approach may assume that structural dynamics of race and gender are accounted for by the very practice of examining groups. However, this approach may mask important aspects of the specific psychological experiences associated with being a member of a particular racial or gender group. For example, racial and gender identity construction are important psychological processes to understand in relation to educational outcomes. Within the field of psychology, there is research that describes and explains race and gender beyond simple categorization. This framing is important since race and gender are described as central axes and privilege within scholarship on intersectionality (e.g., Cole, 2009; Collins, 2015; Crenshaw, 1989).

We define the *psychology of intersectionality* as the mental processes and behavioral choices associated with the meaning and consequences of holding multiple co-constructing categories of social group membership. More specifically, theoretically, the psychology of intersectionality in education explains why some students in STEM fields may have a distinctive experience related to their social identities, particularly with respect to psychological constructs and educational outcomes such as STEM achievement and perceptions of ability (i.e., self-efficacy), belonging, and stereotype threat. Educational psychologists are increasingly concerned with the theoretical and empirical relationship of identity to educational outcomes, such as motivation and persistence (Eccles, 2009; Elmore & Oyserman, 2012; Perez, Cromley, & Kaplan, 2014). The incorporation of intersectionality adds contextual meaning and depth to this area of inquiry, particularly with respect to applications in education research.

Methodologically, the psychology of intersectionality in education considers how our sampling procedures facilitate the obfuscation or illumination of student experiences across and within social groups, how our modes of inquiry allow us to apprehend the personal and social impact or meaning of intersectionality in STEM education, and the sufficiency of our analytic approaches for addressing questions of student beliefs and behaviors in STEM education. Settles and colleagues' (Settles, 2004, 2006; Settles, Jellison, & Pratt-Hyatt, 2009) research on identity interference among Black women and women scientists is an example of a psychometric approach to ascertaining the meaning and consequences of holding multiple co-constructing categories of social group membership—particularly when one experiences difficulty enacting particular identities simultaneously. In their discussion of the future of intersectionality studies, Cho et al. (2013) address the ways that various disciplines have approached methodological standards and practices in the study of intersectionality and Cole's (2009) approach is noted as one of the pathways taken up in the field of psychology. In the subsequent section on the methodology we used to review the literature, we explain how we used Cole's framework, posed as three questions for conceptualizing intersectionality in the research studies, and why this approach is a particularly useful standard for intersectional inquiry in education research.

METHODOLOGY

Our review of the literature on Black women and girls in STEM education was conducted using a three-phase data collection process: literature search, abstract screening, and full text screening. We conducted searches of the following databases: EBSCOhost, Academic Search Complete, PsycInfo, PsycArticles, ERIC, and SocINDEX with Full Text. Our search included combinations of the following keywords: *Black* OR *African American, minority* OR *underrepresented, wome*n OR *girls, women of color, girls of color, STEM, science, technology, mathematics, engineering, physics, biology, chemistry, education, students,* and *intersectionality.* These searches resulted in 1,290 unique sources, which we worked collaboratively to reduce through an iterative process of screening abstracts and full text documents.

Inclusion Criteria and Screening

We originally intended to review conceptual papers and empirical studies from 1976 (the year Malcom et al. published their seminal *Double Bind* report) to date. However, to fully engage with the breadth of research addressing the experiences of Black women and girls in STEM education contexts and also focus our attention on the knowledge generated from this body of work, we removed the restriction on publication date and narrowed our inclusion criteria to include only publications reporting on empirical research or original analyses of secondary data with disaggregated results for Black women or girls in STEM education. We included dissertations in the first phase of our screening process, as they included valuable references; however, dissertations were ultimately screened out in the second phase of our screening.

The following questions guided phase one of our screening process:

Screening Question 1: Does the research (in part or as a whole) include the experiences of Black female students in STEM education?

Screening Question 2: Does the research include at least one of the following student populations, including retrospective accounts of STEM professionals as students: elementary school, middle school, high school, undergraduate school, or graduate school?

Screening Question 3: Does the publication report an original analysis and/or empirical research results?

Screening Question 4: Does the research occur in the United States?

In the first phase of screening, we worked in pairs to review the 1,290 abstracts and determine if the source would advance to a full text review. The first phase of screening resulted in 407 sources, which were distributed among our team for a review of the full text. The second phase of our process entailed a closer review of the document to reconfirm that the source met our inclusion criteria and check that the results were disaggregated such that there were data reported on Black women or girls in STEM education. The second phase of screening resulted in $N = 60$ sources, which were analyzed to address our research questions. Studies that investigated an all-Black and -female sample were $n = 17$ (28%). In the remaining studies, Black women and girls represented a subset of the sample for which results were explicitly reported.

Analytic Process

We set out to analyze the sources by first identifying a priori codes based on theory, the goals of our review, and prior literature. We incorporated emergent codes that were identified as we reviewed content patterns across the sources. Our final codebook consisted of 33 codes, which were categorized as *theory* (e.g., critical race theory, feminist theory, intersectionality theory), *educational level/context* (e.g., elementary school, middle school, high school, etc.), *STEM field* (e.g., biology, chemistry, physics, math, engineering, etc.), *psychological construct* (e.g., identity, achievement, interest, belonging, stereotype threat, etc.), and *research design* (e.g., program evaluation, research study, qualitative methods, quantitative methods, etc.). Additionally, we extracted the research questions, findings, and recommendations from each source to compare and contrast their contributions to the knowledge base. Throughout our analytic coding process, we collaboratively assessed the validity of our codes and our interrater reliability to ensure the accuracy and consistency of our methods.

Cole (2009) describes the importance of interdisciplinarity for advancing our understanding of intersectionality and the benefit of broad perspectives for approaching research problems and questions concerning social categories. We based our evaluation of the way intersectionality was employed with the literature using the criteria established by Cole, which are posed as three questions for conceptualizing intersectionality in the methodology used in the research process: (1) *Who is included in this category?* (2) *What role does inequality play?* (3) *Where are the similarities?* Cole's framework originated from the lens of psychological research but has been cited widely and highlighted by prominent intersectionality scholars (Cho et al., 2013). We believe these three questions provide a holistic basis for assessing the potential for intersectional inquiry through one's methodological choices and are suitable for application among a variety of research disciplines, including education research.

As we analyzed sources using the first question, we considered, does the research attend to diversity within social categories (i.e., are within-group differences among Black women and girls addressed)? For the second question, we considered, does the research address structural inequality, not just individual- or person-level characteristics? For the third question, we considered, does the researcher identify commonalities across different groups, such that the focus of the research is not limited to differences? In our analytic coding process, we established a priori codes for the demographic attributes and psychological constructs; however, we did not break down the three questions posted by Cole (2009) as codes (e.g., types of structural inequality). Instead, for that portion of our analysis, we looked for evidence to confirm whether the authors attended to these three considerations and extracted the evidence if present.

FINDINGS

Themes Within the Literature on Black Girls and Women in STEM Education

To demonstrate how intersectional approaches have produced new knowledge concerning the education of Black women and girls in STEM, we present themes that emerged during the review of the literature. The authors referenced in this section addressed (measured, manipulated, and/or analyzed) psychological constructs within the STEM educational context uniquely influenced by intersections of race and gender. Additionally, these works present Black women and girls as unhidden figures by sampling exclusively or disaggregating data on Black girls and women in STEM education settings to facilitate the visibility of their unique educational experience. These themes include (1) identity; (2) STEM interest, confidence, and persistence; (3) achievement, ability perceptions, and attributions; and (4) socializers and support systems. The section concludes with a presentation of themes unique to specific educational levels.

Identity

Identity, particularly the development of STEM identity,[3] was a key theme throughout the literature on Black women and girls in STEM. Learning opportunities that enhance early exposure to science can be instrumental in fostering a science identity for young girls by creating opportunities to see oneself as a "scientist" (Riedinger & Taylor, 2016). At the elementary and secondary levels, there is a greater focus on cultivating a STEM identity through conceptual understanding and exposure to STEM-related activities (e.g., Buck, Cook, Quigley, Eastwood, & Lucas, 2009; Scott & White, 2013), whereas studies at the collegiate level tend to explore barriers to maintaining STEM identity development (Carlone & Johnson, 2007). Black women in STEM have experienced sexist encounters that foster a sense of disconnection from science and threaten to disrupt their STEM identity development (Carlone & Johnson, 2007). As early as elementary school, Black girls have been shown to disaffiliate (i.e., report not sharing characteristics or behaviors) with peers identified as a "smart science student" (Carlone, Haun-Frank, & Webb, 2011). Still, STEM identity development promotes success among Black women in STEM undergraduate programs (Jackson, 2013). For Black women transferring from community college, environments at historically Black colleges or universities (HBCU) have better facilitated STEM identity development because they are less culturally shocking and composed of other women who look like them (Jackson, 2013).

In addition to STEM identity development, personal identity (or personal definition of self) was also a prominent theme for Black girls and women in STEM. Self-definition and self-valuation (i.e., the content of self-definition) are considered a significant component of the collegiate experience for Black women (Gibson & Espino, 2016). Social perceptions of the self among Black women can be affected by gender and racial stereotypes within one's STEM discipline (Gibson & Espino, 2016). In STEM education settings, Black women experience imposed definitions of who they are and expectations, such as being too feminine or angry (Gibson & Espino, 2016). While grappling with the conflicts between imposed identities and one's true sense of self, Black women may find themselves in situations where they must negotiate how to represent themselves. Black women may adopt the belief that they need to become masculine in order to thrive within a STEM environment (Ong, 2005), or redefine their membership in a stigmatized group to reflect an advantage (Carlone & Johnson, 2007). Black women have also employed strategies to enhance the representation of their blackness on campus to demonstrate resistance to the stereotypical appearance of a scientist (Ong, 2005). For some Black women, personal and family identities are considered more salient than a STEM identity, and a sense of segregation in STEM education settings can potentially affect one's racial, ethnic, and cultural identity, as well as persistence in STEM fields (Ong, 2005).

STEM Interest, Confidence, and Expectations

Prior research has found that identity development is related to students' interest (or intrinsic motivation), competence beliefs, and expectancy for success in STEM education (Perez et al., 2014). Our analysis found patterns of STEM interest, confidence, and expectations for success within the literature on Black women and girls. Varma and Hahn (2008) found a pattern of increased interest in science over time from middle to high school for Black girls in computing majors. However, in higher education, large class sizes and difficulty in chemistry courses have been linked to declining interest in premedical studies among African American female students (Barr, Matsui, Wanat, & Gonzalez, 2010). With regard to achievement expectations, Black girls in high school, relative to boys, have reported greater expectations for success in science but lower expectations for success in mathematics (Else-Quest, Mineo, & Higgins, 2013). Still, Litzler, Samuelson, and Lorah (2014) found Black undergraduate women in engineering demonstrated similar STEM confidence levels as their White male peers after controlling for personal, environmental, and behavioral factors (e.g., student experiences and GPA). Due to divergent findings on the same analyses for African American men (higher STEM confidence than White men) and White women (lower STEM confidence than White men) after controlling for the aforementioned variables, Litzler et al. (2014) discuss the implications for understanding the differences in STEM confidence levels across different ethnic and gender groups of students as well exploring unmeasured factors that might contribute to STEM confidence. We believe that the experience of intersectionality, including its impact on students' mental processes and subsequent behaviors, largely accounts for these differences across and within these social groups.

Achievement, Perceptions of Ability, and Attributions

In educational psychology, the expectancy-value model of achievement motivation illustrates the ways personal and collective identities inform motivational beliefs (i.e., the value students hold for STEM education and the expectations for success in these fields) and that these beliefs in turn mediate students' achievement related choices (Eccles, 2009). Despite some evidence of low performance in secondary school and higher education STEM foundational courses (Chambers, Walpole, & Outlaw, 2016; Farinde & Lewis, 2012; Gilmartin, 1976; Russell & Russell, 2015), the literature also shows Black women have experienced an early recognition of ability in STEM education, stemming from the messages received by others (Rice & Alfred, 2014). However, scholars have found self-ratings of engineering learning outcomes among Black undergraduate women to be significantly lower than those of their White peers—a finding not evident for Black men (Ro & Loya, 2015). Although some research has found no significant difference in science self-efficacy between Black and White women undergraduates (Gwilliam & Betz, 2001), diminished academic self-efficacy is evident for some Black women in graduate programs (Alexander & Hermann, 2016). Over time, Black high school girls also experience declines in math self-efficacy (Chambers et al., 2016).

With regard to math ability, Black women at the collegiate level have reported lower self-ratings than Black boys (Hartman, 1991), but this pattern differs in secondary education. Although not explicitly reporting on perceived ability, Black girls in high school have perceived math to be less of a challenge than do Black boys but perceive greater difficulty in science (Martinez & Guzman, 2013). With regard to classroom performance, a high school study with a predominately Black sample reported that girls and boys receive similar math grades and report a similar level of math self-efficacy (M. H. Jones & Ford, 2014). On the other hand, Black girls' perceptions of their math self-concept, as opposed to math self-efficacy, are lower in comparison to the self-perceptions of Black boys (Else-Quest et al., 2013). Additionally, when it comes to math performance, Swinton, Kurtz-Costes, Rowley, and Okeke-Adeyanju (2011) found math success and failure attributions among Black girls grow more negative over time. Furthermore, Black girls use ability attributions to explain English success more than math and science success, and Black girls are more likely than Black boys to attribute math success to effort (Swinton et al., 2011). Additionally, Swinton et al. did not find gender differences in failure ability attributions in math, but they did find girls were more likely than boys to attribute science failure to lack of effort.

Socializers and Support Systems

Socializers, or socializing agents, are interpersonal influences that provide guidance and structure for the development of STEM identity, confidence, and achievement. Socializing agents and support systems play a critical role in STEM achievement and the development of STEM identity and interest among Black women and girls. A support system consisting of family, teachers, peers, and minority networks is critical for African American women in STEM education (Rice & Alfred, 2014; Tate & Linn, 2005). The research also points to the positive influence of institutional support, particularly mentoring at the graduate level, among Black women in STEM education (Borum & Walker, 2012). Science role model characteristics are also important in STEM identity development, as Black girls have expressed the belief that science role models should be people of color (Buck, Clark, Leslie-Pelecky, Lu, & Cerda-Lizarraga, 2008), and Black female computer-based models are shown to be more effective in impacting Black undergraduate women's engineering attitudes (Rosenberg-Kima, Plant, Doerr, & Baylor, 2010). Furthermore, Stearns et al. (2016) found schools with more female math and science teachers did not influence whether or not Black girls declared a STEM major in college or graduated from a STEM program and noted the larger percentage of White math and science teachers than Black teachers as a possible explanation. With regard to peer influence, young Black girls' social status within a mathematics classroom is more influential in dictating participation during cooperative learning opportunities than their competence beliefs—students with a lower social status are less engaged than those with high social status (Gholson & Martin, 2014).

In addition to teachers, peers, and role models outside the home, parents play a role in promoting STEM achievement and interest. One's home environment, in addition to museums and science fairs, typically provide opportunities for younger children to learn science (McPherson, 2014). In high school, however, these learning opportunities in the home tend to decline for Black girls (McPherson, 2014). Parents' math expectations are also shown to have a positive relationship with math self-concept among Black girls (Entwisle, Alexander, Pallas, & Cadigan, 1987). Furthermore, the correlation between standardized math test performance and high school GPA among students whose parents earned a college degree was relatively low for African American girls (compared to African American and White boys); this correlation among students whose parents earned a high school diploma was as high among African American girls as White girls (Bridgeman, McCamley-Jenkins, & Ervin, 2000). Additionally, through practice with mathematical concepts at home or culturally responsive pedagogy in the classroom, socializing agents, such as parents and teachers, respectively, can enhance Black girls' identity construction and learning outcomes in mathematics (Young, Young, & Capraro, 2017). Self-valuation construction in STEM among Black girls is also fostered by family and community (Gibson & Espino, 2016).

Gendered socialization may also influence STEM attitudes and beliefs. Gilmartin (1976) found 22% of Black high school girls believed that not very often or never could women do the same work as men, an attitude that was most frequently held by Black and Hispanic students. However, O'Brien, Blodorn, Adams, Garcia, and Hammer (2015) found that Black undergraduate women hold weaker beliefs regarding the masculinity of STEM fields than White women. Additionally, when interacting with Black computer-based models, Rosenberg-Kima et al. (2010) found Black women are less likely to endorse gender stereotypes than those interacting with White models. The aforementioned themes were evident across educational levels; however, there are developmental differences between Black girls and women and themes that are particular to their experiences across the STEM education pipeline. The following section will highlight themes unique to levels of education.

Elementary and Secondary Education

STEM interventions and instructional practices. Among the sources reviewed, with the exception of one higher education research-based instructional intervention (Goertzen, Brewe, Kramer, Wells, & Jones, 2011), interventions and instructional practices designed to enhance STEM interest and scientific understanding were more dominant in elementary and secondary schools than higher education contexts (e.g., Buck et al., 2009; Scott & White, 2013). In addition to culturally responsive instructional approaches (e.g., Scott & White, 2013), active learning and hands-on activities enhance STEM identity development and/or increase STEM interest for Black girls in middle school STEM environments (Ferreira, 2002; Riedinger & Taylor, 2016). In addition to instructional practices, structural changes such as single-sex groups and classrooms in elementary and middle school promote a greater understanding of technology concepts (Seay, 2004), as well as increase math achievement (Bowe et al., 2017), for Black girls. Affirmation writing interventions have also been implemented in attempts to minimize stereotype threat for Black girls during mathematics assessments, though the effects were not found to be statistically significant (Bancroft, Bratter, & Rowley, 2017).

College preparedness and STEM major intent. STEM interventions and programming targeted at Black girls are also evident in high schools, but an additional and more dominant theme for high school is college preparedness and STEM major intent. With respect to academic preparedness, studies found that some Black women had inadequate high school preparation for STEM college courses and that students felt underprepared academically while in STEM programs at predominantly White institutions (PWIs; Joseph, 2012; Russell & Russell, 2015). In addition to academic preparedness, high school factors are often measured to determine one's intent to enroll in college and declare a STEM major. Black girls' selected field of study in college is associated with their desired college major as a sophomore in high school, math attitudes, and the number of math and science courses completed during high school (Maple & Stage, 1991). Additionally, achievement test scores and mother's education are positively associated with Black girls' choice of major as high school sophomores (Maple & Stage, 1991).

Undergraduate and Graduate Education

College enrollment and graduation rates. As researchers shift their focus from Black girls in primary and secondary education to Black women in STEM collegiate programs, a theme associated with college preparedness is still evident. There is much in the literature on Black women in STEM regarding enrollment and graduation rates (e.g., Smyth & McArdle, 2004), as well as findings on STEM persistence (Espinosa, 2011). With regard to college enrollment, Espinosa (2011) sampled a racially diverse group of women in STEM majors across varying higher education institutions to compare characteristics and factors influencing persistence for women of color versus their White peers. This analysis found that a greater proportion of African American women were enrolled in private institutions and 4-year colleges than White and Chicana/Latina women but a smaller proportion of African American women were enrolled in highly selective institutions. Additionally, O'Brien et al. (2015) report that Black women at HBCUs are more likely to declare STEM majors than Black women at non-HBCUs and White women overall. Black women have also been shown to declare a computer engineering major at the same rate as Black men (Lord, Layton, & Ohland, 2011) but outnumber White women in electrical engineering programs (Lord et al., 2011). Math anxiety has been found to be a barrier to entering nontraditional careers (Bernstein, Reilly, & Coté-Bonanno, 1992), and Black women have reported technical anxiety as reasons for low enrollment in computing majors (Varma, 2010). Yet, even with the known challenges, Rice and Alfred (2014) found a particular attitude of perseverance among Black women in STEM, as if to say quitting is not an option.

Once Black women declare STEM majors on entry into college, concerns of whether or not they persist and matriculate through their programs become evident in the literature. Depending on the institutional context, 6-year graduation rates in engineering are generally either higher for Black women than Black men, lower, or nearly the same (Ohland et al., 2011). More specifically, in computer engineering, women of all ethnicities have lower graduation rates (Lord, Layton, & Ohland, 2015), but researchers have found Black women to enter the field of chemical engineering at a higher rate than Black men (Lord, Layton, Ohland, Brawner, & Long, 2014). Still, scholars find that, among Black women, the probability of attaining a degree in life science is much higher than of attaining an engineering science degree (Perez-Felkner, McDonald, Schneider, & Grogan, 2012).

Graduation rates among Black women in STEM programs are ultimately the outcome of their persistence. With regard to STEM persistence, Espinosa (2011) reported a 54% persistence rate for Black undergraduate women, compared to 57 for White women and 52% for Latinas. Studies show that Black women understand and acknowledge that academic, psychological, and financial barriers affect their persistence and achievement in STEM, but they are also aware of how STEM learning environments characterized, for instance, by a cooperative rather than competitive peer culture and faculty encouragement can mitigate the effects of such barriers

(Perna et al., 2009). As such, most of the literature on Black women in STEM seeks to illuminate their experiences within collegiate STEM learning environments.

STEM learning environments. Scholars interested in the STEM achievement of Black women acknowledge how the learning environment contributes to academic outcomes (e.g., Charleston, George, Jackson, Berhanu, & Amechi, 2014). In elementary and secondary education, a focus is placed on interventions and instructional practices within the learning environment (e.g., Ferreira, 2002), whereas at the collegiate level, our review of the literature shows a shift to examining the negative educational environments in institutions and STEM departments (e.g., Rincón & George-Jackson, 2016). At the undergraduate and graduate levels, Black women have experienced learning environments characterized by experiences of racial microaggressions (Alexander & Hermann, 2016; Martin, Green, & Dean, 2016), exclusion from study groups (Reyes, 2011; Rosa & Mensah, 2016), encounters with gendered stereotypes (Carlone et al., 2011; Martin et al., 2016), alienation and discrimination (Borum & Walker, 2012; Herzig, 2010), and feelings of isolation (Rosa & Mensah, 2016; Charleston et al., 2014)—acknowledged as a result of being a woman in male-dominated fields and Black in predominantly White fields (Herzig, 2010). In addition to feelings of isolation, Black women have expressed a sense of discouragement in STEM programs fostered by unfulfilled promises regarding academic opportunities, independence, and opportunities to be involved (Callahan et al., 1996).

Black women have also reported feeling invisible at times in STEM learning environments, while other times, due to their otherness, their presence seems highly visible within their STEM program (Herzig, 2010). Though at times, Black women lack the desire to "fit in" with mainstream notions of STEM culture, there is a recognized sense that they do not fit into the culture of their discipline and even within their academic department (Herzig, 2010). This sense of belonging in one's STEM academic department varies by institution; some Black women intentionally seek HBCUs for the well-known success in promoting the achievement of Black women in STEM (Perna et al., 2009). Even for Black women transferring from HBCUs to PWIs, HBCU faculty members are viewed as more hands-on and personal than faculty at PWIs (Joseph, 2012). However, if faced with negative STEM climates cultivated by faculty and/or peers, Black women have been shown to possess more navigational capital than Latinas, which is characterized as a greater ability to navigate educational institutions despite negative contextual factors (Samuelson & Litzler, 2016).

These findings highlight the nuanced nature of racial and gender dynamics in the educational experiences of Black women and girls in STEM fields. Although some findings may not appear unique to Black women in STEM, and possibly common to all women or women of color in STEM, it is important to determine how the intersection of race and gender for specific subgroups of women of color is uniquely or commonly manifested in STEM educational environments. Without attending to the intersections of race and gender or disaggregating data to illuminate trends in specific subgroups, we would not observe that Black girls (not White girls or Latinas) prefer that science role models be persons of color (Buck et al., 2008), or that Black women assess their engineering learning outcomes significantly lower than their White peers—a finding not evident for Black men (Ro & Loya, 2015), or that all girls across ethnic groups, with the exception of Black girls, report higher levels of challenge in math class in comparison to their male counterparts (Martinez & Guzman, 2013). Researchers risk overlooking these psychological manifestations of intersectionality in education without adopting the appropriate lens to explore the experiences of Black women and girls in STEM learning environments.

Evaluating Intersectional Approaches

Although all of the studies included in our review reported on Black women and girls in STEM education, not all employed intersectionality as both a theoretical and a methodological approach. From a methodological standpoint, there was variance among the sources with respect to whether they addressed the aforementioned three questions for conceptualizing intersectionality in the research process established by Cole (2009): (1) *Who is included in this category?* (2) *What role does inequality play?* (3) *Where are the similarities?* Among the sources we reviewed, 22 studies (31%) addressed all three of the aforementioned questions concerning intersectionality. Of those 22, nine studies also stated an intersectional, critical race, or feminist theoretical framework as guiding their inquiry and used an intersectional approach that is aligned with the criteria Cole (2009) established. We proceed to highlight the ways those studies examined the experiences of Black women and girls in STEM education

Buck et al. (2008) used feminist, inclusive, and critical perspectives to investigate cognitive processes involved in girls selecting a science role model. They conducted focus groups with 13 eighth-grade girls that were organized by ethnic group. This method allowed for an examination of similarity and differences across the groups. For example, Caucasian and Hispanic girls agreed that race-matched science role models were not important; however, African American girls strongly expressed that science role models should be persons of color, suggesting race was more salient among Black girls. Additionally, through their interactions with science role models over the course of the study, across all ethnic groups, participants' perceptions of who a science role model is and what scientists do changed and became less gender stereotypical. Through mixed methods, Buck et al. (2009) also explored profiles of African American girls' attitudes toward science. Their investigation found four personality orientations that linked success in school and experiences with science to confidence and importance of science and definitions of science to value/desire. This research also uncovered commonalities among Black girls with respect to the way they define science (the majority defined science according to specific scientific content) and experience science (the majority referenced out of class experiences with science concepts).

Gholson and Martin (2014) used an intersectional frame to examine the mediating role of African American girls' social networks in the mathematics learning environment. Their investigation explored an all-Black elementary school as a context for Black girlhood as well as identity development and interpersonal relationships among these girls in the math classroom. Two third-grade students were studied, and results indicated that throughout the academic year both girls exhibited moments of serving as a "bully" and a "model student," depending on the circumstances. Both girls' experiences were also contrasted by their racial socialization, their physical features (the light-skinned model student versus the dark-skinned bully), and the ways that classroom actors (other girls and the teacher) respond to them. Using a variety of data collection methods (e.g., classroom observations, field notes, audio records, interviews, classroom artifacts, formative and standardized assessment results, etc.), Gholson and Martin (2014) examine the phenomena associated with Black girls learning math, as well as the way these girls navigate their privilege, power, and social relationships in the math classroom setting.

McPherson (2014) conducted individual interviews and reviewed journal entries to examine the P–12 science learning experiences of African American women in science, mathematics, and engineering undergraduate programs. Their critical framing of the study highlighted the importance of a strengths-based approach to examining African American girls' experiences with science, and acknowledged the cultural capital that African American girls acquire both in and outside of the classroom. Results showed that African American girls acquire cultural capital and access to free-choice learning of science through traditional and informal opportunities (e.g., family role models, field trips to museums, science fairs, student organizations and clubs in primary and secondary school). However, in high school, African American female teens had fewer opportunities to engage in everyday science experiences at home than in earlier grades. Similarly, Rosa and Mensah (2016) conducted individual interviews to investigate the educational trajectories of six Black women physicists use a critical race theory framework. Despite their common professional identity, these women had very different family backgrounds, educational timelines, and personal characteristics. However, they traced their start in science to early exposure to science-related school programs and acknowledged the importance of their participation in summer research programs at the undergraduate level, which affected their career choices and provided exposure to the culture of physics. Yet these women also reported experiences of isolation in their graduate programs due to their race, particularly in study groups with peers.

Alexander and Hermann (2016) conducted individual interviews to examine the experiences of eight African American women in graduate programs in biology, chemical engineering, and agriculture. Sampling across a variety of STEM fields allowed the authors to explore within-group differences as well as commonalities shared by these African American women. Borum and Walker (2012) and Charleston et al. (2014) both used focus groups to explore the experiences of Black women in mathematics and computer science graduate programs, respectively. Borum and Walker (2012) addressed within-group differences among Black women in math PhD programs, such as varying experiences between the women who attended an HBCU versus those who attended a non-HBCU for their undergraduate degree.

These interviews revealed the range of challenging experiences each of the women faced through their intersectional lenses, including microaggressions from peers (both White women and White men) in their department, perceived inferiority of their HBCU undergraduate experience by their peers, lack of mentors, and inadequate responses from counseling services or department representatives (Alexander & Hermann, 2016). Conversely, Borum and Walker (2012) found that participants who attended an HBCU noted their positive experiences and the support they received from both faculty and peers, which encouraged them to pursue graduate study in mathematics, while those who had not attended an HBCU reported feelings of isolation, poor advising, and feeling targeted due to race or gender.

Charleston et al. (2014) explored the unique challenges that African American women experience in their respective graduate computing science environments, and how these spaces are navigated among this demographic group. In both studies, the authors' analysis of power and privilege includes a discussion of mathematics and computer sciences as a "White male–dominated" and the reality that non-White, nonmale students have to conform to the norms or face exclusion and isolation. Charleston et al. (2014) noted that for some, racial identity was most salient and they believed they were perceived as Black first and foremost. For others, racial and gender identity were inextricably linked, and thus stereotypes of Black women were unique to those about Black people and women more broadly—a classic demonstration of intersectionality at play.

Ro and Loya (2015) measured quantitative differences in the learning outcomes (three core engineering competencies and three professional skills) of racial-ethnic–minority women and men, compared to those of White women and men in undergraduate engineering programs. Controlling for factors such as institution type (e.g., HBCU vs. PWI), their analysis explored intersectionality as interpreted by a statistical interaction between gender and race effects on learning outcomes. However, their study was framed and results were interpreted by an examination of privilege in engineering education. They found that generally, women in engineering education tended to rate their engineering learning outcomes lower than men but their professional learning outcomes higher than men. The results of their analysis also conclude that the intersection, or statistical interaction, of race and gender had more negative effects for Black women than Black men in engineering education with respect to learning outcomes. The authors note that future research is needed to explain why Black women assess their engineering abilities lower than their White peers. Our analysis of the psychological constructs associated with intersectionality in the prior literature suggests that despite their cultural assets, abilities, and motivations, there are many documented factors, on both the individual and institutional levels, which can undermine Black women's sense of competence and belonging in STEM fields.

Who Is Included in This Category?

In the context of our assertion regarding the importance of identity to the study of intersectionality in the literature, the question of "who" is being researched is key. One of the most useful characteristics of the aforementioned studies is that they each attend to diversity within social categories and explore the particular perspectives of Black women and girls. Through studies on this particular student demographic, we learn about differences in Black girls' socialization in the mathematics learning environment (Gholson & Martin, 2014), their unique preference for science role models of color compared to White and Latina peers (Buck et al., 2008), the distinct personality orientations related to their experiences and values in STEM education (Buck et al., 2009), and the importance of exposure to science education both in and outside of the classroom for Black women from diverse backgrounds (McPherson, 2014; Rosa & Mensah, 2016). In STEM higher education settings, we also glean insights into the particular challenges (e.g., gendered racism) faced by Black women in pursuit of biology, mathematics, and engineering degrees (Alexander & Hermann, 2016; Borum & Walker, 2012; Charleston et al., 2014), as well as the implications for how Black female engineers assess their abilities as compared to the self-assessments of their (non-Black and nonfemale) peers (Ro & Loya, 2015).

What Role Does Inequality Play?

A common critique of the emphasis on identity in intersectionality discourse is that the focus on the individual can obscure the structural and systemic factors associated with power, privilege, and systemic oppression. Though these studies address person-level characteristics among Black women and girls in STEM, they also attend to issues of structural inequality, which affect their educational experience such as stereotypes (Buck et al., 2008), privilege (Gholson & Martin, 2014; Ro & Loya, 2015), overt gender and racial discrimination (Alexander & Hermann, 2016; Borum & Walker, 2012; Charleston et al., 2014; Rosa & Mensah, 2016), as well as issues of educational access (Buck et al., 2009; McPherson, 2014).

Where Are the Similarities?

The illumination of power and privilege through the lens of intersectionality has the potential to focus on difference at the expense of opportunities for building connections and coalition among groups. However, in the aforementioned examinations of similarities across groups we learn of common ways Black girls (and their White and Latina peers) come to understand what science is and what scientists do (Buck et al., 2008; Buck et al., 2009) as well as commonalities among different experiences of Black girlhood within the social hierarchy of the mathematics classroom (Gholson & Martin, 2014). We also learn about common cultural assets and STEM learning opportunities in the retrospective accounts of Black women as they reflect on their educational trajectories in various STEM fields (McPherson, 2014; Rosa & Mensah,

2016). Additionally, we come to understand shared challenges among Black women in undergraduate and graduate programs across a variety of STEM disciplines (Alexander & Hermann, 2016; Borum & Walker, 2012; Charleston et al., 2014), as well as similarities between Black women and Asian men in their assessment of their undergraduate engineering skills (Ro & Loya, 2015).

ADVANCING KNOWLEDGE ABOUT THE PSYCHOLOGY OF INTERSECTIONALITY AMONG BLACK WOMEN AND GIRLS IN STEM EDUCATION

Our review of the literature uncovered four key thematic areas of note with respect to the experiences of Black women and girls in STEM education and highlighted the ways researchers have employed intersectionality theoretically and methodologically. Understanding the nature of identity in STEM education, the importance of STEM interest, confidence, and persistence; patterns of achievement, attributions, and perceptions of ability; and the influence of socializers and support systems for Black women and girls can help illustrate the psychological meaning of intersectionality in STEM education. We found that research samples including a substantial number of Black women and girls or sampling them exclusively allowed for analyses that uncovered common experiences as well as within-group differences among this demographic group. Additionally, statistical methods such as tests of race and gender interaction explored ways to measure intersectionality quantitatively. Furthermore, the results of the studies reviewed point to the necessary consideration of structural factors such as power, privilege, and institutional barriers, which affect the mental processes and educational choices of Black women and girls in STEM education, beyond their individual characteristics. By examining the sampling choices, analytic approaches, and interpretive framing of these studies, we identified examples of how, methodologically, intersectionality has been employed in the research process. We will now share research and practice implications of this review for advancing knowledge about intersectionality among Black women and girls in STEM education.

Research Implication 1: Reframing the "Double Bind"

The multiplicative experiences of racism and sexism that Black women in STEM have endured have been described as "double bind," "double disadvantage," and "double jeopardy" (Malcom et al., 1976; O'Brien et al., 2015); however, the double bind has not been examined sufficiently in terms of the interplay of personal and structural forces acted on Black women versus their response to these forces, including cultural tools and resources that must be deployed in order to survive and thrive. In addition, there are situations and settings in which, because of their gender, or race, or ability, or social class, Black women are advantaged. There are also scenarios in which power and privilege are not limited to the duality of race and gender and in which both race and gender may modulate the effects of other factors. Self-perceptions of identity are not the same among individuals within the same social identity group;

there is no one universal Black identity nor is there a universal woman identity. Future research and theorizing in these areas are warranted. Researchers interested in developing such an agenda might look to the guidance Cole (2009) establishes for conceptualizing intersectionality throughout the various stages of the research process and even consider examples such as the Settles (2006) intersectional framework for the measurement of Black female identity.

Research Implication 2: Increased Integration of Intersectional Scholarship

A greater diversity of researchers and research approaches are needed to operationalize intersectional experiences of Black girls and women in STEM. Beyond the structural constructs and social categories of race and gender, psychological theories of racial identity and gender identity help explicate the meaning students derive from their membership in these social groups, including associated norms, values, collective histories, and positioning within learning contexts. This understanding has been particularly beneficial to research on issues concerning Black students and female students.

In future research, we propose the integration of three bodies of scholarship that to our knowledge have not been integrated: (1) intersectionality scholarship generated in the field of STEM education and workforce development (e.g., McGee & Martin, 2011; Ong et al., 2011; Rincón & George-Jackson, 2016; Samuelson & Litzler, 2016; Settles, 2004, 2006; Smith et al., 2014; Tate & Linn, 2005), (2) gender psychology scholarship produced in the field of psychology (e.g., Cole & Stewart, 2001; Rice, 2008; Stewart & McDermott, 2004), and (3) psychological significance of race scholarship produced in the field of psychology (e.g., Boykin, 1986; Cross, 1971, 1991; Franklin, 1999; Goff, Eberhardt, Williams, & Jackson, 2008; Harrell, 1999; J. M. Jones, 2003; Nobles, 1991; Sellers et al., 1998; Steele, 1997; Sue et al., 2007; C. E. Winston et al., 2004; C. E. Winston & Winston, 2012).

Research Implication 3: Diverse and Complex Research Methods

Examining intersectional experiences is extremely complex, and thus requires research methods that can capture the complexity. Often, that includes the use of multiple and mixed methods, which together can provide more robust information than singular approaches. In addition, qualitative research is particularly suited to examine intersectional experiences given the nuanced and phenomenological nature of intersectionality. The Society of Qualitative Inquiry in Psychology (2017), a section of Division 5 of the American Psychological Association, emphasizes that qualitative inquiry includes "topics such as philosophies of science (e.g., ontology and epistemology), methodologies, methods of data collection/generation, methods of data analysis, criteria for evaluating quality, ethics, reflexivity, and forms of knowledge mobilization and dissemination." Greater development and use of qualitative research (worldviews and methods of inquiry) would benefit the knowledge base as well as exploring ways to implement quantitative methods with the lens of intersectionality.

Practice Implication 1: Culturally Relevant Pedagogy and Curriculum

The thematic focus in the literature on STEM learning environment suggests that pedagogical approaches and teacher education program training are important areas of intervention. There is an encouragement for educators to incorporate more culturally relevant strategies and innovative pedagogical approaches into STEM education (Barr et al., 2010; Chambers et al., 2016; Rankin & Thomas, 2016). Chambers et al. (2016) recommend placing greater attention on racial and gendered aspects of culturally relevant pedagogical techniques in teacher and counselor education programs, as well as teacher professional development. In addition to exposure to new pedagogical techniques, Alexander and Hermann (2016) noted that educators, particularly at the higher education level, should receive training on cultural responsiveness and effective mentoring processes. We believe that attending to these areas of curriculum and instruction will ensure that learning environments are shaped in a way that leverage identity as a cultural asset with cultural integrity (see Boykin, 2010) in STEM education.

Practice Implication 2: Attending to the Psychological Needs

In addition to mentoring opportunities and academic support, resources must be provided to address the psychosocial and emotional needs of Black women and girls in STEM (Alexander & Hermann, 2016). Black women in higher education STEM settings have reported experiencing negative social climates in their STEM departments (Rincón & George-Jackson, 2016). To mitigate these experiences, educational institutions should make efforts to minimize feelings of isolation, promote inclusive learning environments, offer student support groups, as well as foster connections within STEM programs and departments (Borum & Walker, 2012; Charleston et al., 2014; Herzig, 2010; Joseph, 2012; Rosa & Mensah, 2016). Throughout the educational pipeline, counseling resources should be available to students who are having difficulty navigating the social aspects of their educational environments. Additionally, professional staff and educational leadership must prioritize the well-being of their students, which can facilitate more positive educational outcomes.

CONCLUSION

Our review of the literature demonstrated the importance and utility of intersectionality as a theoretical and methodological approach to understanding the educational experiences of Black women and girls in STEM and discussed the *psychology of intersectionality* in STEM education. In addition, our chapter highlighted research that uncovered insights about the education of Black women and girls in STEM and identified common themes throughout this body of work with a focus on psychological processes and educational outcomes. This chapter also evaluated the various ways in which researchers of Black women and girls in STEM education have employed intersectionality as both a theoretical and a methodological framework, including opportunities for intersectionality to advance education research in this area. Intersectionality provides the opportunity to illuminate nuanced experiences and shades of meaning both within and across different social groups that are otherwise obscured in aggregate results of research that include Black women and girls or one-dimensional analyses of the Black female student demographic.

Our analysis of this body of literature encourages researchers and professionals in STEM education to consider how an understanding of intersectional experiences can advance their scholarship and practice toward a future where Black women and girls are unhidden figures and all students feel encouraged to fulfill their highest academic potential.

NOTES

[1]For the purposes of this chapter, we use the terms *Black* and *African American* interchangeably. We follow the term used by specific authors when referencing the subjects of their research.

[2]*Female* is used as a modifier and is not intended to distinguish between sexual identity and gender identity (i.e., female engineering students = women/girls studying engineering). We follow the term used by specific authors when referencing the subjects of their research.

[3]STEM identity is a general form of occupational identity, defined as an individual's personal identification with or relation to a specific career or academic pursuit in science, technology, engineering, or mathematics.

REFERENCES

Alexander, Q. R., & Hermann, M. A. (2016). African-American women's experiences in graduate science, technology, engineering, and mathematics education at a predominantly white university: A qualitative investigation. *Journal of Diversity in Higher Education, 9,* 307–322. doi:10.1037/a0039705

Bancroft, A., Bratter, J., & Rowley, K. (2017). Affirmation effects on math scores: The importance of high school track. *Social Science Research, 64,* 319–333. doi:10.1016/j. ssresearch.2016.10.001

Barr, D. A., Matsui, J., Wanat, S. F., & Gonzalez, M. E. (2010). Chemistry courses as the turning point for premedical students. *Advances in Health Sciences Education, 15,* 45–54. doi:10.1007/s10459-009-9165-3

Bernstein, J. D., Reilly, L. B., & Coté-Bonanno, J. F. (1992). Barriers to women entering the workforce: Math anxiety. *New Jersey Equity Research Bulletin, 3,* 3–6.

Borum, V., & Walker, E. (2012). What makes the difference? Black women's undergraduate and graduate experiences in mathematics. *Journal of Negro Education, 81,* 366–378. doi:10.7709/jnegroeducation.81.4.0366

Bowe, A. G., Desjardins, C. D., Covington Clarkson, L. M., & Lawrenz, F. (2017). Urban elementary single-sex math classrooms: Mitigating stereotype threat for African American girls. *Urban Education, 52,* 370–398. doi:10.1177/0042085915574521

Boykin, A. W. (1986). The triple quandary and the schooling of Afro-American children. In U. Neisser (Ed.), *The school achievement of minority children* (pp. 57–92). Hillsdale, NJ: Lawrence Erlbaum.

Boykin, A. W. (2000). The talent development model of schooling: Placing students at promise for academic success. *Journal of Education for Students Placed at Risk, 5*(1–2), 3–25. doi: 10.1080/10824669.2000.9671377

Bridgeman, B., McCamley-Jenkins, L., & Ervin, N. (2000). *Predictions of freshman grade-point average from the revised and recentered SAT® I: Reasoning test* (ETS Research Report Series No. 00-1). Retrieved from http://research.collegeboard.org/sites/default/files/publications/2012/7/researchreport-2000-1-predictions-freshman-gpa-revised-recentered-sat-reasoning.pdf

Buck, G. A., Clark, V. L. P., Leslie-Pelecky, D., Lu, Y., & Cerda-Lizarraga, P. (2008). Examining the cognitive processes used by adolescent girls and women scientists in identifying science role models: A feminist approach. *Science Education, 92*, 688–707. doi:10.1002/sce.20257

Buck, G., Cook, K., Quigley, C., Eastwood, J., & Lucas, Y. (2009). Profiles of urban, low SES, African American girls' attitudes toward science: A sequential explanatory mixed methods study. *Journal of Mixed Methods Research, 3*, 386–410. https://doi.org/10.1177/1558689809341797

Callahan, C., Adams, C., Bland, L., Moon, T., Moore, S., Perie, M., & McIntire, J. (1996). Factors influencing recruitment, enrollment, and retention of young women in special secondary schools of mathematics, science, and technology. In K. Arnold, K. D. Noble, & R. F. Subotnik (Eds.), *Remarkable women: Perspectives on female talent development* (pp. 243–261). Cresskill, NJ: Hampton Press.

Carlone, H. B., Haun-Frank, J., & Webb, A. (2011). Assessing equity beyond knowledge- and skills-based outcomes: A comparative ethnography of two fourth-grade reform-based science classrooms. *Journal of Research in Science Teaching, 48*, 459–485. doi:10.1002/tea.20413

Carlone, H. B., & Johnson, A. (2007). Understanding the science experiences of successful women of color: Science identity as an analytic lens. *Journal of research in science teaching, 44*, 1187–1218. doi:10.1002/tea.20237

Chambers, C. R., Walpole, M., & Outlaw, N. (2016). The influence of math self-efficacy on the college enrollments of young black women. *Journal of Negro Education, 85*, 302–315. doi:10.7709/jnegroeducation.85.3.0302

Charleston, L. J., Adserias, R., Lang, N., & Jackson, J. (2014). Intersectionality and STEM: The role of race and gender in the academic pursuits of African American women in STEM. *Journal of Progressive Policy & Practice, 2*, 273–293.

Charleston, L. J., George, P. L., Jackson, J. F., Berhanu, J., & Amechi, M. H. (2014). Navigating underrepresented STEM spaces: Experiences of Black women in US computing science higher education programs who actualize success. *Journal of Diversity in Higher Education, 7*(3), 166–176. doi:10.1037/a0036632

Cho, S., Crenshaw, K. W., & McCall, L. (2013). Toward a field of intersectionality studies: Theory, applications, and praxis. *Signs, 38*, 785–810. doi:10.1086/669608

Cole, E. R. (2009). Intersectionality and research in psychology. *American Psychologist, 64*(3), 170–180. doi:10.1037/a0014564

Cole, E. R., & Stewart, A. J. (2001). Invidious comparisons: Imagining a psychology of race and gender beyond. *Political Psychology, 22*, 293–308. doi:10.1111/0162-895X.00240

Collins, P. H. (2015). Intersectionality's definitional dilemmas. *Annual Review of Sociology, 41*, 1–20. doi:10.1146/annurev-soc-073014-112142

Collins, P. H., & Bilge, S. (2016). *Intersectionality*. Malden, MA: Polity Press.

Combahee River Collective. (1995). Combahee River Collective statement. In Guy-Sheftall, B. (Ed.), *Words of fire: An anthology of African American feminist thought* (pp. 232–240). New York, NY: New Press. (Original work published 1977)

Crenshaw, K. (1989). Demarginalizing the intersection of race and sex: A Black feminist critique of antidiscrimination doctrine, feminist theory and antiracist politics. *University of Chicago Legal Forum, 1989*(1), Article 8. Retrieved from http://chicagounbound.uchicago.edu/uclf/vol1989/iss1/8

Crenshaw, K. (1991). Mapping the margins: Intersectionality, identity politics, and violence against women of color. *Stanford Law Review, 43*, 1241–1299. doi:10.2307/1229039

Crenshaw, K. (2016, March). *Kimberlé Crenshaw: WOW 2016 keynote. On intersectionality* [Video file]. Retrieved from https://www.southbankcentre.co.uk/blog/kimberl%C3%A9-crenshaw-wow-2016-keynote

Cross, W. E. Jr. (1971). The Negro-to-Black conversion experience. *Black World, 20*, 13–27.

Cross, W. E. Jr. (1991). *Shades of black: Diversity in African-American identity*. Philadelphia, PA: Temple University Press.

Eccles, J. (2009). Who am I and what am I going to do with my life? Personal and collective identities as motivators of action. *Educational Psychologist, 44*(2), 78–89. doi:10.1080/00461520902832368

Elmore, K. C., & Oyserman, D. (2012). If "we" can succeed, "I" can too: Identity-based motivation and gender in the classroom. *Contemporary Educational Psychology, 37*, 176–185. doi:10.1016/j.cedpsych.2011.05.003

Else-Quest, N. M., Mineo, C. C., & Higgins, A. (2013). Math and science attitudes and achievement at the intersection of gender and ethnicity. *Psychology of Women Quarterly, 37*, 293–309. doi:10.1177/0361684313480694

Entwisle, D. R., Alexander, K. L., Pallas, A. M., & Cadigan, D. (1987). The emergent academic self-image of first graders: Its response to social structure. *Child Development, 58*, 1190–1206. doi:10.2307/1130614

Espinosa, L. (2011). Pipelines and pathways: Women of color in undergraduate STEM majors and the college experiences that contribute to persistence. *Harvard Educational Review, 81*, 209–241. doi:10.17763/haer.81.2.92315ww157656k3u

Farinde, A. A., & Lewis, C. W. (2012). The underrepresentation of African American female students in STEM fields: Implications for classroom teachers. *US-China Education Review B 4(2012)*, 421–430. Retrieved from http://files.eric.ed.gov/fulltext/ED533550.pdf

Ferreira, M. (2002). Ameliorating equity in science, mathematics, and engineering: A case study of an after-school science program. *Equity & Excellence in Education, 35*(1), 43–49. http://dx.doi.org/10.1080/713845242

Franklin, A. J. (1999). Invisibility syndrome and racial identity development in psychotherapy and counseling African American men. *Counseling Psychologist, 27*, 761–793. doi:10.1177/0011000099276002

Gholson, M. (2016). Clean corners and algebra: A critical examination of the constructed invisibility of Black girls and women in mathematics. *Journal of Negro Education, 85*, 290–301. doi:10.7709/jnegroeducation.85.3.0290

Gholson, M., & Martin, D. B. (2014). Smart girls, black girls, mean girls, and bullies: At the intersection of identities and the mediating role of young girls' social network in mathematical communities of practice. *Journal of Education, 194*, 19–33.

Gibson, S. L., & Espino, M. M. (2016). Uncovering Black Womanhood in Engineering. *NASPA Journal About Women in Higher Education, 9*, 56–73. doi:10.1080/19407882.2016.1143377

Gilmartin, K. J. (1976). *Development of scientific careers: The high school years*. Final report. Washington, DC: National Science Foundation.

Goertzen, R. M., Brewe, E., Kramer, L. H., Wells, L., & Jones, D. (2011). Moving toward change: Institutionalizing reform through implementation of the Learning Assistant model and open source tutorials. *Physical Review Special Topics-Physics Education Research, 7*(2), 020105-1–020105-9. doi:10.1103/PhysRevSTPER.7.020105

Goff, P. A., Eberhardt, J. L., Williams, M. J., & Jackson, M. C. (2008). Not yet human: Implicit knowledge, historical dehumanization, and contemporary consequences. *Journal of Personality and Social Psychology, 94*, 292–306. doi:10.1037/0022-3514.94.2.292

Gwilliam, L. R., & Betz, N. E. (2001). Validity of measures of math-and science-related self-efficacy for African Americans and European Americans. *Journal of Career Assessment, 9*, 261–281. doi:10.1177/106907270100900304

Hanson, S. (2008). *Swimming against the tide: African American girls and science education.* Philadelphia, PA: Temple University Press.

Harrell, C. J. P. (1999). *Manichean psychology: Racism and the minds of people of African descent.* Washington, DC: Howard University Press

Hartman, H. (1991, August). *Self-concept and metacognition in ethnic minorities.* Paper presented at the annual meeting of the American Psychological Association, San Francisco, CA.

Herzig, A. H. (2010). Women belonging in the social worlds of graduate mathematics. *The Mathematics Enthusiast, 7*, 177–208.

hooks, b. (1981). *Ain't I a woman: Black women and feminism.* London, England: Pluto Press.

Jackson, D. L. (2013). A balancing act: Impacting and initiating the success of African American female community college transfer students in STEM into the HBCU environment. *Journal of Negro Education, 82*, 255–271. doi:10.7709/jnegroeducation.82.3.0255

Joseph, N. M., Hailu, M., & Boston, D. (2017). Black women's and girls' persistence in the P–20 mathematics pipeline: Two decades of children, youth, and adult education research. *Review of Research in Education, 41*, 203–227.

Jones, J. M. (2003). TRIOS: A psychological theory of the African legacy in American culture. *Journal of Social Issues, 59*, 217–241.

Jones, M. H., & Ford, J. M. (2014). Social achievement goals, efficacious beliefs, and math performance in a predominately African American high school. *Journal of Black Psychology, 40*, 239–262.

Joseph, J. (2012). From one culture to another: Years one and two of graduate school for African American women in the STEM fields. *International Journal of Doctoral Studies, 7*, 125–142.

Ladson-Billings, G., & Tate, W. F. (1995). Toward a critical race theory of education. *Teachers College Record, 97*(1), 47–68.

Litzler, E., Samuelson, C. C., & Lorah, J. A. (2014). Breaking it down: Engineering student STEM confidence at the intersection of race/ethnicity and gender. *Research in Higher Education, 55*, 810–832.

Lord, S. M., Layton, R. A., & Ohland, M. W. (2015). Multi-institution study of student demographics and outcomes in electrical and computer engineering in the USA. *IEEE Transactions on Education, 58*, 141–150.

Lord, S. M., Layton, R. A., & Ohland, M. W. (2011). Trajectories of electrical engineering and computer engineering students by race and gender. *IEEE Transactions on education, 54*, 610–618.

Lord, S. M., Layton, R., Ohland, M., Brawner, C., & Long, R. (2014). A multi-institution study of student demographics and outcomes in chemical engineering. *Chemical Engineering Education, 48*, 231–238.

MacPhee, D., Farro, S., & Canetto, S. S. (2013). Academic self-efficacy and performance of underrepresented STEM majors: Gender, ethnic, and social class patterns. *Analyses of Social Issues and Public Policy, 13*, 347–369.

Malcom, S. M., Hall, P. Q., & Brown, J. W. (1976, April). *The double bind: The price of being a minority woman in science.* Washington, DC: American Association for the Advancement of Science.

Maple, S. A., & Stage, F. K. (1991). Influences on the choice of math/science major by gender and ethnicity. *American Educational Research Journal, 28*, 37–60.

Martin, S. F., Green, A., & Dean, M. (2016). African American women in STEM education: The cycle of microaggressions from P-12 classrooms to higher education and back. In *Critical research on sexism and racism in STEM fields* (pp. 135–143). Hershey, PA: IGI Global.

Martinez, S., & Guzman, S. (2013). Gender and racial/ethnic differences in self-reported levels of engagement in high school math and science courses. *Hispanic Journal of Behavioral Sciences*, *35*, 407–427.

McAdams, D. P. (2001). The psychology of life stories. *Review of General Psychology*, *5*, 100–122. doi:10.1037/1089-2680.5.2.100

McGee, E., & Martin, D. B. (2011). From the hood to being hooded: A case study of a Black male PhD. *Journal of African American Males in Education*, *2*, 46–65.

McPherson, E. (2014). Informal learning in SME majors for African American female undergraduates. *Global Education Review*, *1*(4), 96–113.

National Science Foundation, National Center for Science and Engineering Statistics. (2017). *Women, minorities, and persons with disabilities in science and engineering: 2017. Special report NSF 17-310.* Arlington, VA: Author. Retrieved from https://www.nsf.gov/statistics/2017/nsf17310/static/downloads/nsf17310-digest.pdf

National Science and Technology Council, Committee on STEM Education. (2013). *Federal Science, Technology, Engineering, and Mathematics (STEM) Education 5-Year Strategic Plan.* Retrieved from https://www.whitehouse.gov/sites/whitehouse.gov/files/ostp/Federal_STEM_Strategic_Plan.pdf

Nobles, W. A. (1991). African philosophy: Foundations for black psychology. In R. L. Jones (Ed.), *Black psychology* (3rd ed., pp. 47–63). Berkeley, CA: Cobb & Henry.

O'Brien, L. T., Blodorn, A., Adams, G., Garcia, D. M., & Hammer, E. (2015). Ethnic variation in gender-STEM stereotypes and STEM participation: An intersectional approach. *Cultural Diversity & Ethnic Minority Psychology*, *21*, 169–180.

Ohland, M. W., Brawner, C. E., Camacho, M. M., Layton, R. A., Long, R. A., Lord, S. M., & Wasburn, M. H. (2011). Race, gender, and measures of success in engineering education. *Journal of Engineering Education*, *100*, 225–252.

Ong, M. (2005). Body projects of young women of color in physics: Intersections of gender, race, and science. *Social Problems*, *52*, 593–617.

Ong, M., Wright, C., Espinosa, L. L., & Orfield, G. (2011). Inside the double bind: A synthesis of empirical research on undergraduate and graduate women of color in science, technology, engineering, and mathematics. *Harvard Educational Review*, *81*, 172–208.

Perez, T., Cromley, J. G., & Kaplan, A. (2014). The role of identity development, values, and costs in college STEM retention. *Journal of Educational Psychology*, *106*, 315–329. doi:10.1037/a0034027

Perez-Felkner, L., McDonald, S. K., Schneider, B., & Grogan, E. (2012). Female and male adolescents' subjective orientations to mathematics and the influence of those orientations on postsecondary majors. *Developmental Psychology*, *48*, 1658–1673.

Perna, L., Lundy-Wagner, V., Drezner, N. D., Gasman, M., Yoon, S., Bose, E., & Gary, S. (2009). The contribution of HBCUs to the preparation of African American women for STEM careers: A case study. *Research in Higher Education*, *50*, 1–23.

Rankin, Y. A., & Thomas, J. O. (2016). Leveraging food to achieve 100% student retention in an intro CS course. *Journal of Computing Sciences in Colleges*, *32*, 127–134.

Reyes, M. E. (2011). Unique challenges for women of color in STEM transferring from community colleges to universities. *Harvard Educational Review*, *81*, 241–263.

Rice, D. W. (2008). *Balance: Advancing identity theory by engaging the Black male.* Lanham, MD: Rowman & Littlefield.

Rice, D., & Alfred, M. (2014). Personal and structural elements of support for African American female engineers. *Journal of STEM Education*, *15*(2), 40–49.

Riedinger, K., & Taylor, A. (2016). "I could see myself as a scientist": The potential of out-of-school time programs to influence girls' identities in science. *Afterschool Matters, 23,* 1–7.

Rincón, B. E., & George-Jackson, C. E. (2016). Examining department climate for women in engineering: The role of STEM interventions. *Journal of College Student Development, 57,* 742–747.

Ro, H. K., & Loya, K. I. (2015). The effect of gender and race intersectionality on student learning outcomes in engineering. *Review of Higher Education, 38,* 359–396.

Rosa, K., & Mensah, F. M. (2016). Educational pathways of Black Women physicists: Stories of experiencing and overcoming obstacles in life. *Physical Review Physics Education Research, 12*(2), 020113-1–020113-15.

Rosenberg-Kima, R. B., Plant, E. A., Doerr, C. E., & Baylor, A. L. (2010). The influence of computer-based model's race and gender on female students' attitudes and beliefs toward engineering. *Journal of Engineering Education, 99,* 35–44.

Russell, M. L., & Russell, J. A. (2015). Black American undergraduate women at a PWI: Switching majors in STEM. *Negro Educational Review, 66*(1/4), 1–28.

Samuelson, C. C., & Litzler, E. (2016). Community cultural wealth: An assets-based approach to persistence of engineering students of color. *Journal of Engineering Education, 105,* 93–117.

Scott, K. A., & White, M. A. (2013). COMPUGIRLS'standpoint: Culturally responsive computing and its effect on girls of color. *Urban Education, 48,* 657–681.

Seay, C. (2004). Using a "socio-cultural" approach in teaching information technology to African American students with academic difficulties. *Journal of Information Technology Education, 3,* 83–102.

Sellers, R. M., Smith, M. A., Shelton, N. J., Rowley, S. A. J., & Chavous, T. M. (1998). Multidimensional model of racial identity: A reconceptualization of African American racial identity. *Personality and Social Psychology Review, 2*(1), 18–39.

Settles, I. H. (2004). When multiple identities interfere: The role of identity centrality. *Personal and Social Psychology Bulletin, 30,* 487–500. doi:10.1177/0146167203261885

Settles, I. H. (2006). Use of an intersectional framework to understand Black women's racial and gender identities. *Sex Roles, 54*(9–10), 589–601.

Settles, I. H., Jellison, W. A., & Pratt-Hyatt, J. S. (2009). Identification with multiple social groups: The moderating role of identity change over time among women-scientists. *Journal of Research in Personality, 43,* 856–867. doi:10.1016/j.jrp.2009.04.005

Shetterly, M. L. (2016). *Hidden figures: The untold story of the African-American women who helped win the space race.* New York, NY: Harper Collins

Smith, K. C., Fleming, L., Williams, D., Bliss, L., Moore, I., Burris, S., & Bornmann, F. (2014, June). *Black undergraduate success in engineering: The "prove them wrong syndrome" or social responsibility.* Paper presented at the American Society for Engineering Education's 121st annual conference and exposition, Indianapolis, IN.

Smyth, F. L., & McArdle, J. J. (2004). Ethnic and gender differences in science graduation at selective colleges with implications for admission policy and college choice. *Research in Higher Education, 45,* 353–381.

Society of Qualitative Inquiry in Psychology. (2017, January 31). *Action alert: Tell the APA to include qualitative methods in clinical, school and counseling psychology training!* Retrieved from http://qualpsy.org/action-alert-apa-training-regs/

Stearns, E., Bottía, M. C., Davalos, E., Mickelson, R. A., Moller, S., & Valentino, L. (2016). Demographic characteristics of high school math and science teachers and girls' success in STEM. *Social Problems, 63,* 87–110.

Steele, C. M. (1997). A threat in the air: How stereotypes shape intellectual identity and performance. *American Psychologist, 52,* 613–629.

Stewart, A. J., & McDermott, C. (2004). Gender in psychology. *Annual Review of Psychology, 55*, 519–544.

Sue, D., Capodilupo, C. M., Torino, G. C., Bucceri, J. M., Holder, A. B., Nadal, K. L., & Esquilin, M.(2007). Racial microaggressions in everyday life. *American Psychologist, 62*, 271–286.

Swinton, A. D., Kurtz-Costes, B., Rowley, S. J., & Okeke-Adeyanju, N. (2011). A longitudinal examination of African American adolescents' attributions about achievement outcomes. *Child Development, 82*, 1486–1500.

Tate, E. D., & Linn, M. C. (2005). How does identity shape the experiences of women of color engineering students? *Journal of Science Education and Technology, 14*, 483–493.

Varma, R. (2010). Why so few women enroll in computing? Gender and ethnic differences in students' perception. *Computer Science Education, 20*, 301–316.

Varma, R., & Hahn, H. (2008). Gender and the pipeline metaphor in computing. *European Journal of Engineering Education, 33*, 3–11.

Winston, C. E., Rice, D. W., Bradshaw, B., Lloyd, D., Harris, L., Burford, T., . . . Burrell, J. (2004). Science success, narrative theories of personality, and race self complexity: Is race represented in the self and identity construction of African American adolescents? *New Directions in Child and Adolescent Development, 2004*, 55–77.

Winston, C. E., & Winston, M. R. (2012). Cultural psychology and racial ideology: An analytic approach to understanding racialized societies and their psychological effects on lives. In J. Valsiner (Ed.), *Oxford handbook of culture and psychology* (pp. 559–581). New York, NY: Oxford University Press.

Winston, J. A. (1991). Mirror, mirror on the wall: Title VII, Section 1981, and the intersection of race and gender in the Civil Rights Act of 1990. *California Law Review, 79*, 775–805.

Young, J. L., Young, J. R., & Capraro, M. M. (2017). Black girls' achievement in middle grades mathematics: How can socializing agents help? *The Clearing House, 90*(3), 70–76.

Chapter 11

Intersectionality and Educational Leadership:
A Critical Review

VONZELL AGOSTO ⓘD
ERICKA ROLAND
University of South Florida

In this review of research, we explore intersectionality in the literature on K–12 educational leadership. We seek to understand how researchers have used intersectionality and what their findings or arguments reveal about the work of leading to reduce inequities in education. We ask, What traditions and trends associated with intersectionality have been brought into educational leadership research to inform the development of transformative leadership? The sample includes 15 articles published in peer-reviewed journals between 2005 and 2017. We identify the themes individualism and knowledge relations, which leads us to three interrelated findings concerning conceptions of leadership and intersectionality. We find that intersectionality primarily (1) is used to support micro-level analysis rather than both micro-level and macro-level analysis of the inequities being confronted by leadership practice, (2) is used to focus on individuals' experiences as "leaders" and "leadership" capacity rather than "leading" practices, and (3) serves as an emergent knowledge project in its support of agendas related to transformative educational leadership. We discuss how the use of intersectionality, conceptions of leadership, and leadership and research practices coincide, pointing to the implications for the continued use of intersectionality in educational leadership, and provide recommendations to support the use of intersectionality in future research.

In educational leadership research, various approaches to scholarship are being advanced to help expose and explain the complexity of social injustice and transform education accordingly (Capper, 1989; Horsford, 2012; Quantz, Rogers, & Dantley, 1991). Examples of such approaches include critical race theory (CRT; Capper, 2015), feminist theory (Blackmore, 2013), critical spirituality (Dantley,

Review of Research in Education
March 2018, Vol. 42, pp. 255–285
DOI: 10.3102/0091732X18762433
© 2018 AERA. http://rre.aera.net

2010), and multiculturalism (Santamaría & Santamaría, 2013). This critical review of literature drew from the common theme across these approaches, leading social transformation toward social justice, to focus on transformative educational leadership.

The purpose of this review was to understand the use of intersectionality by researchers studying educational leadership and related inequities. The guiding questions were the following: (1) How is intersectionality used in relation to leadership and intervening in inequities in education? (2) How is leadership conceptualized when intersectionality is used? In the next paragraph, we will introduce theoretical conceptions of leadership in the field of educational leadership and describe the recent turn to a transformative leadership. Then we provide some historical background on intersectionality to expose traditions and tensions that are important for those who seek to use it at this point in the trajectory of its development.

Theoretical Conceptions of Educational Leadership

Research in educational leadership has favored leadership theories that focus on organizational goals and emphasize transactions, management, and efficiency (Larson & Murtadha, 2003; Quantz, Cambron-McCabe, Dantley, & Hachem, 2017). During the 1980s, as the focus shifted from organizational management to leadership, education research introduced new leadership theories that centered human agency rather than organizational structure (Evers & Lakomski, 2013). The focus on the agency of human actors recentered individualism and ushered in a leader-centric view in which leadership was an expression of a single person's influence—the formal leader of an organization. According to Evers and Lakomski (2013), leader-centric accounts involve a commitment to methodological individualism whereby logical structures are reduced in the analysis on how leading is practiced in educational organizations so as to understate the significance of a broader range of influences.

The addition of the principal's office within schools changed the culture and organization of schools to match the traditional social and leadership expectations for men (Rousmaniere, 2007). Even as women began to increasingly enter into educational administrative positions during the start of the 20th century (Blount, 1998, Hansot & Tyack, 1981; Tyack & Hansot, 1982), White, Protestant, heterosexual men remained dominant in the field. Furthermore, notions of masculinity, heteronormativity, and White supremacy informed by their prominence and dominance continue to serve as the basis for theories of leadership (Liang, Sottile, & Peters, 2016). This historiography of educational leadership illustrates how inequities developed to further shape educational leadership theory, practice, and research. Next, we describe how William Foster paired Burns's (1978) *transformational leadership* with Giroux's (1988) *transformative intellectual* to help pave the way for scholarship on leading as a practice involving the analysis of power relations and the use of findings to further educate.

Transformative Leadership Practice

Foster (1989) argued that administration in K–20 education "needed to be recast as a transformational practice where leadership and critique form the basis for establishing true educational communities" (p. 10). He defined critique, based on critical theory, as "a sustained and formal attempt to analyze social relations and the impact of class, power, and ideology on these, with the ultimate, if utopian, goal of freeing people from the conditions that they themselves identify as being repressive" (p. 11). Therefore, as he argued, leadership is educative, and those who serve in leadership roles should perform as "transformative intellectuals" who analyze forms of discourse for how they disguise power relations and use those findings to educate.

Drawing on the work of adult educators using critical social theory (Freire, 1970; Mezirow, 1991), some scholars have theorized transformative leadership in education as a practice of intervening in inequities. For instance, Shields's (2012) approach to transformative leadership in education is grounded in the four critical components of Freire's pedagogy of the oppressed: awareness (conscientization), reflection, analysis, and action or activism. Others have referred to these processes as ways of being, relating, knowing, and doing (henceforth leading) that are needed to respond to a globally changing context (Montuori & Donnelly, 2017). According to Shields (2010), transformative leadership begins by recognizing the ontological dimension of leadership; how "some material realities of the broader social and political sphere" and "the inequities and struggles experienced in the wider society affect one's ability to perform and to succeed within an organizational context" (p. 568).

Transformative leadership is a broad-based framework constituted by the following tenets:

- Acknowledging power and privilege
- Articulating both individual and collective purposes (public and private good)
- Deconstructing social–cultural knowledge frameworks that generate inequity and reconstructing them
- Balancing critique and promise
- Effecting deep and equitable change
- Working toward transformation: liberation, emancipation, democracy, equity, and excellence
- Demonstrating moral courage and activism (Shields, 2011)

There is growing emphasis in the literature on leading to transform education into a more equitable and just system.

Intersectionality as an Oppositional Knowledge Project

Oppositional knowledge projects contest hegemonic or dominant scholarship that "aims to preserve the status quo, ensure social order, and redefine social change as a process of polite gradualism" (Collins, 2016, p. 139). Scholarship supports oppositional knowledge projects when it exposes uneven power relations behind unjust practices that result in patterns of inequity. Intersectionality is an oppositional knowledge project that began in social movement settings and was brought into American higher education to support social awareness and change (Collins, 2009). Across decades, Kimberlé Crenshaw and Patricia Hill Collins have worked to define and use intersectionality. Their ongoing scholarship can inform how researchers/ scholars in educational leadership can proceed when taking up intersectionality. For instance, to expose how Black girls are pushed out, overpoliced, and unprotected in schools, Crenshaw, Ocen, and Nanda (2015) used intersectionality to connect race and gender to zero-tolerance policies, social marginalization, and criminalization. They pointed to the need for leadership at all levels and sectors of society to provide the necessary resources to ensure that Black girls, and girls of color more generally, have equitable opportunities. Given the promise of intersectionality to assist in exposing inequities in K–12 education, its examination in educational leadership research is warranted. Despite the use of intersectionality across various social science fields, it remains underused in educational leadership literature focused on understanding and critiquing inequities in PreK–12 schooling (Capper & Young, 2014). According to Capper (2015), detailed analyses of the use of intersectionality within equity leadership practice would benefit the field.

In conducting this review, we leaned heavily on the historical and ongoing work of Kimberlé Crenshaw and Patricia Hill Collins, including but not limited to what was cited in the literature we reviewed herein. In the following sections, we describe intersectionality, the methodology, and present the findings. We then discuss the findings and offer recommendations to guide the use of intersectionality as a tool that supports research as a dispositionally informed practice involving critique and analysis.

What Is Intersectionality?

The origins of intersectionality can be traced back to early social movements, during the 1960s and 1970s, which analyzed inequities within political, social, and economic structures, including education, employment, and the legal system (Anzaldúa, 1987; Collins & Bilge, 2016; Combahee River Collective, 1981; Harlan, 1957; Shoben, 1980). Inspired by CRT and Black feminism, Crenshaw (1988) coined the term *intersectionality* while exposing the inadequacy of antidiscrimination law to address employment barriers and undo racism and sexism that directly influenced Black women in particular. She relied on the history of Black liberation politics to illustrate the limitations of antiracist and feminist theories to address structural discrimination affecting interactions and marginalization associated with social "categories of experience and analysis" (Crenshaw, 1989, p. 139). In doing so, she broadened her focus from race to include sex/gender in her criticism of antidiscrimination laws and continued developing and applying intersectionality to examine other phenomena such as violence against Black women (Crenshaw, 1991).

Core Ideas About Intersectionality

Intersectionality is a tool researchers can engage analytically and dispositionally in examinations of interlocking educational injustices (Collins & Bilge, 2016; Natapoff, 1995; Scanlan & Theoharis, 2016). It has been described as a way for researchers to highlight the relational aspects of human connections and society (Cho, Crenshaw, & McCall, 2013). Crenshaw (1991) identified three forms of intersectional analysis: structural, political, and representational. These forms refer to overlapping structures of subordination in which marginalized people are situated, the material consequences of interactive oppressions, the erasure of people's experiences at the intersections of multiple oppressions, and the cultural construction of identities that result in negative stereotypes that are used to further discredit marginalized experiences.

In contrast to critiques that intersectionality is simply an identitarian framework (Carbado, Crenshaw, Mays, & Tomlinson, 2013), Hancock (2013) argued that empirical research using intersectionality has gone beyond the politics of identity (i.e., race, gender, and sexuality) to analyze uneven power relations that shape structural manifestations of oppression (i.e., racism, sexism, and heterosexism), but also noted the following issues: a lack of attentiveness to the historical context of experience lived by the participants, the marginalized aspects of their social locations, and the privilege and agential aspects of their social locations. Although descriptions of intersectionality abound, there are few analyses of how it has been used methodologically across the social sciences (Gross, Gottburgsen, & Phoenix, 2016; McCall, 2005).

The core ideas of intersectionality can be applied in educational leadership. Its use in the study of educational leadership could potentially strengthen transformative leadership as an educative oppositional knowledge project focused on intervening in interrelated systems of oppression. First, its emphasis on the experiences of social groups, social structures, and social oppressions challenges methodological individualism with analysis of individual–organizational relationships and practices (Evers & Lakomski, 2013). Second, intersectionality also supports critique and researcher reflexivity on how education and education research is transformed by ways of relating, knowing, being, and leading.

METHODOLOGY

To examine how researchers used intersectionality in articles focused on educational leadership, we drew on the grounded theoretical approach to conducting literature reviews suggested by Wolfswinkel, Furtmueller, and Wilderom (2011). They claimed that "a high-quality review inspires valuable studies that extend the earlier theoretical and empirical repertoire" (p. 9) and "must be a richly competent coverage of a well-carved out niche in the literature" (p. 3), and be informed by the background knowledge researchers bring to the process. An additional criterion by which to judge the quality of reviews or research in general is whether or not it fosters emancipation and provides insight into the structure of human experience

(Clegg, 2005). The five stages of the model are defining, searching, selecting, analyzing, and presenting.

Defining the Parameters for Inclusion and Exclusion

Scope, Criteria, and Field of Study

We focused the review on educational leadership at the K–12 level involving administrative roles, such as superintendents, principals, and assistant principals, rather than nonadministrative leadership roles (i.e., teacher leaders, counselors, or social workers). We included studies of students in advanced educational leadership preparation programs that combined leadership preparation on K–12 and higher education (Welton, Mansfield, Lee, & Young, 2015). We excluded studies of administratively certified teachers, who had not taken an administrative position.[1]

Searching

We used five criteria to conduct the initial search for articles on intersectionality related to educational leadership: (1) the time frame from 1989 to 2017; (2) peer-reviewed journals; (3) research conducted in the United States; (4) the inclusion of the word "intersectionality" in the title, keywords, and/or abstract; and (5) emphasis on K–12 educational leadership and/or educational leadership preparation programs. This 28-year time frame allowed us to capture literature published since the inception of intersectionality in critical legal studies and its entry into the field of education and educational leadership. Initially, we searched for articles using the key terms *intersectionality* and *education leadership* or *administration* in the title, keywords, or abstract. As the search progressed, we expanded the terms to include "intersect" on noticing that some articles used the terms *intersected* and *intersectional*, either with or without intersectionality. We restricted our search to peer-reviewed journals since they provide a review process to evaluate and enhance the quality of published work and excluded dissertations, books, reports, white papers, conference proceedings, and social media, which generally tend to be inconsistently reviewed by other scholars. Geographically, we restricted the search to literature focused on the United States given that its historical context for marginalized groups has been shaped by particular federal and state-level politics and policies, including housing, immigration, desegregation, disability, and (de)colonization.

To begin, we searched using Google Scholar and saved articles we thought met the criteria in our respective Google Scholar Libraries. From there, we each created an Excel table that we populated with the saved articles. After combining our libraries and filtering out doubles, we read the remaining articles' titles, abstracts, and sections of text referencing intersectionality. Then we searched the following library databases: Educational Resources Information Center (ERIC), Academic Search Premier, and Education Source.

We repeated the search by targeting journals specific to educational leadership, such as *Educational Administration Quarterly* (*EAQ*) and the *Journal of School*

Leadership. We found two additional works in *EAQ* that we initially excluded but then included: an essay (Alston, 2005) and a literature review (Capper, 2015). Prior to this review, Capper and Green (2013) reviewed articles on equity and organizational theories published in *EAQ* (2000–2010) but found none that addressed the intersection of multiple identities. They did not include Alston's (2005) article in their analysis, though we eventually did, since she included intersectionality as a keyword and used to theorize about leadership.

Selecting

We organized the initial sample into groups and arranged each group alphabetically; articles reporting on studies with human subjects and articles without human subjects. Using a dialogical process similar to intercoder reliability, we read the first article in a group and discussed our justifications as to why it should or should not be included in the sample. When we had a difference in opinion, offered a weak rationale, or remained tentative about excluding an article, we placed it on hold and then proceeded to read and deliberate on others in the sample. This process allowed us to further define the parameters for including/excluding articles previously placed on hold.

We excluded articles introducing themed issues, articles about leadership outside of formal institutions of education, and studies of women (a single category) in educational leadership engaging intersectionality that met the marginalized identity criteria (gender: women), but did not engage in analysis beyond a single axis. If we found articles focusing on intersectionality, leadership, and the benefits of privilege, while ignoring its harms for those in multiple marginalized social locations affected by social oppression(s), we excluded them. We did this after taking into account the assertion made by Collins and Bilge (2016), that intersectionality exists to expose social inequities that are rarely caused by a single issue (e.g., racism or sexism).

In keeping with our purpose to review research based on a systematic scholarly inquiry, we excluded the *Journal of Cases in Educational Leadership*, since it publishes pedagogical cases rather than case studies. Cases from the 2016 themed issue on intersectionality have been reviewed elsewhere (Roland, 2016), and another case is reflected in an empirical study included in our sample (Witherspoon & Taylor, 2010).

Analyzing

To support our collaborative review, we developed a data extraction tool that helped us systematically extract key segments of text that illustrated the traditions in which intersectionality and leadership were situated, related, and used in the articles we analyzed. We posted the data extraction tool in the form of a table within a virtual shared folder and reproduced it to allow each of us to complete the extraction. Each of us read an article closely and conducted the data extraction independently, which was repeated for approximately three to five articles. This process provided us with an archive consisting of two tables per article and focused our discussions on the data extraction process, outcomes, and weaknesses in order to improve the tool. Once we were comfortable with the process of interpreting based on more defined understandings, we read each article and marked excerpts by hand on paper copies. We then extracted excerpts from the sample and entered them along with our interpretations into the online data extraction tool. The data extraction tool was essential in the process of dissecting each article and identifying themes and gaps across the selected literature.

As the review progressed, we expanded the timeline by 10 years to identify gaps in the publication record (1980s), and then opened the search from 1900 to 2000 to add to the historical record on the use of the term *intersection* alongside inequity in education (e.g., Harlan, 1957). To understand how intersectionality was rooted and used, we focused on how the articles grounded the concept in previous scholarship, discussed its purpose, and used it in relation to educational leadership and inequity. Within the sample, we examined articles that were coauthored and/or included human participants (*n* = 10) to examine how the researchers provided participants with opportunities to engage dialogically in narrating their leading experiences and the opportunities they created for themselves to collaborate with other researchers or scholars in the knowledge process. We identified the themes of (1) individualism and (2) knowledge relations through open coding. Individualism concerns the focus on leadership at the individual level. Knowledge relations concern how leading was conceptualized and how intersectionality was used in research/scholarship.

Presenting

After removing 7 articles that either focused on higher education leadership or failed to substantively discuss intersectionality, even after having used it in the title, keywords, or abstract, we settled on a final sample of 15 articles: 9 qualitative studies, 4 essays, 1 review of literature, and 1 mixed methods study (see Table 1). Overwhelmingly, the selected articles focused on the identities of school-based administrators and how they navigated difficult situations. Black women administrators were the main participants in 10 of the 15 articles.

Limitations

This review is limited by the criterion that restricted the sample to empirical research situated in the United States. We excluded empirical studies from abroad given that school leadership is mediated in the particularities of the policies and practices of each country, and our knowledge of such is limited to the United States. We were willing to include conceptual work; however, we found no published literature that went beyond mentioning intersectionality in a sentence or two.[2] Another limitation is the small sample of articles (*N* = 15), which is not unusual for a review of concepts or practices recently introduced into educational leadership research. For example, an initial review of research literature on "turnaround principals" by Meyers and Hambrick Hitt (2017) included 18 studies.

TABLE 1

Articles Reviewed

Title	Author	Year	Journal	Framework	Intersectionality Origin	Methodology	Approach	Identity Categories	Pages	Themed Issue
Tempered Radicals and Servant Leaders: Black Females Persevering in the Superintendency	Judy Alston	2005	Educational Administration Quarterly	Intersectionality and tempered radicals	Collins (1998), Crenshaw (1991)	Essay	—	Black women	14	No
Fostering an Ethics of Care in Leadership: A Conversation with Five African American Women	Lisa Bass	2009	Advances in Developing Human Resources	Feminist care focused and Black feminist theory	Collins (2000)	Qualitative	Exploratory multicase study	African American Women	14	Yes
Pastoral Care: Notions of Caring and the Black Female Principal	Noelle Witherspoon and Bruce Makoto Arnold	2010	The Journal of Negro Education	Womanist theory	Crenshaw (1991), Collins (1998), Tate (2005)	Qualitative	Spiritual narratives: In-depth interviews	Black women Christian	13	No
Spiritual Weapons: Black Female Principals and Religio-Spirituality	Noelle Witherspoon and Dianne L. Taylor	2010	Journal of Educational Administration and History	Womanist theory	Crenshaw (1991), Collins (1998), Tate (2005)	Qualitative	Spiritual narratives: In-depth interviews	Black women Christian	26	Yes
Leading Through the Challenge of Change: African American Women Principals on Small School Reform	April L. Peters	2012	International Journal of Qualitative Studies in Education	Afrocentric feminist epistemology	McCall (2005)	Qualitative	Instrumental case study: Semistructured and open-ended interviews	Black, women, age (less than 40 years)	16	Yes
The Intersection of Race and Gender in School Leadership for Three Black Female Principals	Latish Cherie Reed	2012	International Journal of Qualitative Studies in Education	Black feminist epistemology	Collins (2000), Zane (2002), Andrews (1993)	Qualitative	Case study: Semistructured interviews	Black women	20	Yes

(continued)

TABLE 1 (CONTINUED)

Title	Author	Year	Journal	Framework	Intersectionality Origin	Methodology	Approach	Identity Categories	Pages	Themed Issue
This Bridge Called My Leadership: An Essay on Black Women as Bridge Leaders in Education	Sonya Douglass Horsford	2012	*International Journal of Qualitative Studies in Education*	Black feminist and critical race feminism	Crenshaw (1989)	Essay	—	Black women	12	Yes
The Subtlety of Age, Gender, and Race Barriers: A Case Study of Early Career African American Female Principals	Gaetane Jean-Marie	2013	*Journal of School Leadership*	Afrocentric epistemology	Collins (2000), King (1995), Crenshaw (1989), Bloom and Erlandson (2003), Loder (2005), Byrd (2009)	Qualitative	Case study	African American, women, age	25	No
The 20th-Year Anniversary of Critical Race Theory in Education: Implications for Leading to Eliminate Racism	Colleen Capper	2015	*Educational Administration Quarterly*	Critical race theory	Crenshaw (1991)	Essay	—	—	43	No
Mentoring Educational Leadership Doctoral Students: Using Methodological Diversification to Examine Gender and Identity Intersections	Anjale D. Welton, Katherine Cumings Mansfield, Pei-Ling Lee, and Michelle D. Young	2015	*International Journal of Educational Leadership Preparation*	Mentoring	None	Quantitative and qualitative	Focus group interview and exploratory survey	—	28	No

(continued)

TABLE 1 (CONTINUED)

Title	Author	Year	Journal	Framework	Intersectionality Origin	Methodology	Approach	Identity Categories	Pages	Themed Issue
Recognizing Postmodern Intersectional Identities in Leadership for Early Childhood	Julie Nicholson and Helen Maniates	2015	Early Years	Intersectionality	Crenshaw (1989), Collins (2000), Núñez (2014)	Essay	—	—	16	No
Understanding Asian American Women's Pathways to School Leadership	Jia G. Liang, James Sottile, and April L. Peters	2016	Gender and Education	Undetermined	Crenshaw (1989), Collins (2000), McCall (2005)	Qualitative	Multi-case study	Asian American women	20	No
Leadership for Chicano/Latino Education and the Politics of Change	Patricia D. López	2016	Association of Mexican American Educators Journal	Chicana feminist epistemology	Crenshaw (1989, 1991)	Essay	—	Chicano/Latino	12	Yes
Out of the Sombra: One Afro-Latino Making His Way in Educational Leadership	Wellinthon García and Monica Byrne-Jiménez	2016	National Forum of Educational Administration and Supervision Journal	Latino critical theory	Anzaldúa (1987), Delgado Bernal (2002)	Qualitative	Narrative	Afro-Latino	19	Yes
"I Am More Than What I Look Alice": Asian American Women in Public School Administration	Jia "Grace" Liang and April L. Peters-Hawkins	2017	Educational Administration Quarterly	Intersectionality	Ritzer (2007), Crenshaw (1991), hooks (1984), Collins (2000)	Qualitative	Multi-case study: Semistructured in-depth interviews and informal observations	Asian American women	30	No

FINDINGS

In reviewing the literature, we asked how intersectionality was used when inequity in education was a concern expressed by the researchers. We subsumed all approaches urging educational leadership to develop more just and equitable education under the descriptor *transformative leadership*, although not all researchers used this phrase. Horsford (2012) advanced a vision of leadership "that engages transformative educational practices, which promote equity, diversity and social justice for all students" (p. 12). Other researchers in the sample provided purpose statements, problems, or questions that reflected an interest in supporting the ideal of transformative leadership, often framed as a contribution to fostering a more equitable and just educational system and society.

Several researchers named and criticized the centrality of Western, Eurocentric styles and theories of leadership based on the normative (White) lens in educational leadership practice and scholarship and positioned their work as support for the reconceptualization of leadership based on the experiences of marginalized groups, their voices, and the ways in which they lead (Alston, 2005; Bass, 2009; García & Byrne Jiménez, 2016; Horsford, 2012; López, 2016; Reed, 2012; Witherspoon & Arnold, 2010; Witherspoon & Taylor, 2010). Liang and Peters-Hawkins (2017) named knowledge suppression as a threat to the economic, political, and social vitalization of Black women and their realities (Bloom & Erlandson, 2003), which reflected Collins's (2016) concern about the depoliticization of oppositional knowledge (i.e., intersectionality). They argued that the absence of historically underrepresented groups and their stories, such as Asian American women within educational leadership, allows for the continuation of discourse that "perpetuates a system that refuses to acknowledge the genuine needs and legitimate concerns of Asian-American women, and fails to provide access and equity to those who aspire to leadership" (Liang & Peters-Hawkins, p. 42).

Witherspoon and Taylor (2010) also situated their study of Black women's knowledge, in the form of spiritual or religious epistemologies, "as powerful counter-narratives to traditional knowledges in educational leadership, schools, and society" rather than as ways of "*not knowing*" (p. 156). We interpreted research that used intersectionality to challenge traditional notions of leadership, make visible and audible the voices and narratives of groups who have been marginalized or rejected, and promote equitable opportunities and outcomes for groups who have been underserved by the educational system, among others, as adding to the oppositional knowledge project we refer to as transformative leadership.

Through a grounded theory process of analysis, three interrelated findings emerged from the data. The first finding on the centrality of "the leader" points to the continued use of a person-centric conception of leading (alone) analyzed at the micro-level—focused on individual(s) and interpersonal experience. Majority of the researchers throughout the sample tended to pose questions about individuals rather than about issues related to oppression. Within five studies, the subfinding exposed how women of color working in school-based administrative positions continued to experience workplace discrimination.

The second finding, evident in a smaller number of empirical studies with and without human subjects, switched between a micro-level and macro-level analysis, as well as between conceptions of leadership and the leader. More specifically, four studies expressed the hybrid conception of transformative leadership involving the leader, leadership, and leading (with others). The active construction, leading, is echoed in the emphasis transformative leadership scholarship places on praxis involving action and change related to the subfinding: contextualized sociopolitical consciousness.

Unlike the previous findings, the third finding speaks to the politics of knowledge affected by research processes and relations between people, theories, and their power to support oppositional knowledge projects. The third finding is that intersectionality is inchoate as an emergent knowledge project in educational leadership research and risks underserving political and research agendas associated with the development of transformative leadership theory/practice. The subfindings are as follows: intersectionality is a floating signifier across the sample, citation practices made questionable the people and traditions supporting the development and application of intersectionality over time, and the tenets or principles of oppositional knowledge projects tended to be ignored in descriptions of design and implementation of studies involving human subjects. This final finding largely concerns how researchers develop and report on studies, including how they illustrate their and others' understandings and applications of intersectionality in relationship to knowledge production processes of power.

Finding 1: Person-Centric Conception of Leading—The Leader

In most studies, researchers used intersectionality to understand experience at the individual and interpersonal levels (Bass, 2009; Horsford, 2012; Jean-Marie, 2013; Liang et al., 2016; Liang & Peters-Hawkins, 2017; López, 2016; Peters, 2012; Reed, 2012; Welton et al., 2015; Witherspoon & Arnold, 2010; Witherspoon & Taylor, 2010). A micro-level analysis was evident in the research questions posed across the sample, such as: "How does African-American women leaders' experiences with intersectionality inform ethics of care in responding to social injustices within the educational system?" (Bass, 2009, p. 621), and "What are the experiences of highly visible, early career African-American principals in a large urban school district? Specifically, how do age, gender, and race intersect in their professional experiences?" (Jean-Marie, 2013, p. 616).

Drawing largely on data from questionnaires and surveys, Welton et al. (2015) studied mentoring experiences and relationships among doctoral students in educational leadership programs based on their intersectional social categories of identity. The researchers noted that "female doctoral students of color experience both racism and sexism, and alleviating this interlocking oppression would require both feminist and race-conscious approaches to mentoring" (p. 59). The researchers' focus on identity politics was evident in their recommendation that programs help develop students' understanding of how their social identities intersect. Crenshaw (1991) argued that intersectionality is not "some new totalizing theory of identity" but rather an analytical tool for making sense of structural power relations (p. 1244). Helping individuals understand their identity intersections, without helping them analyze intersections of oppression linked to power relations, can serve to minimize the significance of group or shared patterns of experience in their perception of the magnitude of oppression.

There was a vague example of leading evident in another study. A principal commented, "When I stopped focusing so much on achievement at my school, our test scores increased by 19%" (Witherspoon & Arnold, 2010, p. 227). Other researchers captured more specific examples of leading among school-based administrators (Jean-Marie, 2013; Peters, 2012; Reed, 2012; Witherspoon & Arnold, 2010; Witherspoon & Taylor, 2010). For instance, a principal attempted to garner the support of the community by switching to a beauty parlor in a part of the town where students and their parents were going, she described how she "tried to become a part of the life they lived" (Witherspoon & Arnold, 2010, p. 227). Bass (2009) described African American women as leaders whose experiences with intersectionality influenced how they "used their power to bend the rules" (p. 629). She attributed their capacity to bend the rules to their personal insights into the system that makes the rules, alluding to how perceptual acuity can be gained through prior experience navigating similar arrangements of institutional power.

The most concrete examples of leading were expressed in quotations made by Black, women school principals related to funding inequities. For instance, to sustain professional development for instructional classes, there was a need to gain district-level finances to implement reform. One principal went to the "district office and asked for $5000" to continue an instructional practice, but when her request "was declined" she had to continue the implementation of the educational reform with limited funds (Peters, 2012, p. 30). Another principal, quoted in two articles, "fought for a laboratory at school" (Witherspoon & Arnold, 2010, p. 227), which she thought "needed it more than the rich school they were trying to give it to" (Witherspoon & Taylor, 2010, p. 146). Also related to economic equity affecting building infrastructure, another principal stated, "What people don't get is that I'm still trying to get sections of this building wired [for the Internet]" (Reed, 2012, p. 53). This quote was in reference to disparities between schools and how she observed that as the enrollment of students of color increased the school's funding decreased, while in suburban schools money was available to fund extracurricular activities. These specific efforts to intervene in the perpetuation of inequities through the reallocation of human and nonhuman capital reflect transformative leadership.

Overall, participants were portrayed as working and persisting alone rather than in alliance or in fellowship with others. Only Reed (2012) provided an example, a single quotation, of a participant describing how they led relationally. She stated, "So we decided as a staff that we would change to uniforms" (p. 49). Reed described this principal's approach to leading as a dispersion of power for the general good of the community rather than "having power for power's sake" (p. 42). While her inclusion of this quotation suggests a distributed *leadership* approach to power used by the participant while *leading* to transform policy and practice to be more equitable and just (Brooks & Jean-Marie, 2007), the majority of the articles and comments made by participants in the study focused on leaders and leadership rather than leading.

Workplace Discrimination

Analyses of individuals primarily focused on how they perceived and responded to workplace discrimination while seeking social justice for themselves and others. Some claimed that, historically, Black women's awareness of self and self-preservation have been intertwined with leadership for social justice in education (Horsford, 2012), and the field of educational administration has reinforced gender norms, including the image of the White, protestant, heterosexual men so that traditional conceptions of upward mobility reflect their experiences (Liang et al., 2016).

Also pointing to workplace discrimination related to institutions and identities, Welton et al. (2015) described how two Asian women with international student status felt discriminated against given that they were ineligible for funding reserved for domestic students and unable to secure employment on campus. Others' feelings and perceptions of discrimination were included in studies that reported on how Asian American women used their individual agency to navigate their employment contexts, while attempting to remain true to their cultural identities and values (Liang et al., 2016; Liang & Peters-Hawkins, 2017). In studying Asian American women principals, Liang et al. (2016) suspected that participants were reluctant to violate leadership norms and risk being perceived as violating social and cultural expectations for Asian women. Although the researchers situated the problem and interpreted the data as evidence of systemic discrimination affecting career mobility, the data generated were in response to the question about individual pathways to school leadership, which were then analyzed for how their experiences differed across the group and in comparison with other women of color. Thus, most data were biographical, focused on mentoring as an interpersonal relationship, and absent description of their work in their leadership positions as principals and assistant principals.

In some cases, an aspect of one's identity was maximized to support leadership and self-preservation. Spirituality (a source of power) was a common focus among studies that centered on the experiences of Asian American women (Liang & Peters-Hawkins, 2017) and Black women (Bass, 2009; Horsford, 2012; Peters, 2012; Witherspoon & Arnold, 2010; Witherspoon & Taylor, 2010) in educational leadership. Witherspoon and Taylor (2010) pointed to the intersectionality of race, gender, and religiospirituality in participants' active resistance aimed at social justice on behalf of the students. Relating the participants' experiences to intersectional identities and social oppressions, they typically described the participants operating independently—though not apart from "a higher being" (Bass, 2009, p. 628).

According to Witherspoon and Taylor (2010), self-preservation strategies used among Black women principals were supported by spirituality and their social justice mission. One participant commented, "I have been discriminated against in every sense of the word and yet I am still here. I would have given up a long time ago if I did not pray and have God" (p. 147). Although this participant did not quit, some participants in others studies did quit their positions. For instance, two African American women left their positions as principals as an act of self-preservation to escape from an unsupportive environment during the reform of the small schools and to resist educational inequities they perceived were being perpetuated by their school district (Peters, 2012). These studies point to what Shields (2012) described as the starting point for transformative leadership, acknowledging that the material reality of leading is affected by inequities.

Finding 2: Hybrid Conception of Leader/Leadership/Leading as Contextualized Consciousness

Transformative leadership is not just about heroic individuals or just about organizations but about participation and collaborative creation (Montuori & Donnelly, 2017). We refer to this individuals–organizations relationship as a hybrid conception that alternates between leader/leadership/leading (people, capacity, and process involving individuals, groups, and organizations affecting the cocreation of one another). While the focus on the leader and leadership was not uncommon in studies of micro-level experience of individuals (Horsford, 2012), we now discuss the literature that addressed the leader, leadership, *and* leading, and the subfinding—contextualized sociopolitical consciousness.

In a subset of articles, researchers challenged the person-centric notion of leadership with a hybrid conception of leader/leadership/leading supported by intersectionality. They most consistently undermined a person-centric framing of problems and solutions around a single "leader," and instead treated leading as an expression of power (i.e., agency) related to the value of relationality and communality rather than individualism (Alston, 2005; Nicholson & Maniates, 2015) involving individual and collaborative efforts (Capper, 2015), and modeled or advocated for a contextualized sociopolitical consciousness (García & Byrne-Jiménez, 2016; López, 2016). The first two articles discussed are essays based in different critical traditions (Indigenous knowledge, postmodern thought; Alston, 2005; Nicholson & Maniates, 2015), followed by a review of research (Capper, 2015); all draw from different traditions associated with intersectionality.

Alston (2005) relied on intersectionality to recapture the ways in which Black women in leadership roles have transferred their multiple marginality status into leadership practice. She paired intersectionality with tempered radicalism and servant leadership to argue that a form of tempered radicalism enacted by Black women has been neglected in leadership theories. She argued that in the historiography of educational leadership, there is evidence that power once intended to serve as a mechanism of oppression was transformed by Black women "into an effective instrument for constructive change" (p. 677). To analyze their form of tempered radicalism, she used a framework centering Afrocentric philosophy involving relationality, agency, identities, and sociopolitical historiography, based on intersectionality as described by Crenshaw (1991) and Collins (2000). Alston (2005) theoretically challenged the person-centric notion of the heroic leader with the communal notion of servant leadership. The essay by Nicholson and Maniates (2015) also referred to tempered radicals (Meyerson, 2001).

Nicholson and Maniates (2015) argued that modernist notions of leadership as rational, simple, and linear must be replaced by postmodern notions of leadership as relational and distributed. Intersectionality as a concept, they argued, can accommodate the complexity of early childhood leadership, where power is shared among professionals with multiple selves/identities. They drew on a multilevel model of intersectionality from the higher education literature, which includes attention to domains of power and the contexts of the past and present. Yet, in describing a first-generation Latina, they used social role descriptors (a small business owner) and general dispositional qualities (i.e., self-confidence in public speaking, nervous), thereby conflating the first level of the model, axes of identity (Crenshaw, 1989), with social contexts (i.e., organizational), and domains of power (i.e., formal positions, relationships). Nicholson and Maniates described her agency as an act of "subverting her state-licensing board's mandated use of bleach by quietly using an environmentally friendly alternative" (p. 74). The example failed to address the confluence of social power that perpetuates oppression, constitutes the marginalization of (some) identities, and influences which ways of being are recognized as enactments of leading.

It should be noted that the Latina they described was a character in the book by Meyerson (2001), who focused on the field of business. Still we wondered how their discussion of her might have been different if their intersectional analysis had been paired with Black and/or Chicana/Mestiza (Indigenous) thought and/or grounded in more recent contributions provided by Collins and Crenshaw. Models and tools can guide but do not ensure that researchers can hold together an analysis of leading within multiple, entangled, and interpenetrating forces.

In reviewing the use of CRT in educational leadership, Capper (2015) described six tenets across the literature, one of which was intersectionality. Citing Crenshaw (1991), she described intersectionality as a way to "consider race across races and the intersection of race with other identities and differences" (p. 795), and referred to the leader and leadership. She provided several descriptions of leading practices in connection to inequities in education and within a collective, such as teams including students and input from their families. Her focus was on intersectionality as a tool to analyze policies, practices, and injustices affecting students.

Sociopolitical Consciousness in Context

López (2016) and García and Byrne-Jiménez (2016) drew on critical race and feminist perspectives (i.e., Black feminist thought, Latino critical theory), related leadership to agency such as resistance and activism, expressed concerns about multiple intersecting oppressions, interpreted problems from the micro-level to the macro-level, and discussed sociopolitical consciousness in context.

López (2016) situated her argumentative essay in critical pedagogical perspectives, Chicana feminist epistemology and Black and Chicana feminist notions of intersectionality, "influenced by Kimberly [*sic*] Crenshaw (1989, 1991)" (p. 133). She advocated for Chicano/Latino students, education, and educational leadership that can "disrupt the talons of corporate interests in and out of education" (p. 137). She switched between person-centric narratives of the educational "leader" to "leadership" as an expression of agency among political actors, in a "culture of control and governmentality" (p. 134). Although at times López advanced the person-centric notion of leadership, she also situated the individual and problem in a broader sociopolitical context (culture of control) across sectors (corporate, education), attended to past conceptions of leadership, and connected leading (to disrupt the talons) to broader social problems such as immigration. The problems toward which she analytically directed intersectionality were not only those experienced or perceived by individuals but also those developed in the context of leading across people and political conditions affected by intersectoral systemic oppressions (corporate, government).

García and Byrne-Jiménez (2016) offered a pointed critique of educational leadership as operating under a normative White, male lens and related intersectionality to leadership, race (Afro/Black), and ethnicity (Latino, Dominicano, Dominican American). In this call to "emerge," they recentered the person-centric notion of leadership as the "Afro-Latino leader" (p. 135). This was the only study describing leadership enacted by a man, who was one of the researchers (García). While they provided detailed descriptions of his life prior to becoming an assistant principal, they offered little explicit description of specific leading activity while in that role and none that exposed (1) how his efforts to challenge social injustice as an Afro-Latino man differed from traditional leadership approaches or (2) how his male privilege and linguistic capital affected how he was able to lead or advance into an administrative role.

They argued that Afro-Latino perspectives can empower disenfranchised communities to join with other communities to transform the education system, which situated race and ethnicity as political and social tools for use in analyzing power dynamics. They concluded by urging educational leadership scholars to "emerge from the shadow of their own complacency" in neglecting the "intersectionality and unique experiences of Afro-Latinos" (García & Byrne-Jiménez, 2016, p. 135), and described how leadership as an agency can be a source of inspiration for collective transformation.

Those who grounded their use of intersectionality in the broader knowledge project of CRT or a variation such as LatCrit, or in combination with philosophical principles and branches of epistemology, such as Black feminist thought based on Afrocentric (Indigenous) knowledge, were able to discuss leaders, leadership, and leading with attention to social consciousness, criticism, and actions that help promote equity and justice. Intersecting identities can also be a source of collective agency, alliance, and political activism to challenge inequities in education, including the person-centric conception of leadership, which can pave the way for a recentering of individualism and narratives of heroism.

Finding 3: Intersectionality as Emergent Knowledge in Educational Leadership

The third finding is informed by the first two on the focus of the analysis (micro-level) and the conceptions of leadership (person-centric), which is that intersectionality is emergent knowledge in educational leadership and its use is inchoate. Subfindings point to how intersectionality's oppositional force and analytical power is at risk of being depleted by its appearance as a floating signifier, its detachment from oppositional knowledge projects, and its separation from philosophical principles that have helped constitute it and guide the development of researchers' dispositions and processes of inquiry.

Conceptual clarity about what intersectionality is, how it is used, and how it is defined through empirical study affects the strength of the knowledge base produced around it and its subsequent use. Concepts represent abstractions and inform theory construction. According to Watt and Van Den Berg (2002), the research community benefits when researchers clarify the meaning(s) and use(s) of concepts. Conceptual clarity

- Allows other researchers to critically examine the definitions or replicate the investigation using the concept(s)
- Allows validity to be enhanced, since other researchers understand the concepts that can be improved and used
- Allows other researchers to use the concept(s) in measuring or devising a conceptual scheme
- Allows other researchers to account for conflicting findings in different studies, focusing on the same phenomenon

In other words, conceptual clarity can support conceptual acuity among researchers in the field and in their reading of scholarship produced by other researchers. Theoretical definitions of intersectionality would clarify its meanings to readers, whereas operational definitions would clarify its use in the study, such as the purpose it serves. The extent to which intersectionality continues as oppositional knowledge in educational leadership depends on how well it serves the construction and maintenance of knowledge, which "is a vitally important part of the social relations of domination and resistance" (Collins, 2000, p. 221).

Floating Signifier

Across this sample, intersectionality was a floating signifier (Hall, 1996). It was not always clear to us when its general use of the term (to describe a condition or relationship) ended and its use as an analytical construct began. Researchers referred to intersectionality as a concept (Peters, 2012; Witherspoon & Arnold, 2010; Witherspoon & Taylor, 2010), framework, theory (Liang & Peters-Hawkins, 2017; Nicholson & Maniates, 2015), or notion (López, 2016). It was sometimes used to qualify perspectives or experiences (Bass, 2009; Horsford, 2012; Liang et al., 2016; Welton et al., 2015). At other times, the term was altered, as in "intersected world" (Liang et al., 206), "intersected" or replaced by terms such as "identity complexities" (Welton et al., 2015). For instance, Welton et al. (2015) referred to "compounded oppression" but did not explain it or cite a resource that offered a definition. Still, we included this article since compounded oppression is an antecedent of intersectionality, and the researchers also used the term "intersected" to describe participants' experiences with social oppression. This was the only study that focused on participants in leadership preparation programs.

Collins and Crenshaw situated their work in the history of broader knowledge projects with which they were engaged (Collins with Black feminist thought, Crenshaw with CRT) and cited previous contributors to those projects. This brings us to the next subfinding associated with intersectionality as an emergent knowledge project within the oppositional knowledge project of transformative leadership: attribution through citation. Attribution concerns the ways in which credit is assigned through citation practices, which has implications for the historical record and the development of careers, legacies, and research agendas.

Citing as a Practice of Power

Academic citing is a knowledge/power practice involved in the marginalization and subjugation of certain types of intellectual labor. Across the sample, we found examples of citation practices that were misleading, such as when the researchers attributed intersectionality to others (Liang & Peters-Hawkins, 2017), or cited Crenshaw in a way that suggested she contributed a feature to intersectionality (Liang et al., 2016; Nicholson & Maniates, 2015). Liang et al. (2016), for instance, wrote "interconnected and constructed social identities" (Collins, 2000), followed by "intersected experiences" (Crenshaw, 1989), before the "concept of intersectionality," which they did not attribute to anyone (p. 5). Then, they described intersectionality as such: "and intersectionality, which examines the multiplicative aspects of a person's identity in informing their experiences (McCall, 2005, p. 25)" (p. 5). This citation pattern may lead readers who are unfamiliar with the history and trajectory of intersectionality to reasonably surmise that Crenshaw and Collins provided some ideas that McCall brought together in order to define intersectionality. Welton et al. (2015) did not cite any of the scholarship that contributed to the development of the concept of intersectionality.

Through citation, intellectual contributions and meaningful connections with broader literatures can be traced (May, 2014), whereas the lack of citation disconnects intersectionality from its genealogical trajectory and the contextual dynamics under which it is paired with other oppositional knowledge projects.

Relating Research to an Oppositional Knowledge Process

Only one researcher described the philosophical underpinnings of their methodology in connection to the work of scholars they cited when describing intersectionality. Jean-Marie (2013) situated Collins's (2000) epistemological tenets of Black feminist thought in her conceptual framework, which was composed of Afrocentric epistemology and gendered racism, which she used to analyze data at the intersection of age, race, and gender. She described how she purposefully designed the study to privilege feminist perspectives and combined case study with a dialogical approach to conducting four group interviews with two participants. She wrote,

A dialogical approach encourages individuals to participate in a pool of shared meanings while reflecting on their perspectives. Since both participants have similar characteristics, the dialogical approach (e.g., group interview) provided them an opportunity to reflect and share their experiences with each other. (p. 620)

It should be noted that the data collection activities spanned a year and a half, which extended the time and opportunities with which the participants were supported to engage in a dialogical process.

In discussing the findings, Jean-Marie (2013) referred back to her data generation process, stating that the two women developed a close relationship, continued to help each other, and stayed connected. The participants began to seek each other out "to obtain moral support" (p. 635). The methodological choices made by Jean-Marie, which were based on philosophical tenets and justified theoretically (i.e., feminist, Black feminist theory), affected the design of the study and the participants. Her research process afforded them opportunities to build a relationship where they could obtain moral support while navigating through common barriers. Her approach reflected what Capper (2015) recommended researchers using intersectionality do; consciously address intersectionality in the formation of the problem, question, design, and process of conducting research.

DISCUSSION

Although CRT, and with it, intersectionality, entered the educational leadership scholarship in the 2000s, transformative leadership has at least a decade longer body of literature from which to draw. The sample of literature reviewed herein suggests that the body of research claiming to use intersectionality remains inchoate in the field of educational leadership and in its support for the development of transformative leadership practice and scholarship. Following Collins's (2016) discussion of what can be done to ensure that intersectionality stimulates oppositional knowledge, we point out the importance of research in examining and documenting transformative leadership as an oppositional knowledge project and the support that intersectionality can offer to studies of educational leadership. This includes, as noted by Collins (2016), how the work of researchers is developed and practiced with regard to identifying, problematizing, and criticizing existing knowledge and the broader social world while attempting to solve or stimulate new ways to solve problems.

Critiques of Power and Oppression

Critiques of oppression and oppressive forces in the sample of articles were more subdued than we anticipated, given that intersectionality is rooted in Black women's liberation politics and CRT in legal studies. More pointed critiques of oppression were evident in articles that situated intersectionality alongside critical theories such as LatCrit, critical pedagogy, and critical (prophetic) spirituality. These few articles exposed uneven power relations beyond the leader's identity related to systemic inequities within education, especially those concerning discipline and funding. For example, López (2016) offered an analysis of structural inequities and framed educational leadership practices as forms of resistance and activism, especially for Chicano/Latino communities. This subset of articles targeted the meso-level (societal norms and practices promoted in the field of educational leadership, school districts, and the curriculum and instruction of educational preparation programs), while deconstructing notions of leadership as a secular performance of an idealized White man devoid of an ethic of care.

Transformative practices in research and leading aim to expose uneven power relations at various levels and contexts of decision making in public spaces or with social movements involving students and communities, as illustrated by Collins's (2016) reference to the #BlackLivesMatter movement. Across the sample, researchers named the intersections of social categories of identity, but often apart from examining structural oppressions (e.g., racism, sexism, and ageism) in conjunction with leading practices. For instance, several researchers neglected to discuss how the individual is shaped by structural systems of power. While pointing out how religion and spirituality guided participants navigating personal and professional expectations, they neglected to describe the power and oppression associated with their systems of belief, such as how those systems contribute to colonization, genocides, racism, and sexism (Grosfoguel, 2016).

Additionally, what participants attempted or wanted to enact were not discussed by the researchers problematically or situated in broader sociopolitical issues. For instance, one participant who attempted to establish a policy requiring that students wear school uniforms described feeling resistance from parents of Black students (Reed, 2012). This effort could have been interrogated or at least situated in the literature that relates mandatory school uniforms to the socialization of students of color to enter the school-to-prison pipeline. In another instance, a participant demonstrated care by asking a student who was being sent to jail if he was hungry (Bass, 2009). This was a missed opportunity to connect the incident, and leading as caring, to disparities in school discipline. It is in such examples, of blurred lines between decisions that will ignore, improve, and/or worsen a situation, where researchers can demystify how educational leadership and scholarship serves as a transformative knowledge project. Otherwise, readers are left to think of leading as a mythical phenomenon. It is important that inequities affecting politically minoritized social groups be erased, and not their presence in the field. In the context of transformative leadership, this also means that their experiences, practices, and belief systems are also open to critique as part of historically situated power relations and systems of domination.

Researching and Leading Relationally

At the onset of the review process, we anticipated that we would learn much about how leadership and intersectionality were being paired to study the inequities affecting groups of students, such as how school- or district-based administrators are involved in issues spanning from classrooms to courtrooms (i.e., discipline, disability, community protest). In retrospect, we were more stringent in our search for "intersectionality" than we were for "leadership." We assumed that leading practices would be made evident through specific accounts and were surprised at how few descriptions were provided to illustrate the daily experiences of leading to connect theoretical understandings of "leadership" with concrete images of "leading." General practices such as building trust, setting a vision, and increasing morale were implicit, but the efforts involved were seldom described. We concur with Witherspoon and Arnold (2010) that "ordinary day-to-day administrative practices must become more of a focal point in understanding how administrators actually engage in the process of social justice" (p. 221).

To emphasize researching as a relational process is to resist the recentering of the individual self (the researcher) apart from others. Research and researchers starting from the assumption that leading is a distributed and relational network of interactions and that encounters can open a window to students' experiences. Methodologically, this was exemplified by Jean-Marie (2013), who produced brief detailed reports of activities involving interactions and encounters based on notes she took during her onsite-based observations of two Black women serving as school principals. Under the heading, "The daily challenge of putting out fires: Caring for children," she provided the following excerpt describing how she and one of the participants responded to an alert that two kindergarten boys had left the school building:

Panicking, Principal Gilbert and I jumped in her car to search the neighboring premises while her security personnel also went searching for the boys. Fortunately, the boys were found unharmed. . . . Principal Gilbert was relieved that her "babies were safe" and she gave them a motherly and tough lecture about their misconduct while waiting to meet [with] the boys' parents. She also had a stern conversation with her security personnel because of the [their] failure to follow specific procedures. I was privy to her interactions with various individuals involved in the situation; her determination to deal with the different stakeholders provided some initial insights about her leadership style: assertive, caring, and decisive. (p. 624)

The use of observations and interviews, coupled with reports from researcher(s) on the praxeology of the study, and decisions made in the process of conducting the study, allowed us to better understand the interconnectedness of this researcher's and her participants' praxis. While the examples of the participants' responses illustrate a web of relations across power differentials, there was no discussion of students' experiences in relation to patterns of inequities or shared decision making.

This sample illustrates how despite the recent trend in educational leadership away from the modernist notion of leading as a linear practice, and toward a conception of leadership as a distributed web of influence focused on structures, programs, and processes (Crevani, Lindgren, & Packendorff, 2010), the person-centric conception is still discursively embedded in the literature. Given that some researchers were able to criticize the field and its contributions to forms of oppression while illustrating the benefits of both person-centric and relational leading, perhaps Capper and Young's (2014) suggestion to blend the heroic and collaborative approaches is a third way forward for using intersectionality to study educational leadership. More specifically, the hybrid conception of leader/leadership/leading may assist those using intersectionality to examine how the problems under study are affected by forces of power and privilege exercised across micro-climates and macro-sectors that influence how just and equitable education is, in its processes and outcomes, for groups.

Resistance to Individualism as a Political Stance

Crenshaw's (1991) articulation of intersectionality assumed that the more comprehensive the analyses of social problems were, the more likely effective social actions would result—redefining the individual, which reshapes the political and reorients the individual (Collins, 2009). Hence, the organizational–individual and the isolated individual divide is blurred in this view of identity and problem re-creation and re-orientation.

By focusing on the individual's experience, the sample illustrated how workplace discrimination at the intersection of marginalized identities continues alongside the growing expectation that school leadership teams will lead alliances and coalitions of educators away from oppressive policies and practices, and toward social justice.[3] By focusing on the individual's experience, the use of alliance building, coalition building, social movements, fellowship, mentoring networks, and other relational practices that provide a collective struggle against shared experiences with oppression remained underrepresented. An oppositional stance to individualism can be taken up in research that examines coordinated action against oppression.

Whereas Capper (2015) pointed to the role of CRT and intersectionality in addressing inequities faced by students rather than by those leading in schools or districts, the main focus in a majority of the articles in the sample was on inequities encountered by those working in educational leadership positions who researchers often described as Asian, Latina, Afro-Latino, and African American/Black women. We were left wondering how Capper's (2015) questions for those using intersectionality while leading might be revised in light of the findings from this sample to consider the barriers and opportunities one can face and overcome when entering educational leadership programs as faculty and/or researchers, alone or as a member of a collective or coalition.

Intersectionality and transformative leadership theory both provide multiple and overlapping recommendations (i.e., engaging in criticism, reflection, and action toward social transformation). Based on the findings of this review, we offer two recommendations (acuity and intersectoral analysis) to support the development of research projects involving analytical focus and critique that is sharp and broad.

RECOMMENDATIONS

The following recommendations take into account the findings, lessons learned, and questions raised in the process of conducting the review, as well as our background knowledge to inspire studies that extend the field's engagement with intersectionality. To the question of how intersectionality and transformative educational leadership can be of service to one another and to what end, we offer two recommendations aimed at documenting and ameliorating historically marginalizing policies and practices that negatively affect groups and individuals: to bring a sharper focus to the issues and a more trenchant criticism when engaging intersectionality in educational leadership. We understand, as Clegg (2005) asserted, criticism is complex and arduous. We recognize that in the attempt to hold together an analysis of multiple forces associated with multiple oppressions, the labor of critique is magnified as is its urgency. The following recommendations are intended to support the field of educational leadership, scholarship and practice, through and beyond its emergent engagement with intersectionality.

Conceptual Acuity

According to Capper (2015), educational leadership scholars interested in transforming education to be more socially just must "consciously address intersectionality in the problem, formation, research questions, and conduct of their studies" (p. 825). This argument expands intersectionality from simply being a way to analyze to being a way to design and conduct studies. Capper (2015) situated intersectionality within an overarching framework of CRT and argued for the study of races and other categories of social identity affected by powers and privileges. In other words, she provided conceptual clarity around intersectionality by positioning it in relationship to broader theoretically based political movements toward social justice. Such clarity provides a more solid grounding for her statement, as well as for the work of those who might respond to her call and design research to explore and explain leading practices associated with transformative leadership. The following recommendations, beginning with conceptual acuity, are meant to be supportive of the developing research on transformative leadership and intersectionality.

Acuity denotes keen thought, vision, and action that can guide researchers in the work of conceptualizing, conducting, reporting, and disseminating research. More specifically, we suggest beginning with conceptual acuity, which stems from clear conceptual and operational descriptions and definitions based on a range of resources. With regard to intersectionality, this means seeking conceptual clarity on what intersectionality is and what one is enlisting intersectionality to do, in addition to other concepts and how they are understood in relationship to intersectionality. Conceptual vagueness regarding intersectionality and its usefulness in educational leadership research places intersectionality at risk of being appropriated in the depoliticization of transformative educational leadership.

Understanding how researchers are engaging intersectionality entails investigating how they are not engaging it to its fullest expression. Looking ahead, researchers might explore (1) how and why other tenets associated with variations of CRT, such as interest convergence, have traveled into educational leadership unaccompanied by intersectionality and (2) why critical race feminism (mentioned by Horsford, 2012) has not yet seen the same flight across fields and into educational leadership. Conceptual acuity can support perceptual acuity, and together can support a sharper critique of oppressive forces. To that end citing more recent examples of work by Collins and Crenshaw applying intersectionality across sectors (i.e., media, juvenile justice) can be informative beyond describing its historical development. This brings us to our second recommendation, which is to focus intersectionality on complex problems associated with inequity by considering the forces emerging from various sectors of society.

Intersectionality Across Sectors (Intersectoral Analysis)

The majority of leading activities described in the sample concerned economic inequities, which suggests a need for researchers to pay attention to macroeconomic sectors (e.g., household, business, government, foreign) that affect what is consumed, produced, and regulated, within and outside of the educational organizations. We recommend future studies of educational leadership take an intersectoral analysis approach, which means examining how educational inequities are influenced by multiple sectors, paired with intersecting social group identities and social issues (Agosto & Rolle, 2014). For instance, issues about which school has its laboratory funded, how many buses are available to transport which students, and which students' Internet searches via school-based computers will be surveilled are all part of elaborate funding structures involving taxation, property, and access to virtual/physical places such as learning modules, schools, or science laboratories. Implicated in these issues are housing, technology, and science sectors to name a few. Intersectoral analysis paired with intersectionality can bring attention to the complexity of injustice and deliberation over which interventions will alleviate or exacerbate it. For example, how one responds to chronic student absenteeism depends on how one understands the cause of it. Students who are the primary caregivers for adults may be compensating for inequity in the health care system that underserves racially minoritized families. Thus, caring, compassion, and grant seeking to support home tutors or transition to a full-service model of schooling are options one might consider over others.

In addition to an intersectoral analysis, we encourage researchers in educational leadership to point intersectionality analytically across micro- to macro-levels, as others have done across the social sciences. This could include studying how the lack of choice in housing and choice options in education contribute to displacement or excessive mobility associated with poor school performance, or how public planners of urban landscapes reimagine them when students participate in mapping a community's wealth and desires. Researchers in educational leadership and practitioners might learn from youth leadership research using intersectionality at multiple crossroads of being, such as queer activists involved in social movements from various locations in the crosshairs of immigration reform.[4] Intersectionality and transformative educational leadership share common aims and features that, if further supported by conceptual acuity and intersectoral analysis, can be used in research to better understand the past, monitor the present, and foreshadow the future.[5]

ACKNOWLEDGMENT

We would like to acknowledge the editorial team and reviewers for their vision and support throughout the process.

NOTES

[1]For examples of studies mentioning intersect or intersectional, and focused on multiply, marginalized identities and leadership career paths, see Davis, Gooden, and Bowers (2017) and Reed and Evans (2008).

[2]In our initial search, we found a conceptual paper presented by Lumby (2014) at a conference that focused on intersectionality. However, it was later published by Lumby and Morrison (2010) with much less attention to intersectionality.

[3]For an example of current research engaging intersectionality focus on workplace prejudice, see Jones et al. (2017).

[4]For an example of intersectionality used in a study of queer youth leadership in the immigrant rights movement, see Terriquez (2015).

[5]Gibson and Tarrant (2010) describe leadership toward organization resilience and argue that how organizations respond to that which enhances or degrades their resilience will depend on how they exercise acuity (understand the past, monitor the present, and foreshadow the future).

ORCID ID

Vonzell Agosto (iD) https://orcid.org/0000-0002-6970-7376

REFERENCES

References marked with an asterisk indicate studies included in the literature review.
Agosto, V., & Rolle, R. A. (2014). An intersectoral policy framework: Technology and obesity intersecting on schoolchildren. In C. A. Grant, & E. Zwier (Eds.), *Intersectionality and urban education: Identities, policies, spaces & power* (pp. 293–310). Charlotte, NC: Information Age.

*Alston, J. A. (2005). Tempered radicals and servant leaders: Black females persevering in the superintendency. *Educational Administration Quarterly, 41*, 675–688.

Andrews, A. R. (1993). Balancing the personal and professional. In J. James, & R. Farmer (Eds.), *Spirit, space, and survival: African American women in (White) academe* (pp. 179–195). New York, NY: Routledge.

Anzaldúa, G. (1987). *Borderlands/La Frontera: The new Mestiza*. San Francisco, CA: Spinsters/Aunt Lute.

*Bass, L. (2009). Fostering an ethics of care in leadership: A conversation with five African American women. *Advances in Developing Human Resources, 11*, 619–632.

Blackmore, J. (2013). A feminist critical perspective on educational leadership. *International Journal of Leadership in Education, 16*, 139–154.

Bloom, C. M., & Erlandson, D. A. (2003). African American women principals in urban schools: Realities, (re)constructions, and resolutions. *Educational Administration Quarterly, 39*, 339–369.

Blount, J. M. (1998). *Destined to rule the schools: Women and the superintendency, 1873–1995*. New York: State University of New York Press.

Brooks, J. S., & Jean-Marie, G. (2007). Black leadership, White leadership: Race and race relations in an urban high school. *Journal of Educational Administration, 45*, 756–768.

Burns, J. M. (1978). *Leadership: Transformational leadership, transactional leadership*. New York, NY: Harper & Row.

Byrd, M. Y. (2009). Telling our stories of leadership: If we don't tell them they won't be told. *Advances in Developing Human Resources, 11*, 582–606.

Capper, C. A. (1989). *Transformative leadership: Embracing student diversity in democratic schooling* (ED 305 714). Madison: University of Wisconsin Press.

*Capper, C. A. (2015). The 20th-year anniversary of critical race theory in education: Implications for leading to eliminate racism. *Educational Administration Quarterly, 51*, 791–833.

Capper, C. A., & Green, T. L. (2013). Organizational theories and the development of leadership capacity for integrated, socially just schools. In L. Tillman, & J. J. Scheurich (Eds.), *Handbook of educational leadership for equity and diversity* (pp. 62–82). New York, NY: Routledge.

Capper, C. A., & Young, M. D. (2014). Ironies and limitations of educational leadership for social justice: A call to social justice educators. *Theory Into Practice, 53*, 158–164.

Carbado, D. W., Crenshaw, K. W., Mays, V. M., & Tomlinson, B. (2013). Intersectionality. *Du Bois Review: Social Science Research on Race, 10*, 303–312.

Cho, S., Crenshaw, K. W., & McCall, L. (2013). Toward a field of intersectionality studies: Theory, applications, and praxis. *Signs: Journal of Women in Culture and Society, 38*, 785–810.

Clegg, S. (2005). Evidence-based practice in educational research: A critical realist critique of systematic review. *British Journal of Sociology of Education, 26*, 415–428.

Collins, P. H. (1998). It's all in the family: Intersections of gender, race, and nation. *Hypatia, 13*(3), 62–82.

Collins, P. H. (2000). *Black feminist thought: Knowledge, consciousness, and the politics of empowerment* (2nd ed.). New York, NY: Routledge.

Collins, P. H. (2009). Piecing together a genealogical puzzle: Intersectionality and American pragmatism. *European Journal of Pragmatism and American Philosophy, 3*, 88–112.

Collins, P. H. (2016). Black feminist thought as oppositional knowledge. *Departures in Critical Qualitative Research, 5*, 133–144.

Collins, P. H., & Bilge, S. (2016). *Intersectionality*. Hoboken, NJ: John Wiley.

Combahee River Collective. (1981). A Black feminist statement. In C. Morága & G. Anzaldúa (Eds.), *This bridge called my back: Writings by radical women of color* (pp. 210–218). Watertown, MA: Persephone Press.

Crenshaw, K. W. (1988). Race, reform, and retrenchment: Transformation and legitimation in antidiscrimination law. *Harvard Law Review, 101*, 1331–1387.

Crenshaw, K. (1989). Demarginalizing the intersection of race and sex: A Black feminist critique of antidiscrimination doctrine, feminist theory, and antiracist politics. *University of Chicago Legal Forum, 1989*, 8. Retrieved from https://chicagounbound.uchicago.edu/uclf/vol1989/iss1/8/

Crenshaw, K. (1991). Mapping the margins: Intersectionality, identity politics, and violence against women of color. *Stanford Law Review, 43*, 1241–1299.

Crenshaw, K., Ocen, P., & Nanda, J. (2015). *Black girls matter: Pushed out, overpoliced, and underprotected.* New York, NY: Center for Intersectionality and Social Policy Studies, Columbia University.

Crevani, L., Lindgren, M., & Packendorff, J. (2010). Leadership, not leaders: On the study of leadership as practices and interactions. *Scandinavian Journal of Management, 26*, 77–86.

Dantley, M. E. (2010). Successful leadership in urban schools: Principals and critical spirituality, a new approach to reform. *Journal of Negro Education, 79*, 214–219.

Davis, B. W., Gooden, M. A., & Bowers, A. J. (2017). Pathways to the principalship: An event history analysis of the careers of teachers with principal certification. *American Educational Research Journal, 54*, 207–240.

Delgado Bernal, D. (2002). Critical race theory, LatCrit theory and critical raced-gendered epistemologies: Recognizing students of color as holders and creators of knowledge. *Qualitative Inquiry, 8*, 105–126.

Evers, C. W., & Lakomski, G. (2013). Methodological individualism, educational administration, and leadership. *Journal of Educational Administration and History, 45*, 159–173.

Foster, W. (1989). Toward a critical practice of leadership. In J. Smith (Ed.), *Critical perspectives on educational leadership* (pp. 39–62). New York, NY: Routledge, Falmer.

Freire, P. (1970). *Pedagogy of the oppressed.* New York, NY: Continuum.

*García, W., & Byrne-Jiménez, M. (2016). Out of the sombra: One Afro-Latino making his way in educational leadership. *National Forum of Educational Administration & Supervision Journal, 33*(2–3), 121–143.

Gibson, C. A., & Tarrant, M. (2010). A "conceptual models" approach to organisational resilience. *Australian Journal of Emergency Management, 25*(2), 6–12.

Giroux, H. A. (1988). *Teachers as intellectuals: Toward a critical pedagogy of learning.* Westport, CT: Greenwood.

Grosfoguel, R. (2016). What is racism? *Journal of World-Systems Research, 22*(1), 9–15.

Gross, C., Gottburgsen, A., & Phoenix, A. (2016). Education systems and intersectionality. In A. Hadjar, & C. Gross (Eds.). *Education systems and inequalities: International comparisons* (pp. 51–72). Chicago, IL: University of Chicago Press.

Hall, S. (1996). *Race: The floating signifier.* Northampton, MA: Media Education Foundation.

Hancock, A. M. (2013). Empirical intersectionality: A tale of two approaches. *UC Irvine Law Review, 3*, 259–296.

Hansot, E., & Tyack, D. (1981). *The dream deferred: A golden age for women school administrators* (Policy Paper No. 81-C2). Stanford, CA: Stanford University School of Education, Institute for Research on Educational Finance and Governance.

Harlan, L. R. (1957). The Southern Education Board and the race issue in public education. *Journal of Southern History, 23*, 189–202.

hooks, b. (1984). *Feminist theory: From margin to center.* Boston, MA: South End Press.

*Horsford, S. D. (2012). This bridge called my leadership: An essay on Black women as bridge leaders in education. *International Journal of Qualitative Studies in Education, 25*(1), 11–22.

*Jean-Marie, G. (2013). The subtlety of age, gender, and race barriers: A case study of early career African American female principals. *Journal of School Leadership, 23*, 615–639.

Jones, K. P., Sabat, I. E., King, E. B., Ahmad, A., McCausland, T. C., & Chen, T. (2017). Isms and schisms: A meta-analysis of the prejudice-discrimination relationship across racism, sexism, and ageism. *Journal of Organizational Behavior, 38*, 1076–1110.

King, D. K. (1995). Multiple jeopardy, multiple consciousness: The context of a Black feminist ideology. In B. Guy-Sheftall (Ed.), *Words of fire: An anthology of African American feminist thought* (pp. 294–317). New York, NY: New Press.

Larson, C. L., & Murtadha, K. (2003). Leadership for social justice. *Yearbook of the National Society for the Study of Education, 101*, 134–161.

*Liang, J. G., & Peters-Hawkins, A. L. (2017). "I am more than what I look alike": Asian American women in public school administration. *Educational Administration Quarterly, 53*, 40–69.

*Liang, J. G., Sottile, J., & Peters, A. L. (2016). Understanding Asian American women's pathways to school leadership. *Gender and Education*. Advance online publication. doi:1 0.1080/09540253.2016.1265645

Loder, T. L. (2005). Women administrators negotiate work-family conflicts in changing times: An intergenerational perspective. *Educational Administration Quarterly, 41*, 741–776.

*López, P. D. (2016). Leadership for Chicano/Latino education and the politics of change. *Association of Mexican American Educators Journal, 10*(3), 129–140.

Lumby, J. (2014, March). *Intersectionality theory and educational leadership: Help or hindrance?* Paper presentation at the British Educational Leadership, Management and Administration Special Interest Group, Gender and Leadership, Birmingham, England.

Lumby, J., & Morrison, M. (2010). Leadership and diversity: Theory and research. *School Leadership and Management, 30*(1), 3–17.

May, V. M. (2014). "Speaking into the void"? Intersectionality critiques and epistemic backlash. *Hypatia, 29*, 94–112.

McCall, L. (2005). The complexity of intersectionality. *Signs: Journal of Women in Culture and Society, 30*, 1771–1800.

Meyers, C. V., & Hambrick Hitt, D. (2017). School turnaround principals: What does initial research literature suggest they are doing to be successful? *Journal of Education for Students Placed at Risk, 22*(1), 38–56.

Meyerson, D. (2001). *Tempered radicals: How people use difference to inspire change at work.* Boston, MA: Harvard Business School Press.

Mezirow, J. (1991). *Transformative dimensions of adult learning.* San Francisco, CA: Jossey-Bass.

Montuori, A., & Donnelly, G. (2017). Transformative leadership. In J. Neal (Ed.), *Handbook of personal and organizational transformation* (pp. 1–33). Dordrecht, Netherlands: Springer.

Natapoff, A. (1995). Anatomy of a debate: Intersectionality and equality for deaf children from non-English speaking homes. *Journal of Law & Education, 24*, 271–278.

*Nicholson, J., & Maniates, H. (2015). Recognizing postmodern intersectional identities in leadership for early childhood. *Early Years, 36*(1), 66–80.

Núñez, A. (2014). Employing multilevel intersectionality in educational research: Latino identifies, contexts, and college access. *Educational Researcher, 43*(2), 85–92.

*Peters, A. L. (2012). Leading through the challenge of change: African-American women principals on small school reform. *International Journal of Qualitative Studies in Education, 25*(1), 23–38.

Quantz, R., Cambron-McCabe, N., Dantley, M., & Hachem, A. H. (2017). Culture-based leadership. *International Journal of Leadership in Education, 20*, 376–392.

Quantz, R. A., Rogers, J., & Dantley, M. (1991). Rethinking transformative leadership: Toward democratic reform of schools. *Journal of Education, 173*, 96–118.

*Reed, L. C. (2012). The intersection of race and gender in school leadership for three Black female principals. *International Journal of Qualitative Studies in Education, 25*, 39–58.

Reed, L., & Evans, A. E. (2008). What you see is [not always] what you get! Dispelling race and gender leadership assumptions. *International Journal of Qualitative Studies in Education, 21*, 487–499.

Ritzer, G. (2007). *Contemporary sociological theory and its classical roots: The basics*. Boston, MA: McGraw-Hill.

Roland, E. (2016, November). *Understanding intersectionality to promote social justice in education leadership*. Paper presentation at the University Council for Educational Administration Annual Convention, Detroit, MI.

Rousmaniere, K. (2007). Presidential address: Go to the principal's office: Toward a social history of the school principal in North America. *History of Education Quarterly, 47*(1), 1–22.

Santamaría, L. J., & Santamaría, A. P. (2013). *Applied critical leadership in education: Choosing change*. New York, NY: Routledge.

Scanlan, M., & Theoharis, G. (2016). Introduction to special issue—Intersectionality: Promoting social justice while navigating multiple dimensions of diversity. *Journal of Cases in Educational Leadership, 19*(1), 3–5.

Shields, C. M. (2010). Transformative leadership: Working for equity in diverse contexts. *Educational Administration Quarterly, 46*, 558–589.

Shields, C. M. (2011). Transformative leadership: An introduction. *Counterpoints, 409*, 1–17.

Shields, C. M. (2012). *Transformative leadership in education: Equitable change in an uncertain and complex world*. New York: NY: Routledge.

Shoben, E. W. (1980). Compound discrimination: The interaction of race and sex in employment discrimination. *New York University Law Review, 55*, 793–837.

Tate, W. F., IV. (2005). Ethics, engineering and the challenge of racial reform in education. *Race, Ethnicity and Education, 8*(1), 121–127.

Terriquez, V. (2015). Intersectional mobilization, social movement spillover, and queer youth leadership in the immigrant rights movement. *Social Problems, 62*, 343–362.

Tyack, D. B., & Hansot, E. (1982). *Managers of virtue: Public school leadership in America, 1820–1980*. New York, NY: Basic Books.

Watt, J. H., & Van Den Berg, S. (2002). *Elements of scientific theories: Concepts and definitions. Research methods for communication science*. Boston, MA: Allyn & Bacon.

*Welton, A. D., Mansfield, K. C., Lee, P. L., & Young, M. D. (2015). Mentoring educational leadership doctoral students: Using methodological diversification to examine gender and identity intersections. *International Journal of Educational Leadership Preparation, 10*(2), 53–81.

*Witherspoon, N., & Arnold, B. M. (2010). Pastoral care: Notions of caring and the Black female principal. *Journal of Negro Education, 79*, 220–232.

*Witherspoon, N., & Taylor, D. L. (2010). Spiritual weapons: Black female principals and religio-spirituality. *Journal of Educational Administration and History, 42*, 133–158.

Wolfswinkel, J. F., Furtmueller, E., & Wilderom, C. P. M. (2011). Using grounded theory as a method for rigorously reviewing literature. *European Journal of Information Systems, 22*(1), 1–11.

Zane, N. (2002). The glass ceiling is the floor my boss walks on: Leadership challenges in managing diversity. *Journal of Applied Behavioral Science, 38*, 334–353.

Chapter 12

Intersectionality Dis/ability Research: How Dis/ability Research in Education Engages Intersectionality to Uncover the Multidimensional Construction of Dis/abled Experiences

David I. Hernández-Saca
University of Northern Iowa

Laurie Gutmann Kahn
Moravian College

Mercedes A. Cannon
Indiana University-Purdue University Indianapolis

The purpose of this chapter is to systematically review the research within the field of education that explicitly examined how various social constructions of identity intersect with dis/ability to qualitatively affect young adults' experiences by asking the following question: What are the key findings in education research focusing on youth and young adults with disabilities who are multiply situated in terms of race, gender, social class, sexual orientation, or other social markers? Our conceptual framework included a sociohistorical approach that culled from intersectionality and disability studies in education that centered on the intersectional lived experiences of youth within K–16 educational contexts. In our research, we found 10 qualifying studies that illuminated how youth create meaning along the lines of their disabilities and their intersections, and we summarized these within the following three themes: (a) navigate intersectional disability discourses, (b) present their dis/ability oppression as intersectional, and (c) engage in their identity meaning making as a form of intersectional discourse. We conclude by situating these findings within the larger body of intersectionality disability studies in education research and provide future implications.

Review of Research in Education
March 2018, Vol. 42, pp. 286–311
DOI: 10.3102/0091732X18762439

"Ain't nobody gonna get me down!" —Kiesha (Petersen, 2009, p. 434)

Critical special education and disabilities studies in education (DSE) scholars have called for an adoption of an intersectionality framework to better understand the political, emotional, sociocultural, and historical contexts of dis/ability[1] and its effect on lived experience within schools (Blanchett, Klingner & Harry, 2009; García & Ortiz, 2013). The formation of dis/abled, racialized, gendered, sexualized projects are mutually constituted and shape the education of youth and young adults with dis/abilities. We view the intersectionality framework as necessary to be fully inclusive of these identities. Intersectionality, a term Kimberlé Crenshaw (1991) coined in her work examining how women of color, particularly Black women, experience employment discrimination and violence, explains how the experiences of individuals who occupy multiple marginalized identities can be silenced by intersectional forms of oppression.[2] Intersectionality theorists argue that locations of oppression and discrimination interact and shape the multiple dimensions of those experiencing them in a way that is not fully captured by separate examinations of each hegemonic system.

Despite the critical special education and DSE community's efforts toward understanding how disability is inextricably linked with ideologies of race, gender, sexual orientation, and other markers of difference, most theories of inequity within the educational landscape have ignored disability in its analysis (Artiles, 2013; Ferri, 2010). We situate the interlocking nature of disability and other markers of identity from a sociohistorical approach to draw attention to how these markers have influenced the education of students with dis/abilities. In other words, by a sociohistorical approach, we frame youth and young adults' intersectional identities as being socially constructed and positioned within historical, economic, political, and emotional contexts of their unique identities. These do not only involve the historical legacies of such identity groups but how they and others have made sense of such identities in the now—the latter of which influence how they phenomenologically make sense of who they are at their intersections. The purpose of this chapter is to systematically review empirical studies that examined how social constructions of identity intersect with dis/ability to qualitatively affect youths' and young adults' experiences in schools and classrooms *on the ground*.[3] In this review, we ask: *What are the key findings in education research focusing on youth and young adults with disabilities who are multiply situated in terms of race, gender, social class, sexual orientation, or other social markers?*

After centering the significance of this work during the contemporary societal and political changes within the United States, we outline our conceptual framework and present our own positionalities. We then present our methods, followed by our findings, which we intertwine with the actual voices of multiply oppressed individuals with dis/abilities, and then discuss their implications. Finally, we end with our conclusions for theory, research, and praxis—the coupling of both critical reflection and action—for policy and practice on the ground.

To answer our review question, the synthesis of existing education research on youth and young adults with dis/abilities is of significance for several reasons. First, students of color and their families live and are being educated in the most segregated settings since the 1970s, compared with their White and/or Asian and middle-class counterparts (Frankenberg, Hawley, Ee, & Orfield, 2017). Second, the neoliberal and capitalist logic of the U.S. political climate is jeopardizing the advances in civil rights that have resulted from the *Brown v. Board of Education* decision, the 1964 Civil Rights Act, the 1965 Elementary and Secondary Education Act, and the Individuals with Disabilities Education Act (Baglieri & Shapiro, 2012; Trent et al., 2014). This hegemony of neoliberalism threatens all students' opportunities to fair, appropriate, equitable, and accessible educations. For example, the U.S. Department of Education under Betsy DeVos has recently released a memo outlining its plans to limit the scope of civil rights investigations and has terminated more than 50 positions in the civil rights office of the U.S. Department of Education (Harris, 2017). That said, from our perspective, current civil rights laws do not sufficiently address the intersectional experiences of youth and young adults with dis/abilities (Crenshaw, 1991; see also Harris & Leonardo, 2018, this volume).[4] We concur with Annamma's (2017) recent critique of DeVos and call for a disability justice that is intersectional:

We can work toward this intersectional approach to dismantling entrenched inequities by committing to disability justice. . . . Disability justice is not to replace other frameworks, but to be integrated in our fights against the systems of colonialism, White supremacy, cisgender heteropatriarchy, and capitalism as each of these contributes to a normative standard and punishes those that do not meet those standards. . . . (p. 1050)

Conceptual Framework

We begin by situating our conceptual framework that helped us make sense of the studies included in this review. Again, our conceptual framework is a sociohistorical approach. More specifically, by sociohistorical, we not only account for the history of disability at its intersections (Artiles, Dorn, & Bal, 2016) but also for the ways students with disabilities, who are multiply situated, recount their everyday experiences at their intersections in contemporary times. In other words, these youths' accounts of their intersectional identities are shaped by the deep histories of race, disability, and other social categories of difference in the United States. In addition, our framework has been influenced by past and present academic scholars' discourses and disciplinary discussion at the boundaries between special education and DSE. This is important since our conceptual framework is interdisciplinary in nature at the intersection of disability, influencing our understanding of disability justice as intersectional (Annamma, 2017). Specifically, we culled from critical theory, social constructivism, DSE, and intersectionality for our sociohistorical approach at the intersectionality of disability and race, ethnicity, gender, sexual orientation, religion, and so on.

Disability Models

As a category and a label, disability is diverse, unclear, and open to interpretation, yet the presence of a disability label may lead to unequal outcomes in one's ability to

access education, housing, health care, transportation, and other aspects of independent functioning (Gold & Richards, 2012; Savaria, Underwood, & Sinclair, 2011).
Our sociohistorical approach is founded on the idea that disability must be seen from
a social model of disability that distinguishes between the impairment (biological and
functional limitation) and the disability (the social oppression that results from the
category). Although the social model of disability is widely recognized in the
International Disability Rights movement, it has had minimal influence over U.S.
institutions (including education, politics, etc.) and cultural ideas and practices that
continue to view disability through the medical–psychological model, which emphasizes the individual's pathology and interventions that attempt to normalize the individual (Connor, Gabel, Gallagher, & Morton, 2008). In contrast, the social model of
disability focuses on the disabling consequences of social exclusion (Stevenson,
2010). This latter theoretical framework allows us to explore how the field of education research has examined the lived experiences of youth and young adults with dis/
abilities who also identify with more than one marginalized identity. Nevertheless, it
is important to explain how DSE has historically engaged with intersectionality due
to the fact that we are coming from both a sociohistorical approach that culls from
DSE and intersectionality frames, among others.

Disability studies in education and intersectionality. Again, despite the critical
special education and DSE community's efforts to shift toward understanding how
students with disabilities experience intersectionality in schools, most theorists who
speak to the production of inequity have ignored disability in their analyses (Ferri,
2010). DSE theorists and researchers argue that disability is a social construct that
is reproduced by inequitable social structures and arrangements. They point out
that definitions of what constitute a disability are unstable and shifting categories.
In addition, similar to DSE, traditional special education has historically ignored
issues of intersectionality (Artiles, 2013; Erevelles, 2000; Gill & Erevelles, 2017). In
turn, those engaging with intersectionality have been guilty of ignoring the salience
of disability (Erevelles & Minear, 2010). Failing to take into account the intersectionality of race *and* disability within both scholarly communities has intended and
unintended epistemological, ontological, axiological, and etiological consequences
for how we have come to know the nature of human experience within U.S. society
and schooling (Ferri, 2010). Some of the consequences of the former include contribution to the reproduction of White Supremacy and institutionalized racism along
the intersections of identity markers, given its own—special education—hegemonic
and positivist underpinnings (Artiles, 1998; Heshusius, 2004; Patton, 1998).

Within our field of special education, one major example of the intersection of
race and disability is the over 60-year-old problem of the disproportionate placement
of minority students within more subjective and high-incidence categories of special
education labels such as intellectual disabilities, learning disabilities (LD), and emotional behavioral disabilities (Artiles, 2011; Collins, 2000; Skiba, Artiles, Kozleski,
Losen, & Harry, 2016). Artiles (2011) has pointed out that due to the lack of an

intersectional understanding of disability as racialized, special education and special education law have failed to recognize the hierarchical functions of these intersections. For example, civil rights efforts for students with disabilities through Individuals with Disabilities Education Act became a tool of inclusion for White students, but a tool of exclusion for historically marginalized students, with the same disability (Artiles, 2011). This is particularly so, if seen through an intersectionality lens that acknowledges the qualitatively different ways in which racial minority groups experience schooling contexts versus racial majority students at the intersection of disability and race. Hence, we can no longer ignore dis/ability intersectionality and its sociohistorical nature and contexts and must give explicit attention to power relations and the other side of the dialectic that is both discursive and material (Artiles, 2017; Erevelles & Minear, 2010; Ferri, 2010) given that racial disparities in special and general education continue to discursively and materially structure the experiences of some students qualitatively differently.

Sociohistorical approach of dis/ability intersectionality. When we view dis/ability at its intersections as a process within a sociohistorical context, wherein human bodies are represented and organized within social structures and everyday practices that are socially constructed, we can begin to understand how dis/ability is a fluid construct, concurrently a (re)presentation of what it signifies while its meaning is created and recreated over time and spaces (Artiles et al., 2016; Garland-Thomson, 2002). One of these spaces is schools. While primarily understood as a space for gaining academic knowledge, schools cannot ignore the social and emotional processes that also take place within educational contexts. For example, schools can be crucial environments for establishing a student's sense of self and community. However, schools can also be locations of violence and oppression. Within the social sciences, Wetherell (2012) has coined the term *affective intersectionality* to foreground how our intersectional identities are not only embedded with the cognitive ways in which they influence our self-concepts, but how the role of affect and emotionality is structured by our experiences of oppression at the intersections.

This systematic review of the literature will allow us to understand how these disability labels and identities are co-constructed through the lens of intersecting identity categories in schooling contexts. By doing so, we can come to a deeper understanding of how our construction of disability is shaped by intersecting systems of privilege and oppression at the personal, political, and structural levels in educational spaces. Applying a sociohistorical lens, therefore, allows us to view the duality of the labels we use in their appropriate contexts. In particular, in this review, how we understood the salience of a sociohistorical lens was by framing the experiences of the participants of the studies as windows into their intersectional realities. In other words, by exploring the experiences and voices of youth and young adults with dis/abilities who simultaneously identify with multiple marginalized identities in the disability research in education that engages intersectionality, we can better affect transformational change in school cultures as well as support individual students

(Hernández-Saca, 2017; Kozleski & Artiles, 2015). We start this exploration with our own critical reflexivity of our positionalities at our disability intersections.

Our Positionalities

We approach this review as a situated cultural practice, from conceptualization to feeling–meaning making (Lemke, 2013) of the knowledge and (re)presentations of the literature and the findings that are (co)produced (Arzubiaga, Artiles, King, & Harris-Murri, 2008). Conducting research as cultural work means that our personal assumptions, values, and biographies, as well as our social interactions between ourselves as scholars and the studies we analyze and our ideological frameworks are embodied in our work (Arzubiaga et al., 2008).

Author 1

I am a 35-year-old (author DIH) bilingual in Spanish and English, gay male of El Salvadoran and Palestinian descent labeled with an auditory LD. My family and I immigrated to the United States when I was 2 years old because of the civil war in El Salvador during the 1980s and for economic reasons. During that journey, I developed a fever of 105 degrees. As a result, I experienced seizures and convulsions throughout my childhood, which led to my diagnosis of an auditory LD and being tracked into special education from kindergarten through college. These early childhood experiences introduced me to the world of dis/ability at my intersections, and even though I experienced seizures and convulsions that took over my body with uncontrollable energy, I was always myself. Nevertheless, the trauma of these events were compounded by the symbolism and negative perceptions that our culture and educational system have inculcated into me about the meanings of "disability," "LD," and being in special education (e.g., "special needs kid," "not smart," "never learning to read and write") and other self-deprecating false messages about myself (e.g., "not having long-term memory and not being able to quickly recall information"), that is, the labels of special education. Other dominant discourses perpetuate fears about people who are immigrants to the United States. For example, for me coming from a war-torn country and having to listen to negative messages about my home country of El Salvador, in addition to Palestine, within the U.S. context has been problematic to say the least. My identities of El Salvadoran and Palestinian have made me sensitive to the projections that others have placed on me. In other words, experiencing speech therapy for my auditory LD and being a dual language learner within K–12, and a person of color of El Salvadorean and Palestinian descent, I am sensitive to the dominant stereotypes about how I speak English and the microaggressions I receive from native speakers at their intersections. Nevertheless, my identities and the languages I speak represent pride in my communities as opposed to being predicaments that cause "special" treatment. Such intersectionalities are only causes of "trouble" within the hegemonic order in a society and schools of White-supremacist and assimilation, English-speaking, able-bodied norms, among others.

Author 2

As the second author, my background as a special education teacher provides me with the firsthand knowledge of special education environments, processes, and experiences described in this research. I am also an individual with a disability, having been diagnosed with attention deficit hyperactivity disorder (ADHD) and LD in adulthood. Although I never experienced the special education system as a student, I have navigated the process of identity, disclosure decision-making processes, and understanding accommodations as a person with a disability. I am afforded the power and privileges that come with privileged identities. As a heterosexual, cisgender, middle-class White Jewish woman with a graduate education who is not the parent of a student with a disability, I bring with me an awareness of a set of values and beliefs that have been shaped by these positions. As I strive to continuously develop as an ally with historically oppressed and marginalized identity groups, I try to deliberately work at understanding how White supremacy, heterosexuality, and classism manifest as a set of institutional practices that marginalize and subordinate others.

Author 3

As the third author, I too intersect several identity markers: Black, heterosexual, woman of faith in Christ, mother, and a person labeled with a speech and language disorder. At 4 years old, my mother's sudden death left me traumatized (Cannon, & Morton, 2015), and I did not speak for well over a year. Once I started school, I had to meet regularly with the school's speech pathologist. Throughout my adult life, this mental and emotional memory was suppressed and emerged during the last semester of my master's program when readings about the marginalized treatment of individuals with disabilities in schools and broader society. As I read, I consciously connected my thoughts to the historical treatment of Black folks and the pseudoscientific experiments conducted on them, such as the Antebellum Medical Experiment, the Tuskegee Syphilis Study, Eugenics/Reproduction Control, and Radiation Experiments With Plutonium, just to name a few (Washington, 2006). The purpose behind how I disclosed my positionality is twofold: (a) to provide the intersectional perspectives of a Black, woman, with a dis/ability label,[5] which lacks (re)presentation in the educational literature (Cannon, 2016) and (b) to examine *othering* conversations about intersectionality that usually obscures Blacks and Black women's perspectives of how they view their dis/abilities.

METHOD

Below we detail how we identified the studies included in this review as well as our methods of analysis.

Data Collection

We conducted a systematic search for educational studies that utilized an intersectionality framework, centering on the lived experiences of youth and young adults with disabilities focusing on youth with marginalized identities within K–16 educational contexts. By studies that use an intersectionality framework, we refer to research that analyzes the intersection of social identity markers of difference by examining intersecting systems of power (McCall, 2005). Using a collaborative online platform (Google Docs), we created a list of 71 keywords and descriptive terms that explored issues of young adults with disabilities at various intersections. We used the following six search engines: *SearchOne Portal* from the University of Northern Iowa, *Journal Storage (JSTOR)*, *PsychINFO*, *Google Scholar*, *EBSCO Academic Search Premier*, and *EBSCOhost*. We used the keywords and descriptive terms in various combinations with connectors such as "and" or "or" to yield potential studies. Some of these combinations included the following: *disability and dis/ability, intersectionality, school(ing), lived experience, education labels, gender, youth, learning disability, special education, qualitative research, ethnography, stories,* and *narratives.*

The inclusion and exclusion criteria included the following:

1. *Timeframe:* To critically examine and survey the most current disability and intersectionality published work in the field of education research we focused on studies published between 2000 and 2017.

2. *Type of Study:* We restricted our sample to studies that were qualitative, utilized a critical lens,[6] were conducted in the United States and explored the lived experience of the student participants themselves. It was through content analysis of the studies' design, theoretical, and conceptual framework that we were able to review if the study came from a critical lens. Our sample included the following research designs and data collection methods: ethnographies, in-depth interviews, case studies, including multiple case study, and narrative poem co-construction. We excluded quantitative and mixed-methods studies because they do not necessarily capture the voices of the students or represent the youths' lived realities on the ground, and they foreground the etic perspectives of researchers as opposed to the emic voices of youth with dis/abilities at their intersections.

3. *Source of Publication:* We focused on peer-reviewed journal articles to ensure the quality of the research studies because peer-reviewed studies are vetted by scholars who are experts in the field.

4. *Population and Focal Social Identity Markers:* Our sample of studies were focused on youth and young adults—students aged 14 to 26 years—who have a disability and have other social identity markers of difference with analysis that specifically analyzes that intersection. Ages 14 to 26 was chosen because it spans adolescence to emerging adulthood (Arnett, 2000). In addition, we wanted to explore this formative time for this group given their in-depth identity exploration as individuals and as part of social groups.

We conducted a total of 50 searches, which produced 153,245 articles. Collectively, we skimmed these articles' titles and/or abstracts to determine whether or not they met our inclusion and exclusion criteria. As many of the titles made it clear that they would not meet our criteria, there were fewer abstracts to read. If the titles and/or abstracts did not provide us with the evidence necessary to include or exclude the study, we reviewed the relevant sections of the published article that would provide us with the evidence.

Individually, we identified the articles that we felt met the criteria listed above. After omitting duplicates, we had 32 potentially eligible articles. We reviewed these 32 articles and together decided an article's inclusion or exclusion in the final sample. This provided the opportunity for cross-examination of the 32 articles and a reexamination of the ones we each gathered to ensure they met all four of the inclusionary and exclusionary criteria. After cross-reviewing the 32 articles, we identified and decided on 10 articles that met all of the above criteria.

Data Analysis

Our data analysis processes and procedures were systematic, critical, iterative, and recursive (Bogdan & Biklen, 2011). First, we created a data matrix that served as a document to divide the data analysis processes and included the following columns that represented the research study elements that we wanted to code for each of the 10 studies: (a) coded by; (b) author and title; (c) confirmation that the selected study met the inclusionary and exclusionary criteria or not; (d) purpose and research questions; (e) methods of data collection; (f) images/tables/figures; (g) methods of data analysis; (h) discussion of findings, implications, and conclusions; (i) narratives or quotes by the researchers and youth and young adults that spoke to us; (j) our systematic literature review question; and last (k) space to memo and reflect as we coded the 10 studies. Second, each researcher input the content from the articles within the matrix. During this phase of the review process, we carefully read all of the studies in the database, which assisted in filling out the matrix. Third, we created separate online collaborative matrices to analyze, synthesize, and engage with the studies around our research question, allowing us to inductively and collaboratively analyze for themes that emerged from the research in our database. Finally, all of the authors collaboratively and iteratively discussed, reflected upon, and analyzed the findings of the review as well as the feeling–meaning making of the findings and the connections to existing research and theory.

Through this systematic, iterative, and recursive data analysis, we co-constructed the data in the spirit of "slow scholarship" (Mountz et al., 2015). Each author was acutely aware of the different positionalities and perspectives that we each brought to the review process(es) and were mindful in how we interacted with one another to co-construct our understandings, access, and participation within the cultural practice of completing this review. We now turn to the presentation of our findings.

FINDINGS

Our research question allows us to explore what knowledge has been created by on the ground experience of youth and young adults with dis/abilities at their intersections. In our research, we found that youth create meaning along the lines of their disabilities and we summarized these within the following three themes: (a) navigate intersectional disability discourses, (b) present their dis/ability oppression as intersectional, and (c) engage in their identity meaning making as a form of intersectional discourse. The powerful quote at the beginning of this systematic review, "Ain't nobody gonna get me down!" was from one of Petersen's (2009) study participants, Kiesha, an African American woman who was labeled with ADHD and an anxiety disorder during her sophomore year of college. In it she centers her voice in the context of her experiences as an individual who is multiply oppressed. Therefore, we felt it exemplifies many of the sociohistorical dimensions of the youths' disability discourses. For Kiesha, we specifically noticed that her use of "Ain't" is not ahistorical due to the fact that "Ain't" is reminiscent of "Ain't I a Woman" from Sojourner Truth's famous speech against her intersection of, at the time regarding racism, slavery, and patriarchy. Kiesha's choice of "Ain't" in contemporary times evokes the legacies that we argue connect her to past generations of Black women fighting for their freedom such as Sojourner Truth.

First, at the structural level, our analysis revealed dominant discourses—intersectional disability discourses—related to particular materialities (e.g., the special education classroom, the short bus, etc.) within and across time, space, and contexts that the youth and young adults with disabilities experienced at the intersections. The second finding was focused at the political level, and highlighted how youth and young adults experienced dis/ability oppression as intersectional. The third, at the personal level, revealed that youth and young adults' discourses and narratives about their intersections are interconnected to the first two findings as the individuals engaged in questioning, resisting, and subverting dehumanizing internal and external structures and systems. We understood these as the studies' participants understanding of disability identity as intersectional discourse because their discourses and narratives involved intersectional experiences.

Intersectional Disability Discourses

Findings from this review revealed key dimensions of the dominant discourses around the intersections of disability and race, gender, sexual orientation, class, and language and how the individual(s) navigated and made sense of these discourses. On a structural level, this synthesis showed the complex ways youth's experiences within dominant dis/ability discourses and material reality is intersectional. These dominant discourses of disability identity expose *special education symbolism* (the myths that circulate within society and special education and general education) that have become rumors and half-truths about what it means to be a student with a special education category at their intersections (Hernández-Saca, 2017). In other words, as we unpacked what we know from education research, we came to the conclusion that youth and young adults with dis/abilities need to make sense of what it means to be labeled within special education categories and at their intersections of gender, race, ethnicity, and so on. The latter was part and parcel of the dominant discourses and the stories about what it meant to be—the symbolism—a student with a dis/ability at their intersections. To illustrate, Kiesha states, "if it's not my race, it is other things, like being a woman or my disability" (Petersen, 2009, p. 436). These dominant narratives about dis/ability at their intersections have structured how individuals experience the present—*history matters and influences the present lived experiences of students at their intersections* (Artiles, 2017; Artiles et al., 2016; Hernández-Saca, 2017; Munyi, 2012).

Three of the 10 studies collectively and individually conducted on the life experiences of Black females and males with dis/abilities were included in the database and illuminated insights about the intersectional nature of dis/ability (e.g., Annamma, 2014; Connor, 2006; Ferri & Connor, 2010). More specifically, Annamma, Connor, and Ferri's body of work illuminated the power of intersectional disability discourses. For example, Annamma (2014) centered the experiences of 10 young girls and women of color with special education dis/ability categories within juvenile incarcerated facilities, illuminating the effects of institutional practices and processes of control and compliance related to how *deviant behavior* was understood and documented. The young girls and women's "deviant behavior" was framed as an academic need within the institutional context of the juvenile justice system. This rationalizing in the name of their academic needs was unraveled by Annamma through the students' voices as socializing practices. For example, Veronica was one of the 10 participants in Annamma's (2014) study who together with the other females "had a variety of experiences with disability labels . . . and felt that [she was] in special education because [she] could not intellectually contend with [her] peers" (p. 317). Within the context of Annamma's (2013) larger dissertation study, she described Veronica as "a self-identified lesbian female of color . . . [who] 'never saw' people like her in the curriculum. Nor did she see the practices exercised by this historically oppressed community taken up in schools" (p. 127). Within the context of Annamma's (2014) study, Veronica stated the following:

I don't care who says no or what, if I'm comfortable with it, I'm going to sit the way I want. And I'll just do what I do and I never got in trouble for it. And when I did, I would just close them back and spread (my feet) again. (p. 314)

This quotation is representative of the youth and young adults who experience dis/ability socializing practices. As another example, Annamma (2014) illuminated this "subordination" from Veronica as gendered, given that she was violating the standards of "normative femininity." For example, Veronica had "short spiky cut" hair, and she was described within an official school document as having "a mannish posture" (Annamma, 2014, p. 319), demonstrating how disability intersects with other dimensions of marginalized identities. We argue that not only the participants' singular-dimensional experiences of race, disability, and/or gender were clearly informing the institutional actors in the reviewed research. But, in contrast, the participants experienced intersectional disability discourses that enacted violence and erased their voices. In addition, this finding fills a gap in the literature, illuminating the intersections of disability, race, and gender. In other words, intersectional disability discourses, documented in Petersen (2009) and Annamma's (2014) studies, create a social construction of reality and identities that leads to the erasure of people's humanity.

From a sociohistorical perspective, we can see how the legacies of slavery, capitalism, eugenics, and patriarchy constrain the agency of youth due to their intersections within and across markers of difference (Erevelles, 2011). We do not suggest that educational literature ignores this complexity, but more studies need to illuminate the complexity that students experience due to race, gender, sexual orientation, dis/ability relations within U.S. educational contexts and society. For example, Veronica's voice attests to these structural, intersectional disability discourses, whose characteristics are embedded within individuals as ideologies or paradigms and institutions through social practices, routines, and hence cultures (Annamma, 2014). These structural, or negative intersectional disability discourses, can be understood as part and parcel of the deficit-oriented thinking that has a long history within U.S. society and schooling (Valencia, 2012). Ferri and Connor (2010) further highlight these intersectional disability discourses that youth experienced at the intersection of gender, dis/ability, and special education—what we call *special education symbolism*—that other historically marginalized youth with dis/abilities at their intersections must navigate. *Special education symbolism* refers to how students have negatively experienced and felt the meaning of special education on their psyches. Historically, the master narratives of special education (Hernández-Saca, 2016) have framed these negative feelings, emotions, and meanings as *subjective*, temporary, or irrational. Nothing could be further from the truth—the damage caused by special education symbolism has deleterious effects on students at their intersections. Moreover, we argue that *special education symbolism* is intersectional in nature because dis/ability and identity are not single-dimensional. Furthermore, it is important to emphasize then that this is a way that the intersectional lives of youth are shaped by such structural intersectional identities and in particular the unintended consequences of special education labels and placement have on students' conceptualizations of self.

Across the 10 studies reviewed here, 6 illuminated how youth with dis/abilities at their intersections needed to actively navigate presumptions about not only their dis/abilities but also about their other identity markers while experiencing special education across time and space (e.g., Annamma, 2014; Connor, 2006; Ferri & Connor, 2010; Kahn & Lindstrom, 2015[7]; Madigan, 2005; Petersen, 2009). In Petersen (2009), a couple of young adult Black women with disabilities were profoundly aware of the school personnel's assumptions about their disabilities. For example, Shana talked about her school counselor's view of her and the limitation of her ability: "He wouldn't let me go on college visits because he didn't think college was for me. He looked at me and saw just another young, single, poor, black woman. A woman going blind at that!" (Petersen, 2009, p. 433). Similarly, Courtney was aware of race, gender, and disability assumptions:

I thought sharing my visual chart with [my personal wellness professor] would fix things for me, but that wasn't the case. Now I was the pitied, disabled, black woman. If it wasn't one thing, it would be something else. I just couldn't win. (Petersen, 2009, pp. 435–436)

She continued, "At least I knew what I was up against" (p. 436).

Similarly, Ferri and Connor (2010) open their study by acknowledging the "youth crisis," the dominant narrative that circulates within society and schooling about girls: "Like the phrase 'failing schools,' the terms 'youth' and 'crisis' have become so intertwined that it is difficult to think about one without the other" (p. 105). Ferri and Connor illustrated how dominant intersectional disability discourses, about the "youth crisis," are often gendered and have created the social construction of the "girl problem." Much of Ferri's body of work has highlighted the issue of gender as it intersects with special education disability categories (Ferri, 1997; Ferri & Connor, 2010; Ferri & Gregg, 1998). For example, we know very little about what it means to be the "only girl of color in special education" (Ferri & Connor, 2010) given that there is not only a paucity of studies that focus on the experiences of females of color with dis/abilities or critically examine how being a girl shapes their experiences as students across time and space (Cortiella & Horowitz, 2014). This theme was also described by Madigan (2005), who explored the intersections of gender, ethnicity, disability, and a coed special education classroom versus a single-gender special education classroom. Our review found that females of color experienced disability as qualitatively different than males of color, but at the same time, there were overlaps across gender (e.g., individualized attention, modification, and accommodations along with shame and frustration about the myths and meanings of LD and special education within society). This finding points to the urgency of utilizing an intersectionality framework when understanding and creating knowledge concerning the experience of youth and young adults with dis/abilities at their intersections. Significantly, this first finding shows us that the dominant narratives and discourses at the structural dimensions of society shape the lived experiences of youth and young adults with disabilities on the ground in oppressive intersectional ways.

Most of the research in this review demonstrated a forceful method for rejecting dominant oppressive ideologies that involved participants developing critical consciousness around the intersections of their identities. For example, Petersen (2009) found that young Black women with dis/abilities who participated in her study actively sought liberation through developing (a) an awareness of how the discourses surrounding race, gender, or dis/ability may have led to limited or restricted opportunity; (b) an ability to reject the dominant ideologies and subsequent messages surrounding race, gender, or disability; and (c) an awareness of how race, gender, and dis/ability interconnect to limit opportunity. By developing an *intersectional critical consciousness* and rejecting dominant ideologies of "deficient," "abnormal," and "broken," these youths and the communities they navigate are concurrently experiencing and redefining the dominant discourse of dis/ability at its intersections. In other words, by validating youths' sociohistorical knowledge, researchers construct dis/

ability feeling–meaning making in a manner that rejects the negative messages about people at their intersections. This is critical to recognize and positively respond to the structural ways in which disability at its intersections shape youth's experiences in schools and future life trajectories.

Youth's Dis/ability Oppression as Intersectional

As we conducted the analysis of our 10 studies to answer our research question, our second finding focused on the interaction between the structural and the personal levels of intersectionality (Crenshaw, 1989). The synthesis of these studies revealed that the youth and young adults exposed how oppression was rooted in the social construction of the intersection of their identities that they experienced, witnessed, and made feeling–meaning of. From a DSE framework, we found that even impairment labels that the youth claimed or were given were not only biological but also socially, historically, emotionally, and politically constructed (Gallagher, Connor, & Ferri, 2014; Shakespeare, 2013).

For example, race, disability, and other intersections were significant to the well-being of students in some of the studies. Connor (2006) shares the voice of Michael, a Black, young adult male, labeled with an LD. Connor illuminated the intersections of Michael's identity at the dominant discourses of race, socioeconomic status, and LD. In Connor's (2006) study, Michael's voice and narratives highlight the intersectional nature of his experiences and feeling–meaning making of oppression and violence exposing the over 60-year-old problem of overrepresentation of students of color within special education settings (Artiles, Kozleski, Trent, Osher, & Ortiz, 2010). Michael described the disturbing phenomenon that many Black males get into so much "trouble just by walking" as they navigate U.S. communities and schools. Michael's comments evoke how Black girls, women, boys, and men are overrepresented in shootings at the hands, fears, and misunderstandings of police officers in the United States. Furthermore, this experience parallels how Black and Brown bodies with dis/abilities are disproportionately recipients of "zero-tolerance" and "discipline" policies within educational contexts (Losen, Ee, Hodson, & Martinez, 2015; Morris, 2016). Michael addresses these dominant discourses and stereotypes of Blacks as criminals when he wrote through poetry:

People suspect us.

They stereotype Black people as thieves, criminals and

all that—you're gonna steal.

So people really don't trust you.

They'll take your bag before you go into the store.

It makes you not wanna shop.

Being a Black person is hard because you get stopped by the police constantly. (Connor, 2006, p. 157)

However, Michael's words above—that is, his *truth*—pushes back on these dominant discourses even as they try to colonize his mind and (re)present him as one of these "enemies." Similar to Michael, Chanell, a Black, young woman, with an LD "positions herself among a legacy or genealogy of Black women who have survived positions of seeming powerlessness and the direst of consequences" (Ferri & Connor, 2010, p. 118) in her poem:

A Slave Woman's Voice:

Hear me and hear me good for Which I, the woman is speaking.

Take these shackles off my legs (!!)

Which you have installed upon me

Let me be free to talk, run and play with me

People for which I am human just like you.

If you cut me, don't I bleed?

If I am sad, don't I cry?

If I'm happy, don't I laugh?

Don't I have feelings just like you?

So take these shackles from my feet

Open up these doors

Show me some

R-E-S-P-E-C-T

For we the women

The creator of all of you,

And God's the creator of all.

So I say with my last breath

Take these shackles off my feet.

Open the gate and let me free. (Ferri & Connor, 2010, p. 118)

Both Michael and Chanell remind us that poetry is a way to convey one's knowledge of their experiences at our intersections, while shedding light on other ways of knowing, experiencing, and expressing that are not promoted by hegemonic discourses. The power of such hegemonic discourses—productive, oppressive, and capillary—is distributed within and across people and social institutions through language and emotion (Gannon & Davis, 2012). Both Michael and Chanell's poems are reflective of their sociohistorical contexts as they relate to how others have treated them at their multiple intersections. Hence, we argue students and human beings do not experience socially constructed ideologies of race, gender, class, and disability neutrally or as a *matter of fact*.

Within this second theme, *youth's dis/ability oppression as intersectional*, we also found that the majority of the youth and young adults described how the intersection of their identities affected the social, emotional, and spiritual aspects of their person-hood. For example, Ferri and Connor (2006) found the following themes based on the experiences of their five participants: (a) issues around privacy and positionality within and across school spaces; (b) negotiating their multiple selves in relationships; (c) barriers to their education related to issues of power and control within special education and general education that affected their motivation and well-being in schools; (d) gendered experiences outside of school; and (e) being aware of the inter-sectionality of social reality due to their multiple identities within these structures. Regarding the lack of privacy, Ferri and Connor (2006) concluded:

Despite guarantees of privacy, schools regularly convey students' disability status in direct and indirect ways. The derogatory names given to accessible busses (i.e. "the short bus" or the "tard bus") illustrate how the stigma associated with special education spreads even to the physical structures of schools. Many of the young women in this study talked about how parts of the school building came to be associated with special education. This unofficial marking off of special education zones within schools underscores the level of segregation students who receive special education services experience on a daily basis. (pp. 107–108)

Therefore, dis/ability and gender intersectionality segregation was not only external but also internal (Hernández-Saca, 2016, 2017). Understanding the importance of how youth and young adults with dis/abilities make sense of their internal and exter-nal worlds is critical to creating new knowledge that contributes to educational equity reform movements and praxis on the ground. For school reform efforts, a focus on historically marginalized youth voices that take an intersectional lens of disability is warranted given the paucity of this research (see Gonzalez, Hernández-Saca, & Artiles, 2017, for a systematic literature review on student voice research).

Youth's Dis/Ability Identity as Intersectional Discourse

Our last finding was that the researchers of the studies included in this review overwhelmingly described the identity formation of dis/ability as mutually constitu-tive of intersectional identities. Kahn and Lindstrom (2015), for instance, reported that the young adults who identify as lesbian, gay, bisexual, transgender, queer, and/ or intersex (LGBTQI) and as people with dis/ability labels described how the con-struction of disability and queer narratives mutually constituted each other within school contexts, concurrently influencing and being influenced by each other. Desi, a transgender student and a person of color in Miller's (2015) study, dealt with stig-mas from dis/ability and other labels within school contexts.

Because depression and anxiety disorders are still really stigmatized, it's harder for me to bring that up in an academic context with my teachers, because they're less likely to understand and they're usually going to be in the mindset of, "You need to come to class anyway, because this is a grade. No matter what your feelings are, you need to come." I don't bring it up, because I often feel like they put the lazy label on me or just the overly emotional label on me, which feels really terrible. It adds to feeling stigmatized. (Miller, 2015, p. 386)

Desi's identity discourse explicates his personal feeling and experiences with stigmas from teachers about identity categories. To further illustrate in another study, a gay man with a disability (i.e., Cerebral Palsy) who also has LD, and is a person of color, was not comfortable talking about his identity and experiences (Henry, Fuerth, & Figliozzi, 2010). "If I would have had counseling all of my college career, I would be a different person" (p. 5). These experiences set a foundation for how the participants navigated normality within their own identities and within the school environment if he would have had the opportunity for identity development in an institution that supported him at the intersection of his identities. Instead, the institutions he was socialized within approached support as if his identities were additive and unidimensional, causing him difficulty and pain.

In Connor (2006, p. 155), Michael continues to shed light on his experience, illuminating how youth created intersectional meaning of dis/ability identity:

I write backwards . . .

. . . I was born in Brooklyn.

I'm nineteen going on twenty.

Dyslexia . . . I still have it.

I think it is natural

Everyone is born with something, so it's not like a disability.

People say, you have dyslexia, da-da-da-, but to me it

Really didn't do anything.

I just had to work harder.

If people understood they wouldn't make fun of

learning disabilities.

People really won't know about what learning

disabilit[ies] are.

I think in this society, learning disability—

It's like a downfall, it makes you look bad . . .

"It's not like a disability."

"It's natural."

Within Michael's poetry, we can see how dominant discourses, intersectional disability discourses, about what it means to be Black, LD—specifically, dyslexic—and poor create a "matrix of oppression" that students like Michael (and others in the included studies) needed to navigate internally and externally about their sense of self and multiple selves, such as their academic identities (Cannon & Morton, 2015; Collins, 2000). These dominant discourses—beliefs and ideas or even tropes about who these particular students are—were persuasive, ideational, emotional, and, hence, sociohistorical and political realities in which youth were forced to be aware of, and could not just "ignore." Michael's poetry, and hence, voice, above demonstrates how he navigated these structural domains that tried to tell him who he was. In another example, in Kahn and Lindstrom (2015), Sarah, who is diagnosed with a specific learning disability, states,

'Cause I just want to be what other people expect me to be. I just want to do . . . what I feel is good, what I feel is okay, just not, like, social norm. I don't want to be like everybody else, I want to be different. (p. 367)

In other words, the youth's oppressed positionality keeps them from full citizenship and belonging within U.S. society and schooling, due to the power of these dominant structures that are simultaneously being experienced and (re)produced by their experiences. Given that Sarah clearly asserts her embrace of difference, this understanding helps us counter deficit-oriented ideologies structured within U.S. society and schooling about historically marginalized youth and their communities. Connor (2006) and Kahn and Lindstrom (2015) help us humanize historically marginalized youth like Michael and Sarah and call for a dismantling of these violent structures within educational contexts.

In another example, Lambert's (2015) research on young Latina/o's experiences in the mathematics classroom explores how disability and ability are constructed within school settings. Lambert presents tensions that exist between professional pathologizing and the lived experiences of the individual with the lived intersectional experience. With a system steeped in systematic oppression, this discourse is highly racialized and gendered. This scenario brings to light the importance of valuing the students' articulation of their sociohistorical narratives. This research also explores how dis/ability is constructed by the gendering of the students' feeling–meaning making. For example, consider Ana, bilingual in Spanish and English, "Dominican and American . . . [and was] identified by the school as learning disabled . . . [and] approached mathematics learning differently" (Lambert, 2015, p. 2).

Ana's self understanding frames her as different from the boys in interests, not intelligence. Her narrative echoes those of high-achieving girls in other studies who downplay their own ability in mathematics, actively constructing identities that exclude mathematics despite their success. (Lambert, 2015, p. 13)

This quote exemplifies how the researcher constructs the narrative around dis/ability and gender identity and how the experiences of her participants were intertwined. For example, although Ana frames her lack of interest in math as different from boys and having nothing to do with intelligence, the researcher points to the larger gender pattern of girls having to downplay their intelligence in fields that are traditionally dominated by stereotypes of who is smart and who is not. Within the field of math, the question of who is smart at math and who is not happens to be along gender lines. In addition, from a sociohistorical intersectional disability discourse analysis, Ana's self-understanding is indeed intersectional in nature since she is experiencing doing math along the structural identities of gender, ethnicity, and being a student with a disability. This points to the salience of dominant discourses defined earlier within this section but also within this review in the theme *intersectional disability discourse*.

DISCUSSION

The findings described above contribute to a critical understanding of the experience of dis/ability at its intersections for historically marginalized youth within educational contexts. The findings demonstrate how disability is intersectional, constructed within dominant sociohistorical *discourses and material realities* within U.S. society and schooling that stem from legacies of oppression and injustice that fall along intersectional lines. Our findings lead us to argue that disability experience and identity can no longer be considered separate from youths' other socially constructed intersectional identities because they have real material consequences for their lived experiences within everyday cultural practices (Erevelles, 2011). Historically, theory, research, and policy have ignored complexity, which we argue students are already experiencing within educational contexts, including special education (Artiles et al., 2016; Erevelles, 2011; Hernández-Saca, 2017). From our findings, we contend that academic (e.g., learning and literacy) and educational spaces and contexts are not devoid of social, emotional, and spiritual identification processes related to race, dis/ability, gender, socioeconomic class, sexual orientation, masculinity, and other differences that intersect and interlock with the experiences of students at their intersections (Baker, Andriessen, & Järvelä, 2013; Lemke, 2013; Nasir, 2011).

Across the 10 studies reviewed, the theoretical and conceptual frameworks grounding these topics and the feeling–meaning making of the participants were framed within their intersectional identities. The usual *identity badges* of disability, race, gender, sexual orientation, among other differences, do not only encompass the experiences of youth with disabilities at their intersections. Therefore, the role of culture and learning needs to be taken into account since culture mediates human development and all human activity (Artiles, 2015; Rogoff, 2003). Furthermore, the focus on disability at its intersections is similar to the framing of dis/ability critical race studies theory (Annamma et al., 2013), which foreground the false and oppressive ideology of Whiteness and heteronormativity with that of normalcy and ableism. Similarly, our research aligns with theories of how oppressive ideologies structures the experiences of Black, Brown, and disabled females and males—Black or Brown Disabled bodies—at the macro level within U.S. society. Therefore, educational contexts undergird who and how one counts as a person and who has symbolic, cultural, social, and economic capital or legitimacy (Bourdieu, 1986). As we incorporate our findings from this review into the epistemological work of intersectionality, Kiesha's voice (Petersen, 2009), "Ain't nobody gonna get me down!" deeply resonates and represents the other youth and young adults included in this research, serving as a powerful representation of the strength, emancipation, and resistance that intersectionality as a framework provides as it centers the experiences of those who are at the fringes of societal imaginaries within U.S. society and schooling.

IMPLICATIONS

Our review has demonstrated that as education researchers, advocates, and professionals continue to construct disability as unidimensional, they continue to contribute to the master narrative of disability that shames and marginalizes. As Henry, Fuerth, and Figliozzi (2010) noted, "Contemporary diversity advocates are challenged to reexamine disability within a precise and interwoven context that can also account oppressive experiences of the disabled based on sexual orientation, gender, race, and class" (p. 378). By centering our analysis on qualitative studies that focus on youths' voices to illuminate the intersection of ableism with racism, sexism, cissexism, ethnocentricity, and other forms of systematic oppression, this research explored the divide that often manifests between *the professional and the lived experience*. For the implications, we will focus on ways to operationalize an intersecting lens that incorporates students' articulation of their sociohistorical narratives.

Personal

Fostering critical consciousness (the ability to understand and actively challenge oppressive social and political hegemonic powers) also has the potential to support the development of resilience, empowerment, and full integration of all aspects of personal and group identities for youth with dis/abilities who experience intersectional systematic oppressions (Freire, 2008). By engaging in an ongoing examination of their experiences to determine how disability and race, gender, sexual orientation, ethnicity, and so on interact on micro, meso, and macro levels in society, teachers and education researchers have the opportunity to support youth as they come to understand the interaction of these characteristics within multiple ecological contexts. Hence, this is why student voice research is of paradigmatic importance to lead to individual and societal transformation through systems change (Gonzalez et al., 2017). The latter acknowledges the psychological contributing to sociohistorical frameworks, not just purely framing individual identity as pathological and psychological (Kozleski & Artiles, 2014).

How the researchers operationalized the construction of intersectional dis/ability communicated the loss of social, cultural, and economic capital that manifests in the denial of educational opportunity. This supports Bourdieu's (1986) description of capital as the symbolic and concrete resources acquired by the individual's connections, communities, and relationships that was repetitively described by researchers who discussed the deletion of capital due to intersecting of dis/ability and other marginalized identities. This review's finding of the stigmatizing and overincarceration of Black and Brown youth and its systematic intersection with gender is both a result of and contributing to the diminished social capital of the described intersectional identities. This key finding of the connection between the personal and the structural ecological level had major on the ground implications for the participants' lives in these studies, yet the concept of cultural and social capital is not used commonly in discussions around dis/ability and education (Trainor, 2008, 2017).

Structural

The knowledge and voices from this research support the argument that we must go beyond *identity badges* to move toward justice for all. We consider students as human beings. We recognize that students' identities matter and are not identity-less or culture-less (Artiles, 2015).[8] This helps us counter deficit-oriented ideologies structured within U.S. society and schooling. We argue that traditional theory, research, and practice and the canon of special education has failed to take advantage of the intersectionality framework given that they do not recognize social identity markers or culturally responsive or sustaining pedagogy (Ladson-Billings, 1994; Paris & Alim, 2017) as relevant to teaching, literacy, and learning and to the nature of dis/ability (Artiles, 2015; Artiles, 2011; Waitoller & King-Thorius, 2016).

Again, our review approached our research question from a sociohistorical lens by centering the voices of the youth and young adults along disability, race, and gender and other markers of difference to reveal the complex ways dis/ability is experienced intersectionally. In particular, we explored the youth and young adults' voices at the structural, political, and personal levels of society and schooling. We found that education research focusing on youth and young adults with dis/abilities who are multiply situated in terms of race, gender, social class, sexual orientation, or other social markers understood disability in terms of (a) intersectional disability discourses, (b) dis/ability oppression as intersectional, and (c) engage in their identity meaning making as a form of intersectional discourse. In sum, our review highlights the importance of using an intersectional framework to better understand how multidimensional identities affect our students and our research. Our review also reminds us to rely on the voices of the marginalized and oppressed to see how schools, policy, and labels can inflict harm on the individuals that are supposed to be provided with a fair and appropriate education.

ACKNOWLEDGMENTS

All three authors are thankful and greatly appreciative for the professional copyediting by Dr. Stephanie McBride-Schreiner. The authors are mindful and grateful of the peer-reviews that they received before and during the 2016 annual American Educational Research Association conference on an earlier draft of the current project and preliminary findings presentation. The authors are extremely thankful to Drs. Jeanne M. Powers, Gustavo E. Fischman, and Adai A. Tefera for their review of our proposal and feedback as it greatly influenced the focus of this systematic literature review. Last, the authors are mindful of the mentor-text they used to model this review off of: Waitoller and Artiles (2016).

NOTES

[1] Throughout the chapter, we use *dis/ability* to define disability as being a social construction and constructed by its political, historical, social, emotional, and economic contexts regarding ability and disability at the same time. We use *disability*, without the dash (/) between *dis* and *ability*, to denote and acknowledge the existence of disability as impairment or being a real predicament (Shakespeare, 2013).

[2] A foundational force for the framework of intersectionality, Black feminism examined how the interlocking systems of power, social inequities, socially constructed identities, and social problems and their solutions are constructed through the intersection of race and gender (Collins, 2000).

[3] By on the ground, we mean how youth and young adults experience their intersectional identities in their everyday lives within tangible, situated contexts, such as inside of schools.

[4] For example, critical theorist researchers face conflict when using labels and social categories because, on the one hand, these labels and social categories are necessary to participate in the political and civil rights conversations that are built on hegemonic structures. On the other hand, critical researchers feel these terms harm the individual since they also may be used to sort and segregate individuals. Using an intersectionality framework allows the researcher to first understand, and then question, how social groups are defined and constructed and how those groups are understood (Penrose, 1999) and how intersectionality is used. Furthermore, McCall (2005) acknowledges the contradictory relationships that identity categories can create.

[5] As a critical scholar, I (author MAC) am aware of the sociohistorical construction of the terms, such as Black, female, and disability. I chose to list a few of my identity markers the way that I did to bring attention to the concept that my identities are all separate in essence but intersectional in function. To illustrate my view, I use the words of a participant in Petersen's (2009) study name Kiesha, here is her words, "If it's not my race, it is other things, like being a woman or my disability" (Petersen, 2009, p. 436).

[6] By *critical lens*, we mean having a critical theory (Freire, 2005) approach at the analysis of disability at its intersections that foreground issues of power relations. This was important to ensure that the studies did not take a medical–psychological model of disability and foregrounded the importance of power relations in social identities in the lives of their student participants. This, in turn, indexes our own conceptual framework that we brought to the review and the importance of a sociohistorical intersectional analysis.

[7] It is important to note that this included study was conducted by the second author of this literature review.

[8] We choose to use *identity-less* and *cultureless* as opposed to *colorblindness* given that the term *colorblindness* reproduces an ablest assumption about those who are blind as deficit.

REFERENCES

References marked with an asterisk were studies included in the analysis and database of this systematic literature review.

Annamma, S. A. (2013). *Resistance and resilience: The education trajectories of young women of color with disabilities through the school to prison pipeline* (Doctoral dissertation, University of Colorado Boulder). Retrieved from https://scholar.colorado.edu/educ_gradetds/33/

*Annamma, S. A. (2014). Disabling juvenile justice: Engaging the stories of incarcerated young women of color with disabilities. *Remedial and Special Education, 35*, 313–324.

Annamma, S. A. (2017). Not enough: Critiques of Devos and expansive notions of justice. *International Journal of Qualitative Studies in Education, 30*, 1047–1052.

Annamma, S. A., Connor, D., & Ferri, B. (2013). Dis/ability critical race studies (DisCrit): Theorizing at the intersections of race and dis/ability. *Race Ethnicity and Education, 16*(1), 1–31.

Arnett, J. J. (2000). Emerging adulthood: A theory of development from the late teens through the twenties. *American Psychologist, 55,* 469–480.

Artiles, A. J. (1998). The dilemma of difference: Enriching the disproportionality discourse with theory and context. *The Journal of Special Education, 32,* 32–36.

Artiles, A. J. (2011). Toward an interdisciplinary understanding of educational equity and difference: The case of the racialization of ability. *Educational Researcher, 40,* 431–445.

Artiles, A. J. (2013). Untangling the racialization of disabilities: An intersectionality critique across disability models. *DuBois Review, 10,* 329–347.

Artiles, A. J. (2015). Beyond responsiveness to identity badges: Future research on culture in disability and implications for RTI. *Educational Review, 67*(1), 1–22.

Artiles, A. J. (2017, October 19). *Re-envisioning equity research: Disability identification disparities as a case in point.* Presented at the Fourteenth Annual AERA Brown Lecture in Education Research. Retrieved from http://www.aera.net/Events-Meetings/Annual-Brown-Lecture-in-Education-Research

Artiles, A. J., Dorn, S., & Bal, A. (2016). Objects of protection, enduring nodes of difference: Disability intersections with "other" differences, 1916–2016. *Review of Research in Education, 40,* 777–820.

Artiles, A. J., Kozleski, E., Trent, S., Osher, D., & Ortiz, A. (2010). Justifying and explaining disproportionality, 1968–2008: A critique of underlying views of culture. *Exceptional Children, 76,* 279–299.

Arzubiaga, A., Artiles, A. J., King, K., & Harris-Murri, N. (2008). Beyond research on cultural minorities: Challenges and implications of research as situated cultural practice. *Exceptional Children, 74,* 309–327.

Baglieri, S., & Shapiro, A. (2012). *Disability studies and the inclusive classroom: Critical practices for creating least restrictive attitudes.* New York, NY: Routledge.

Baker, M., Andriessen, J., & Järvelä, S. (Eds.). (2013). *Affective learning together: Social and emotional dimensions of collaborative learning.* Abingdon, England: Routledge.

Blanchett, W. J., Klingner, J. K., & Harry, B. (2009). The intersection of race, culture, language, and disability: Implications for urban education. *Urban Education, 44,* 389–409.

Bogdan, R. C., & Biklen, S. K. (2011). *Qualitative research for education: An introduction to theories and methods* (5th ed.). Upper Saddle River, NJ: Prentice Hall.

Bourdieu, P. (1986). The forms of capital. In J. G. Richardson (Ed.), *Handbook of theory and research for the sociology of education* (pp. 241–258). New York, NY: Greenwood Press.

Cannon, M. A. (2016). From homeless to hopeful: Overcoming tragedy to preserver. In Y. D. Ford, L. J. Davis, M. T. Scott, & Y. Sealey-Ruz (Eds.), *Gumbo for the soul: Liberating memoirs and stories to inspire females of color* (pp. 51–57). Charlotte, NC: Information Age.

Cannon, M. A., & Morton, C. H. (2015). God consciousness enacted: Living, moving, and having my being in him. *Western Journal of Black Studies, 39,* 147–156.

Collins, P. H. (2000). *Black feminist thought: Knowledge, consciousness, and the politics of empowerment* (2nd ed.). New York, NY: Routledge.

*Connor, D. J. (2006). Michael's story: "I get into so much trouble just by walking: Narrative knowing and life at the intersections of learning disability, race and class. *Equity & Excellence in Education, 39,* 154–165.

Connor, D. J., Gabel, S. L., Gallagher, D. J., & Morton, M. (2008). Disability studies and inclusive education: Implications for theory, research and practice. *International Journal of Inclusive Education, 12,* 441–457.

Cortiella, C., & Horowitz, S. H. (2014). *The state of learning disabilities: Facts, trends and emerging issues.* New York, NY: National Center for Learning Disabilities.

Crenshaw, K. (1989). Demarginalizing the intersection of race and sex: A Black feminist critique of antidiscrimination doctrine, feminist theory and antiracist politics. *University of*

Chicago Legal Forum, 1989(1): 139–167. Retrieved from https://chicagounbound.uchi cago.edu/uclf/vol1989/iss1/8/

Crenshaw, K. (1991). Mapping the margins: Intersectionality, identity politics, and violence against women of color. *Stanford Law Review, 43*, 1241–1299.

Erevelles, N. (2000). Educating unruly bodies: Critical pedagogy, disability studies, and the politics of schooling. *Educational Theory, 50*(1), 25–47.

Erevelles, N. (2011). *Disability and difference in global contexts: Enabling a transformative body politic.* New York, NY: Palgrave MacMillan.

Erevelles, N., & Minear, A. (2010). Unspeakable offenses: Untangling race and disability in discourses of intersectionality. *Journal of Literary & Cultural Disability Studies, 4*, 127–145.

Ferri, B. A. (1997). *The construction of identity among women with learning disabilities: The many faces of the self* (Doctoral dissertation). University of Georgia, Athens.

Ferri, B. A. (2010). A dialogue we've yet to have: Race and disability studies. In C. Dudley-Marling & A. Gurn (Eds.), *The myth of the normal curve* (Vol. 11, pp. 139–150). New York, NY: Peter Lang.

Ferri, B. A. & Connor, D. J. (2006). *Reading resistance: Discourses of exclusion in desegregation and inclusion debates* (Disability Studies in Education). New York, NY: Peter Yang.

*Ferri, B. A., & Connor, D. J. (2010). "I was the special ed. girl": Urban working-class young women of colour. *Gender and Education, 22*, 105–121.

Ferri, B. A., & Gregg, N. (1998). Women with disabilities: Missing voices. *Women's Studies International Forum, 21*, 429–439.

Frankenberg, E., Hawley, G. S., Ee, J., & Orfield, G. (2017). *Southern schools: More than half-century after the civil rights revolution.* Retrieved from https://www.civilrightsproject.ucla.edu/research/k-12-education/integration-and-diversity/southern-schools-brown-83-report

Freire, P. (2008). *Education for critical consciousness* (Continuum impacts). London, England: Continuum.

Freire, P. (2005). *The pedagogy of the oppressed* (Continuum impacts). London, England: Continuum.

Gallagher, D. J., Connor, D. J., & Ferri, B. A. (2014). Beyond the far too incessant schism: Special education and the social model of disability. *International Journal of Inclusive Education, 18*, 1120–1142.

Gannon, S., & Davis, B. (2012). *Postmodern, post-structural, and critical theories.* In S. N. Hesse-Biber (Ed.), *The handbook of feminist research: Theory and praxis* (2nd ed., pp. 65–91). Thousand Oaks, CA: Sage.

García, S. B., & Ortiz, A. A. (2013). Intersectionality as a framework for transformative research in special education. *Multiple Voices for Ethnically Diverse Exceptional Learners, 13*(2), 32–47.

Garland-Thomson, R. (2002). Integrating disability, transforming feminist theory. *NWSA Journal, 14*(3), 1–32.

Gill, M., & Erevelles, N. (2017). The absent presence of Elsie Lacks: Hauntings at the inter-section of race, class, gender, and disability. *African American Review, 50*, 123–137.

Gold, M. E., & Richards, H. (2012). To label or not to label: The special education question for African Americans. *Educational Foundation, 26*, 143–156.

Gonzalez, T., Hernández-Saca, D. I., & Artiles, A. J. (2017). In search of voice: Theory and methods in K–12 student voice research in the US, 1990–2010. *Educational Review, 69*, 451–473. doi:10.1080/00131911.2016.1231661

*Haight, W., Kayama, M., & Gibson, P. (2016). Out-of-school suspensions of Black youths: Culture, ability, disability, gender, and perspective. *Social Work, 61*, 235–243.

Harris, A. (2017, June 15). Memo outlines education dept. plans to scale back civil-rights efforts. *The Chronicle of Higher Education.* Retrieved from http://www.chronicle.com/blogs/ticker/memo-outlines-education-dept-plans-to-scale-back-civil-rights-efforts/118937

Harris, A., & Leonardo, Z. (2018). Intersectionality, race-gender subordination, and education. *Review of Research in Education, 42,* 1–27.

*Henry, W., Fuerth, K., & Figliozzi, J. (2010). Gay with a disability: A college student's multiple cultural journey. *College Student Journal, 44,* 377–388.

Hernández-Saca, D. I. (2016). *Re-framing the master narratives of dis/ability through an emotion lens: Voices of Latina/o students with learning disabilities* (Doctoral dissertation). Arizona State University, Tempe.

Hernández-Saca, D. I. (2017). Re-framing the master narratives of dis/ability at my intersections: An outline of a research agenda. *Critical Disability Discourses/Discours critiques dans le champ du handicap, 8,* 1–30. Retrieved from https://cdd.journals.yorku.ca/index.php/cdd/article/view/39723

Heshusius, L. (2004). From creative discontent toward epistemological freedom in special education: Reflections on a 25-year journey. In D. J. Gallagher, L. Heshusius, R. P. Iano, & T. M. Skrtic (Eds.), *Challenging orthodoxy in special education: Dissenting voices* (pp. 169–230). Denver, CO: Love.

*Kahn, L. G., & Lindstrom, L. (2015). "I just want to be myself": Adolescents with disabilities who identify as a sexual or gender minority. *Educational Forum, 79,* 362–376.

Kozleski, E. B., & Artiles, A. J. (2014). Beyond psychological views of student learning in systemic reform agendas. In E. B. Kozleski & K. King-Thorius (Eds.), *Ability, equity, and culture: Sustaining inclusive urban education reform* (pp. 63–79). New York, NY: Teachers College Press.

Kozleski, E. B., & Artiles, A. J. (2015). Mediating systemic change in educational systems through socio-cultural methods. In P. Smeyers, D. Bridges, N. Burbules, & M. Griffiths (Eds.), *International handbook of interpretation in educational research* (pp. 805–822). New York, NY: Springer.

Ladson-Billings, G. (1994). *The dreamkeepers: Successful teachers of African American children* (2nd ed.). San Francisco, CA: Jossey-Bass.

*Lambert, R. (2015). Constructing and resisting disability in mathematics classrooms: A case study exploring the impact of different pedagogies. *Educational Studies in Mathematics, 89*(1), 1–18.

Lemke, J. L. (2013). Thinking about feeling: Affect across literacies and lives. In O. Erstad & J. Sefton-Green (Eds.), *Learning lives: Transactions, technologies, and learner identity* (pp. 57–69). Cambridge, England: Cambridge University Press.

Losen, D., Ee, J., Hodson, C., & Martinez, T. (2015). Disturbing inequities: Exploring the relationship between racial disparities in special education identification and discipline. In D. Losen (Ed.), *Closing the school discipline gap: Equitable remedies for excessive exclusion* (pp. 89–117). New York, NY: Teachers College Press.

*Madigan, J. (2005). The intersection of gender, race, and disability: Latina students in special education. *Multiple Voices for Ethnically Diverse Exceptional Learners, 8*(1), 45–60.

McCall, L. (2005). The complexity of intersectionality. *Signs, 30,* 1771–1800.

*Miller, R. (2015). "Sometimes you feel invisible": Performing queer/disabled in the university classroom. *Educational Forum, 79,* 377–393.

Morris, M. (2016). *Pushout: The criminalization of Black girls in schools.* New York, NY: New Press.

Mountz, A., Bonds, A., Mansfield, B., Loyd, J., Hyndman, J., Walton-Roberts, M., . . . Curran, W. (2015). For slow scholarship: A feminist politics of resistance through collective action in the neoliberal university. *ACME: An International Journal for Critical Geographies, 14,* 1235–1259.

Munyi, C. W. (2012). Past and present perceptions towards disability: A historical perspective. *Disability Studies Quarterly, 32*(2). doi:10.18061/dsq.v32i2.3197

Nasir, N. I. (2011). *Racialized identities: Race and achievement among African American youth.* Palo Alto, CA: Stanford University Press.

Paris, D., & Alim, S. H. (2017). *Culturally sustaining pedagogies: Teaching and learning for justice in a changing world.* New York, NY: Teachers College Press.

Patton, J. M. (1998). The disproportionate representation of African-Americans in special education: Looking behind the curtain for understanding and solutions. *Journal of Special Education, 32*(1), 25–31.

Penrose, J. (1999). Using personal research to teach the significance of socially constructed categories. *Journal of Geography in Higher Education, 23,* 227–239.

*Petersen, J. A. (2009). "Ain't nobody gonna get me down": An examination of the educational experiences of four African American women labeled with disabilities. *Equity & Excellence in Education, 42,* 428–442.

Rogoff, B. (2003). *The cultural nature of human development.* Oxford, England: Oxford University Press.

Savaria, E., Underwood, K., & Sinclair, D. (2011). If only I had known . . . : Young people's participation in the construction of their learning disability labels. *International Journal of Special Education, 26*(3), 92–105.

Shakespeare, T. (2013). *Disability rights and wrongs revisited.* Abingdon, England: Routledge.

Skiba, R., Artiles, A. J., Kozleski, E. B., Losen, D., & Harry, B. (2016). Risks and consequences of over simplifying educational inequities: A response to Morgan et al. (2015). *Educational Researcher, 45,* 221–225.

Stevenson, M. (2010). Flexible and responsive research: Developing rights-based emancipatory disability research methodology in collaboration with young adults with Down syndrome. *Australian Social Work, 63*(1), 35–50.

Trainor, A. A. (2008). Using cultural and social capital to improve postsecondary outcomes and expand transition models for youth with disabilities. *Journal of Special Education, 42*(3), 148–162.

Trainor, A. A. (2017). *Transition by design: Improving equity and outcomes for adolescents with disabilities.* New York, NY: Teachers College Press.

Trent, S. C., Driver, M. K., Rodriguez, D., Oh, K., Stewart, S., Kea, C., & Artiles, A. J. (2014). Beyond Brown: Empirical research on diverse learners with or at-risk for specific learning disabilities from 1994–2012. *Multiple Voices, 14*(2), 12–29.

Valencia, R. R. (Ed.). (2012). *The evolution of deficit thinking: Educational thought and practice.* New York, NY: Routledge.

Waitoller, F. R., & King-Thorius, K. A. (2016). Cross-pollinating culturally sustaining pedagogy and universal design for learning: Toward an inclusive pedagogy that accounts for dis/ability. *Harvard Educational Review, 86,* 366–389.

Washington, A. H. (2006). *Medical apartheid: The dark history of medical experimentation on black Americans from colonial times to the present.* New York, NY: Harlem Moon.

Wetherell, M. (2012). *Affect and emotion: A new social science understanding.* Thousand Oaks, CA: Sage.

About the Editors

Gustavo E. Fischman is a professor of education policy and director of edXchange, the knowledge mobilization initiative, at Mary Lou Fulton Teachers College, Arizona State University. His scholarship has been distinguished with several awards, and he has been a visiting scholar in several universities in Europe and Latin America. Dr. Fischman has authored more than 100 articles, chapters, and books. He has been the lead editor of *Education Policy Analysis Archives* and is the editor of *Education Review*. Among his best-known works are *Imagining Teachers: Rethinking Teacher Education and Gender*, *Dumb Ideas Won't Create Smart Kids* (coauthored with Eric M. Haas), and *Made in Latin America: Open Access, Scholarly Journals, and Regional Innovations* (coedited with Juan P. Alperin).

Jeanne M. Powers is an associate professor in the Mary Lou Fulton Teachers College at Arizona State University. Dr. Powers received her PhD in sociology from the University of California, San Diego. Her research agenda is oriented around issues of equity and access in education policy. Recent projects have focused on school segregation, school choice, and the educational achievement of immigrant students. She has published in the *Review of Research in Education*; *American Educational Research Journal*; *Educational Policy*; *American Journal of Education, Equity and Excellence in Education*; and *Law and Social Inquiry*. In 2015 Dr. Powers was awarded the AERA Review of Research Award for her article "From Segregation to School Finance: The Legal Context for Language Rights in the United States" (2014). She is currently the president of the Arizona Educational Research Organization.

Adai A. Tefera is an assistant professor in the School of Education at Virginia Commonwealth University. Her scholarship focuses on how educational policies aimed at improving equity among students at the intersections of race, disability, language, and other sociocultural differences are enacted and experienced by educators, leaders, and students, particularly within complex classroom, school, and community contexts. Her work has been included in journals such as *Teachers*

Review of Research in Education
March 2018, Vol. 42, pp. 312–313
DOI: 10.3102/0091732X18769562
© 2018 AERA. http://rre.aera.net

College Record, Urban Education, and *Theory Into Practice*. Her commitment to educational equity and justice is rooted in her experiences as the proud daughter of Ethiopian immigrants, her upbringing in New Mexico, and her work with students of color labeled with disabilities, including her sister, who remain her greatest teachers.

About the Contributors

Vonzell Agosto, PhD, is an associate professor at the University of South Florida. Her research focuses on curriculum leadership and anti-oppression related to race, gender, and disability.

Sonya M. Alemán, PhD, is an associate professor at the University of Texas at San Antonio. Her research focuses on representations of race, racism, and whiteness in the media; reimagined journalism pedagogical models that result in more inclusive and authentic coverage of Latina/o communities; media products created by Chicana/o students; and the educational experiences of students of color.

Subini Ancy Annamma, PhD, is an assistant professor in the Department of Special Education at the University of Kansas. Her research focuses on increasing access to equitable education for multiply marginalized students, particularly students of color with disabilities. Specifically, she critically examines the social construction of race and ability, how the two are interdependent, how they intersect with other identity markers, and how their mutually constitutive nature impacts education experiences.

Erika C. Bullock, PhD, is an assistant professor of mathematics education and curriculum studies at the University of Wisconsin-Madison. She uses critical theories of race, poststructural theories, and concepts from urban sociology, critical geography, and science and technology studies to interrogate the politics of mathematics education and STEM education.

Tamara T. Butler, PhD, is an assistant professor at Michigan State University in the Department of English and the African American and African Studies Program. Her research focuses on the connections between place-making, storytelling, and memory among Black girls and women. As a member of the English education and African American studies core faculty, she teaches undergraduate and graduate courses that focus on artistic forms of activism, Black women's and girls' storytelling, and practices of justice and equity that are rooted in communities of color. She is the recipient of the 2017 Woodrow Wilson Career Enhancement Fellowship and a member of the National Council of Teachers of English's 2012–2014 cohort of Cultivating New Voices Among Scholars of Color fellowship program. In 2016, the National Council of Teachers of English awarded her the Promising Researcher Award for her research

Review of Research in Education
March 2018, Vol. 42, pp. 314–318
DOI: 10.3102/0091732X18768228
© 2018 AERA. http://rre.aera.net

on youth activism among high school girls of color in Columbus, Ohio. She holds a doctorate in multicultural and equity studies in education from The Ohio State University.

Mercedes A. Cannon, MS, is an associate director of outreach, compliance, and services at Indiana University–Purdue University Indianapolis. Her research focuses on centering the voices (narratives) and perspectives (consciousness) of individuals with disabilities (e.g., Black women) while underscoring their educational experiences at the intersections of race, gender, and disability oppression. She is also interested in transition processes and resources, which provides access to and completion of college for students with disabilities.

David J. Connor, EdD, is a professor at Hunter College, City University of New York. His research focuses on learning disabilities, intersectionality, inclusive education, and expanding disability studies in education.

Kendra D. DeLaine, MEd, is a doctoral student in the Educational Psychology program at Howard University. Her research focuses on achievement motivation and academic self-perceptions of African American students in STEM learning environments.

Beth A. Ferri, PhD, is a professor of inclusive education and disability studies in the Department of Teaching & Leadership, Syracuse University. Her research focuses on the intersection of disability, race, and gender; feminist disability studies; narratives; and inclusive education.

Kimberley Edelin Freeman, PhD, is an associate professor of educational psychology and chair of the Department of Human Development and Psychoeducational Studies in the School of Education at Howard University. Her research focuses on motivation and achievement of African American students, the preparation of science and mathematics teachers at historically black colleges and universities, culturally responsive pedagogy, and mixed-methods research.

Laurie Gutmann Kahn, PhD, is an assistant professor at Moravian College. Her research and practice interests include the intersection of identity, culture, and disability in education research; the emancipatory possibilities of disability studies in special education practices; and the education of teachers working with students with disabilities from a social justice framework. Her work also explores how we can create supportive learning and living communities for the transition from school to adult life for young adults with disabilities.

Angela Harris, JD, is professor emerita at the School of Law at University of California, Davis. Her research focuses on critical race theory, feminist theory, and law and political economy.

David I. Hernández-Saca, PhD, is an assistant professor at the University of Northern Iowa. The nucleus of his research agenda is problematizing the common sense assumptions of what learning disabilities are. His three lines of research are (a) the emotional impact of learning disability labeling on conceptions of self, (b) the role of emotion and affect in teacher learning about social justice issues, and (c) transition plans and programming for historically marginalized youth with disabilities at their intersections and their families.

Danyelle T. Ireland, PhD, is associate director of the Center for Women in Technology at the University of Maryland, Baltimore County. Her research focuses on the interrelatedness of social, academic, and occupational identities among students in STEM education, and psychosocial factors that influence the motivation and persistence of underrepresented student groups in computing and engineering fields. She is particularly interested in the theoretical and methodological applications of intersectionality toward advancing psychological scholarship on the achievement of Black women and girls in secondary and higher education settings.

Zeus Leonardo, PhD, is a professor at the Graduate School of Education and faculty of the critical theory designated emphasis at the University of California, Berkeley. His research focuses on ideology critique of race, whiteness, and class in education.

Stacey McDonald Lowe, MS, is a doctoral student in the Howard University Department of Human Development and Psychoeducational Studies. Her research interests include exploring issues related to impacting teaching practice in economically challenged schools and school districts with a focus on the impact of various interdisciplinary contexts (educational, socioeconomic, psychological, physical, and political) have on the development of minority, underrepresented, and marginalized students' motivation, persistence, and self-efficacy for the purpose of improving access to postsecondary education leading to degree completion with a special interest in women and African Americans in STEM.

Bach Mai Dolly Nguyen, PhD, is an assistant professor of education at Lewis & Clark College, Portland, Oregon. Her research focuses on racial stratification, racial heterogeneity, and organizational change.

Thai-Huy Nguyen, PhD, is an assistant professor of education at Seattle University, Seattle, Washington. His research focuses on social inequality, postsecondary education, and workforce stratification.

Ayesha Rabadi-Raol has an MA in early childhood education and early childhood special education. She is a doctoral student, doctoral research fellow, instructor, research assistant in the Department of Curriculum and Teaching at Teachers College, Columbia University, New York City. Her research focuses on equity issues in early childhood education and teacher education. She is specifically interested in how students of color and teachers of color have been positioned by educational institutions in and through standardization.

Sarah A. Robert, PhD, is an associate professor at the University at Buffalo's Graduate School of Education. Her research focuses on how teachers *enact* policy and how teachers' work is transformed in the process. She is particularly concerned with all the work teachers do in addition to facilitating learning in the classroom. She blends ethnography with archival research and policy and media analysis to theorize policy enactment in local contexts with attention to historical and contemporary power dynamics. She aims to mediate the often diverging interpretations of what "problems" a policy should address and forge a more inclusive policymaking process to bring forth equity. Her work is interdisciplinary, appearing in journals such as *Educational Policy Analysis Archives, Anthropology & Education Quarterly, British Journal of Sociology of Education, Gender and Education*, and *DISCOURSE: Cultural Politics of Education*. She is the author and editor of multiple books, including the ethnography of teachers' policy work, *Neoliberal Education Reform: Gendered Notions in Global and Local Contexts* (Routledge, 2017).

Ericka Roland, MS, is a doctoral candidate at the University of South Florida. Her research focuses on critical approaches to the development and enactment of leadership in educational organizations and communities.

Lauren Schudde, PhD, is an assistant professor at the University of Texas at Austin. Her research focuses on the impact of postsecondary educational policies and practices on educational attainment and labor market outcomes, with a primary interest in how education can be better leveraged to ameliorate social inequalities in the United States.

Mariana Souto-Manning, PhD, associate professor at Teachers College, Columbia University, is an early childhood teacher educator committed to racial and cultural justice. From a critical perspective, her research examines in/equities and in/justices in early childhood teaching and teacher education, (re)centering methodologies and pedagogies on the lives and experiences of people of color and other historically minoritized communities. She considers questions such as "critical for whom?" and "according to whom?" as she investigates issues pertaining to equitable teaching and learning, focusing on languaging and literacy practices in pluralistic settings. She has published eight books and more than 60 articles in journals such as the *Journal of Teacher Education* and *Teachers College Record*. She is the recipient of a number of research awards, including the 2011 AERA Division K Innovations in Research on Diversity in Teacher Education Award and the 2017 AERA Teaching and Teacher Education (Division K) Mid-Career Award.

Cynthia E. Winston-Proctor, PhD, is a professor of psychology in the Howard University Department of Psychology. Her research focuses on narrative personality psychology theory and method development to advance understanding of the relationship among narrative identity, race self-complexity, achievement motivation, and the psychology of success within the lives of adolescents, women, and African Americans in STEM.

Kamilah M. Woodson, PhD, is an associate professor of counseling psychology in the Department of Human Development and Psychoeducational Studies in the

School of Education at Howard University. Her research focuses on HIV/AIDS, substance abuse, violence exposure, trauma, victimization, psychological functioning, and colorism with women and girls of color, from professional to those who are incarcerated. Specifically, she examines the complex mosaic resulting from the intersection of culture, race, social class, gender, and sexual orientation within social, political, and historical contexts. This integrated approach to research, scholarship, program development, and community activism is the vehicle by which her work addresses health disparities and promotes social justice and equity. She also examines women of color in academia from the perspective of the ways in which they are marginalized and invisible in the ivory tower, to inform retention and mentoring efforts, and to ensure that women scholars are healthy and productive.

Min Yu, PhD, is an assistant professor in the Teacher Education Division in the College of Education at Wayne State University. Her research focuses on how changing social, political, and economic conditions affect schools serving migrant and immigrant families and communities. Her work appears in journals such as *Review of Research in Education*; *Diaspora, Indigenous, and Minority Education*; and *Curriculum Perspectives*; as well as chapters in various edited volumes. She is the author of the book *The Politics, Practices, and Possibilities of Migrant Children Schools in Contemporary China* (Palgrave Macmillan, 2016).